BEYOND PSYCHOTHERAPY

Recent Titles in
Developments in Clinical Psychology
Glenn R. Caddy, Series Editor

Child Multimodal Therapy
Donald B. Keat II

Psychophysiology for Clinical Psychologists
Walter W. Surwillo

Strategic Health Planning: Methods and Techniques Applied to Marketing and Management
Allen D. Spiegel and Herbert H. Hyman

Behavioral Medicine: International Perspectives, Volume 1
Don G. Byrne and Glenn R. Caddy, editors

Behavioral Medicine: International Perspectives, Volume 2
Don G. Byrne and Glenn R. Caddy, editors

The MMPI: A Contemporary Normative Study of Adolescents
Robert C. Colligan and Kenneth P. Offord

Adult-Child Research and Experience: Personal and Professional Legacies of a Dysfunctional Co-Dependent Family
Robert E. Haskell

Behavioral Medicine: International Perspectives, Volume 3
Don G. Byrne and Glenn R. Caddy, editors

Reprogramming Pain: Transform Pain and Suffering into Health and Success
Barry Bittman, M.D.

Personal Construct Therapy: A Handbook
Linda L. Viney

The Natural Limitations of Youth: The Predispositions That Shape the Adolescent Character
John J. Mitchell

Distance Writing and Computer-Assisted Interventions in Psychiatry and Mental Health
Luciano L'Abate, editor

BEYOND PSYCHOTHERAPY

Programmed Writing and Structured Computer-Assisted Interventions

Luciano L'Abate

Developments in Clinical Psychology
Glenn R. Caddy, Series Editor

ABLEX PUBLISHING
Westport, Connecticut • London

Library of Congress Cataloging-in-Publication Data

L'Abate, Luciano, 1928–
Beyond psychotherapy : programmed writing and structured computer-assisted interventions / Luciano L'Abate.
p. cm.—(Developments in clinical psychology)
Includes bibliographical references and index.
ISBN 1–56750–654–2 (alk. paper)
1. Written communication—Therapeutic use. 2. Psychotherapy—Problems, exercises, etc. 3. Psychotherapy—Computer-assisted instruction. 4. Internet in psychotherapy. I. Title. II. Series.
RC489.W75L325 2002
616.89'14—dc21 2001031648

British Library Cataloguing in Publication Data is available.

Library of Congress Catalog Card Number: 2001031648
ISBN: 1–56750–654–2

First published in 2002

Ablex Publishing, 88 Post Road West, Westport, CT 06881
An imprint of Greenwood Publishing Group, Inc.
www.ablexbooks.com

Printed in the United States of America

The paper used in this book complies with the Permanent Paper Standard issued by the National Information Standards Organization (Z39.48–1984).

10 9 8 7 6 5 4 3 2 1

Copyright Acknowledgments

The author and publisher gratefully acknowledge permission for use of the following material:

Material for Tables 1.2, 1.3, 1.7, and 7.2 and Figures 5.1 and 5.5 from L'Abate, *A Theory of Personality Development.* New York: John Wiley & Sons, Inc. Copyright © 1994. Reprinted by permission of John Wiley & Sons, Inc.

Material for Tables 1.5 and 1.6 from M. D. Weintraub, *Verbal Behavior: Adaptations in Psychopathology.* New York: Springer Publishing Company, Inc., 1981. Used by permission.

Material for Table 5.1, Copyright 1998 from L. L'Abate, "Discovery of the Family: From the Inside to the Outside," *American Journal of Family Therapy, 26*, 265–280. Reproduced by permission of Taylor & Francis, Inc., http://www.routledge-ny.com.

Figure 5.7, Copyright 2001 from L. L'Abate, R.G. Lambert, P. W. Schenk, "Testing a Theoretical Model of Psychopathology with the MMPI-2," *American Journal of Family Therapy, 29*, 221–238. Reproduced by permission of Taylor & Francis, Inc., http://www.routledge-ny.com.

Material for Table 6.2 from L. L'Abate, P. De Giacomo, F. McCarty, A. De Giacomo, and G. Verrastro, "Testing Three Models of Intimate Relationships," *Contemporary Family Therapy: An International Journal, 22*, 2000: 103–122. Used by permission.

Material for Table 6.3 from P. Lindaver, "Le persone in relazione: Tre modelli Teorici a confronto," *Famiglia, Interdisciplinarita', Ricerca, 3*, 1998: 101–114. Used by permission.

Table 6.4 printed with permission of the Family Psychology Service of the Research Institute "Eugeneo Medea" in the Association "La Nostra Famiglia," Bosisio Parini (Lecco), Italy.

Material for development of some workbooks from R. D. Davis and T. Millon, "Models of Personality and Its Disorders," in T. Millon, T. H. Blaney, and R. D. Davis (Eds.), *Oxford Textbook of Psychotherapy* (pp. 485–522). New York: Oxford University Press, 1999.

Contents

Preface

A revolution is taking place in the field of psychotherapy. This revolution lies in how mental health systems will be delivered in the coming century. After the invention of the wheel, clock, printing press, electricity, photography, telephone, radio, motion pictures, television, transistor and solid state electronics, compact disks and magnetic recordings, wireless communication, personal computers, and now the Internet, each invention is based on the discovery and universal application of previous ones. For instance, the Internet owes its origin and development to all of the inventions found in the past, especially the telephone, television, compact disks, and personal computers. With these technologies, especially the personal computer and the Internet, it is now possible to reach more people in distress per unit of professional time than it was possible heretofore.

Furthermore, in every human enterprise except current mental health practices, progress is based on written memoranda, blue-prints, x-rays, laboratory results, histories, etc. In mental health, which includes, among others, the fields of prevention, psychotherapy, and rehabilitation, we are trying to change people for the better using a very expensive, relatively ineffective, and clearly uncontrollable medium, talk. There is no denying that talk-based psychotherapy may be effective in at least 66% of the cases, even though there may be those who dispute this percentage. Yet, we need to ask ourselves: "How about the other 33%?" Additionally, could we help those who are helped by talk more efficiently, if, above and beyond talk, we use another medium, namely: distance writing (DW) and computer-assisted interventions (CAI)? We need to remember that the previously mentioned 66% represents people who terminated treatment. What about those who dropped out prematurely during treatment, or those who never sought treatment, for whatever reasons there may be? Could it be that there are people in need of psychological help who could profit by using DW/CAI rather than talk? Could we obtain synergistic, that is, faster and less expensive results if we were to combine face-to-face talk with DW/CAI? What about readmissions, people who come back for therapy because the earlier treatment was not effective enough to allow them to lead successful lives? Could they profit by media other than talk? What about recidivism in our correctional institutions? Could offenders be helped with a medium like DW/CAI that may help improve deficits in how they feel, think, and act? Talk therapy with the latter has met with uniformly negative results.

Another issue is worthy of mention, and that is: replicability of interventions. As long as many psychotherapeutic practices are the outcome of personal interests and opinions of professionals, it will be difficult if not impossible to replicate and find which approach helps and which does not. Even though most psychotherapeutic approaches seem to be equal in effectiveness, which approach will be eventually superior to others in outcome? Everything else being equal, the approach that is equally effective as others but less expensive than all the others will eventually be superior. How are we going to find out if we do not know which approach is replicable and which is not? Talk in psychotherapy is difficult to replicate and expensive to research, a commodity left to a handful of dedicated researchers. Most of our living standards, comforts, and discomforts are due to objects and operations that are infinitely replicable. Even the most delicate surgical operations are replicable from one surgeon to another and from one medical center to another. Thus, the present proposal is unabashedly and unapologetically mechanistic in its major characteristic, and that is its replicability from one professional to another and its relatively inexpensive structure.

One type of distance writing (DW), programmed distance writing (PW) as represented by workbooks, the focus of this work, can be paired with any other preventive, psychotherapeutic, and rehabilitative approach, regardless of theory and regardless of personal bias. This pairing with any other approach should yield synergistic results. Otherwise, workbooks would not be worth the paper (or computer) they are printed on.

Although this author has published in this area of intervention, especially programmed writing (PW), this issue has never been addressed as directly as it is here. The first chapter aims at clarifying and classifying a variety of issues in the field of psychotherapy. First of all, psychotherapy can also be viewed along a continuum of care, that is: primary, secondary, and tertiary prevention or crisis intervention and rehabilitation. Psychotherapy as tertiary prevention can also be viewed as a science and as an art, according to the two major overlapping dimensions of human enterprise: indeterminism-determinism and dialectical-demonstrative, respectively. From these dimensions, which represent two aspects of the same coin, derive viewpoints that lead to two seemingly antagonistic psychotherapeutic practices and interventions, the artistic and the scientific. Current and traditional psychotherapeutic practices have been based mainly on talk.

It is proposed here that another medium, DW and especially PW, can be added for working at a distance from respondents and for structured computer-assisted interventions (SCAI), to be included in current interventional practices.

Chapter 2 attempts to demonstrate the values (economy, efficiency, and objectivity) of working at a distance from people in distress using PW/SCAI. Both DW, PW, and SCAI imply writing away from the professional's eyes and presence, in one's own home or office. In some instances, in this writer's experience, written homework assignments have been completed in cars, bars, restaurants, and public parks. There is no denying that there are definite dangers and certain disadvantages in trying to help people at a distance. Hence, psychotherapists and mental health professionals will need to become doubly careful in how they work with people in this way. However, the economic and practical advantages of DW/CAI overshadow its possible disadvantages.

Writing is classified according to three major, overlapping dimensions, varying between structured and unstructured interventions. While psychotherapy may be conceived as a mainly unstructured intervention, no one can predict what respondents (clients, patients, individuals, couples, and families) will say and how professional practitioners will respond. DW/CAI and especially PW, the use of workbooks, can be conceived as secondary prevention. Workbooks are targeted and specific to individual, couple, and family issues and symptoms. Especially in comparison with talk, which is nonspecific and uncontrollable, workbooks can be conceived as being parapreventive and paratherapeutic because they can be applied as additions, supplements, or alternatives to either primary or tertiary prevention.

DW, and especially PW, reviewed in Chapter 3, include a relatively new phenomenon in the mental health field, the introduction of workbooks for mental health purposes as software for computer and Internet interventions. This chapter, therefore, will introduce the use of workbooks as an intermediate step between no intervention ("Nothing," in the title of Chapter 1) and psychotherapy, including the much sought-after link between evaluation and interventions, including prescriptiveness.

Chapter 4 introduces summaries of available workbooks classified according to their applications to individuals (children, adolescents, and adults), couples, and families. They can be classified according to whether they are based on a single test score or a psychological test profile or on the referring questions or symptom. Furthermore, workbooks are classified according to whether they apply to two major dimensions of dysfunctionality, internalization and externalization, as well as normalization and psychopathological extremes.

Chapter 5 summarizes a contextual, developmental theory of interpersonal competence. The purpose of this theory is to show how it is possible to link theory with research and practice in much more specific ways than it has been the case with past theories. Many workbooks are either theory-independent, based on generic clinical experience, or model-derived, as in many workbooks developed from a variety of test instruments. However, some workbooks are also theory-related, allowing a comparative evaluation among workbooks derived from competing theories or models. This step will allow comparative testing of theories and models beyond sterile laboratory research, dealing instead with real interventions.

Chapter 6 shows how it is possible to link theory with research and practice, provided the theory is specific enough to link specific models with specific laboratory research and with specific primary, secondary, and tertiary prevention practices. The two watchwords here are specificity and explicitness. The dictum followed in this enterprise is: "It is better to be specific and wrong, rather than being generally vague and right."

Chapter 7 attempts to tie together all the loose ends left over from previous chapters in terms of implications for conducting the practice of psychotherapy in the future rather than in the past, the effects of managed care on the profession of psychotherapy, ethical and professional issues that will undoubtedly arise from working at a distance from respondents, as well as a hierarchical structuring of mental health personnel needed to deal with the many mental health problems facing our and other nations. The psychotherapy and mental health communities will have to decide whether to remain in the past century or enter into the new twenty-first century. The conclusion of this chapter epitomizes and summarizes all of the preceding pages and chapters by presenting a successive sieves and stepped-treatment approach set within the context of a continuum of care, going from the least to the most expensive intervention.

This work might be of interest to most mental health workers in the various disciplines of counseling, pastoral or otherwise, social work, psychiatric nursing, clinical psychology, psychotherapy, and psychiatry. It would be of interest to students and professionals in those disciplines as well as to researchers. The latter will be able to intervene with people and, at the same time, evaluate the outcome of different workbooks derived from different theoretical or therapeutic schools. For instance, given the availability of seven workbooks dealing with depression, which workbook derived from which theory will be more effective than other workbooks in the long run? Hence, workbooks provide a method of evaluating competing theoretical models in a more active, dynamic, and interactive fashion than has been the case in the past, when only test instruments were and are still used to evaluate competing models. Workbooks can also be used by beginning students as scripts for structured interviews as a way to learn without the anxiety provoked by lack of structure.

It is also an intriguing possibility that DW/CAI as well as PW/SCAI could be used by primary care physicians and clergy who need very concrete and specific assistance in dealing with a plethora of mental health problems that might not usually come to the attention of mental health professionals. An even more intriguing possibility is that most institutions, schools, mental health clinics, hospitals, and especially libraries may be all connected with each other through computers to help as many people at risk of breakdown and in need of assistance who cannot or do not want to receive help verbally and face-to-face.

1

Between Nothing and Psychotherapy

> Required for social transformation are new visions and vocabularies, new visions of possibilities, and practices that in their very realization begin to chart an alternative course.
>
> (Gergen, 1994, p. 60)

The purpose of this introductory chapter is to lay the groundwork for the rest of this book. The last century has seen a proliferation of ways to improve the distressed human condition based on talk, face-to-face psychotherapies, and paratherapies. The latter are preventive approaches composed of social skills training programs that, in the last quarter of a century, have intervened between "nothing" and psychotherapy. It is the purpose of this work to suggest ways and means of going beyond the spoken word in face-to-face psychotherapy and to fill the gap between nothing and psychotherapy. To start filling this gap, it is important to attempt a systematic schematization, that is, to lay the groundwork, to make sense of and understand this proliferation that, at first blush, would seem a veritable and bewildering Tower of Babel. The proliferation of psychotherapies is so mindboggling that it does need a systematic framework to make sense of it, in order to go beyond it (Ehrenwald, 1991; Freedheim, 1992; Norcross & Goldfried, 1992).

In many lay people's minds there is no other help available except psychotherapy, medication, hospitalization, incarceration, or a combination of two, three, or four. Thus, the purpose of this chapter, as well as this whole book, is to dispel the notion that nothing except those four options is available for many human problems as well as for criminal and psychopathological conditions. Between nothing and psychotherapy there are many ways of helping people in distress, provided that the writing medium, rather than talk, is used.

The thesis of this book is that as long as modalities of intervention (and theory testing) rely on the spoken word, it will be practically difficult if not impossible to test any theory or method of treatment. Is it possible to match treatment with a psychological problem or symptom? The answer to this question is affirmative provided the modality of intervention is written down rather than verbal or nonverbal (medication, diet, exercise, massage, etc.). By definition, psychological interventions to help people include the psychotherapies as well as other structured helping approaches—the paratherapies. Both types of interventions are based on personal, face-to-face contacts and relationships between professional helpers and dysfunctional people in need of psychological or psychiatric help. This face-to-face, verbally based approach is not only expensive but is also difficult to verify. Consequently, we will need to find ways and means of helping people in other ways than just talk. To achieve this goal we will need to review American mental health needs and attempt a classification of psychological interventions to make sense of them. We will also need to relate them, if possible, to cost-effective interventions and to a developmental theory of interpersonal competence in order to link theory with practice.

AMERICAN MENTAL HEALTH NEEDS

What could constitute an intermediate level of intervention between no intervention whatever, that is, "nothing," and psychotherapy? Perhaps using the term "nothing" may be overstating the case unnecessarily. It may well be a misnomer. However, there are some grounds for using this term advisedly. Most people (individuals, couples, and families) wait, in other words, "do nothing" until a crisis develops, before seeking professional help. Typically—depending, of course, on the nature and severity of the crisis—nonmedical professionals will use a face-to-face approach based on the verbal medium, that is, talk. Consequently, most people at risk, but not yet in crisis, might need some kind of intervention, preventive but not necessarily therapeutic. Unless there is a crisis, they will do nothing to deal with the problem at hand. They will wait until the problem has reached critical, clinical, or criminal proportions before seeking help. Oftentimes, the problem may be so severe that it may have reached irreversible extremes. Hence, it is either nothing, or medication, psychotherapy, and, in the most severe cases, hospitalization or incarceration.

In case this writer is overstating this point, a recent report about American mental health needs from the Surgeon General of the United States (U.S. Department of Health and Human Services, 1999) concluded that: "One in every five Americans experiences mental disorder in a given year, and half of all Americans have such disorders at some time in their lives, *but most of them never seek treatment*. Many people cannot afford treatment because they lack insurance that would cover it. . . . [Apparently, there is] a huge gap between the need for mental health services and their availability" (italics added). Treatments for mental disorders cost more than $69 billion in 1996. It would not be surprising if this estimate reaches the $100 billion mark by the end of this century.

Another way to look at the vacuum between nothing and psychotherapy is to consider the vast availability of self-help, self-improvement books and manuals, as well as motivational gurus. These materials and charismatic preachers, in addition to television, pulpits, and workshops, have now entered the Internet. One famous guru's motivational tapes are part of a company whose shares are now available on the stock market (*Atlanta Journal & Constitution*, January 8, 2000). None of these materials or methods, of course, have an ounce of empirical or rational evidence to support their use. They are strictly related to the exhortative, hortatory, seductive, and suggestive powers of their presenters, who, in their ways, are no different from many tele-evangelists. Yet, the fact that so many people are attracted to them attests to the need to fill the gap between nothing and psychotherapy.

Existing psychological interventions, in addition to psychotherapy, include prevention and rehabilitation. They are the most innovative methods developed in the past century for helping people in distress (Albee & Guillotta, 1997; Bond & Wagner, 1988). As we look at the beginning of this new century, we have to ask ourselves: "Are these practices the only nonmedical, psychological approaches to helping people in distress?" By now these practices are a part of the accepted mainstream of professional mental health practices. They are the vehicles through which clients/patients—hereafter called respondents—gain and regain their sanity, mental health, and even happiness. As yet, we do not know of other efficacious ways to help distressed people besides life-style changes like exercise and better diet. However, prevention has lagged behind psychotherapy in the effort to help people at risk avoid becoming even more dysfunctional than they are (L'Abate, 1986a). Hence, even though preventive approaches could fill the gap between nothing and psychotherapy, they have not been able, as yet, to fulfill their promise. The medium applied to helping people falling into the void between nothing and psychotherapy is still talk.

Psychotherapy, because of its success, is so embedded in our culture that by now it has become institutionalized within the context of societally accepted methods used to help control and change troubled people. To question its effectiveness is to go against the status quo. Trying to question this status quo may be suicidal professionally (Cummings, 1999; Hoyt, 1999). As already noted, psychotherapy and other psychological interventions are characterized by a bewildering and mystifying array of different approaches, methods, and forms of intervention that have varying degrees of respectability, replicability, and claims of effectiveness (Abt & Stuart, 1982; Bergin & Garfield, 1994; Corsini, 1984; Lynn & Garske, 1985; Norcross, 1986; Prochaska, 1984; Sperry & Carlson, 1996). Inspite of their immense diversity and seeming success (Perry, Banon, & Ianni, 1999; Sperry, Brill, Howard, & Grissom, 1996), most current and traditional psychotherapy practices are based on talk. This medium still remains the major if not the only medium of communication and healing among human beings, professionally and otherwise. Before suggesting an alternative to talk, however, we need to look at the current state of affairs in the psychotherapy community.

In spite of their claimed cost-effectiveness (Clay, 2000), the major issue with psychotherapeutic interventions is still cost. The cost of face-to-face therapy can be prohibitive for many people. Hourly fees may range from $10 or $15 for therapy with a student intern to 10 times as much and more for an experienced therapist. How might costs be reduced without reducing effectiveness? How can a therapist's effectiveness be improved without reducing workload? How can the present number of clinicians and organizations offer more cost-effective therapeutic services to millions of individuals, families, and couples who need help? The number of mental health professionals is not sufficient to accommodate and heal the mental health needs of this and other nations. More cost-effective ways of helping people in distress will be needed.

THE STATUS OF PSYCHOTHERAPY

Many people do go to their clergy for help. However, as popular articles have argued, members of the clergy are poorly prepared to deal with people in crisis. Most often than not, they serve as referral sources for many mental health professionals, as do lawyers and primary care physicians (Hendrick, 1998), and fulfill a crucial and important social function. Expanding on the recent Surgeon General's report cited earlier, one could estimate with little fear of contradiction that for every individual, couple, or family in psychotherapy or psychiatric treatment, there are up to 10 individuals, couples, or families who need some kind of help, but not necessarily verbal, face-to-face psychotherapy. They do not know how to find it, are afraid of it, and do not know whether this help will indeed be beneficial to them. If help is needed, they do not know what kind of help to seek, except for their clergy, primary care physicians, friends, or lawyers. Will they need a psychiatrist and, consequently, be thought of as "crazy"? They will avoid seeking professional help until a breakdown, either personal, marital, or familial, takes place. Even then, they will find it very hard to change long-established ways of feeling, thinking, and relating (Cullari, 1996). Should they seek a psychologist, a social worker, or a professional counselor? Furthermore, among the many available mental health specialties, which one is best qualified? Should they seek a pastoral counselor, a family therapist, a psychiatric nurse, and so forth? Hence, seeking professional help is not as easy as we (mental health professionals) may think. It takes a lot of suffering and strength to seek professional help. What about people in distress in rural areas, where professional help is not readily available? What about criminals in penal institutions; what kind of help and rehabilitation are they receiving? What about missionary or military couples and families, Peace Corps volunteers, or stay-at-home handicapped people? In these populations, "nothing is available" is still the answer.

What has been happening to the psychotherapy community in recent years? First of all, there are the pressures and restraints of managed care, limiting access, decreasing number of sessions, demanding accountability, and requiring cost-effectiveness. The criteria demanded by managed care companies have never really been considered worthy by many psychotherapists. Self-determination, that is, what is good for the patient and for economic survival of the professional, were the two main motivating factors in past clinical and psychotherapeutic practices. How can delicate, difficult, ephemeral personal (Derlega, Hendrick, Winstead, & Berg, 1991) and interpersonal processes in face-to-face talk sessions be subjected to external and objective scrutiny, and, God forbid, quantification? Clearly, demands from managed care have changed the complacent, taken-for-granted view that psychotherapists from whatever mental health discipline, once licensed in their state, were only responsible to themselves and to their patients. Hence, the use of the term "private practice." No external interference was acceptable nor required. This position, of course, is no longer tenable because we psychotherapists can no longer claim to live and practice in a safe, self-contained cocoon of "independent" and even less "private" practice. We are no longer independent, and our practices are no longer private. Our practices are now open to the scrutiny of peer reviews and other intrusions and interferences from managed care.

Second, the face-to-face verbal, professional contact is so expensive that unless patients receive support from managed care companies, many professionals have had to lower their fees or find additional sources of income outside therapy sessions. Private practice is no longer a sinecure for academic clinicians who have reverted to it after failing to achieve tenure. Clinicians who do go directly into private practice, bypassing academic possibilities, can no longer hope to become solvent immediately. Some might have to spend one to two or more years making connections, networking, and spending a great deal of their time on public relations and marketing. Even established practitioners can no longer take for granted that their referral sources will continue to send them patients unless they make a concerted effort to keep these sources informed and satisfied. Private practice, therefore, is just as competitive as academia, where there are usually over one hundred applicants for any clinical position open.

Third, in spite of their progress and their many successes, talk therapies have had little impact in reducing rates of recidivism among criminals (Cellini, Hinze, Speaker, & Wood, 2000; Hughes, 2000; Simon, 1998) or readmissions to psychiatric hospitals (Bergin & Garfield, 1994). Also, they have improved the overall levels of functioning in relatively few cases in comparison to the staggering mental health problems faced by this and other countries (Bickman, 1999). Face-to-face, talk-based psychological interventions are a drop in the bucket in view of the overwhelming mental health needs of this and other nations. These needs will remain unfulfilled as long as the status quo of face-to-face personal, verbal contact is the mainstream, an uncritically accepted and even rewarded norm.

As Bickman (1999) concluded in his review of expenditures for mental health practices, these expenditures "have plummeted in the past decade. Concurrently, psychologists have been unable to muster scientific evidence for the effectiveness of typical services." After reviewing relevant scientific literature, he concluded that there is "little or no evidence to support . . . six myths [of mental health] . . . that more effective services are assured by (1) more experienced clinicians, (2) advanced degree programs, (3) continuing education, (4) licensing at the state level and board examinations at the national level, (5) accreditation from national professional organizations, and (6) clinical supervision" (p. 965). He found no evidence to support these myths.

Bickman's conclusions tend to support Dawes's (1994) scathing criticisms of psychotherapy. These criticisms have prompted full rebuttals, among the most recent from Fishman (1999). Fishman suggested pragmatism as a way out from and as an intermediary position between blatant scientism on one extreme and uncritical acceptance of psychotherapy on the other. Unfortunately, Fishman's suggestion, as well reasoned as it may be, is not only utopian, given the present state of affairs in psychotherapy, but it is still grounded on talk as the only means of communication and healing. Thus, it would preserve the status quo while trying to change it, an impossible solution. Nothing less than the Internet revolution (Barak, 1999; L'Abate & Kern, in press) as the new vehicle of mental health service delivery will change that status quo. How do we go from psychotherapy to the Internet? This book aims to give one of many possible answers, provided distance writing (DW) is applied as the middle ground between nothing and psychotherapy.

Dawes's criticisms, however, seem mild in comparison to Watters and Ofshe's (1999) brutal, but perhaps necessary, diatribe against "psychodynamic psychotherapy." Fortunately, they do exclude behavioral-cognitive psychotherapy from their strong criticisms. These writers support, instead, biological psychiatric treatments, that is, medication over psychodynamic therapies. This view, of course, is strongly contradicted by Breggin (1991) and by Ross and Pam (1995). Breggin suggested that in therapy, empathy and love would supplant biological treatments. Perhaps the latter qualities may be necessary to begin a psychotherapeutic relationship. They may work well with certain individuals (Luborsky, Crits-Christoph, Mintz, & Auerbach, 1988). However, it is doubtful whether empathy and love, including Rogers' (1957) warmth, empathy, and unconditional regard, will carry over after three sessions of therapy, especially with couples and families (L'Abate, 1997b).

In addition to Bickman's distressing conclusions, supporting, in part, Dawes's criticisms and Watters and Ofshe's attacks, we must take into consideration the pessimistic results of a survey conducted by *Parade* magazine (1995) about the profound distrust in which the mental health community is held by the population at large. At least in the United States, "16% have sought help from mental-health professionals, but 59% (of that percentage) have no faith in them." In addition, the majority of those surveyed (1792 people above 18 years of age) preferred to change their diets to treat a health problem rather than take medication. Depression was the 3rd most common "disease," while 49% self-medicated "to avoid paying for a doctor's visit." We need to find more cost-effective ways that will allow us to reach people who cannot be reached through expensive and sometimes ineffective verbal, face-to-face interactions with mental health professionals.

Very likely, this distrust of mental health help is widespread everywhere else in the world. This distrust may stem also from the wide semantic gap between mental health professions and the lay public. Professionals' descriptions of mental, emotional, and behavioral disorders are clouded by technical jargon and seemingly professional, semiscientific terms that may mystify people who do not know or understand what those terms mean. Rather than finding defensive rationalizations and facile externalizations for such distrust, it behooves us, as mental health professionals, to find ways and means to help people whose distress and distrust are even greater than the general population, that is, people affected by mental illness. These are the very ones who most need help but who most often deny or refuse it. Apparently, face-to-face confrontation may be too painful and possibly too shameful for these people. Can we find better ways to help them? Talk may really not improve behavior, especially with truly dysfunctional people. Talk is cheap and expensive at the same time: inefficient as a means of communication, uncontrollable inside and outside the professional's office, and liable to be either forgotten or distorted. In addition to these inadequacies of the verbal medium, there are other sacred cows that have been accepted wholesale and uncritically by the psychotherapy community. They are (1) seeing a professional face-to-face will improve behavior, (2) the professional's talk and personality as well as the therapeutic alliance will improve behavior, (3) the more family members involved the better, and (4) the more therapy sessions the better (L'Abate, 1999f).

Last but not least, one must consider recent criticisms leveled by one therapist (Mahrer, 1999) against the psychotherapy community. He argued that this field has "some embarrassing problems that are collectively denied" (p. 1147). He enumerated and expanded on 11 problem areas:

1. The field of psychotherapy is reluctant to admit that there really is a problem in the field of psychotherapy.
2. Many mental health professions insist on exclusive ownership rights over the field of psychotherapy.
3. Psychotherapists have virtually no subject matter of their very own.
4. Psychotherapists try to fix problems that are mainly unreal fictions concocted mainly by psychotherapists.
5. Psychotherapy is a pseudoscience of nonexisting unrealities measured with rigorous precision.
6. Instead of learning by observing and studying the work of fine psychotherapists, students are supposed to learn how to do psychotherapy without observing and studying the work of fine psychotherapists.

7. Psychotherapists are licensed, registered, certified, and accredited without having to demonstrate that they can do psychotherapy.
8. A program to train a person to do what psychotherapists do takes about two or three days.
9. Most psychotherapists are distinguished by their skill in speaking psychobabble.
10. The results of psychotherapy research have essentially made no significant differences in the field of psychotherapy.
11. Psychotherapy rests on a foundation of absolute truth, beyond questioning, examination, and falsification.

There is a great deal to argue about concerning the validity of each provocative point presented by Mahrer. His criticisms are mild in comparison to those leveled by L'Abate (1999f), and, some time ago, by Bodin and Ferber (1972) about the efficacy of the verbal medium. In at least one point, this writer (L'Abate, 1983b) agrees with Mahrer, and that is, psychotherapists are accredited without having to show whether they produce therapeutic results or not. They are credentialed on the basis of paper evidence rather than actual presentation of in vivo therapy cases with pretreatment and posttreatment evaluations, a level of proficiency required to pass examining boards.

Consequently, one could argue that the six shortcomings ("myths") found by Bickman (1999), the report from the Surgeon General, *Parade* magazine's survey, L'Abate's "five sacred cows," and Mahrer's (1999) 11 embarasssing problems point to the fact that drastic changes need to be made in how mental health services, that is, psychotherapy, are to be delivered in this century. It will be necessary to rely on additional media, rather than just talk, to help people in distress at a distance. In comparison to talk, the written medium, when programmed, is cost-effective, can be mass-produced, replicated by one professional for another and from one mental health setting to another as well as from one communication channel (e.g., fax, TV) to another (e.g., Internet). More specifically, the subtitle of this work, Programmed Writing and Structured Computer-Assisted Interventions, among other, less structured avenues, suggests some possible alternatives for help. Talk may fail, be too expensive, and not be available to those who may not need psychotherapy or crisis intervention, but who still need help, not necessarily through talk. The mental health needs of this and other nations will not and cannot be met as long as talk remains the main medium of communication and, in some cases, healing. A drastic change, perhaps an evolutionary if not paradigmatic shift, will occur when we start using all three media for communication and healing—nonverbal communication and writing—not just talk.

WHY A CLASSIFICATION FOR PSYCHOTHERAPY?

Why do we need to classify psychotherapy and psychological interventions? In addition to traditional classifications, this section considers dimensions that are relevant to an understanding of both therapeutic and preventive enterprises in the mental health field. Every human endeavor has attempted to classify itself, using either physical, scientific, artistic, or religious categorizations. Psychotherapy and the paratherapies (prevention and rehabilitation) have attempted to do so in the past. However, as we shall see, previous attempts have been limited, and, in the main, unsuccessful, in achieving some degree or semblance of satisfactory systematic order (Fishman, 1999; Zeig, 1997). There are few references (e.g., Bergin & Garfield, 1994) devoted to issues of classification for the psychotherapies and the paratherapies, which will be reviewed below.

Classifications are one way of organizing knowledge. One can therefore rationalize this attempt at classification on at least five grounds: as ways of

1. Making sense of reality and of the whole enterprise of helping people, which is confusing and unyielding
2. Categorizing ways of helping in a manner that would allow better understanding of the whole process
3. Finding a more specific link between evaluation and interventions, once we have a catalogue and classification of which treatments are applicable to which problem
4. Linking theory with practice, a process that can be achieved if a theory is comprehensive enough to be applicable to practice
5. Establishing distance writing and computer-assisted interventions as legitimate ways of helping people in distress, either as supplementary adjuncts or as sole alternatives to talk psychotherapy.

The first point represents the rationale for most if not all classificatory systems, which is, the need to allow for a more or less rational categorization of a plethora of psychotherapies and paratherapies that is now practically and conceptually unmanageable (Freeman, Simon, Beutler, & Arkowitz, 1989; McMullin, 1986; Norcross, 1986; Norcross & Goldfried, 1992; Talley, Strupp, & Butler, 1994). The last point indicates that writing needs to be placed within a psychotherapeutic framework to present an acceptable rationale for its clinical and nonclinical, preventive, and rehabilitative applications. A classification of the psychotherapies would give a context for the use of distance and programmed writing as a medium of intervention different from and in addition to talk.

A rationale for classification would allow comparisons and contrasts among various therapeutic and paratherapeutic methods. It would represent the baseline for commonalties and differences among methods or techniques. This baseline would allow us to comprehend a field that, even to the experienced eye, has reached practically incomprehensible proportions. Hence, classification would allow us to consider the basic dimensions that characterize various psychotherapeutic and paratherapeutic approaches. The identification of these dimensions may eventually allow us to map out their limits and their specific functions.

Hopefully, once this identification is even partially achieved, we might be able to use different approaches synergistically. If two different methods claiming to be therapeutic produce optimal results independently of each other, their combination should produce an even better outcome.

As Andrews, Bonta, and Hoge (1990) argued in regard to a classification system for offenders that applies as well to nonoffenders and to psychotherapy as well as to rehabilitation:

> Principles of classification for rehabilitation describe how particular classes of offenders may be linked with particular classes of discretionary service so that *effectiveness* of service is enhanced. "Effectiveness" has to do with achieving reductions in recidivism, "classes of offenders" refers to preservice differentiations based on the circumstances of offenders, and "discretionary service" refers to direct correctional service such as supervision, counseling, training, and treatment. (p. 19)

We need to know which therapy and paratherapy works for which problem at what cost, and with which therapist or facilitator. To answer these vexing questions, which have bothered mental health professionals since the various psychotherapies and paratherapies came into being (L'Abate, 1969b), we will need to know what we are doing and how we are doing it. A more or less rational classification of the psychotherapies and the paratherapies may be one step in the direction of answering such questions. This classification may allow us to understand what we are doing in a more specific manner than we would without it. Such understanding would give us greater certainty in our enterprise. We need to know what has happened in the past as we embark and get ready for the future. But the future is here! As a result of classification, we may become more flexible and specific in our use of both psychotherapeutic and paratherapeutic methods, since we would at least know which methods made up our armamentarium. Once we do have a catalogue, so to speak, of such methods, we might be able to pick and chose which method fits our professional interests and sensitivities as well as the needs of people in distress, allowing for greater specialization, specification, and, hopefully, cost-effectiveness.

Ultimately, a classification might allow us to match specific interventions with specific problems, including the issue of dual diagnosis. For instance, one may want to use a humanistic, present-oriented, feeling-focused approach with an individual who needs it, but become contextual and even paradoxical in dealing with that individual's family. How can we pick and choose if we do not know what we can pick and choose from? Before attempting a classification proper, however, we need to ask what the aims are of psychotherapy, and, for that matter, of any psychological intervention.

THE AIMS OF PSYCHOTHERAPY

There is really no agreement about the aims of psychotherapy among its practitioners (Bergin & Garfield, 1994; Freeman, Simon, Beutler, & Arkowitz,

1989; McMullin, 1986; Norcross, 1986; Norcross & Goldfried, 1992; Talley, Strupp, & Butler, 1994). Hence, whatever is submitted here is only one person's opinion, open to disagreement from other professionals. At least provisionally, the purposes of psychological interventions are to help individuals, couples, and families

1. Become able to express what they feel, especially their hurts
2. Become more aware of their historical/developmental/situational antecedents, which have, in part, determined their self-defeating, hurtful behaviors
3. Define themselves according to who they are in addition to what they do or what they have
4. Move from reactively repetitive or abusively apathetic (neglectful) styles to more conductively creative styles
5. Balance their extreme, contradictory, and inconsistent approach-avoidance and discharge-delay tendencies more appropriately and creatively
6. Reach selful definitions that will allow them to establish win-win rather than lose-win, win-lose, or lose-lose relationships and
7. Reorganize their priorities in ways that are going to be more rewarding to themselves and their loved ones.

In short, as argued in Chapters 5, 6, and 7, the purpose of any psychological intervention, directly or indirectly, is to help people learn how to love themselves and selected others who reciprocate the same feelings of love, and learn how to negotiate with them as well as with others outside their families (L'Abate, 1990, 1994a, 1997c, 1998a).

PAST CLASSIFICATIONS OF PSYCHOLOGICAL INTERVENTIONS

Psychotherapies and paratherapies are differentiated from each other in terms of their structural dimensions. Psychotherapies are open to what people bring into the therapy session, while the paratherapies do not give this choice. The former are usually open to the number of sessions needed and their content, with the exception of the brief therapy movement (Wells & Giannetti, 1990). The latter is very specific, stating beforehand the number of sessions necessary to complete a program and their contents. People who want paratherapeutic help such as assertiveness training or parenting skills, know beforehand what the topic of a program is, how long is going to last, and how much it will cost. Each lesson or session has a definite theme, topic, or goal, a characteristic that is not present in therapy sessions. Hence, we need to consider that possible classifications of psychotherapies may not apply to the paratherapies. The latter are structured beforehand, including the cost for the whole program. The former are left pretty much unstructured in terms of length, contents, and costs, except for the per-session professional fee. The referral question, of course, should orient the treatment. However, even when this question is present from the outset, it may not change the course of therapy, because as long as psychotherapy is based on talk, it will not be as specific and explicit as is necessary to address that question (Seligman, 1998).

For instance, past classifications of the psychotherapies concerned themselves very practically, concretely, and structurally with frequency of sessions (more than once a week, once a week, once every two weeks, once a month, etc.), composition (individuals, couples, families, or groups), duration (short versus long), intensity (supportive versus confrontational), temporal focus (past, present, and future-oriented), and therapeutic schools. L'Abate (1986b, 1994a, 1997c) has classified therapeutic schools according to what aspects of an information-processing cycle follow an ERAAwC model, to be reviewed further in Chapter 5. For instance, the humanistic school stresses Emotionality, psychodynamics stresses Rationality, behaviorism stresses Activity, gestalt and similar approaches stress Awareness, and family therapies stress Context.

Royce and Muehlke (1991) found some evidence to support the validity of the first three components (ERA) in selection of interventions strategies. Part of the same ERAAwC model was applied by L'Abate, Ulrici, and Wagner (1983) to a classification of psychoeducational skill training programs. In fact, these programs can be used as a criterion of fruitfulness and usefulness for various therapeutic schools. For instance, only humanistic and behavioral schools have generated preventive, psychoeducational skill training programs, the paratherapies. Psychoanalytic and systems-oriented schools have failed to produce such programs, for whatever reason (L'Abate, 1990).

The ERAAwC model is supported and elaborated further by Karasu (1996). He stressed the relationships among specific techniques of different psychotherapy schools in a similar fashion. He differentiated among Affective Experiencing (E), Cognitive Mastery (R), and Behavioral Regulation (A), in a way that is consistent with the ERAAwC model. For instance, *Affective Experiencing* consists of the following techniques: encounter, flooding, meditation, shared dialogue, body manipulation, group regression, massage, free association, isolation, role playing, and intravenous drugs. These techniques are represented by the following schools: existential analysis, implosion therapy, Arica, gestalt therapy, Rolfing, Erhard seminars, primal scream, psychodrama, and narcotherapy. *Cognitive Mastery* consists of techniques such as interpretation, clarification, attacking irrational ideas, providing information, thought stopping, search for meaning, correcting false beliefs, analysis of transference, paradoxical intention, analysis of body armor, confronting decisions. Schools representing these techniques are psychoanalysis, supportive therapy, rational therapy, sex therapy, behavior therapy, logotherapy, cognitive therapy, character analysis, and direct decision therapy. *Behavioral Regulation* consists of the following methods: conditioning, teaching and coaching, direct feedback, giving rewards, direct modeling, suggestion, punishment, relaxation. These techniques are matched by the following schools: behavior therapy, assertiveness training, biofeedback, token economies, modeling therapy, hypnotherapy, aversiveness training, and systematic desensitization. Awareness was included, instead, among the affective therapies. Karasu did not consider marital or family therapies, which would encompass the contextual (C) dimension not included in his otherwise apt classification.

A major systematic classification was devised by Howard, Nance, and Myers (1987). By using the two dimensions of high-low directiveness and high-low support, they were able to classify most methods of therapy into a fourfold matrix. For example, behaviorism would tend to be high in directiveness and support, while rational-emotive therapy would be high in directiveness and low in support. Rogerian nondirectivism would be low in directiveness and high in support, while psychoanalysis would be low in both directiveness and support. As ingenious as this classification is, it needs to be bolstered by evidence to support its validity. This evidence will be difficult to obtain as long as the main and only medium of exchange between therapist and respondent is talk.

CLASSIFICATIONS OF INSTITUTIONAL APPROACHES TO HELPING

There have been quite a few classifications of institutionalized approaches to helping. Some of these (Gibbs, 1989; Horwitz, 1990) consider helping people a form of control or power. Among these classifications, the most influential has been proposed by Brickman, Rabinowitz, Karuza, Coates, Cohen, and Kidder (1982). It consists of four models of interventions: (a) moral, religious or punitive, (b) medical or physical, (c) enlightenment or educational, and (d) compensatory or psychotherapeutic. According to Dunst, Trivette, and Deal (1988), each of these models predicts a different outcome, negative for the first three models and positive for the fourth—the compensatory model. When the locus of responsibility for past behavior and for improvement is added, only the compensatory model, equated with psychotherapy, wins out, because it avoids blaming the individual for past behavior but puts responsibility on the individual for improvement. This conclusion, however, will be questioned below.

Horwitz (1990), categorizes styles of social control according to four dimensions: harm, liability, goal, and solution. Using these four dimensions he obtains four different styles: (a) *penal*, where the solution is punishment, (b) *compensatory*, where the solution is payment, as in the welfare system, (c) *conciliatory*, where the solution lies in negotiation, and (d) *therapeutic*, where the solution is "treatment" of "personality" (p. 22). Thus, these two classifications differ in their definitions of "compensatory." While Brickman et al. equate the compensatory model with the psychotherapies, Horwitz does not. Nonetheless, both classifications do include the psychotherapies as one form of control or help, indicating, therefore, their already institutionalized nature. Once we see how the psychotherapies and paratherapies are embedded in cultural and societal frameworks, we can begin to make sense of them according to past and present modes of classification.

Perhaps both Brickman et al. and Horwitz's classifications could be reconciled if one were to suggest pleasure-pain and punishment-reward as orthogonal dimensions yielding a fourfold classification. The moral model is represented by some religions and the penal systems, using punishment and its infliction of pain as motivating forces. The medical model essentially deals with pain and suffering, trying to alleviate them, through amelioration and possibly rewarding through medications or operations. Some types of welfare systems are based on alleviating pain and perhaps giving some pleasure to people who have received so much punishment, that is, abuse, in their lives that they are unable to function on their own. The enlightenment model, exemplified by the self-help movement, tries to help people find more legitimate, rewarding, and socially acceptable ways of dealing with pleasure such as education and support groups. Within the same quadrant, the compensatory model is exemplified by the psychotherapies and paratherapies. They attempt to make up for what the other three models supposedly cannot do, and that is, help people find rewarding ways to achieve pleasure and to avoid pain.

Bohart and Tallman (1999) have argued that there are two major models of psychotherapy. They criticized the medical model for being too materialistic and mechanistic because it puts the physician in charge of treatment, with patients passively complying with instructions, directions, and prescriptions related to the referring symptom or disease. Treatment is differentially tailored to improving or "curing" the disease, regardless of the patient's mental state or the physician-patient relationship (p. 8). These authors even attack the term "intervention" as implying "intrusion or invasion" from "an external force" (p. 13). One could take exception to this definition, since this term, at least in the title of this book, is given a more benign connotation—"protective" rather than "interfering." Interventions presented in this book are only administered after respondents sign a full Informed Consent Form. They must agree to this type of intervention—programmed writing—with full knowledge of its experimental nature and its possible advantages and disadvantages. These interventions are not intended to intrude or invade any more than Bohart and Tallman say they do in their model of therapy. One cannot help but not intrude.

Instead of the medical model, which they set up as a scarecrow, Bohart and Tallman suggest a "Client-as-Active-Self-Healer" model that makes "clients" responsible for being active and creative agents of change: "Therapy is not like medicine; exercises and procedures are not surgical techniques that 'operate on' clients" (p. 20). These procedures, that, to these authors' credit, include writing and written homework assignments, "facilitate clients to focus on their own active self-healing strategies" (p. 20). Here, Bohart and Tallman create an arbitrary and questionable dichotomy that eventually, again to their credit, becomes a continuum of how to help people in distress. If the medical model is valid, then, these authors "would expect [among others] evidence that there are differential treatment effects with specific approaches producing different effects" (p. 25). Furthermore, within this model, "interventions would be powerful, potent, and specific" (p. 25). In contrast to the medical model, in their client-as-self-healer model, the relationship between therapist and client is all-important and all-healing: "Techniques will neither be the primary causes of therapeutic change nor be seen by clients as that important" (p. 26).

If this writer understands and interprets Bohart and Tallman's suggestions, the major issue between what they call the "medical model" and their "client-as-self-healer" model is one of specificity. The medical model favors it, while the so-called client-as-self-healer model is against it, supporting instead a rather general, vague, and nonspecific approach. Yet, if Seligman (1998) is correct, most psychotherapies, indeed, lack "specificity." The model promoted by Bohart and Tallman stresses relationship factors between therapist and patient and the active involvement of patients in the treatment process. As we shall see, PW/SCAI stress exactly the point they criticize, specificity of intervention, and do encourage respondent's involvement in the writing process. This goal of specificity is difficult if not impossible to obtain as long as therapists rely on talk. Respondents have to take responsibility for completing written homework assignments, and, to that extent, they follow a medical model because homework assignments, as will be shown in the following chapters, are very specific.

In spite of its nonspecificity and questionable evidence compared with the medical model, the client-as-healer model is advocated as the only way to help people in distress. The evidence, which, to Bohart and Tallman's credit, is cited and thoughtfully considered (Luborsky, Singer, & Luborsky, 1975), shows that there are really very few differences in outcome among the various psychotherapy schools. This conclusion, however, is still open to additional evidence that cannot be considered here. The jury is still out on which approach is more effective, even though the more focused and specific the model, the better the outcome (Clay, 2000).

Indeed, a point that is completely left out from Bohart and Tallman's otherwise seductive arguments is costs. These authors seem to forget that given equal results from two different treatments, the cheaper treatment wins out in the long run. For instance, given the choice of feeling better from depression after two to three weeks of medication in contrast to months and even years of psychotherapy, which treatment will respondents choose? Bohart and Tallman, allegedly, would still recommend psychotherapy. However, given the choice, which one will respondents pick? How many people just in the United States, let alone in the world, use antidepressants in contrast to the number of people using psychotherapy for the same condition? Unfortunately, this choice means that medication becomes a life-long procedure, while psychotherapy may produce longer lasting effects than medication. Drop-out rates and relapses indicate that verbal psychotherapy is not the appropriate choice for everyone. This approach could be bolstered by using either of the other two media, nonverbal communication and writing. Furthermore, most psychotherapeutic approaches seem to still ignore or entirely forget populations in hospitals, homes, jails, and penitentiaries who could use some interventions, but not necessarily those that are verbal. If, after months and years of psychotherapy, depression is still present, then what? Can Bohard and Tallman be so sure of their model that they will not suggest medication, knowing full well that a combination of psychotherapy and medication is still the best treatment for this and many other clinical conditions?

As this work develops, it will become clear that the approach advocated here supports the medical model because of the very specificity that Bohart and Tallman attack and decry. The model presented here, as will be shown, is not mutually exclusive or even antagonistic to the client-heal-yourself model. The use of PW/SCAI is definitely mechanistic and, as such, it follows the medical model. Hence, putting talk in its rightful perspective does not mean doing away with it. In many circumstances, indeed, it may well be the only source of communication and healing. Within that context, PW/SCAI are seen as synergistic with traditional talk-based psychotherapies when included in them, not exclusive of them. Furthermore, Bohart and Tallman seem to forget that the medical model is still helping millions of people to a level of functioning that psychotherapy will never reach as long as it is talk-based. We cannot forget that this model is responsible for advances undreamed of a century ago, which have changes the course of humanity. One needs to think about the control of infections like tuberculosis and polio as just a few of the many accomplishments of the medical model. These advances have taken place because of the very specificity that Bohart and Tallman so vehemently criticize. The model they denounce is not only "medical." It is a universal human model. If we live in the present world of material, technical, and communication advances, we owe it (for better or for worse) to mechanical operations that are replicable and specific in industry, science, and technology, not just in medicine. To criticize one model to advance one's own favorite model is creating a false dichotomy that is contrary to the realities of everyday life. However, just because this writer finds the medical model useful in PW/SCAI interventions does not indicate a lack of advancement and support for different models in other contexts (L'Abate, 1986b, 1990, 1994a, 1997a, 1998a).

THE CONTINUUM OF CARE AND PSYCHOTHERAPY

Psychological interventions are embedded and by now institutionalized within the context of societal, institutional methods to "help" control and change troubled people for the better. Both fields of psychotherapy and paratherapy are characterized by a bewildering and mystifying array of different approaches, methods, and forms of intervention with varying degrees of respectability, replicability, and varying claims of effectiveness (Abt & Stuart, 1982; Corsini, 1984; Harper, 1975; L'Abate, 1990; L'Abate & Milan, 1985; Lynn & Garske, 1985; Prochaska, 1984). How is one to make sense out of such a confused and confusing state of affairs? Classification is one way to attempt clarification for such a state. Perhaps, as suggested earlier, out of this classificatory effort a more discriminating ability to acknowledge the value of major therapeutic and paratherapeutic dimensions, their cultural context, and their limitations may emerge. Facing the future with a house somewhat in order rather than in disarray may allow psychotherapists to obtain greater professional credibility, if we are able to make sense of ourselves and of our endeavors (Cummings, 1987). Before becoming more specific, however, it may be important to embed both psychotherapies and paratherapies within the larger cultural context of how our American society deals with two of the basic dimensions of our humanity, namely pain-pleasure and reward-punishment (as discussed earlier).

Admittedly, in addition to education, as in family life education, there are at least two intermediate levels of preventive interventions that need to be considered between "nothing" and medication. There are at least two levels of intervention available before resorting to psychotherapy, crisis intervention, medication, hospitalization, incarceration, or combinations of either two, three or all four. Before psychotherapy, there are primary and secondary prevention, producing a continuum of care extending from education at one extreme to primary, secondary and tertiary prevention or psychotherapy (Table 1.1).

In the first place, in spite of all the programs included in this continuum, they remain a drop in the mental health delivery systems bucket, in comparison to the overall and overwhelming mental health needs of this and other nations (Bickman, 1999; U.S. Department of Health and Human Services, 1999), as already discussed. We have to find more cost-effective ways to prevent distress and help people in distress. In the second place, there are no sufficiently visible and well-known prevention programs—except perhaps, family life education, sex education, and pregnancy prevention—available to make a difference. Hence, there is very little help available to most people at risk or in need before a crisis looms large enough to require professional attention. In the third place, most people do not know about primary or secondary prevention programs. Indeed, there are many mental health professionals who do not know about these programs and who do not even advocate them. Most therapists, as far as this writer knows, avoid using primary prevention approaches to the point of avoiding referring their clients/patients to other professionals who use them.

In the fourth place, in many rural areas or small towns such programs are not available, producing a vacuum of nothing being available other than seeking therapeutic help. In the fifth place, many populations, such as incarcerated criminals, shut-ins, handicapped individuals, the poor and disenfranchised, are not sufficiently psychologically minded to seek face-to-face, verbal treatment or even prevention. At best, they will require medication and nothing else, even though we do know that, in most cases, as noted earlier, a combination of medication and psychological interventions will produce synergistic effects. Thus, as long as talk is our sole mode of intervention, we are not going to reach

Table 1.1
Criteria Used to Differentiate Among Preventive Approaches According to a Continuum of Care

Criteria	**Levels of Prevention**		
	Primary	*Secondary*	*Tertiary*
	Proactive Pre- or Post-therapeutic	Para-active Paratherapeutic or pre-post-therapeutic	Reactive Therapeutic
	Universal	*Selective (targeted)*	*Indicated**
1. Risk:	Low to minimal	High: in need but not critical	Very high: critical
2. Reversibility:	High: 100% to 66%	Medium: 66% to 33%	Low to very low: 33% to 0%
3. Probability of Breakdown:	Low but potential	Medium but probable	High and real (actual)
4. Population:	Nonclinical: labeled but not diagnosable	Pre-clinical and diagnosable	Clinical: critical and diagnosed
5. Ability to Learn:	High	Medium	Low
6. Goals:	Increase competence and resistance to breakdown	Decrease stress and chance of crisis	Restore to minimum functioning
7. Type of Involvement:	Voluntary: many choices	Obligatory: decrease in choices	Mandatory: no other choices are available
8. Recommendations:	"Could benefit by it" "It would be nice"	"You need it before it's too late" "Recommended strongly"	"It is necessary" "Nothing else will do" "Other choices would be more expensive (i.e. hospitalization, incarceration)"
9. Costs:	Low	Low to medium	High to very high
10. Effectiveness:	High	Medium	Medium to low
11. Personnel:	Lay volunteers Pre-paraprofessionals	Middle level professionals Professionals	Professionals and supervised personnel
12. Types of Interventions:	General strengthening:	More specific:	Specialized:
Example(s):	Social skills training	Workbooks	Psychotherapy
13. Degree of Structure:	High to medium	High with workbooks	Medium to low
14. Degree of Specificity:	High	High to medium	Medium to low

Source: L'Abate (1990)
* Mrazek & Haggerty (1994).

many populations who do need help of some kind, help that may not require talk and face-to-face contact with a professional.

One way of differentiating and classifying psychotherapies and paratherapies is to view them from the point of view of prevention. Preventive approaches have been classified according to extent of risk:

1. Primary, to take care of populations who are at risk as a whole, to avoid possible future breakdown. For instance, we all need skills to get along with others. Social skills training is usually one way to produce these skills for as many people as want them.
2. Secondary, to take care of people who are in need of further help but who are not as yet either diagnosed or in crisis, for instance, adult children of alcoholics—they are labeled, but they may not as yet show clinical or critical conditions
3. Tertiary, to take care of people who are in crisis and who demonstrate a diagnosable clinical or critical symptom or condition

Fourteen criteria can be used to differentiate among these three types of preventions (Table 1.1). Paratherapies could be used to strengthen the process of psychotherapy if therapists and preventers were able to talk with each other and started using their approaches synergistically rather than separately.

Paratherapies can be classified according to their degree of structure and of specificity of content (L'Abate, 1981a, 1986a). For instance, instructions for trainers of structured enrichment programs (L'Abate & Weinstein, 1987; L'Abate & Young, 1987) are given verbatim, while instructions for other well-known psychoeducational programs, like Parent Effectiveness Training (Gordon, 1970) and others, are given in general terms or in training manuals (Berger & Hannah, 1999). The result of this decreasing structure defines the role of the facilitator. The less structured the program, the greater the responsibility of the facilitator. For instance, facilitators of the Association for Couples Enrichment differ little from other group therapists (L'Abate, 1990). As far as composition is concerned, paratherapeutic skill training programs differ in their focus and content according to the type of participant, for instance, groups of individuals, premarital couples, couples as partners, couples as parents, children present or children absent, and so forth (L'Abate, 1990; L'Abate & Milan, 1985).

Primary Prevention

Primary or universal prevention consists of approaches, usually called psychoeducational skill training programs (PE-SST), designed to diminish the chances or risk of future breakdown. Examples are marital preparation and parenting programs (Bloom, 1996; L'Abate, 1983a, 1983b, 1990). This level of prevention may be conceived as being proactive, voluntary, and pretherapeutic. It aims at intervening before any need for intervention or crisis develops. These programs range from structured enrichment programs to various social skills training programs for individuals, premarital couples, marriage, and family issues (L'Abate & Milan, 1985; L'Abate & Weinstein, 1987; L'Abate & Young, 1987; Levant, 1986; McFarlane, 1991). These approaches are proactive and pretherapeutic and have been called, together with secondary prevention, the paratherapies. They have a specific content, focus, or topic, a predetermined number of sessions in a pre-set sequence, and a cost known before starting primary prevention (Table 1.1). Primary prevention is universal to the extent that even well-functioning individuals, couples, and families can profit from it, helping people at risk for possible future trouble (Berger & Hannah, 1999; L'Abate & Milan, 1985; Levant, 1986).

Primary prevention programs can be classified according to two separate program types (L'Abate, 1990). There are those that help to support and give a sense of community, like the many available self-help support groups, Alcoholics Anonymous being the primary example. These groups, part of primary prevention, help avoid the exacerbation of any dependency. However, most self-help support groups, by definition, do not teach new skills and are nontherapeutic in their orientation. Yet, they perform an admirable function in keeping their members sober or free of illegitimate or dangerous dependencies.

However, for everyone who attends support groups, there are still many other addicts and traumatized individuals who do not like the intimate confrontation of their dependencies. Furthermore, there are many other individuals, such as sex offenders, who are too ashamed to be stigmatized and to admit and subject their deviancy to public confrontation. In addition, there are many incarcerated individuals who receive minimal and mostly ineffective individual or group psychotherapy and who could use some form of intervention, not necessarily psychotherapy (Cellini, Hinze, Speaker, & Wood, 2000; Hughes, 2000; Simon, 1998). Therefore, primary prevention approaches, as helpful as they may be, still do not reach as many people who are at risk as may be necessary.

Another type of primary prevention, instead, stresses skill training, whether psychosocial, educational, or even technical. The last three decades have seen the development of new structured intervention approaches that have developed into the psychoeducational social skills training (PE-SST) movement. This movement looks at maladjustment and deviant behavior as straightforward skill deficits rather than amplifications of inferred conscious and unconscious motivations (Phillips, 1990). Hence, people with skill deficits need training rather than "therapy." This training consists of a specific presentation of concepts through lectures, experiences, and/or skill building using rehearsals, manuals, homework assignments, and printed course materials that guide the presentation. Rehearsals consist of (a) repeated practice of newly acquired skills, (b) open discussion and direct, active participation, that is, repetition of skills, by all participants, and (c) trying to increase generalization from the practice setting to other settings, like home, work-place, or leisure-time activities. Generalization means the ability to transfer newly learned skills acquired in one setting to another setting, either with similar effects or, usually, greater implied usefulness outside of the training setting (Bellack & Hersen, 1979; L'Abate & Milan, 1985; O'Donohue & Krasner, 1995; Singleton, Spurgeon, & Stammers, 1979; Sprafkin, Gershaw, & Goldstein, 1993).

A variation of this movement has been competence training—that is, if people lack skills, whether personal or interpersonal, what is needed is training to ameliorate these skills deficits (Bond & Rosen, 1980; Marlowe & Weinberg, 1985; Wine & Smye, 1981). If there are deficits, proper training, matched to those deficits, will improve competence and can be generalized to other situations. Hence, most PE-SST programs have been created with training around a specific deficit, for example, assertiveness, anger, anxiety, with (a) a predetermined number of training sessions, and (b) with a specific cost also known beforehand. In some instances, when this type of training has taken place in psychiatric institutions and clinical settings, costs are not billed to participants. Most PE-SST takes place in groups of individual, couples, and families. From functional or semifunctional individuals, this approach was extended and expanded to psychiatric, in-patient populations (Gordon & Gordon, 1981; Lieberman, DeLisi, & Mueser, 1989).

Parallel with this movement involving groups of individuals, there was also the development of marital (Berger & Hannah, 1999; L'Abate & McHenry, 1983) and parental programs (Levant, 1986) based on the same assumption of skill deficits. At its outset, this movement, as may be the case in many mental health movements in the last century, claimed to prevent mental health deficits and deviations. However, because of its inability to demonstrate long-term effects for these programs, the claim of prevention was eventually dropped. Nonetheless the term is still alive in the exortatory writings of its most ardent advocates (Cahalan, 1991; Lofquist, 1983; Pransky, 1991), in spite of the absence of long-term evidence to support its practice (L'Abate, 1986a; Russell, 1986). Consequently, even without the preventive label, PE-SST has become an important addition to the interventional armamentarium of approaches to individuals, couples, and families, between "nothing" and psychotherapy.

It is difficult if not impossible to draw a line between PE-SST programs and preventive efforts (Albee & Guillotta, 1997; Bloom, 1996; Kagan, Powell, Weissbound, & Zigler, 1987; Kessler, Goldston, & Joffe, 1992). Both fields have received a great deal of attention during the same period of time. Their overlap is such that no clear distinction between the two fields can be made. From the vantage point of prevention, the PE-SST movement qualifies as primary prevention, which in the last decade has seen the growth of a variety of preventive programs for children, adolescents, and their families (Bond & Wagner, 1988; Holman, 1992; Roberts & Peterson, 1984). There is no conceptual or theoretical basis for the introduction of these programs into any interventional armamentarium. Unfortunately, many of these programs have failed to be introduced as a part of most graduate training programs and therapeutic clinical practices, probably because therapists and preventers do not speak with each other and are unable to learn from each other, a failure that the whole mental health community must share.

Secondary Prevention

Secondary, selected, or targeted prevention consists of approaches designed to decrease the chances of breakdown in designated populations already in need of help, whose conditions, however, have not yet reached critical, chronic, or clinical proportions (Kaplan, 2000). One of the best examples of such populations is alcoholics. This level of prevention can be conceived as being para-active, somewhat obligatory, and paratherapeutic, if and when this type of prevention is available. Seeking help is still in the hands of those who want it, regardless of need (Table 1.1).

The quality of being targeted in parallel with other activities also implies that secondary prevention approaches could be added to either primary or tertiary prevention activities. Grown-up children of alcoholic parents, victims of past abuse, trauma, and stress, children of divorced parents, or pregnant adolescents would be relevant examples of populations that fit into this level. However, the most common method of intervention here has been based on face-to-face verbal interaction with a professional.

One example of secondary prevention is distance writing (DW). Writing can be viewed as being either paratherapeutic or parapreventive. It can be administered as a supplementary addition or as an alternative to either primary or tertiary prevention approaches. It can be used as either preliminary, preparatory, or parallel to either primary or tertiary prevention, thus becoming one type of secondary prevention (L'Abate, 1990; L'Abate, 1992b). Through the systematic use of DW/CAI, this method can be adapted to current mental health delivery services. Schools could incorporate psychoeducational modules of written homework assignments. Outpatient and partial hospitalization programs could easily incorporate a DW/CAI approach, especially PW (defined in the next chapter). Future applications might also include interactive TV and personal computer systems in public or university libraries, clinics, penitentiaries, and hospitals. Thus, the present work can and should be considered squarely as a contribution to secondary prevention approaches.

Having said the above, one can change the focus, as Kaplan (2000) critically indicated. One could recognize populations at risk and use at least distance writing as a preventive approach. Pennebaker (1997, 2001; Esterling & Pennebaker, 2001), for instance, used his expressive writing approach (to be explained in Chapter 2) with incoming freshmen at Southern Methodist University. This approach was used to decrease the number of drop-outs that typically occur during the first quarter of the first year of college.

Tertiary Prevention

Tertiary, necessary, or indicated prevention, like psychotherapy, is designed to help populations who have reached a crisis level in their lives (Table 1.1).

These populations require treatment, either psychological and/or medical. This level, in comparison to the two previous ones, can be conceived as reactive, that is, requiring immediate attention to the point of being necessary and, in some cases, mandatory. No other choices are available except psychotherapy and/or medication. Of course, in worst cases, hospitalization/incarceration may be necessary. Any delay in treatment would exacerbate the condition. Tertiary prevention approaches include all kinds of psychotherapies, which, at least in the United States, comprise hundreds of different schools, techniques, gimmicks, and gurus, that have, thus far, defied classification. So much has been written about the psychotherapies that it is unnecessary to go on about them any further, except in terms of their classification.

No more will be mentioned about this classification, except to stress that paratherapies could be used to strengthen and perhaps shorten the process of therapy and make it less expensive. Thus far, we have seen there are at least three levels of intervention available before resorting to psychotherapy, medication, hospitalization, incarceration, or combinations of two, three, or four. In addition to education, there are at least two intermediate types of preventive interventions, primary and secondary steps available between nothing and psychotherapy. Because DW/CAI are targeted and can be added to or combined with either primary or tertiary prevention, they are included in secondary prevention approaches.

DETERMINISM AND INDETERMINISM IN PSYCHOTHERAPY

The purpose of this section is to show how both determinism and indeterminism are necessary for helping people in distress. Helping people is the goal of different belief and value systems held among therapists and preventers. As Giacomo and Weissmark (1987) indicated, there are two major value systems (contexts) available to theorists and scientists as well as therapists: indeterminism and determinism (Table 1.2). Both contexts can be seen as either two sides of the same coin—as a continuum—or as two separate, mutually exclusive value systems. To help people, however, one would argue that both value systems are necessary (L'Abate, 1986b), and that they distribute themselves along a continuum well articulated by Bohart and Tallman (1999). Bohart and Tallman identified five different levels of collaboration with clients (pp. 139–164): (1) maximal therapist control of the change process, minimal client collaboration, (2) therapist's technique is primarily responsible for change, compliance with therapist's instructions is the only form of client's collaboration, (3) therapist's techniques provide the context for learning but client is an active, collaborating, and fully participating agent in the process, (4) active client collaboration by complying and participating in techniques that "liberate" the "client's creativity and generativity," and (5) the client is an active self-healer, codirector, and collaborator in the process of change by being the "primary generator." Of

Table 1.2
Determinism and Indeterminism in Psychotherapy

Indeterminism		**Determinism**
(Unpredictability of Random Behavior)	(Giacomo & Weissmark, 1987)	(Predictability of Lawful Behavior)
Discovery	(Reichenbach, 1936)	Justification
Speculation	(Polanyi, 1964)	Verification
Dialectic	(Rychlak, 1975)	Demonstrative
Heuristic	(Nystrand, 1977)	Explicative
Aesthetic	(Keeney & Sprenkle, 1982)	Pragmatic
Experiential/qualitative/subjective	(L'Abate, 1986b)	Empirical/objective/quantitative/operational
"Mythos" human emotions	(Labouvie-Vief, 1990)	"Logos" logic and rationality
Experiential	(Epstein, 1994)	Rational
Discovery-oriented	(Bohart & Tallman, 1999)	Prescriptive-tutorial
Hermeneutics/social Constructionism	Pragmatism (Fishman, 1999)	Logical positivism/empiricism
Intuition/holism	(Kimble, 1999)	Empiricism/analysis
Narrative	(McAdams, 1996)	Empiricism

Source: Updated from L'Abate (1994a).

course, Bohart and Tallman favor the last level, while the present formulation favors levels 3 and 4.

This continuum, therefore, illustrates and indicates various degrees of determinism and indeterminism, with level 1 representing the extreme of determinism and level 5 the extreme of indeterminism. This continuum will be presented dichotomously for illustrative purposes. However, these seeming dichotomies could, again, be considered two sides of the same coin (L'Abate, 1986b). Two major areas of knowledge and professional skills are necessary to explicate this dimension.

Knowledge

A major distinction to be made consistently and repeatedly about knowledge is derived from the dimension of determinism-indeteminism. The most interesting and important aspect of knowledge pertains to its dualistic nature. That is, most sources agree that there are two kinds of knowledge (L'Abate, 1986b; Rychlak, 1975). One is dialectic and based on directly personal, subjective aesthetic grounds. The other is demonstrative and based on pragmatic, objective grounds. Nystrand (1977) bases both kinds on linguistic usage, equating dialectics with the heuristic use of language and the right hemisphere, oriented toward discovery, and the demonstrative with the explicative use of language and the left hemisphere, oriented toward justification. The former belongs to the realm of indeterminism. The latter belongs to the realm of determinism (Table 1.2).

The heuristic belongs to the personally subjective and phenomenologically receptive side of experiencing, while the explicative belongs to the intersubjectively objective, visibly expressive side. Whether one sees these two as extreme polarities of one dimension of knowledge or two sides of the same coin, there is no doubt that one kind cannot operate without the other. Both are necessary to the whole human enterprise, including and especially psychotherapy (L'Abate, 1986b). As summarized in Table 1.2, various sources have contributed to this distinction. Of course, additional dichotomies could be used (Gergen, 1994), such as narrative versus verifiability, antiscientific nihilism versus demonstrability, metaphors versus literalities, and critique versus construction.

Once this duality of knowledge acquisition and dispersion is accepted, we need to concern ourselves with the skills necessary to "do" psychotherapy. Here, again, we meet another duality, which can be considered either as a continuous dimension with two extremes or as a dichotomy—two sides of the same coin. In dealing with ways of helping people we need to stress differences between style and method in both the psychotherapies and the paratherapies, as summarized in Table 1.3. Bruner (1990) distinguished between two ways of thinking, a paradigmatic one favoring a rational, logical, and fact-oriented view of reality, and a narrative one, favoring human intentions and desires based on personal whim and will. These two modes of thought may be related to the different hemispheric localizations that may be needed in writing, requiring left-hemispheric functions, versus the right-hemispheric functions needed in talk and psychotherapy (L'Abate, 2001a; Ornstein, 1997). These different modes of thinking and their respective hemispheric functions may explain the gap between hard-headed, evidence-based therapists primarily using structuring skills, versus soft-hearted therapists favoring relationship skills (Bohart & Tollman, 1999; L'Abate, in press).

Professional skills derive from whatever knowledge, training, and experience have been acquired by therapists in the course of becoming credentialed, full-fledged professionals. As such, they deserve and require a separate section.

RELATIONSHIP AND STRUCTURING SKILLS IN PSYCHOTHERAPY

Therapeutically, the two different value systems of determinism-indeterminism can be seen in the major differentiation for therapeutic skills, divided into relationship skills or style dear to the heart of humanistic therapists and structuring skills dear to the heart of behavioral therapists (Table 1.3). Therapeutically, especially when working with couples and families, we need both sets of skills. It would be very difficult if not impossible to work with one set of skills without the other set. However, do relationship skills require personal, verbal contact and presence? Elsewhere (L'Abate, 1999f, 2001a, in press), this writer has argued that one does not need to be present face-to-face to be emotionally available to someone in crisis. It can be done at a distance on the phone

Table 1.3
Relationship and Structuring Skills in Psychotherapy

Relationship		Structuring (Writing)
(Style/Community)	(Bakan, 1968)	(Method/Agency)
One shot deal		Sequence of repeatable steps
Dependent on and specific to each therapist		Independent of therapist's style
Nonreplicable or difficult to replicate		Easily replicable
Asserting clients' inherent worth and importance		Assessing objectively the nature of referral problem and symptom
Dealing with respondents as persons and not as objects		Dealing specifically with the symptom or referral question
Global, holistic, and subjective		Detailed, particularistic, and objective
Necessary to start and to maintain relationship but insufficient to help produce changes in respondents		Perhaps insufficient to start and maintain relationship but necessary to help produce changes in respondents
Being available emotionally to self and verbally and nonverbally to respondents		Systematic written homework assignments (programmed writing)
Impressionistic		Reductionistic
Anedoctal		Factual
Extreme variability		Narrowed variability
Unplanned		Planned
Nonprogrammable		Programmable
Nonrepeatable from one therapist to another		Repeatable from one therapist to another
Immediate (mainly for office use)		Delayed (mainly for home use)
Specific to the person and style of the therapist		Specific to the symptomatic behavior to be improved
Idiographic		Nomothetic as well as idiographic

Source: L'Abate (1991, 1994a) and L'Abate & Platzman (1991).

and on the Internet, as is already done every day right now by an ever-increasing number of cyberspace professionals.

Professional Skills

Psychotherapeutic and paratherapeutic processes, therefore, are the outcome of two sets of therapeutic skills. The first set, relationship skills, represents what therapists do and say in the office in front of and in contact with respondents. The second set, structuring skills, represent what therapists do and say to help respondents change where it matters the most, that is, in the home, in the office, or in leisure-time activities. Skills related to the relationship—Rogers' (1957) warmth, unconditional regard, and empathy—take place in the professional's office. Skills related to structuring interventions are designed to direct behavior outside of the therapy office, through task assignments (Levy & Shelton, 1990), paradoxical injunctions, ordeal work, and prescriptions such as marital and family conferences (L'Abate, Ganahl, & Hansen, 1986; Weeks & L'Abate, 1982).

These sets of skills represent the omnipresent distinction between the soft-hearted, aesthetically dialectical style of the therapist in dealing with the relationship, and hard-headed, pragmatically demonstrative methods for dealing with symptomatic behaviors (reviewed earlier). Style is both general and particular to each therapist's person and personality. It varies from one therapist to another. Method, as a series of repeatable and reproducible steps, is specific and applies to the treatment of symptomatic behavior, supposedly regardless of the therapist's personality. Both sets of skills, style and method, are necessary for a positive therapeutic outcome (L'Abate, 1986b). Relationship skills, by definition, focus on the person and personalities of respondents. To that extent, they are vague and general, as indicated by Bohart and Tallman (1999). They are important for establishing rapport and maintenance of the therapeutic relationship in some but not all cases. Structuring skills, on the other hand, focus on dealing with problematic or symptomatic behavior.

The first set of relationship skills is dear to the hearts of individually oriented humanistic therapists and preventers (Miller, 1989; Rogers, 1957). The second set of structuring skills is basic to a more systematic approach to symptoms and problems through repeatable methods of step-wise interventions. These methods are found in more expressively active, even intrusively directive modes of intervention based on written prescriptions, task assignments, and homework assignments away from the therapist's office. This approach is favored by behaviorally and empirically oriented therapists (Dobson & Craig, 1998; Hayes, Follette, Dawes, & Grady, 1995; Nathan & Gorman, 1998). The latter are mostly academic researchers who also support a more deterministic approach to therapy based on structuring its process. One characteristic of structuring approaches that seems lacking in relationship-focused approaches is matching problem with solution, a level of specificity denied by an indeterministic viewpoint.

While we may agree about the need for relationship skills to establish rapport and trust with respondents, we need to elaborate on what constitutes structuring skills. These skills deal with how we organize treatment, from setting fees and appointment times to how we deal with problems presented to us. While the number of receptive relationship skills is fairly limited by how we relate to respondents, structuring skills comprise an extremely wide repertoire of interventions, more or less specific, more or less concrete, and more or less helpful. Supposedly, the wider our repertoire of structuring skills, the better the chance of matching problem with solution. To look at this repertoire of skills, however, we need to combine both therapeutic, pretherapeutic, and paratherapeutic skills. Combining psychotherapies and paratherapies would lead to a complete catalogue and classification of all the structuring skills we may ever need.

SPECIFICITY VERSUS GENERALITY

One of the major controversies in the field of psychotherapy (Bergin & Garfield, 1994; Frank, 1973; Karasu, 1996) has been whether there are specific or nonspecific factors that determine therapeutic outcome. For instance, is the success of a therapeutic approach due to the therapist's warmth, unconditional regard, and empathy, or is it due to the theoretical allegiance held by the therapist? Karasu (1996), as reviewed above, tried to solve the controversy by identifying the "three therapeutic change agents that all schools of therapy share as the basis of their different techniques" (p. 687), namely, affective experiencing, cognitive mastery, and behavioral regulation. Bradley (2000), as well as this writer, would support this position, but would stress that affective experiencing would need to be regulated behaviorally through cognitive mastery.

On the basis of the previous classifications, it would seem that the issue could be dealt with in a different fashion. Specificity must be applied to a symptom or referring question or problem in determinate and deterministic ways that have been planned, prepared, tested, and rehearsed. Symptoms need to be dealt with using objective, standardized, and, therefore, nomothetic methods based on structured, systematic plans and programs set out in writing. Generality (nonspecificity), on the other hand, deals with persons and personalities in a reactive, unplanned, and unprepared manner. This approach refers to the style of the therapist or facilitator, which is subjectively spontaneous and individualized in an idiographic fashion. Specificity deals with structuring skills. Generality deals with relationships (Table 1.3).

Hence, the two sets of skills reviewed here reflect Bakan's (1968) distinction between community and agency. The seeking of community and closeness is part of relationship style, while the seeking of agency is part of structuring style. As noted earlier, whether the wide gap between therapists on main streets and researchers in ivory towers is due to different hemispheric localizations is an intriguing possibility also related to different value systems, information processing, and differences between spoken and written media (L'Abate, 2001a). Therapists who stress therapy as an unique art based on faith, which needs no questioning because art is what an artist calls art, would tend toward a community orientation. Therapists who stress therapy as science that needs continuous and repeated evaluation tend toward an agentic orientation. The emphasis of the present work stresses the latter orientation. However, the stress that is necessary here for purposes of full exposition does not deny the importance of the former orientation. The issue with a community orientation lies in how to do it. Is face-to-face contact between a patient and a professional necessary to establish a trusting relationship and a successful outcome? This writer would argue that it is not.

Psychotherapy as Art and Community: Nonreplicable Relationship Skills?

Little needs to be said here that has not been said already in all the many psychotherapy texts available on the market. The whole issue of psychotherapy as art will be left in the hands of those who want to pursue that particular aspect. Nonetheless, L'Abate (1997b) suggested that the common factors among all the various therapies available on the market are not warmth, unconditional regard, and empathy. These qualities, although noble, may help some individuals sometimes, but would not last beyond the third session of therapy with couples and families. Instead, the common factors of most talk therapies consist of three classes of behaviors: (1) in the emotional intensity of a novel situation, finding someone who listens to our feelings and validates them in a positive rather than negative fashion, as had occurred in the respondent's past, (2) predictability in the repetition of agreed-upon appointments, like duration of sessions and their weekly frequency, and (3) direction of whatever is the agreed-upon goal to reach as an outcome of therapy. The first factor relates to *community*: being together in a relationship with someone who listens to us and seems to care, even for a fee, as stressed by Bohart and Tallman (1999) among many others. The second and third factors combined relate to structuring, or *agency*. The latter is of special interest to this work and will be expanded throughout it.

Psychotherapy as Science and Agency: Structuring Skills as Replicable Methods

In a study of the relationship between therapist competence and the outcome of cognitive-behavioral therapy, Shaw, Elkin, Yamaguchi, Olmstead, Vallis, Dobson, Lowery, Sotsky, and Watkins (1999) concluded that: "The component of competence that was most highly related to [psychotherapy] outcome is a factor that reflects the therapist's ability to structure the treatment" (p. 837). More to the point, they concluded: "Thus, of key importance in this study was the therapist's ability to deal competently with setting an agenda and assigning relevant homework while pacing the sessions appropriately" (p. 844). This conclusion supports similar findings stressing the importance of outcome in relation to homework compliance (Burns & Nolen-Hoeksema, 1992; DeRubeis & Feeley, 1990; Fennel & Teasdale, 1987; Kazantzis, 2000; Kazantzis, Deane, & Ronan, 2000). Hence, the most basic issue here seems to be structuring treatment and administration of relevant homework assignments.

In summary, both sets of relationship and structuring skills are necessary in psychotherapy to produce change. The issue remains as to who will benefit by relationship skills and who will benefit by structuring skills? Who will profit by both and who will not profit by either? Probably, internalizing disorders may benefit by relationship skills, while externalizing disorders may benefit by structuring skills. Severe psychopathologies might benefit by both as well as medication. Some, unfortunately, will not profit by any approach.

The rest of this section will deal with the whole issue of homework assignments.

Prescriptive versus Exploratory, Reactive versus Nonreactive Therapies

Ultimately, the function of a classification should facilitate the task of prescription, a task that thus far has taken place along subjective and difficult-to-replicate lines (Beutler, 1989; Howard, Nance, & Myers, 1987; Perry, Frances, & Clarkin, 1990; Seligman, 1990). As long as talk remains the major modality of exchange between therapists and respondents, this goal of prescription will remain unrealistic and difficult to reach. In using written homework assignments, especially programmed ones, however, one can achieve a level of prescription otherwise unreachable verbally (L'Abate, 1990, 1992b, 2001a). As Barkham, Shapiro, and Firth-Cozens (1989) suggested, it may be possible to use prescriptive therapy at the beginning of therapy followed by more exploratory, relationship-oriented therapy later. The same approach could be recommended in working with character disorders. Respondents may have to finish working on written programs to demonstrate their willingness and motivation to change. If change is demonstrated in writing, they may then benefit by a personal relationship based on talk. As in medicine, one goes from cheaper to more expensive approaches—what this writer has called "successive hurdles" or "sieves" (L'Abate, 1990; Reed, McMahan, & L'Abate, 2001).

Active versus Passive Psychotherapy

Another dimension that seems crucial to the process of helping people is the degree of activity necessary for the therapist or facilitator. Rather than considering one aspect of the dimension, activity-passivity, as being better than the other, one would argue instead that both are necessary for positive outcome. There are times when professionals need to be active. There are times when professionals need to be passive. Activity for professionals means to be directively prescriptive and conductively confrontational about issues, symptoms, and problem-solutions, requiring, therefore, structuring skills. Passivity in helping people does not mean apathy and lethargy, giving up or abandoning people, as exemplified by "active listening." It means being nondirectively reflective of their problems and reactively supportive of their hurts, requiring relationship skills of warmth, unconditional regard, empathy, and the ability to reframe positively what are perceived by respondents as being negative issues. Therefore, activity can be related to but not equated with structuring skills, while passivity can be related to but not equated with relationship skills or style. Neither quality needs face-to-face, verbal contact to be helpful.

Matching Problem with Solution

Why classification? In addition to the need to order and review psychological interventions, classification is one form of understanding. If we are able to classify an array of interventions, this will be one way of understanding them: by organizing and ordering them according to their most salient characteristics. There is another advantage that should derive from classification: the possibility of matching a specific type of intervention with a specific human problem. In spite of planners and treatises that attempt to link a specific clinical condition with a matching type of intervention (Jongsma & Peterson, 1995; Jongsma, Peterson, & McInnis, 1996; Jongsma & Stout, 1997; Oher, Conti, & Jongsma, 1998; O'Leary, Heyman, & Jongsma, 1998; Perkinson & Jongsma, 1997; Schultheis, 1998), as long as the major medium of intervention is based on talk, it will be difficult and expensive to demonstrate that such a link has taken place.

The problem of matching problem with solution has been searched and researched since the beginning of psychotherapy research (Bergin & Garfield, 1994). More recently there has been a whole series of contributions (Beutler, 1979, 1989; Beutler & Clarkin, 1990; Hayes, Nelson, & Jarett, 1987; Hill, 1989; Howard, Nance, & Myers, 1987; Hurt, Reznikoff, & Clarkin, 1991; Luborsky, Crits-Christoph, Mintz, & Auerbach, 1988; Okun, 1990; Perry, Frances, & Clarkin, 1990; Seligman, 1990) attempting to match specific interventions with specific problems.

However, the empirical bases of previous attempts at matchings between problem and solution have been brought into question by the critical review of Moncher and Prinz (1991). These contributions represent the culmination of efforts over the last quarter century attempting to answer the troublesome question that has haunted the field of psychotherapy since its inception, and that is: "Which patient will profit most by which method or combination of methods by which therapist at what price?" (L'Abate, 1969b, p. 487). The same question can be rephrased in the present context as: "What kind of intervention will be beneficial for which problem at what cost?" Among the many issues that this question has generated is one that does not seem to have interested past contributions, and that is: "How can we match problem with solution if we do not have a catalogue of available solutions?" Nowhere in the contributions listed above, nor in other basic references dedicated to the whole issue of matching problem with solutions, is there concern about a catalogue or classification of available methods of interventions. This concern would be a starting point toward dealing with, if not solving, the whole problem of matching (Corsini, 1984; Freedheim, 1992; Hersen, Kazdin, & Bellack, 1991; Weiner, 1976). We need to have classifications to make differentiations and choices that could not be made otherwise, including answering the two questions asked above. Hence, we need to classify solutions to achieve a match between problem and solution. Such a catalogue of "solutions," that is, workbooks matching various clinical and nonclinical problems and symptoms, is given in Chapter 4.

Assuming, then, a continuum of care ranging from: (1) relationship only, (2) structure only, and (3) relationship plus structure, we need to find who will benefit by relationship only, who will benefit by structure only, and who will benefit by both, as well who will benefit by one before the other in tandem, or together. Of course, this process implies finding who does not benefit by any interventions of this kind. At this juncture, for instance, one can hazard the possibility that depressed and anxious individuals might benefit mainly by relationship, and acting-out and impulsive character disorders might benefit mainly by structuring.

Severely dysfunctional individuals might benefit by both relationship and structuring combined plus medication. Of course, it is the very nature of severe dysfunctionality to reject any kind of intervention, including and especially medication. These possibilities, however, may not hold water with couples and families who want immediate and practical solutions to their problems. Relationship factors may last up to the third session of therapy. After that session, people in distress, whether individuals, couples, or families, want clear directions and plans that would address their initial concerns, the referral question. Hence, relationships skills may be useful with certain kind of individuals. These skills may be useful at the beginning of couple and family therapy. However, after a few sessions, people in distress need some kind of structure, even if it consists only of weekly appointments, without any content assigned. Given that both relationship and structuring are necessary, the basic question here is: "What kind of structuring?" The rest of this work will be devoted to answering this question. What is meant by "severely dysfunctional" individuals will be explained further in Chapter 5.

MEDIA OF INTERVENTION IN PSYCHOTHERAPY

As we are moving conceptually from the larger cultural context to more restricted and limited therapeutic contexts, we need to concern ourselves with the most immediate contexts for interventions. The media through which we communicate and exchange resources are: (a) verbal, (b) nonverbal, and (c) writing. If we consider that psychological development starts with the nonverbal medium, progresses then to verbal, and ends with the written medium, each medium possesses characteristics and functions of its own that may or may not be shared by the other two media. Traditionally, psychotherapy started by relying mainly on the verbal medium. With the advent of humanistically oriented therapeutic practices, nonverbal therapies were added to the therapeutic armamentarium, as advocated elsewhere (L'Abate, 1997b). Only recently has the written medium been added to complete the full implement of approaches needed to communicate and help people change for the better. Writing, as will be shown, allows a

Table 1.4
Media of Intervention and Functions of Settings Inside and Outside Psychotherapy

Channels of Intervention	**Settings**	
Media	*Inside Therapist's Office*	*Outside Therapist's Office*
Verbal	Evaluation interview Direction of treatment Confrontation of issues Motivation for change Generalization to outside Emotional support	Talking with self Dialogue with partner, relatives, family of origin, friends, older children, coworkers
Nonverbal	Awareness exercises Nonverbal communication Body movements Dance, art, play Biofeedback Kinesiology Virtual reality	Sports and exercise Nutrition-diet Vitamins Meditation Medication
Written	Evaluation through questionnaires and test instruments	Distance writing and workbooks

Source: L'Abate (1994a, p. 227).

degree of specificity, explicitness, and individualization that is not present in paratherapies and certainly not, as Seligman (1998) has argued, in talk-based psychotherapy (L'Abate, 1990, 1992b; Mahoney, 1991; Pennebaker, 1997).

Isomorphism between Inside and Outside the Professional Office

Any intervention, whether therapeutic or paratherapeutic, is designed to help people improve their behavior at home and at work, if not in their leisure activities. Ideally there should be some isomorphism between what happens inside the professional office and on the outside. This, of course, represents the whole issue of generalization or transfer of training that is the desideratum of psychological interventions. Consequently, we need to classify what usually happens in the professional office and what should ideally happen outside of it. Table 1.4 shows how these three media have isomorphic parallels between the therapist's office and behavior outside of it. How does behavior (insights, understanding, experiences, etc.) supposedly learned in the therapist's office generalize to settings outside of that office? Is that not the goal of all therapies—to improve behavior outside of the therapist's office? All three media of communication, not just talk, can be used synergistically to improve behavior outside of our offices.

No matter which theory determines which treatment, as long as treatment is based on talk, links between the two domains are going to be difficult if not impossible to obtain and to prove. Only when treatment is linked with evaluation through writing will we be able to link the two domains to achieve the match we have been looking for through the last generation and longer (Howard, Nance, & Myers, 1987; Seligman, 1990). We have been looking for the Holy Grail of match between theory and treatment without critically questioning whether our quest was appropriate or worth doing. This classification allows us to see that treatment needs to take place using a variety of modalities and that, in combination, these modalities may allow us to intervene with more people in a more discriminating manner than has been the case heretofore.

In addition to this developmental comparison, we need to consider a structural comparisons of the three media—how these three media are used inside and outside the psychotherapist's office. For instance, some therapists may be able to influence a patient's habits in diet, exercise, and use of vitamins, impacting also the nonverbal medium outside of the therapist's office. The majority of therapists, however, do not enter into this nonverbal field. Often, emphasis on talk without any other requirements takes place at the expense of the other two media, which are not yet part of mainstream practices in mental health. While the nonverbal medium shares some problems with psychotherapy in terms of being difficult to record, codify, and classify, DW has a long, mostly unknown history of having been used for preventive and therapeutic purposes.

Nonverbal Communication

"Nonverbal" communication refers to facial, gestural, postural, and locomotor movements that are observable. Unfortunately, we cannot usually observe internal, psychophysiological reactions that may or may not be expressed nonverbally. Studies of Davis and Hadiks (1990) and Hill and Stephany (1990), among many others not cited here, do suggest that the nonverbal modality needs to be acknowledged as another way to access people who may not be otherwise or verbally accessible. Art, dance, and play therapy, among others (Table 1.4), can be conceived of as nonverbal avenues of intervention that could be used synergistically with talk and writing. Again, for reasons of space and relevance, the reader is referred to external sources to evaluate this modality as a potentially powerful way to intervene helpfully with people in trouble.

Verbal Communication

Speech has been traditionally equated with psychological treatment (Nathan & Gorman, 1998; Russell, 1989). We tend to forget that the two other media, nonverbal communication and writing, can no longer be ignored or avoided. Since most of the literature on psychotherapy using the verbal medium is quite extensive, to the point that the two—psychotherapy and talk—are used synonymously, there is no point in belaboring its relevance here. The major point

Table 1.5
Comparisons Among Modalities of Intervention

Nonverbal	Spoken*	Written*
Earliest to be learned	Learned earlier in life at home	Learned later in life in school
Easiest form of information	Easier than written language	Harder than spoken language
Automatic/effortless	Takes less effort	Takes more effort
Extremely informative on few cues	More productive per unit of time	Less productive per unit of time
Learned automatically Spontaneous	Learned automatically Spontaneous	Has to be taught Deliberate
Dependent on immediate context	Dependent on immediate social context	More autonomous of social context
Restricted and limited to few channels	More ideas per unit of time	More ideas per number of words
No permanent record (unless videotaped)	No permanent record (unless tape recorded)	Permanent record
Relatively simple	Less syntactically complex	More syntactically complex
Fairly concrete	Less abstract	More abstract
Immediate	Less time needed for planning and encoding	More time needed for planning and encoding

Source: *Adapted from Weintraub (1981).

about talk, however, relates to the extensive research by Pennebaker and King (1999). They found that "immediacy" is the major characteristic of language, as argued elsewhere by L'Abate (1999f). If this is the case, psychotherapy does not leave room for the development of cognitive controls. It would be easier, less expensive, and perhaps more cost-effective to achieve these controls through DW and programmed writing at pre-set times.

Communication through Writing

Writing is third in development. Since it is the subject of this work, there is no need to repeat explanations about its use in psychotherapy. Its nature and its classification will be discussed in the next chapter.

COMPARING THE THREE MEDIA

Each medium performs specific functions that are different from the other two media (Table 1.5). Each medium has its peculiar advantages and disadvantages. Sometimes one medium may take over for another medium. However, the specificity of functions still remains for each medium. Whichever functions are fulfilled by one medium usually cannot be taken over by another medium.

Hence, it is important to compare the three media in order to understand how each medium can help people in distress.

Advantages of Nonverbal over Spoken Medium

If the nonverbal medium is based directly on our body, then it is also the most primitive or earliest medium of communication. Developmentally, the nonverbal medium takes place earlier than the other two media. Hence, this medium could become a depository of stored memories. Witness the (admittedly impressionistic) report from respondents who are undergoing "body work" such as Rolfing or massage (L'Abate, 1994a). The many different expressions of nonverbal behavior allow us to enlarge our practices as much as they would allow us to widen the range of problems we may be able to deal with. The use of art, dance, play, movement, and other awareness-directed activities in groups would allow us to help more respondents per unit of therapist's time than when we rely solely on the spoken word. Many nonverbal techniques lend themselves to group activities than would not be feasible through the spoken word, except, of course, group psychotherapy. Many character or personality disorders that are typically resistant to verbal therapy may benefit by nonverbal approaches before any other medium of intervention is attempted (L'Abate, 1997b).

Advantages of Nonverbal over Written Medium

The written word is not as immediately available as the body is. The body may allow access to stores of painful memories imprinted on it that may not be as immediately accessible through spoken, face-to-face contact. Many nonverbal awareness exercises may open up a flood of past experiences that may need to be followed up through the written medium. Both media, of course, may complement each other. While nonverbal activities lend themselves to group interventions, written experiences, as shown below, may lend themselves to a more individualized approach.

Advantages of Written over Spoken Medium

In comparison to talk, writing is more explicit and can be more specific than words (Table 1.6). Writing can become definite and finite, whereas talk is indefinite and infinite, subject to and liable to create obfuscations, confusions, misunderstandings, deletions, distortions, and unwarranted generalizations. Writing can be determinably explicit, whereas talk is indeterminably liable to distortions, deletions, and misinterpretations. The explicit specificity of writing makes it controllable, while talk is noncontrollable. We cannot predict and, even less, control what respondents and therapists are going to say. Even training manuals for therapists may limit the therapist's variability, but they do not limit clients' variability. Talk is essentially infinite, while writing, especially when

Table 1.6
Comparisons between Speech and Writing

Speech is learned earlier in life than writing.
Speech is easier to learn than writing.
Writing must explain a situation fully in order to be understood by the reader, this completeness may not be necessary in speech.
Learning to speak is automatic whereas writing must be taught systematically.
Speech takes less effort, and therefore, is more productive than writing per unit of time.
Speech is spontaneous whereas writing is deliberate.
Language is dependent on immediate social context whereas writing is more autonomous of the immediate context.
There are more ideas in speaking per unit of time whereas in writing there are more ideas per number of words.
There is no permanent record in speech, but there is one in writing.
Speech is syntactically less complex than writing.
Speech is more concrete (or less abstract) than writing.
Less time and planning are necessary to speak than to write.
There is more retention in reading and writing than there is in speaking because writing can be repeatedly accessed but speech, unless recorded, cannot.
More issues can be confronted in writing than can be confronted verbally per unit of therapist's time.

Source: Paraphrased from Weintraub (1981, pp. 139–141), Nystrand (1986), and Vetter (1970).

programmed, is finite. Depending on its structure, content, and focus, writing can be controlled, while talk cannot be controlled (L'Abate, 1999f).

Through Programmed Writing (PW), as represented by workbooks (as will be argued for the rest of this work), treatment plans become intersubjective and amenable to verification from other colleagues rather than by professionals alone, without any corrective feedback. The best way treatment plans can become intersubjective and liable to verification from others is through writing. The written medium allows us to work at a distance from respondents, while talk does not, unless we use the phone. Working at a distance from people means enlarging and expanding the written medium to the following populations:

1. Existing respondents, who can and do use written homework assignments on a pre-, during-, or post-therapy basis
2. Respondents no longer available, who have completed verbal, face-to-face psychotherapy but could benefit by written "booster-shots"
3. Respondents who cannot afford therapy fees but could profit by a limited number of visits on a once-a-month or once-every-few-months basis, provided they are administered prearranged weekly or biweekly written homework assignments
4. Incarcerated felons, who have logistical and economical difficulties with talking face-to-face

5. Handicapped individuals or shut-ins who do not want or are unable to leave their homes
6. American citizens in foreign lands, like the military and missionary individuals and their families, who cannot relate to therapists in another language.

Finally, homework writing assignments can be administered while the therapist is on vacation, keeping respondents in control of themselves.

Furthermore, writing allows for comparative testing of theoretical and therapeutic approaches that would be expensive using the spoken word. Such intersubjective testing can take place when treatment plans are detailed in writing (L'Abate, 1992b). When writing is programmed, it allows therapists to link evaluation with treatment in a way that is difficult if not impossible to do with the spoken word. For instance, once programmed workbooks are based on each of the fifteen content scales of the Minnesota Multiphasic Inventory-2 (MMPI-2), each workbook can be administered on the basis of the scale that matches the highest peak elevation. By the same token, given specific symptoms like sibling rivalry, among others, where no test but only the referral question is available, it is possible to administer a workbook that has been specifically written for that symptom and no other symptoms (L'Abate, 1992b; L'Abate & Platzman, 1991). These and other workbooks will be discussed in detail in Chapter 4.

A written workbook can be "debugged" and improved, just like any software program. However, it is very difficult to improve therapists since we do not even have, as yet, minimal, uniform standards for defining what a competent therapist is. They are out of reach once they become credentialed on the basis of paper evidence rather than actual proof of therapeutic effectiveness. As argued years ago, the process of granting licenses and degrees is based on paper credentials that do not take into account the proven therapeutic effectiveness of many therapists (L'Abate, 1983b). How can we improve therapists if we do not know how they should be improved? Workbooks can be improved in ways that therapists cannot. Therapists, therefore, may be able to improve workbooks better than they can improve themselves.

Advantages of the Spoken over the Written Medium

Admittedly, the spoken word may be necessary for rapport-building and motivation-imparting. However, this generalization needs to be qualified. There are externalizing borderline, character-disordered, acting-out, and criminal individuals who use the spoken word for "conning" and manipulating by saying what they think the therapist will want to hear. Language is used here to make a good impression, not to think or to be introspective. If there is a seeming rapport, this quality is used to manipulate rather than to change. Hence, these individuals may benefit by nonverbal and written interventions rather than interventions based on talk. From all the evidence we have available, talk is wasteful and highly inefficient with these individuals (Reed, McMahan, & L'Abate, 2001).

By the same token, affective and depressive conditions, where internalization and ruminative introspection are present and persistent, seem to benefit the most by talking. However, the comparative efficiency of the spoken versus written media in depressed and anxious conditions has not been tested. One could argue that affective conditions such as internalizations of anxiety and depression make for willing respondents who could benefit by almost any kind of help, be it spoken, nonverbal, or written. Schizophrenic individuals and their families, on the other hand, may benefit by skill-training, structured psychoeducational programs (the paratherapies) rather than face-to-face psychotherapy, no matter what form that psychotherapy may take (Anderson, Reiss, & Hogarty, 1986; Gordon & Gordon, 1981; L'Abate, 1990; Liberman, DeRisi, & Mueser, 1989).

Furthermore, the value of talk in rapport-building and motivation-imparting does not rely on either verbal or face-to-face contact. There are now countless examples of how both can be acquired long-distance through the Internet. Only comparative testing of therapeutic effectiveness of the three media will tell which clinical group will benefit by which medium and which sequence of media. For instance, as suggested earlier, depressed individuals may benefit by a sequence of verbal, nonverbal, and written interventions, while criminal and character disorders may benefit by a sequence based first on nonverbal and then written interventions. If both media "take" and there is positive change, eventually talk can be added, provided it is not used to manipulate.

In conclusion, from this classification a model of psychotherapy results that yields a matrix of help-giving that includes four major components: (1) group composition (individual, couple, family, group), (2) a continuum of preventive approaches (primary, secondary, and tertiary) in addition to education, (3) modalities of intervention (verbal, nonverbal, and written), and (4) deterministic (method) and nondeterministic (style) interventions. In addition, one needs to consider (L'Abate, 1997a) issues of novelty, predictability, repetition, duration, direction, and intensity in any professional relationship, whether face-to-face with or at a distance from respondents (as considered in Chapter 7).

ISSUES OF CONTROL: STRUCTURING PSYCHOLOGICAL INTERVENTIONS

The most relevant aspect of structuring any intervention is control, that is, to help establish or reestablish control in out-of-control systems, whether individual, dyadic, or multirelational. The major issue with control, however, in spite of a burgeoning literature on the subject (Gibbs, 1989; Horwitz, 1990; L'Abate, 1984, 1986b, 1994a, 1997b) lies in not relying on academic treatises but on the reality of control. The new buzz-word for control is now "regulation."

Therapists vary as to their notions of control. On one hand, we have humanists who limit control to the professional office and require very little else outside of it. On the other hand, we have behaviorists who want to determine generalization from the professional office to the home or place of work through sequences of appropriate reinforcements and consequences (Bandura, 1989; Shapiro & Astin, 1998). Most therapists, fairly likely, fall in somewhere along this continuum. Thus far, however, few therapists seem to understand that control is achieved through: (a) regulation of routine, pre-set, prearranged appointments to complete written homework assignments, (b) implementation of cognitive controls through written homework assignments, and (c) feedback from the therapist about the nature and quality of completed homework. Thus, issues of control and regulation would be another dimension along which methods of intervention can be classified.

However, little attention has been paid in the psychotherapy literature to issues of control. They are crucial if we want to help people who are either out of control or have too much of it (L'Abate, 1984, 1986b, 1994a; Shapiro & Astin, 1998). To help respondents, it is important to convince them—and to be convinced ourselves—about the necessity for respondents to approach what they have avoided for a long time, and that is, memories of painful feelings, hurts, traumas, and events from their past (Bradley, 2000; Esterling & Pennebaker, 2001; Gross, 1999; Hayes, Strosahl, & Wilson, 1999; Lepore, 1997; Mayer & Salovey, 1995, Pennebaker, 2001).

As discussed at greater length in Chapters 5, 6, and 7, we need to teach people in distress how to regulate their lives by keeping pre-set appointments in which they are going to approach hurt feelings they have avoided most of their lives according to prearranged plans of written homework assignments. Without the establishment of self-regulation and personal commitment to change from respondents, it is going to be very difficult to assign homework that will induce respondents to become actively involved in the process and take responsibility for positive change.

Definite prescriptions about time, frequency, rate, content (topic), and duration of written homework assignments will be helpful, because this model of control mimics real life. We cannot stop undesirable behavior without first starting it. We need to help respondents approach extremely painful topics that need to be brought into the open carefully, slowly, and responsibly (Esterling, L'Abate, Murray, & Pennebaker, 1999; Hayes, Wilson, Strosahl, Gifford, & Follette, 1996; Pennebaker, 1997). Exposure to threatening, feared, or painful stimuli, as is utilized in many behavioral procedures, represents an application of both principles; (1) approach rather than avoid, and (2) start rather than finish. Exposure therapies approach painful or fearful memories from the past. As Foa and Kozak (1986) concluded: "Some form of exposure to fearful situations is common to many psychotherapies . . . and that confrontation with fearful objects or situations is an effective treatment" (p. 20). In addition to "fearful objects," one would also add painful experiences with people and events from the past.

Using written homework assignments under controlled conditions—that is, under previously stated, predetermined, and agreed-upon times, frequencies, rates, and duration of written assignments—is one way of achieving greater control and teaching respondents how to achieve it in their lives. How can we help people in distress achieve control if we professionals do not know what control consists of? If we do not know, how can we help people learn to obtain it? To achieve this goal, we need to ask ourselves how we are controlled and how we control others in the "real" world. We go to work and we leave work, either when our employer tells us, or when we have satisfactorily finished whatever job we have undertaken. While we are at work, we perform chores requested of us by following established criteria, meeting appointments, deadlines, demands, and commitments. In other words, regulation is obtained when we start and follow a routine of assigned tasks and when we practice behavior needed to survive to a criterion of mastery. ("If you want to stop the behavior, start it!") Without routine appointments with ourselves and with loved ones to practice new skills, there would be little if any regulation over ourselves and over our environment (L'Abate, 1984, 1994a, 1997b).

Consequently, if we want any therapeutic approach to succeed, we need to have respondents follow routine homework assignments at prestated times, practicing desirable behavior repeatedly to achieve a level of mastery. The link between our office and external settings (home, work, leisure) cannot be achieved verbally because words are subject to unexpected distortions, inevitable deletions, and unwarranted generalizations. Consequently, if we want to help people change, we had better give them instructions in writing to be answered in writing at pre-established times and for specified durations. The viewpoint that if you want to stop certain undesirable behaviors, respondents have to start them (L'Abate, 1984) is in keeping with the position that to control behavior we need to regulate its beginning, not just its end.

Do Respondents Need Control? Can We Have Change without Regulation?

Regulation from a behavioral viewpoint has essentially concentrated on regulating consequences and reinforcements to shape the output, that is, the performance of respondents. There is no question that this approach has been successful in a variety of ways and with a variety of individuals, couples, and families. However, by stressing the output, this approach has essentially ignored the beginning input and the process that develops after the beginning. Hence, we need to look at regulation throughout the whole sequence, from beginning input, through the process developing from it, and the final outcome (L'Abate, 1984, 1986b).

Once we look at the whole process of regulation from its beginning to its end, from a systemic viewpoint in real life, we need to ask ourselves: "How is regulation established in ourselves and our respondents?" The answer to that question is as follows: "We are usually controlled and regulated by prescheduled routines in our home, work, and leisure time." In the first place, if we want to stop undesirable behavior, for instance, intruding thoughts (IT), we need to learn to start IT in order to have control over its entire sequence! If we do not want IT to regulate us and if we want to learn to control IT, we need to approach IT rather than avoid IT. Avoiding undesirable behavior does not necessarily make IT disappear. On the contrary, when avoided, IT will control us even more. If IT is in our usual repertoire, avoiding IT will only postpone its reoccurance, not lead to its disappearance. This is essentially the principle behind most exposure treatments. Helping people approach what they have avoided, whether: (1) IT is a painful feeling, which is the most frequent source of avoidance (as discussed in Chapter 5), (2) IT is a disturbing habit, or (3) IT is a feared object or animal or a loved one, friend, neighbor, or one's own boss or coworker. Of course, we do not want respondents to start noxious or suicidal behavior that is hurtful to self or others. We may not be able to regulate hurtful behavior from others, but we may able to help regulation of feelings and thinking about it.

Hence, the beginning of change is to help people in distress regulate themselves by scheduling appointments that determine if, when, where, how, and what to approach what has been avoided for a long time. Especially in dealing with painful feelings, the more one wants to avoid being depressed, anxious, fearful, and so forth, the more depressed, anxious, fearful, and so on, one becomes. Avoidance and procrastination are not going to make that painful feeling go away. Feelings, and especially painful feelings, cannot be swept under a rug. Once appointments are scheduled routinely at prearranged, pre-set times at least 24 hours ahead (7 P.M. 8 P.M. etc.), according to agreed-upon frequency (once, twice, or three times a week), and duration (for 15, 20, 30, 45, or 60 minutes), it is then possible to start having control over one's life. Additionally, however, we must have a record of what respondents say they did and whether it has been done. Hence, they should be encouraged to approach IT by writing about IT allowing whatever is inside their self-systems to come outside and leave room for new ideas or information. A summary of guidelines necessary to lean self-regulation is found in Table 1.7.

CONCLUSION: TOWARD A SCIENCE OF PSYCHOLOGICAL INTERVENTIONS

Psychotherapy, no matter how helpful it may be to many, is not enough. It is a drop in the bucket in view of the many people in distress who need help. A complex classification of psychotherapies according to traditional and more recent categories or dimensions allows us to see what we need to learn to help people in distress and in trouble. Long gone are the days when we could draw conclusions about the effectiveness of any form of treatment on a dichotomous, black or white, true-false, applicable-nonapplicable basis. With so many forms of psychological treatment available, we can no longer base our choices and selections of treatment(s) on an all-or-nothing basis, psychotherapy or medication. Instead, we need to choose one or more forms of treatment on the basis

Table 1.7
Guidelines for Learning Self-Regulation

1. *Regulation*: If you want to stop IT (unpleasant thoughts, destructive thinking, tensions, painful feelings, etc.), START IT; that is, arrange weekly or bi-weekly appointments at specific, pre-set times at least 24 hours ahead and for pre-set durations (15, 20, 30, 45, or 60 minutes at the most).
2. *Approach*: If you want to get rid of IT, approach IT instead of avoiding IT. Avoiding IT, as done in the past, will only continue to keep IT inside, still controlling you.
3. *Write*: During the time set to start IT, approach IT by writing about IT, instead of stewing, worrying, or obsessing and ultimately being controlled by IT. Writing has the following advantages over thinking or talking: (a) clears the mind, taking away cobwebs from it, (b) resolves traumas from the past that stand in the way and interfere with the completion and accomplishments of important tasks in the present, (c) helps in recalling, acquiring, considering, and remembering new information, (d) fosters problem solving by clarifying and integrating information at hand by allowing one to focus and concentrate on it in a way that cannot be done by just thinking or talking about it, and (e) freewriting promotes forced writing, by allowing one to improve on a first draft written about anything; one can then go back and add more details and specifics that may have been lacking in the first draft.

Source: Adapted from L'Abate (1994a, p. 234).

of specificity of treatment and matching of respondents' needs with specific treatment. Nonetheless, one cannot dismiss any legitimate and professionally available form of treatment on grounds of specificity or fruitfulness only. There are other scientific and professional criteria to be considered, like cost-effectiveness, uniqueness in respondent-treatment matching, and personal and interpersonal relevance.

Of course, we will need to rely on other professions and on a hierarchy of personnel for whatever their particular contribution may be. If one respondent is extremely upset, s/he may need medical treatment, such as a prescribed tranquilizer or medication, and routine, nonmedical approaches like massages or dancing sessions. These approaches are provided as long as it is understood that they are temporary "crutches" that cannot be used for life, unless that is what the respondent wants (another form, albeit legitimate, of avoidance and possible addiction). An appropriate and effective course of treatment for any dysfunctionality would involve multiple treatment modalities used together synergistically rather than exclusionarily, with a variety of specialized personnel (as discussed in Chapter 7).

Psychotherapy will become a science when it is demonstrated that relationship skills, in addition to structuring skills, can be administered at a distance from respondents. One way to demonstrate this possibility is to do away with face-to-face relationship skills altogether and start studying what outcome, if any, is obtained with structured approaches such as workbooks and their administration

Table 1.8
Toward a Science of Psychological Interventions

Criteria	**Requirements**	**Processes and Outcomes**
Verifiability (Scientific)	Verifiability	Breakdown of component parts Pre-post-intervention evaluation
	Accountability	Follow-up evaluation
Generalization (Professional)	Transfer	Positive carry-over of behavior to other settings Positive spread of effect to other Behaviors
	Duration, Frequency, Rate, Direction	Learning selected criteria of mastery Lasting Effects

through the Internet. Hence, we need to consider (Table 1.8) that the criteria of a science are different than those of a profession. While scientists value empirical testability and long-term accountability of outcomes, practitioners may value positive changes outside of their offices and generalization to other people and settings. Even though their value systems may differ (as do, perhaps, their hemispheric functions), as long as talk is the major medium of communication and, at least partially, healing, very little progress is going to take place in the delivery of mental health services. If psychotherapy wants to become a science, it will have to rely on repeatable operations such as those found in writing.

2

Writing and Its Applications in Psychotherapy

The purpose of this chapter is to introduce the many uses of distance writing (DW) for therapeutic, paratherapeutic, preventive, and parapreventive purposes. DW means having respondents write away from the presence of a mental health professional, either in the waiting room of the therapist's office or at home. Ideally, it consists of systematic homework assignments with written instructions and forms to be answered by respondents in writing. Although DW as a preventive and therapeutic tool is not new, systematic investigation of its efficacy has occurred only recently. Overall, there is a robust and increasingly coherent body of literature that points to the widespread use and benefits of DW. It is one of a growing repertoire of adjunct DW techniques used to support preventive and psychotherapeutic processes and improve coping abilities and perceptions of control over stressful and traumatic events (Esterling, L'Abate, Murray, & Pennebaker, 1999; Esterling & Pennebaker, 2001; L'Abate, 1992b, 2001a; Pennebaker, 1997; Smyth, 1998; Smyth & L'Abate, 2001).

DW can be considered as secondary prevention because it can be applied alongside (before, during, or after) preventive (primary) and therapeutic (tertiary) interventions. Therefore it can be applied parapreventively as well as paratherapeutically to targeted populations. DW suggests that this is the only form of clinical treatment used with dysfunctional respondents that produces possibly beneficial results. This claim is a possibility that is still to be demonstrated fully. Most supporting evidence has thus far been gathered from undergraduate respondents rather than clinical cases (L'Abate & Kern, in press). Paratherapeutic means that DW is used in conjunction with face-to-face psychotherapy. Preventive means that DW is the only form of prevention used without any other intervention with functional or semifunctional respondents. Parapreventive means that DW is taking place in conjunction with a preventive program.

When DW is used as an additional, complementary, or supplementary medium with face-to-face, verbal therapy, its application should be made clear to respondents as a condition for treatment from the very outset of a professional consultation. Even when DW is used as the sole medium of intervention, a clearly worded contract is necessary for ethical and professional reasons (as discussed in Chapter 7). Otherwise, one will meet a great deal of resistance, especially if DW is suddenly sprung on unsuspecting respondents who have not agreed to it beforehand. (The contract might state, "In my practice, I assign homework assignments to be answered in writing as part of the way I work. There are many therapists who do not work this way and you should consult them if you do not want to do any written homework.") It is imperative to have a signed, written contract to cover this practice at the end of at least three initial evaluation sessions. It is just as important to have a pre-post-intervention evaluation and follow-up to assess objectively whether any improvement has occurred as a function of workbook assignments.

DW has only recently been considered as an additional or alternative adjutant to the verbal medium—an avenue of psychological intervention and service delivery in prevention or psychotherapy (Esterling, L'Abate, Murray, & Pennebaker, 1999; L'Abate, 1986b, 1990, 1991, 1992b, 1994a; Riordan, 1996). Indeed, once writing is performed at a distance from a professional (DW), it can become the basis for computer-assisted interventions (CAI). Either through DW or CAI, mental health professionals can reach populations that cannot ever be reached through talk.

RATIONALE FOR THE USE OF DISTANCE WRITING IN PSYCHOTHERAPY

The historical background of advocacy for and research with DW has been reviewed repeatedly in other sources (L'Abate, 1992b, 1997a, 1999c, 1999d, 1999f, 2001a; MacMahan & L'Abate, 2001) and does not need to be repeated here. Suffice to say that DW does have a long, distinguished history. However, its empirical underpinnings are relatively short and recent (Esterling, L'Abate, Murray, & Pennebaker, 1999; L'Abate, 2001a, in press; L'Abate & Kern, in press; Smyth, 1998; Smyth & L'Abate, 2001).

Progress in many fields of human endeavor is based on written records rather than on talk. No business or human enterprise can flourish and advance without a written record of its transactions. Furthermore, the written medium has an advantage over talk because it possesses explicit and specific qualities that become confused in speaking, no matter how clearly one may talk. Psychotherapy is one of the few enterprises in which the process (and assumed progress) is based predominantly on talk. The combination of either two or even all three media—nonverbal, verbal, and written—should provide synergistic outcomes.

Figure 2.1
Media of Intervention

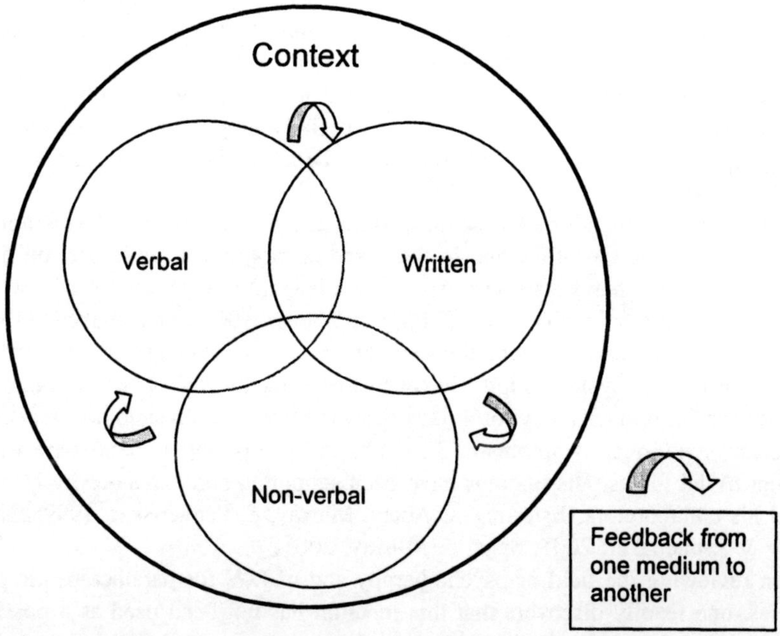

This synergy might hopefully increase the efficiency and efficacy of most therapeutic approaches, regardless of theoretical predilection. No matter what medium is accessed, if the medium is effective, there will be reverberations through feedback loops from one medium to the other two, as shown in Figure 2.1.

DW, in its various applications (to be reviewed below), is but a skip and a jump from CAI and preventive psychoeducational social skill training programs (discussed in the previous chapter). As Bloom (1992) concluded in his review on this topic: "Even those who are quite disturbed interact very successfully with computers, including many patients who are unable to interact with mental health personnel" (p. 169). Therefore, DW can be used as a therapeutic or preventive medium in its own right or can be seen as a precursor or as preliminary software to its use in CAI.

The use of DW/CAI enlarges the therapeutic and preventive armamentarium exponentially making it possible to help many more respondents per unit of therapist's time than can be accomplished individually in face-to-face verbal interactions. Even in group or family psychotherapy, DW/CAI can be administered and individualized before, in parallel with, or after face-to-face interaction. This combination has been utilized for many years by Gould (2001). In preventive programs with less disturbed respondents, DW/CAI could be administered without face-to-face contact, through the mail or Internet (L'Abate,

1999f). Thus, DW/CAI has the potential to decrease costs and increase efficiency in current mental health and psychotherapy practices. Whether these approaches are as effective as verbal ones remains to be seen. Hereafter DW will be considered as a part of CAI. The reader who wants to learn more about recent developments in this field should consult Bloom's (1992) and Gackenbach and Ellerman's (1998) excellent reviews and L'Abate's edited work (2001a). For an historical introduction to the same area, especially programmed instruction and teaching machines that predated computers, the reader is referred to Brown and L'Abate (1969).

DW is one application of structuring skills designed to increase the therapist's influence outside the office and in the home or workplace. Its impact on therapeutic outcome has yet to be fully realized beyond the experience of few clinicians (Bastien & Jacobs, 1974; Phillips & Wiener, 1966). Pennebaker's (1997) contribution of research with focused, expressive writing has highlighted its potential use in psychotherapy. He found that students who wrote on traumatic topics for 20 minutes a day for 4 days showed improved physiological reactions and fewer physical symptoms at 3 months follow-up than students who wrote about trivial topics. His findings have been supported and expanded by Murray and his collaborators (Esterling, L'Abate, Murray, & Pennebaker, 1999; Esterling & Pennebaker, 2001; Segal & Murray, 2001).

In reviewing the field of psychotherapy and of DW for paratherapeutic purposes, one readily discovers that this medium has not been used as a possible method of intervention and is not part of mainstream psychotherapy practices (Ammerman, Last, & Hersen, 1993; Freeman, Simon, Beutler, & Arkowitz, 1989; Bergin & Garfield, 1994). At best, it has been used for single-shot, ad hoc purposes or to log behavior (Levy & Shelton, 1990; Shelton & Levy, 1981). Therefore, to include DW in the practice of psychotherapy, a conceptualization of the therapeutic process was found necessary, as discussed in the previous chapter. We needed a responsible rationale and a relevant context for the insertion of DW within the therapeutic armamentarium.

When DW/CAI are used within the context of a caring and compassionate therapeutic relationship, they can enhance, strengthen, and possibly shorten the length and costs of psychotherapy. In some cases, it has been claimed anecdotally as a real breakthrough in dealing with difficult problems perhaps untreatable through talk. Clearly, its advantages have yet to be fully explored, along with its limitations. In spite of preliminary evidence already gathered and published by this author (L'Abate & Kern, in press; McMahan & L'Abate, 2001; Reed, McMahan, & L'Abate, 2001; Smyth & L'Abate, 2001) and others (Esterling, L'Abate, Murray, & Pennebaker, 1999), more empirical evidence needs to be gathered to justify and support its wider applicability within the context of preventive and psychotherapeutic interventions. Because of its cost-cutting and time-saving potential, it deserves more attention from the psychotherapeutic community than it has received heretofore.

To save time and energy as well as to avoid inevitable distortions from respondents, it is much more efficient to put instructions in writing to be followed step by step, matching one hour of homework for each hour of therapy, or whatever ratio of face-to-face sessions with homework assignments is affordable and comfortable for both parties. The ratio of homework to face-to-face therapeutic interaction is variable according to the logistic and financial needs of respondents. In some cases, face-to-face verbal interaction may be unnecessary, irrelevant, or countertherapeutic, for instance, with incarcerated felons (Reed, McMahan, & L'Abate, 2001).

Often, in this writer's past clinical practice, when using talk for structuring directions, instructions, or prescriptions, it was necessary to repeat the same instructions whenever the same problem was presented. To avoid misunderstandings, selective forgetting, and the blatant distortions that were taking place, as well as to save the therapist's time and energy, it became useful for professionals of various persuasions to write down various instructions to respondents (Levy & Shelton, 1990; Norcross, 1986; Shelton & Levy, 1981). Initially, most instructions consisted of ad hoc, one time only, single-shot interventions. Eventually, they progressed to a more systematic and consistent use of DW in an interactive fashion with respondents (L'Abate, 1986b, 1992b, 1996).

The process of DW, in general, produces four possible change-related feedback loops from: (1) questions asked in an assignment given to individual respondents, putting them in a meta-position to think about themselves in a different way than talking about themselves; (2) individuals reciprocally to and from partners or other family members; (3) respondents (individuals, couples, or families) to therapists; and (4) therapists back to respondents. Whether these feedback loops are stronger than any loop achieved verbally is an important empirical problem in need of evaluation.

DISTANCE WRITING IS A MEDIUM DIFFERENT FROM TALK

To support the position that DW is a medium different from talk (in addition to the arguments given Chapter 1), it seems relevant to introduce an Input-Output Model of Information Processing (L'Abate, 1969a). This model differentiates between receptive input, obtained mainly through the eyes and ears, and expressive output, obtained through the hands and mouth. The skin and body, of course, furnish other input channels that are more relevant to nonverbal interventions (Figure 2.1). This distinction parallels a similar one made between feelings, at the receptive, internally experiential side of emotionality and emotions, at the expressive, externally observable output side (L'Abate, 1997c, 1999a). This distinction will be expanded in Chapter 5.

Talk and writing derive from both aural and visual reception. However, relatively and neurologically speaking, talk is more connected to hearing while writing is more connected to seeing. Receptive functions are determined largely by biological functioning. Expressive functions are determined largely by ex-

Figure 2.2
Hypothetical Relationships Between Hemispheres (Right–Left) and Input–Output Functions

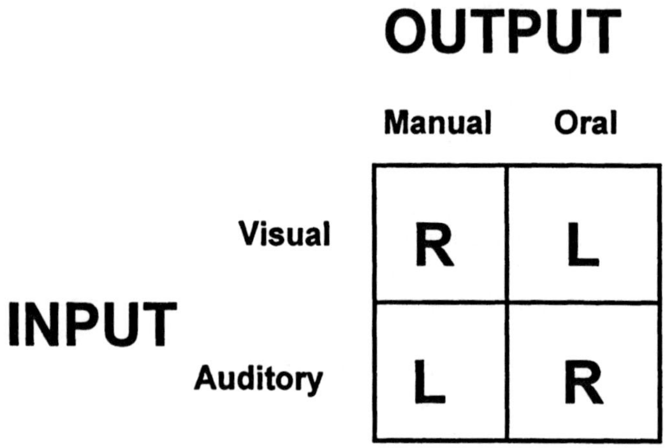

ternal, cultural, and environmental functions like socioeconomic background, socialization practices, and education (L'Abate, 1969a, 1971). Reception is determined mostly by nature. Expression is determined mostly by nurture. However, there is a feedback loop from expression to reception that needs to be included (Figure 2.2), and that will be considered in greater detail in Chapter 5.

Additionally, there is the possibility that talk may rely relatively more on right hemisphere functions, while writing may rely relatively more on left hemisphere functions (L'Abate, 2001a; McMahan & L'Abate, 2001; Ornstein, 1997). If this is the case, this possibility adds an even more compelling reason to couple talk with DW to help people in distress, because of the different nature of the two media. Of course, one needs to consider socioeconomic and educational levels, among other factors. Psychotherapy has been conducted successfully mainly with white, college-educated, middle-to upper class, relatively well-functioning, mostly anxious or depressed respondents who are verbally facile and articulate (Leon, Kopta, Howard, & Lutz, 1999). How about respondents from lower socioeconomic classes? Are they as articulate verbally as respondents from medium to upper classes? One, of course, could argue that, if one cannot talk too well, one also cannot write particularly well. DW is just as determined by socioeconomic and educational background as talk. Yet, this is the very reason for suggesting that DW would be more useful for respondents who cannot either talk or write well, especially spontaneously. As discussed in the previous chapter, talk is spontaneous whereas writing is more deliberate. Certain types of DW, on the other hand, could prompt certain respondents, yet to be identified, to answer in ways that are difficult to access verbally.

Furthermore, one needs to consider incarcerated individuals who cannot talk or write, possibly because of different hemispheric functions. In these individuals, visual-motor skills and eye-hand coordination are usually more pronounced than verbal, ear-mouth ones. These individuals do not like to talk or to think except for purposes of manipulation (Reed, McMahan, & L'Abate, 2001). They may not like to use a pen or a pencil to write. However, in this writer's experience, for whatever reason, they are willing and desirous of writing using a computer. Scott (1998), for instance, found creative writing about private fairy tales to be extremely productive and, impressionistically, of therapeutic value in prisoners. If not valuable in and by itself, the writing process allowed Scott to build a bridge between himself and prisoners that was supposedly of therapeutic value. Hence, there is an even more compelling reason to believe that this population can be accessed through a technology that does not get bored, manipulated, or frustrated, as many mental health professionals working with this population have experienced (Fishbein, 2000; Reed, McMahan, & L'Abate, 2001; Simon, 1998).

Information processing, therefore, is inferred from the relationship between input (ears-eyes) and output (hands-mouth) channels and from variability among the four channels. Input is most affected by biological defects, while output would be affected mainly by environmental and cultural deficits. Socioeconomic status (SES) would affect both output channels, with high SES affecting verbal output favorably, whereas low SES would effect manual output more favorably (L'Abate, 1971; L'Abate, Norman, & Aurandt, 1972; Wildman & L'Abate, 1979). Emotionality and emotional disturbance would increase variability within and between various channels of input and output in an inconsistent, sometimes contradictory manner. For instance, an emotionally disturbed individual may do well on one measure of verbal skills and poorly on another measure evaluating the same skills. A physically handicapped individual, on the other hand, would perform consistently poorly in the same area of functioning, no matter how that area is measured (L'Abate, 1969a).

This model was originally evaluated (L'Abate, 1971) by a test specifically designed to evaluate children between the ages of 9 and 12 years in groups rather than individually. This test was developed to measure input (competence/comprehension) as well as output (performance/production) visually, auditorily, verbally, and manually, using the same stimuli to measure functioning in all four channels. Input was measured by recognition (yes-no; true-false; one out of two, three, or four possibilities; or multiple-choice pointing, as in: "Which of these four pictures is a table?"). Output was measured by a chain of responses that are connected with each other into a meaningful pattern, as in manually drawing a table or verbally defining what a table is. The Auditory Visual Oral and Manual (AVOM) test was drawn from two forms (A and B) of the Peabody Picture Vocabulary Test employing 45 words (nouns) that were concrete enough to be used as stimuli for both input (reception) and output (expression). To measure visual input, the same words were scrambled into meaningless patterns, with the correct word embedded into four choices. Visually, choices were printed for recognition (1 out of 4). Auditorily, the same list of words was audiotaped for consistency and ease of administration. To measure output, the words were reproduced manually by drawing them, or were defined orally, as in a vocabulary test.

Wildman and L'Abate (1979) validated the AVOM by testing 67 fourth-graders, 73 fifth-graders, and 71 sixth-graders of approximately equal numbers of each sex in a regular elementary school within a large metropolitan public school system. Ages ranged from 9 years and 6 months to 11 years and 5 months. Results were an expected and significant main effect for grade placement. The higher the grade, the greater were the AVOM scores on all four channels. In addition, there were significant correlations between the four measures of intellectual functioning and academic grades. There were no significant gender differences. Ethnic origin did affect auditory input and manual and verbal output, but not visual input. There was a significant interaction between grades and ethnic origin for manual output only. A side benefit of this study was the identification of two children whose visual and auditory deficits had not yet come to the attention of their teachers.

Baggett (1980) tested this model using the AVOM to identify mildly handicapped—33 behavior disordered and 37 learning disabled—children in fourth and fifth grades divided according to high and low socioeconomic backgrounds. She advanced three hypotheses: (1) learning-disabled children would be most affected in receptive (input) functioning, (2) children from high socioeconomic backgrounds would perform better than children from low socioeconomic backgrounds on both receptive (input) and expressive (output) measures, and (3) behaviorally disordered children would exhibit variability and inconsistency on all measures of receptive and expressive functioning.

Using Multiple Analysis of Variance (MANOVA) to analyze intra- and inter-individual differences, Baggett found that learning-disabled children were significantly lower on visual input. Children from high socioeconomic backgrounds performed at a significantly higher level on all measures of receptive and expressive functioning than children from low socioeconomic backgrounds. Behavior-disordered children were not significantly more variable than learning-disabled children on any measure of receptive and expressive functioning, even though there was a slight trend toward greater variability and inconsistency in the former. Children from low socioeconomic backgrounds were significantly lower on expressive functioning than on receptive functioning, supporting the results obtained by L'Abate (1971) and Wildman and L'Abate (1979).

What is the point of presenting this information here? It is to suggest that we process information differentially. Some people are more auditory than visual, some can express themselves verbally better than manually, and so forth. Talk is a favorite medium for people from middle- and upper-class backgrounds. Manual output and expression are more prominent in lower socioeconomic classes (L'Abate, Norman, & Aurandt, 1972). Hence, interventions based on talk are limited to special classes of respondents and discriminate against classes of respondents who communicate through channels other than talk. We must find ways and means of accessing people in distress through media different from talk, for instance, through computers, television, and DW.

A CLASSIFICATION OF DISTANCE WRITING FOR HELPING PURPOSES

Writing in general and DW in particular can be classified according to a variety of dimensions (Table 2.1) rather than by seeming dichotomies. These dimensions bring to mind differences between style and method discussed in the previous chapter. One major dimension of writing is defined by one *expressive* extreme, consisting of creative, artistic, and spontaneous story constructions on one hand, versus an *instructive* extreme. This extreme deals with mechanically contrived characteristics of vocabulary usage, spelling style, logic, sentence construction, and sentence combination. A second dimension of writing that may overlap with the first is *structure*, as seen, for instance, in unstructured automatic writing at one extreme, and *structured* writing at another. This section will concern itself solely with structured DW, leaving unstructured writing outside of this work.

"Structured" refers to how free, restricted, or constricted the request is for DW. It varies along five often overlapping dimensions: structure, content, goals, specificity, and abstraction. Within each dimension, DW varies from one extreme of little if any structure to an extreme of a great deal of structure, as in:

1. Least structured or *open-ended* writing (OW) as in, "Write anything that comes into your mind," as is done in diaries or journals. (Progoff, 1975, 1980)
2. *Focused* or expressive writing (FW), as in "For 20 minutes a day for 4 days, write about all the hurts (traumas) you have received in your life, including those that you have never shared with anyone else." (Esterling, L'Abate, Murray, Pennebaker, 1999; Esterling & Pennebaker, 2001; Pennebaker, 1997)
3. *Guided* writing (GW), as in "I have read what you wrote and I want you to answer the following written questions in writing during the next week." The process that de Vries, Birren, and Deutchman (1990) called *guided* writing is located between focused and programmed writing in degree of structure.
4. *Programmed* writing (PW), on the other hand, lies at the most structured extreme. It consists of a systematic series of assignments around a specified topic, forming a workbook, to be completed at home over a period of time. It may continue for as many weeks as are necessary to deal with whatever troublesome issue, problem, or symptom is presented (L'Abate, 1986b, 1987, 1990, 1991), as in: "After you have read, considered, and signed an Informed Consent Form, I want you to work on this workbook for depression. This workbook consists of eight homework assignments. I am giving you the first assignment to work on for next week. Make sure you make

Table 2.1
A Classification of Writing

Expressive/Instructive versus Creative/Spontaneous (contextual, constructive of stories) versus Contrived (vocabulary, spelling, style, syntax, logic, sentence construction and combination)
Unstructured/Structured
  Open-ended (journals, diaries)
  Focused (one topic, as in autobiographies and Pennebaker's expressive format)
  Guided (questions about written compositions)
  Programmed (as in workbooks)
Goals (prescriptive/cathartic)
Specificity (general/specific)
Content (traumatic/trivial)
Abstraction (high/low)

Source: L'Abate (2001a, p. 8).

an appointment with yourself to work on this assignment. Bring the completed assignment to the next session. I am looking forward to seeing what you wrote."

A second dimension of writing is *Content*. It can vary from one extreme, *traumatic*, as in the case of Pennebaker's (1997) work (already cited), to *trivial*, as in writing about one's closet or car. Content can also vary from general, about the meaning of life, to specific, about the ingredients used in all the dishes eaten in the last meal. Trivial content DW can be used as control for experimental uses of traumatic content.

A third dimension of writing consists of its *goals*, ranging from *cathartic* to *prescriptive*. Cathartically, respondents write about sad or painful feelings, without having to do anything else. DW about past traumas does have a cathartic effect (Esterling, L'Abate, Murray, & Pennebaker, 1999; Esterling & Pennebaker, 2001; Pennebaker, 1997). Some workbooks have a prescriptive component, suggesting that certain behaviors need to take place and be repeated in specific ways, between therapy sessions or through distance contacts (phone, Internet, fax) with a professional helper. Respondents need to follow a step-by-step sequence requiring doing or not doing something according to specified instructions. A prescription, usually, needs to be programmed to achieve the desired effect. Among the four levels of structure, open writing, for instance, runs the risk of being the most trivial. A respondent, unless told otherwise, could detail whatever has happened superficially in a daily diary without getting down to innermost feelings and thoughts.

A fourth dimension consists of *level of abstraction*, ranging from very abstract ("Write about the meaning of life") to very concrete ("List all the articles of clothing in your closet"). However, this dimension can be controlled better in programmed writing (PW) than in the other three structures. It would be difficult to control the level of abstraction in the open, focused, or guided DW, unless specific instructions were given, making the format a programmed one.

CLINICAL APPLICATIONS OF FOCUSED WRITING

The rest of this chapter illustrates various applications of focused writing (FW) in either preventive or therapeutic interventions. Open-ended (OW) and guided writing (GW) will not be considered here because their applications are secondary to the purposes of this chapter and work. FW suggests one specific topic that should be the major focus of concern as, for instance, writing about one's autobiography, depression, past hurts, and so forth. From reading the written outcome of this assignment, therapists have at least three choices available: (1) discuss the assignment, using it as grist for the therapeutic mill: (2) proceed to the next step of guided writing by writing specific questions to be answered also in writing, for instance, elaboration of unclear passages in FW, or (3) depending on what transpired during the face-to-face session, proceed to the administration of a workbook. As we shall see (Chapter 4), this choice can be made on the basis of age, marital or family status and composition, a test, or the referral question. These choices would not be available if the therapist were to rely solely on talk.

FW is usually ad hoc, that is, directed toward a specific issue or topic for which there is no program or workbook. The therapist may need to give specific instructions on how respondents need to deal with a particular problem in writing, in addition, of course, to face-to-face sessions. A basic issue concerning differentiation of applications between FW and PW relates to the comparative effectiveness of either approach. Is FW just as effective as PW? Perhaps in the future, we shall be able to specify under what conditions either type of DW should be used, as suggested below.

Focused Writing at the Beginning of Therapy

By definition, FW takes place when a definite topic or assignment has been prescribed between therapy sessions. For instance, in his past clinical practice, this writer routinely asked respondents, whether individuals, couples, or families, to write about their "hurts." They were asked to list them as these hurts would occur to them during pre-set times devoted to answering such assignments ("20 minutes a day for 4 days."). These hurts include all of the possible traumas, rejections, failures, painful and troublesome experiences that may come to their minds in the weeks following the second therapy appointment.

The first three sessions of therapy are framed as "evaluation," based on reciprocity between professional and respondent in the process ("You are going to evaluate me, and eventually decide whether I can be of help to you or not."). Whatever test instruments are administered from the first to the second session are scored between the second and third session, with feedback on the third session. At this point, if there is agreement over a therapeutic contract, respondents need simply to list their hurts, between the third and the fourth therapy session. After this listing is accomplished between these sessions, respondents are to rank these hurts in order of intensity, selecting those that were the most traumatic, expanding and elaborating on them in the following week(s).

In one instance, a middle-aged professional man who for many on-and-off years of therapy had avoided emotional confrontation, was able to recall (through writing) the painfulness of remembering a house he and his family moved to when he was just a few years old. The painfulness of the experience, the coldness and emptiness of the house, brought tears to his eyes as well as a recounting of the many times he felt abandoned as he and his family of origin moved from one place to another without firm foundations. He repeated this experience with his family of procreation, who was now protesting and resisting yet another of the many moves he had made throughout his career. In another instance, a verbally resistant truck driver was able to write and to get in touch with the verbal and physical abuse he had received during his childhood from his alcoholic father, something he had not been able to reveal for years either to himself, his wife, or, more recently the therapist.

The rationale for this initial step can be found in the position that hurts and the fear of being hurt are at the bottom of our human existence. The sharing of past hurts and of fears of future hurts stands at the bottom of intimacy (as discussed in Chapter 5). In addition to this theoretical rationale, there is practical, if not scientific, rationale for the use of this focused assignment at the outset of therapy. Pennebaker (1997; Esterling & Pennebaker, 2001), in his research on the use of expressive writing about traumatic (i.e., hurtful) events, found that undergraduates writing about past traumatic experiences showed a significant improvement in physiological and immune system measurements in comparison to undergraduates who wrote about trivial topics. This study has been replicated many times with the same results (Esterling, L'Abate, Murray, & Pennebaker, 1999).

In this writer's past clinical practice, FW assignments asked respondents to concentrate on listing their defeats; who defeated whom in their family of origin and/or in their family of procreation. They were to list what defeats they produced and what defeats they received. From individual lists, couples and families were to combine them in one grand list that would allow them to know who defeated whom. Sometimes, these defeats were prescribed to help respondents achieve control over them. It remains to be seen whether it is more therapeutic to concentrate on hurts first, and later on, if necessary and relevant, on defeats, or whether the reverse process is more helpful. This practice covers the receptive, experienced aspects (hurts) of functioning, whereas defeats cover the expressive side of an experiencing-expressing continuum (considered in the next section of this chapter and in Chapter 5).

Focused Writing during Therapy

For instance, when dealing with partners for whom issues of being "right" are equated with "good," and being "wrong" is equated with being "bad," instructions can be given as follows, from one week to another, towards the end of therapy sessions:

Week 1. "I want you to write down as many instances as you can remember about how often you were either "right" (or "good") in the past. Write down what happened and especially what happened to the person you were "right" with or "good" to. List as many persons as you can remember. Keep this list open throughout next week and even later by adding to it as you think of others who were involved with you in being "wrong" and "bad" in the past. You are free to discuss this list with each other if it makes you happy, but you will have to make an appointment with each other at least 24 hours in advance. Whether you meet or not, bring a copy of this list to our next session."

After discussing the homework, with whatever implications and repercussions this homework may have brought about, and congratulating whoever has done the homework, the therapist needs to consider whatever else may have happened that needs to be brought into the therapy session. At the end of this session, the therapist may give the second assignment.

Week 2. "I want you to write as many letters of apology as necessary to as many people who were judged by you to be "wrong" or "bad." You may choose not to mail these letters, but their writing is necessary for forgiveness to take place. Your writing these letters is one way of showing that you may have forgiven yourself but you may need the forgiveness of those you love and who love you. If we cannot forgive ourselves for our mistakes, how can we forgive others? Discuss these letters with one another, if you are comfortable, at a meeting pre-arranged 24 hours in advance. If you do no find it comfortable to meet, just bring copies of these letters to the next session."

At the next session, after a discussion of the process of letter-writing, including the issue of whether to mail or not to mail these letters, confront whatever issues ensue afterwards, and, at the end of the session, give the third set of instructions:

Week 3. "Between today and next time we meet, I want you to monitor and write down all the situations where you were either "right" or "good." What provoked you into being like that? What led into it and what followed from it? How did you feel afterwards? If you cannot find it in yourself to be "right" or "good," pretend to be "right" or "good" and see what happens. In other instances, write down situations where you felt that you were right or good but chose to avoid being either. Instead, choose to be helpful and effective. Write all of these experiences down and discuss them among each other if you are comfortable. If you have given up being right or good, write what would have happened in the future if you had continued to define yourself that way. Either way, bring a list of your notes about these situations to our next session."

Once these homework assignments are completed, respondents may be ready for completing as homework the first two written assignments of a Depression workbook concerning the Drama Triangle and Distance Regulation (L'Abate, 1986b), described in Chapters 4 and 5.

Progressing from Experiencing to Expressing Emotions

Another application of FW that was commonly used in this writer's past clinical practice relates to the experiencing-expressing continuum (considered in greater detail in Chapter 5). This continuum is basic to personality and interpersonal functioning (L'Abate, 1994a, 1997c, 2001a, in preparation). Many dysfunctional individuals, for instance, jump immediately from experiencing to expressing. They discharge physically or verbally, without an intermediate, usually cognitive, step that would allow them to experience and process an emotional event before expressing it. In these individuals, experiencing painful feelings is equated and fused with expressing them. Usually, this expression occurs in a destructive fashion, through externalizations, accusations, and recriminations, or even worse, acting out, as in criminal behavior. When the emotional experience is short-circuited, that is, without precipitating immediate external action, then there may be an expansion of cognitive processing, ultimately resulting in obsessions and ruminations. Where cognition is also bypassed, in addition to bypassing emotionality, then there is an expansion of activity, either through impulsive or compulsive acting-out behavior (L'Abate, 1986b). In the latter case (as explained in greater detail in Chapter 5), the individual cannot stand the pressure of withstanding, and even less experiencing, pain, discomfort, and unpleasant tension. Consequently, immediate discharge of painful or uncomfortable feelings is seen as the only way to get rid of those feelings, usually through anger, hostility, and acting out. These individuals are unable to process feelings rationally and to wait before saying or doing something that will be inevitably destructive, since no corrective reflection or cognitive processing has taken place about how such feelings should be expressed in an helpful manner.

The therapist's task here is to help these individuals learn to differentiate between experiencing feelings from expressing them ("I am entitled to feel whatever I happen to feel. However, I am not entitled to beat you over the head because of the way I feel"). Once an awareness about the destructiveness of this pattern is reached, the decision of what to do about it has to be reached by respondents: ("I need for you to think and write about this pattern between today and next time we meet. Then let me know whether you want me to help you with it or not.") After a decision in favor of abandoning this pattern is reached, one can prescribe the following assignments during three consecutive weeks between therapy sessions:

Week 1. "I want you to write down all the past instances when you jumped immediately from feeling something painful to expressing it by jumping into action or attacking an external target. Write down as many of these incidents as you can think of and add them to this list as they come into your mind. Discuss this list with your family if you like. Bring this list to the next session." After a discussion of past instances when respondents jumped from experiencing to expressing without using an intermediate, rational step, plus whatever respondents may bring to the session spontaneously, at the end of this session, the therapist can say (or write):

Week 2. "During the next week, I want you to write letters of apology to whoever was the target of your attack. Do not mail these letters, discuss them with your family if you like, but bring them to the next session so that we can go over them and improve them if necessary." During this session, letters are gone over. Editorial suggestions may be given by the therapist to ensure that their style and content are helpful and effective, following commonplace guidelines of helpful communication. After dealing with whatever else respondents may be bringing in to this session, the therapist can say (or write):

Week 3. "During next week, I want you to pay attention to when you jump from feeling something unpleasant or painful to expressing it immediately with anger. Write down what happened, what lead into it and what the outcome was for you and whoever was the target of your expression. I want you also to think of what would happen to you and those you love if you were to continue or persisted in expressing immediately whatever you feel at the time. If possible, record instances, where instead of jumping into expressing the feeling, you processed, and thought about ways and means of expressing it helpfully rather than hurtfully. Discuss your notes with your family if you like, but bring your written notes to our next session." This assignment could be broken up into two parts, dealing with the immediate present and the distant future, in terms of implications for the future if this pattern were to persist.

After this session it is important to administer to respondents assignments on how to express feelings nondestructively. An in-session exercise that was used quite often consisted of the "Appreciation Game," in which the therapist starts by modeling how to express and share appreciation: "What I appreciate about myself is. . . . What I do not appreciate about myself is. . . ." After speaking about self, respondents then take turn expressing feelings of appreciation toward themselves and toward other family members. These feelings, however, have to be couched toward the performance or behavior of self and others, but never about the person or personality. The same exercise can then be administered to families as an introduction to family conferences.

IMPLICATIONS OF FOCUSED WRITING FOR HELP-GIVING

A practical implication of this approach refers to how we as individuals want to assert our importance (as discussed in greater detail in Chapter 5). We can do it by asserting our inherent righteousness and goodness and denying either quality in those we love and who love us, or we can chose to assert our importance through relationally helpful and effective self-definitions. We may jump immediately into action or we may reflect on how we want to express what we feel. We choose either direction and we pay the price for its relative consequences. In FW, the overall process is the same even though the specific content may vary from one respondent to another. The sequence of instructions from one week to the next progresses from dealing with and learning from the past (Week 1) to the process of asking for forgiveness from past targets (Week 2). The last assignment could be broken up into dealing with the present (Week 3) and dealing with the future (Week 4).

Thus, FW is different from PW in so far that it is constructed for the immediate and individualized needs of specific respondents (individual, couples, or family). Responsibility for change lies in their hands and not in the therapist's head. If respondents want change, they can work for it by completing in writing assignments administered to them. In this approach, FW assignments flow directly and idiographically from the problem. In addition to the examples given here, there are many other conditions that could benefit by this approach.

DIFFERENCES BETWEEN PSYCHOTHERAPY, FOCUSED WRITING, AND PROGRAMMED WRITING

Differences between FW, PW, and traditional psychotherapy are summarized in Table 2.2. Here, we need to start differentiating between stylistic and structuring skills. DW, after all, is one way of structuring therapy. While some authorities believe that style and personal relationship between the therapist and client is mostly responsible for change (Bohart & Tallman, 1999), others believe that in addition to the personal relationship between therapist and patient, there needs to be structuring for change to take place (Nathan & Gorman, 1998). Furthermore, some would argue that relationship skills may be necessary for change to take place in individuals (L'Abate, 1999f). However, another would argue that these skills may be insufficient for helping acting-out character disorders as well as couples and families. Additional structuring skills, such as DW, may be necessary for those who cannot be helped just through talk (L'Abate, 1986b, 1991, 1992b, L'Abate & Platzman, 1991).

The major issue with FW is no longer finding out whether it helps or not. The evidence cited elsewhere (Esterling & Pennebaker, 2001; Pennebaker, 1997; Smyth, 1998) fairly well supports its use as ancillary to talk therapy or as an alternative medium of intervention, used instead of talk. The major issues here lie in whether it will be used (1) by both the prevention and psychotherapy communities, and (2) to identify what kind of individuals, issues, and problems will be helped by what approach.

In conclusion, FW is introduced through examples as an approach that requires a setting of personal, dyadic, or multirelational prearranged meetings. In

Table 2.2
Differences between Traditional Talk Psychotherapy, Focused, and Programmed Writing

Traditional Talk Psychotherapy	**Focused and Programmed Writing**
Style more important than method	Method more important than style
Reliance on style more than method	Reliance more on method than on style
Style varies from one therapist to another	Little variance in method; style is either secondary or irrelevant
Process is idiographic	Both idiographic and nomothetic
Content varies	Content can be varied or fixed
Free-wheeling/Flexible	Somewhat rigid
Vague/nonspecific	Very specific and explicit
Costs: high	Costs: relatively minor

these meetings, written instructions for homework assignments are followed up, completed in writing, and then discussed with loved ones as well as with the therapist. From FW, once more information has been gathered, one can then switch to PW. Neither approach is mutually exclusive of the other. Both can be administered in a sequentially flexible fashion. Which approach precedes the other depends very much on the particular needs of respondents at the moment, as perceived by therapists and by respondents themselves. Both approaches, however, expect respondents to work at these assignments in writing, matching one or more hours of homework for one hour of face-to-face or personal contact. With this approach, however, one of the major issues lies in finding evidence to support its responsible and responsive professional practice.

There is virtually no topic that cannot be dealt in DW that is not already dealt with in speaking. In fact, some people, with certain character disorders, for instance, tend to reveal in writing more than they can disclose orally. Addicts have a hard time writing about painful events in their lives. This avoidance demonstrates that one of the major tasks of our lives is to confront, face, and deal with our hurts by expressing and sharing them with loved ones (as discussed in Chapter 5). As Scott (1998) suggested, it is possible to reach prisoners with DW in ways that cannot be obtained through talk. With addicts, it may be helpful to start them writing about generally unpleasant events and then gradually increase the intensity to hurtful and even traumatic ones, as found in the Self-Awareness workbook (described in Chapter 4). Many addicts fear DW because they equate it with losing control. Hence, this fear needs to be confronted before assigning written homework.

DW in any of its four structures does not decrease or eliminate the need for a professional. Rather, it provides a way in which a professional's time and energy can be used more effectively, thereby decreasing the time and costs of psychotherapy. DW is seen as complementary and supplementary to the therapist's personal contribution. Depending on its degree of structure and directives, DW is free from theoretical bias. For example, a central aim of cognitively oriented therapists is to uncover self-defeating thought patterns and self-statements. In contrast, therapists with psychodynamic or humanistic orientations could use DW to aid respondents in reflecting on feelings associated with particular memories or psychological states (e.g., depression).

There are several conceptual bases from which to explain the beneficial effects of FW. One psychosomatic theory of inhibition, avoidance, holds that repression of one's thoughts, feelings, or overt behaviors, particularly those that are traumatic or troubling, takes up both physiological and psychological energy (Esterling, L'Abate, Murray, & Pennebaker, 1999). The effort of inhibition or avoidance produces short-term increases in autonomic nervous system activity that, over time, increase the likelihood of stress-related disease, or exacerbation of concurrent disease (L'Abate, 1994a). Such inhibition also reduces individuals' ability to cognitively process or effectively work toward resolution of their difficulties. Verbally labeling and describing a trauma through DW, as a form of helpful rather than hurtful discharge, allows individuals to cognitively process the event and gain a sense of control, thus reducing the influence of inhibition or avoidance. Properly framed, FW could assuage obsessive internal ruminations and allow expression (i.e., discharge) of painful emotions that can exacerbate physical health and psychological problems. This rationale repeats what was recommended in the previous chapter, and that is, approach rather than avoid and discharge rather than delay. Both functions will be considered in greater detail in Chapter 5.

POSSIBLE ADVANTAGES OF DISTANCE WRITING

The following list is strictly suggestive and based on anecdotal, clinical experience. It should not be taken as a given. Experiences with DW in its four different structures may vary a great deal from one therapist to another and from one respondent to another. That said, DW in its various structures may provide the following advantages:

- Saves time in clinical practice by maximizing effectiveness of interventions
- Conserves energy and effort by maximizing respondents' involvement in the treatment process
- Reaches underserved populations (home-bound, handicapped, military, missionary, Peace Corps volunteers, incarcerated felons, juveniles, etc.)
- Serves respondents who cannot afford weekly face-to-face interventions
- Maintains the continuum of care between therapy sessions
- Conforms to managed care requirements
- Decreases the number of unproductive sessions
- Conducts controlled research inexpensively

POSSIBLE DISADVANTAGES OF DISTANCE WRITING

For respondents (clients, patients, consumers, individuals, couples, families), these possible disadvantages are to be kept in mind:

- Respondents may be too upset to complete assignments.
- Illiterate respondents can be helped by putting workbooks on one tape and allowing them to answer on another tape, or using volunteers to read questions and write down the answers.
- Lack of motivation on the respondent's part—assignments are seen as irrelevant to the process of change—and responsibility for change rests and remains on the therapist's shoulders.
- Possibility of side effects, that is, eliciting painful memories that increase the level of distress in individuals, couples, or families.
- Failure to structure the integral use of writing with verbal psychotherapy from the very beginning. Writing assignments should not be sprung on unsuspecting respondents during the course of therapy. If at all possible, a contract should be drawn at the very beginning.

Therapists should be mindful of ethical and professional limitations and guidelines governing therapeutic practices as conditions for their state license. In addition, they should pay attention to the following personal and professional fears (rather than the reality) of change:

- Resistance to the use of DW in psychotherapy: Fear of change? Fear of losing respondents? Fear of lowered income through the shortening of therapy length?
- Use of DW may become another power struggle with respondents.
- Resistance to complete written homework assignments may indicate dependency needs, fears of change, inability to take responsibility, etc., in respondents. Of course, the sources of resistance should be explored. However, a great deal of resistance can be overcome when written homework assignments are made as a condition for acceptance into a therapeutic contract.

The issue, therefore, consists of trying to help people at risk, in need, and even in crisis in ways that may not require direct, face-to-face referral to a professional. Most estimates, either subjective or objective, find that there are not enough mental health professionals to take care of the multifarious mental health needs of our nation. Can this problem be solved? No single proposal can and will solve the many mental health problems facing us.

Of course, the present proposal is not so grandiose or unrealistic as to suggest that it will solve all the mental health needs of today's society. It might solve some but certainly not all of these problems. At present, it is difficult to envisage how many could be helped through existing technologies (L'Abate & Odell, 1995). However, it will be argued here that to reach as many people who want help, and even those who need it but do not want it, mental health professionals will need to work at a distance from them. Why? Because talk, heretofore the major form of transaction among humans and clearly the major source of interaction in psychotherapy, is relatively inefficient, usually expensive, often uncontrollable and, therefore, unpredictable and impossible to prescribe.

HELPING PEOPLE AT A DISTANCE

To help people at a distance is a very dangerous enterprise, chock full of ethical and professional issues (L'Abate, 1997a) that will be discussed in Chapter 7. There are dangers of misdiagnosis—putting an inappropriate label on an individual. There are dangers in offering misleading treatment that does not match the referral question. There are dangers in not knowing whether the respondents (couples or families) who are supposed to help at a distance, without seeing them, are the very ones therapists are thinking they are helping. Furthermore, what kind of treatment are we going to give if we do not see the patient face-to-face? How about fees? What kind of fees should we charge when no face-to-face contact took place or contract was made? With the overwhelming number of suits against professionals increasing at a frightening pace, who is going to risk one's practice, livelihood, and reputation on something as chancy as working at a distance from respondents?

The above are just a few questions raised by adopting DW as a component of one's practice. Are real or feared dangers (L'Abate, 1997a) overshadowed by ethical and professional considerations? Should we stop helping people because of fears or because of reality? This is clearly a professional minefield, where many professionals "fear to tred." In spite of all these risks, apparently, there are sufficient numbers of professionals who are willing to operate at a distance from respondents through telephone, correspondence, faxes, computers, and even videotapes. Why should we and our respondents not avail ourselves of all avenues of communication and healing?

Can we really and effectively change people's behavior without even seeing them? If words have power, then any argument about their limitations will be seen as threats to the therapist's power and, therefore, rejected. When speaking into a microphone and writing about past traumas are compared experimentally in their effectiveness with control groups that write about emotionally neutral events, there is no denying that the microphone is slightly superior to writing (Esterling, L'Abate, Murray, & Pennebaker, 1999; Smyth, 1998; Szell, 1994). However, this difference is not sufficiently significant statistically to justify its superiority over writing. Furthermore, as Weintraub (1981) argued then—and it has been argued ever since (L'Abate, 1990, 1991, 1997a, 2001a, in press)—speech needs to be transcribed into writing, a process that is expensive. Consequently, at least in that respect, talk is more expensive than DW. Perhaps, if talk is inefficient, it is effective? If it is effective, then, it is an expensive way to help people change.

Any deviation from traditional, mainstream practice may be viewed as antitherapeutic and, therefore, suspect. This proposal does not include, as yet, an individual-differences approach that assumes mental disturbances present themselves along a continuum of severity. Some disturbances can be dealt with without face-to-face contact. Some may not be dealt with in any way except face-to-face, verbal contact. However, we will never know which respondent will be helped with which issue unless we explore alternatives. Psychotherapy is not seen by many therapists along a continuum of care that includes education, primary, and secondary prevention approaches, as presented in the previous chapter. Consequently, if psychotherapy remains the sole method of intervention, we will never access populations in need of psychological help, but not necessarily face-to-face help. The gap between nothing and psychotherapy is not only present in the population at large, it is also present in the psychotherapy community, which controls many of the policy decisions made about working at a distance from respondents. This writer submits respectfully that these decisions may be based more on fears than on realities. These fears restrict our practices and do not allow us to enlarge them to meet the diverse needs of diverse populations.

DISCUSSION

Among the many advantages of DW over talk, in addition to costs, lies its potential to reach masses of individuals for both preventive and paratherapeutic purposes (L'Abate, 1990). Studies using DW or PW were conducted with a minimum of cost. They utilized part-time research assistants, mailings, and data analyses provided by the institution. Thus, DW could be used in epidemiological and preventive interventions in ways that would be difficult, expensive, and practically impossible to achieve through talk.

The combination of talk with DW, that is, the influence of the therapist's own style, which is mainly verbal and nonverbal, with the application of a replicable method of treatment through DW, should result in synergistic effects between the three media, as shown in Figure 2.1. This synergism, which thus far is only a personal impression formed during the writer's past clinical practice, could accelerate the process of research about therapeutic change. This approach could increase the number of clinicians who could become involved in research activities.

How much evidence will be necessary to change traditional therapeutic practices based mainly on talk to also include both nonverbal and written modalities? No matter how much research evidence one may muster, it is very doubtful whether any amount of evidence will hold sway over current verbally mediated psychotherapeutic practices. Ultimately, the decision to change and to incorporate new or even more cost-effective practices may be mandated by third parties, since change in current therapeutic practices will not take place otherwise. Resistance to the use of DW in psychotherapy practice and research, either by itself or in conjunction with talk, is inevitable (L'Abate, 1997b).

Some psychotherapists may be as resistant to change as some of the very respondents they want to help, if not more so (L'Abate, 1997b). However, if the process of therapeutic change consists of at least the three components listed below (elaborated on in Chapter 7), then the process of change for psychotherapists should possess the same characteristics.

1. Emission of new responses that were not present in the past repertoire, either an emotive, cognitive, or behavioral response of an individual (*novelty*)
2. This new response needs to be of a *positive* nature, defined as self-enhancing and rewarding behavior that does not damage anyone else (*positivity*)
3. frequent repetition, practice, and rehearsal to increase the habitual preeminence of this new behavior in the repertoire of an individual (*strength*).

Professional change will take place if and when—only if and when—psychotherapists start practicing new, positive techniques with sufficient intensity and strength to make a difference for themselves and for their clients. These changes imply cost-effectiveness, that is, greater effectiveness in preventive and therapeutic procedures and smaller costs for respondents. This change, of course, implies frequently using new, positive practices that we have not used in the past, such as DW in its different forms.

Matching Dysfunctionalities with Available Help-giving Approaches

An attempt will be made here to begin matching media of exchange with extent of dysfunctionality. This attempt is admittedly general and preliminary. To link problem characteristics with specific interventions for clinical dysfunctionalities, we need to take into consideration two major factors that define them: (1) extent or severity of dysfunctionality, as in acute versus chronic, and (2) type of dysfunctionality, as in externalization and, internalization (Cicchetti & Toth, 1991). The extent or severity of a clinical condition or symptom would determine in part the duration (brief versus prolonged therapy) and frequency of treatment (weekly, biweekly, monthly). In dealing with acute or chronic disorders, medication and even hospitalization or incarceration may be needed. Hospitalization is usually reserved for disorders of internalization, whereas incarceration is usually reserved for disorders of externalization.

With severe to mild disorders one needs to distinguish again between externalization and internalization. With externalizing character disorders, for instance, one would use PW/SCAI and nonverbal group approaches before attempting verbal psychotherapy. With internalizing affective disorders, one would want to use PW/SCAI in parallel with psychotherapy, as demonstrated by Gould (2001) and by DeGiacomo and De Negris (2001).

With disorders of externalization, social skill training, medication, and nonverbal approaches may be necessary before attempting any verbally based therapies. With these disorders, as with most criminalities or acting-out disorders, talk is extremely inefficient (Reed, McMahan, & L'Abate, 2001). Talk is used to manipulate and to make a good impression. Talk, on the other hand, is used differently in internalizations. It is used as introspection, reflection, meditation, thinking, and, often times, rumination and obsession. Verbal psychotherapy with externalization problems is the last resort one wants or needs to use (Reed, McMahan, & L'Abate, 2001; Simon, 1998). Nonverbal group approaches and individualized writing assignments would seem to be much more effective ways of helping than verbally based psychotherapy.

Additionally, changes brought about by the impact of managed care must be considered. This is probably the most significant development to have affected not only mental health practices but the entire field of medicine. Cost-effectiveness and accountability have become the new watchwords. The number of visits to mental health professionals are limited by fiat from external, often unknown agents. It is clear that the days of prolonged psychotherapy are long gone, except for those few who can afford it out of their own pockets or hospitalized patients who need it. In the second place, managed care does not usually pay for prevention. Perhaps things may change once it is understood that prevention is cost-effective, even though its long-term effects have not been established as yet (L'Abate, 1986a). In the third place, very little attention has been paid in the mental health literature to issues of control (as already discussed in the previous chapter). These issues are crucial if we want to help people who are either out of control or have too much of it.

The two *sine qua non* prerequisites for working at a distance from respondents are (1) informed consent, and (2) pre-post-intervention evaluation.

Informed Consent Form: Workbooks must be administered with Informed Consent forms. These can be adapted, lengthened, or shortened to suit the specific needs of respondents. Some parts of these forms can be administered verbally in face-to-face professional relationships, provided a signed waver is obtained. The length and complexity of this form is due to its discussion of legal, ethical, and professional issues designed to protect both patients and professionals alike.

Pre-Post-Intervention Evaluation: This issue will be considered in greater depth in the next chapter.

CONCLUSION

As long as psychotherapy is based mainly on talk, progress in psychotherapy will be slow and difficult to achieve, limited mostly to those few researchers who can receive research grants. It is possible to: (1) study comparatively different therapeutic models in the treatment of many clinical and nonclinical conditions through various types of structured DW and especially programmed workbooks in different populations, (2) possibly increase coping skills in former respondents, and (3) link and match evaluation with treatment through test scores or specific referral questions. These issues will be expanded the next chapter.

There have been many developments under the umbrella of DW in psychotherapy during the last few years: Open-ended, Focused-expressive, Guided, and Programmed DW. Combined with CAI, DW has the potential to reach populations through the Internet that heretofore have been neglected or have been underserved by the mental health and psychotherapy communities.

3

Applications of Workbooks in Psychotherapy

The purpose of this chapter is to introduce a rationale for applications of workbooks as representatives of PW, and as additions or alternatives to existing preventive, rehabilitative, or psychotherapeutic approaches. The creation of workbooks, of course, finds its historical roots in teaching machines and programmed instruction (Brown & L'Abate, 1969). Workbooks consist of a series of assignments containing a variety of questions, exercises, and tasks to be answered in writing around a specific topic, that is, anxiety, depression, negotiation, and so forth. Assignments can be completed by respondents at home between therapy sessions or through computer-mediated contacts between professionals and respondents. Depending on the severity and nature of the condition, these assignments can be administered without face-to-face contact but through correspondence—with written feedback from the therapist—through mail, fax, or e-mail. In this way, a permanent, replicable record is retained by both parties (L'Abate, 1986b, 1990, 1991, 1997a, 2001a, in press; L'Abate & Kern, in press). Conceivably, there should little room for distortions, deletions, or displacements through these assignments even though therapists can be as deceived and manipulated through this medium, as they can be through talk (L'Abate, 1992b; Reed, McMahan, & L'Abate, 2001). Clinicians can easily assess the outcome of these workbook anecdotally, while researchers can perform evaluation studies much more easily and economically than with talk.

Workbooks represent a relatively new phenomenon that supports the thesis of increasing formalization in the practice of psychotherapy and psychological interventions (L'Abate, in press, submitted for publication, b). We need to give respondents definite, concrete, and specific treatment plans, including length, duration, frequency, and costs, to keep them involved until the end of the prescribed treatment. Through these assignments, respondents are responsible for whatever changes they want to make for the better. This may minimize attrition rates and improve outcomes.

Results reviewed by Esterling et al. as well as others (L'Abate & Kern, in press; Smyth & L'Abate, 2001) tentatively support this contention. This evidence was gathered from cooperative undergraduate students rather than clinical cases. When clinical (De Giacomo & De Nigris, 2001; Gould, 2001) or criminal (Reed, McMahan, & L'Abate, 2001) cases were involved, controls were either missing or inadequate. More evidence will be needed to specify under what conditions workbooks are helpful and under what conditions they are not. Furthermore, given the plethora of available workbooks (Chapter 4) dealing with similar clinical conditions, for example, depression, it will be critical to find which workbook based on which theoretical model or empirical evidence is more effective than other workbooks dealing with the same topic.

The critical question here, of course, lies in defining "What kind of written homework assignments?" The last decade has seen the publication, at least in the United States, of a plethora of workbooks that represent the essence of Programmed Writing (PW) (L'Abate, submitted for publication, a). Recently, the Psychological Corporation has published workbooks for empirically-supported treatment programs for such conditions as drug and alcohol dependence, panic disorder, anxiety, phobias, major depression, sexual deviations, obsessive-compulsive disorder, and eating disorders (TherapyWorks*, 1998). Other mental health workbooks have been produced by New Harbinger Publications of Oakland, California, Learning Publications Inc., of Holmes Beach, Florida, and John Wiley & Sons.

The goal of workbooks is to act as the first line of defense (or attack?) in decreasing the debilitating effects of clinical, semiclinical, and quasiclinical conditions. Whereas traditional, verbally based, face-to-face psychotherapy or even just medication is administered to individuals, workbooks can be added to the whole treatment package with couples and families as well. An individual with a dual diagnosis, for instance, could be asked (provided an informed consent form is signed at the outset of treatment) to complete weekly assignments about anxiety or depression. A parental couple may complete assignments in a workbook about temper tantrums for one child, or the Negotiation workbook for themselves. If one partner is depressed, both partners may profit by the Depression in Couples workbook (L'Abate, 1986b). If the other partner is a driven individual, he or she may profit from a workbook by matching MMPI-2 Type A Content Scale (Chapter 4) to reduce the impact of such a condition on the couple.

Workbooks, therefore, address individual, couple, and family issues that may be time-consuming and difficult to confront in face-to-face interactions, especially in comorbid, dual diagnoses conditions. Workbooks permit professionals to tailor-make interventions for the specific and explicit needs of individuals, couples, and families. They enlarge the therapeutic armamentarium in areas where therapists may not be knowledgeable.

Admittedly, the major issue with most workbooks relates to their not having been subjected to repeated empirical verification from separate and independent sources in terms of their clinical usefulness. The rapid production of workbooks has not been matched by research evaluating their clinical usefulness (L'Abate, submitted for publication, a). Only homework assignments in general have been subjected to controlled studies, These studies do support the usefulness of homework assignments in shortening the length of treatment, and by extension, the use of written homework assignments (Burns & Spangler, 2000; Detweiler & Whisman, 1999; Kazantzis, 2000; Kazantzis, Deane, & Ronan, 2000; L'Abate, submitted for publication, b).

However, homework assignments do not always include systematic workbooks. Although considered mass-produced and cost-effective in their clinical applications, workbooks are still in dire need of empirical support. To help correct this inadequacy, Smyth and L'Abate (2001) evaluated physical and psychological benefits through a meta-analysis of 18 workbooks. Results showed a +.44 effect size estimate for mental health workbooks compared to a +.25 effect size for physical health workbooks. In spite of this preliminary evidence of a middle-sized effect, it is important to continue to study the effects of workbooks used without psychotherapy. As long as psychotherapy and homework assignments are administered together, it will be practically impossible to separate which process, psychotherapy or workbooks, is related to which outcome (Kazantzis, 2000; L'Abate, submitted for publication, b).

Additional evidence to support clinical and non-clinical applications of workbooks is crucial because, in some studies conducted by this writer and his associates, control groups produced higher mean change scores than experimental groups, an unexpected and paradoxical outcome (L'Abate, in press, submitted for publication, b).

WORKBOOKS AND THEORY TESTING

DW at a distance from a therapist, using workbooks based on different theoretical perspectives, would allow a comparison of these perspectives. More than 100 commercially available workbooks, for instance, cover most areas of individual, couple, and family relationships, both clinical and nonclinical. The large number of workbooks available to deal with a rather wide range of problems and symptoms makes it possible to match intervention with evaluation or diagnosis in a way that is difficult if not impossible to obtain through talk. An increasing number of publications from different sources attests to their marked, but mostly anecdotal, evidence as helpful adjuncts to talk-based, face-to-face psychotherapy (Riordan, 1996).

Workbooks written from different theoretical, therapeutic, or empirical perspectives may well become the next dynamic step in the comparative evaluation of different approaches. For instance, the workbook about anxiety and panic developed by Barlow and Craske (1994) could be compared with an anxiety workbook developed from the *Diagnostic Symptom Manual IV* (DSM-IV) (L'Abate Boyce, Fraizer, & Russ; 1992). The Depression workbook developed by Weissman (1995), based on interpersonal psychotherapy, could be compared with workbooks developed from Beck's Depression Inventory or Hamilton's Depression Scale (presented in Chapter 4). A sexuality workbook developed by Wincze and Barlow (1997) could be compared to a sexuality workbook developed by Russ and L'Abate (Chapter 4).

Hence, comparative testing of contrasting theoretical models through workbooks could take place dynamically above and beyond artificial laboratory testing of psychometric measurement properties of instruments without interventions. If this link is valid, then workbooks developed from existing and validated test instruments would become as valid and reliable as the instruments from which they were developed. Of course, this equation in itself needs empirical evaluation.

Objective comparisons among workbooks written from different and even antagonistic theoretical perspectives would allow finding which perspective is "better" (i.e., more cost-effective, greater outcome) than others in treating certain clinical conditions (L'Abate, 2001a). For instance, L'Abate, Boyce, Fraizer, and Russ (1992) compared the effectiveness of three workbooks in undergraduates who claimed to be depressed, as measured by the Beck Depression Inventory (BDI) and the Center for Epidemiological Studies Depression Scale (CES-D). One workbook was derived from Beck's cognitive model of depression, a second was derived from a strictly empirical model of depression, the MMPI-2 (L'Abate, 1992b), and a third from L'Abate's (1986b) interpersonal model of depression, as discussed later on in this chapter. At a 6-month follow-up, students who had completed the three workbooks had improved significantly over controls (L'Abate, submitted for publication, b). These results replicated those obtained in psychotherapy, where no one theoretical viewpoint seems to be superior to others (Bergin & Garfield, 1994). The cost of this study, however, was a fraction of what it takes for research with talk-based psychotherapy.

These considerations suggest that (1) workbooks are inexpensive ways to conduct research, (2) it is now feasible and possible to help some people at a distance without seeing them, and (3) workbooks allow elimination of confusing and perhaps interfering "common" factors in therapy (L'Abate, 1999f). Certainly, as any physician worth his or her salt knows, "good bedside manners" do count at the outset of any professional relationship in order to establish a modicum of rapport. However, does this factor matter if the operation or prescription were not matching the symptom or the medicine itself was not sufficient to deal with it? No operation or prescription for medication is effective on the basis of good bedside manners alone. Does a surgeon need to meet patients before operating? Given a surgeon with excellent bed-side manners and 30% mortality rate and one with poor manners but 10% mortality rate for the same condition, which one would be picked? Furthermore, some prescriptions can be given over the phone, especially if the physician knows the patient. Would the operation or prescription produce better effects if doctors operating or prescribing them met patients beforehand?

Presence, one of the major arguments for the direct, face-to-face therapeutic alliance between a professional and a respondent, can be established and even measured through the Internet (Darken, Bernatovich, Lawson, & Person, 1999; Draper, Kaber, & Usher, 1999; Heeter, 1999; Huang, 1999). If this measurement is possible, it would take away some of the mystique of personal, face-to-face contact dear to the hearts and minds of some mental health professionals (L'Abate, 1999f).

While Pennebaker's (1997, 2001) FW approach (reviewed in Chapter 2) is practically universal—it can be applied to most human beings—the advantage of workbooks lies in their specificity, explicitness, and versatility. As shown in the next chapter, they can be tailor-made to the specific needs of a particular individual, couple, or family. For instance, if an individual is depressed, there are now more than a handful of workbooks available to deal with this condition. The diagnosis of depression can be made by history and symptoms alone or by high scores on single-dimension scales like the Beck Depression Inventory, or by high peaks in the profiles of various clinical, objective personality tests like the MMPI-2, the Personality Assessment Inventory (PAI), or other inventories. Workbooks to match each of the content scales of the MMPI-2 or the clinical scales of the PAI or Neuroticism, Extraversion, Openness (NEO) are available. Hence, the specific match between a clinical condition and a workbook can be achieved much more easily through workbooks than through talk.

For couples, workbooks can be administered according to either a symptom or peak scores on a marital inventory. An example of the former is found the workbook about Arguing and Fighting (Chapter 4). An example of the latter is found in workbooks derived from the Marital Satisfaction or the Marital Conflict Inventories. Depression, negotiation, and intimacy workbooks for couples and families are discussed in Chapter 4). The same process can take place with families.

An evaluation instrument was even created with matching homework assignments, the Problems in Relationships Scale (PIRS). It consists of a 240-item questionnaire matching the same dyadic dimensions covered by isomorphic assignments with the same dimensions (L'Abate, 1992b). A series of 20 conflict areas frequently cited in the couple therapy literature (dominant/submissive, expressive/inexpressive, open/closed, etc.) provided the basis for the 240 items rated on a 5-point scale by each partner. Scores for each partner are meaningful only when compared with those of the other partner. The test profile (produced through a computer program) shows which dimensions for each couple have the widest discrepancy. Thus, the profile of each couple is specific to that couple and to no other couple.

Depending on the number of conflict areas, each couple is administered homework assignments that match dimensions with the greatest discrepancy scores. Discrepancies among the 20 scales are added to obtain a total discrepancy score. This score correlated significantly and negatively with two subscales, Dyadic Satisfaction ($r = -.57$, $p < .01$) and Dyadic Cohesion ($r = -.53$, $p < .05$) of the total score of the Spanier Dyadic Adjustment Scale ($r = -.51$, $p < .05$) in 32 married couples (McMahan & L'Abate, 2001).

The PIRS illustrates how a nomothetic (for all couples) evaluation instrument can be applied in an idiographic manner (specific to one couple) to match homework assignments isomorphic with dimensions measured by the evaluation instrument. This process would be impossible to achieve verbally.

The major among the many dangers (Chapter 7) related to workbooks lies in the mismatch between a condition and the workbook administered to deal with it. For instance, a paranoid individual may appear anxious, asking help for that claimed condition, not disclosing from the outset the extent of his/her paranoia. He or she may be administered an anxiety workbook, the referral question being taken at face value. That workbook may eventually elicit either more florid symptoms of paranoia or produce no positive outcome. Since no improvement has taken place, this individual may blame the therapist who administered the anxiety workbook for no improvement and even sue the therapist for damages, that is, the workbook produced the paranoia.

A couple may hide the extent of physical abuse and be accepted for working at a distance through a workbook while the abuse may still be going on. Many potential dangers of using workbooks and Structured Computer-Assisted Interventions (SCAI) may be minimized (although never eliminated) by a careful, objective evaluation of the referral symptom as given not only by respondents but also from family members or friends. Unless careful, objective, and multidimensional screening is performed from the very outset, the danger of administering a mismatched workbook is very real and potentially very destructive, not only to respondents but also to professionals. This conclusion leads to a critical discussion about the current state of evaluation in current mental health practices.

Evaluation in Current Clinical Practices: Critical Remarks

Evaluation is not as valued by the mental health establishment as it needs to be. This conclusion should not detract or distract us from stressing its importance in spite of its consistent devaluation in mental health and psychotherapy (L'Abate, 1990). Most evaluative practices in these fields consist, at best, of a history and the nature of the referral question obtained through interviews (L'Abate, 1994b; L'Abate & Bagarozzi, 1993). Why should we waste professionals' and respondents' time, energy, and money to evaluate above and beyond an interview? That interview is sufficient to evaluate anybody. Why not accept as given existing evaluative practices, that is, an interview, no matter how inadequate, and go with the flow, accepting things as they are? Willingness to conform to currently accepted evaluation practices, no matter how inadequate, would be tantamount to accepting the status quo without questioning it.

The status of evaluation in the mental health field, whether with individuals, couples, and families, is unacceptable. This harsh conclusion is especially relevant to the attempt to link and connect evaluation with workbook interventions. This is one of the major failings of evaluation as traditionally practiced. If we cannot link evaluation with treatment, why should one evaluate? Combining evaluation with intervention is not part of standard operating procedure in the mental health field, either in training or in practice. Apparently, objective evaluation is seen as an unnecessary requirement and an irrelevant, time-consuming chore rather than a necessary and crucial part of any intervention. The whole treatment process takes place through talk and no other options seem necessary. As suggested repeatedly, with the written, programmed medium it is possible, easy, and inexpensive to achieve a link between evaluation and treatment.

Evaluation and PW/SCAI

As already discussed in previous chapters, the verbal, face-to-face relationship may be critical in dealing with respondents as people, to establish rapport, trust, and communication, using warmth, unconditional regard, and empathy. This approach includes the style of the therapist. DW, on the other hand, can be used as a method and workbooks used as a technology for dealing with referring symptoms or problems. The treatment of symptoms, if it is to become an intersubjective, scientific method, needs to be established through detailed, specific, and explicit written-out plans. These plans or scripts, ideally, should have been already tested on nonclinical populations. Consequently, as long a part of treatment occurs in writing, it can be evaluated from one therapist to another and from one clinical setting to another.

Some workbooks were tried out with a nonclinical population of undergraduates, who scored high on tests of depression and anxiety (L'Abate, Boyce, Fraizer, & Russ, 1992). It was found that, indeed, these workbooks significantly reduced high levels of depression and anxiety to normal levels, suggesting that the same workbooks can be administered without harm to a clinical population (Bird, 1992). In addition, it was possible to administer a well-known personality test (MMPI-2) and prescribe those workbooks that matched high peaks (highest deviance) on any of the 15 Content Scales (L'Abate, Boyce, Fraizer, & Russ, 1992). Unpredictably and paradoxically, in the latter study, as well as in a study of seminarian couples (McMahan & L'Abate, 2001), control groups showed a greater improvement in mean change scores than experimental groups. These results, therefore, raise the question of whether, indeed, workbooks can be used as ameliorative vehicles of change. On the other hand, the meta-analysis of mental health workbooks mentioned earlier (Smyth & L'Abate, 2001), did find a middle-sized effect, pushing the weight of supporting evidence on the plus side for their implementation with clinical populations (L'Abate, submitted for publication, b).

Of course, written homework assignments beg the question: "If these homework assignments are administered on the basis of the presenting symptom, what do we need an evaluation for?" This is an important issue that needs highlighting. Prescription of a workbook should be based, ideally, on both an objective test profile and on the contextual nature of a presenting symptom as surmised from an interview. Linking evaluation with treatment has been a crucial problem since the historical beginnings of the testing movement (Weiner, 1976). Supposedly, tests are to be used to understand the extent and type of dysfunctionality. They also provide relevant recommendations for a specific match with the most appropriate form of treatment. This ideal, however, although desired and desirable, has not been reached, as far as this writer knows, and will not be reached as long as talk is the preferred medium of treatment (Howard, Nance, & Myers, 1987; Hurt, Reznikoff, & Clarkin, 1991; Kennedy, 1992; Moncher & Prinz, 1991; Okun, 1990; Perry, Frances, & Clarkin, 1985; Seligman, 1990).

Ultimately, objective evaluation serves as a baseline for the evaluation of outcome, whether a result of talk or of writing. Qualitative and anecdotal evidence of the type gathered from an interview is not going to furnish an adequate pre-post-comparison, as do objective tests.

Evaluation and Workbooks for Individuals

This approach can be accomplished with individuals using an objective test like the MMPI-2. To determine the effectiveness of PW in lowering the peak scores on the MMPI-2 content scales, 54 undergraduate respondents were administered this test on a before-after basis. They were randomly assigned to one of three groups: (1) control without homework assignments, (2) an experimental group given workbooks designed to match each of the 15 Content scales (L'Abate, 1992b), and (3) another experimental group that in addition to MMPI-2 assignments received written feedback about and after each assignment was turned in completed. As in all the previous studies, personal contact between respondents and experimenters was either nonexistent or minimized. One-way Multiple Analysis of Variance (MANOVA) was used to examine mean differences in peak scores subtracted from the average profile elevation of the remaining 14 scores on the content scales on a pre-post treatment basis. Although between-groups effects yielded no significant difference ($F = 2.03$; df. 2,5, $p > 14$) among the three groups, the within-effect yielded a significant difference among the same groups ($F = 24.12$; df. 2,51, $p < .001$). Although the mean peak scores decreased significantly in this study, the control group's mean peak scores went down as well as those of the two experimental groups, decreasing the validity of the results.

Some additional findings concerned the validity of the content scales as related to the students' behavior during the study. For instance, students scoring highest on the Type A scale were the most prompt in returning assignments, whereas those scoring highest on the Antisocial Practices scale handed in incomplete assignments, made the most excuses, were often late, and dropped out most often from the study. Nonetheless, in spite of the control group decreasing peak scores more than the two experimental groups, these results supported the feasibility of linking evaluation with test scores on a prescriptive-idiographic basis. Why the control group "improved" as much as the experimental group, as was also the case with seminarian couples, is an intriguing but still unanswered issue (McMahan & L'Abate, 2001)

Evaluation and Workbooks for Couples

We can obtain the same link between evaluation and treatment with couples using two different instruments to measure the same dimensions from two different vantage points, direct versus indirect, and a nomothetic approach used in an idiographic manner. A program in this context means the combination of tests with an isomorphic series of programmed assignments, as in the case of the PIRS described earlier.

To evaluate the reliability of the PIRS, 18 couples drawn from the undergraduate volunteer pool at a large urban university were administered the PIRS twice, at the beginning and at the end of the quarter, with a minimum interval of about four to six weeks (L'Abate & Kunkel, 1988). This inventory indirectly evaluated four personality characteristics: selful, selfish, selfless, and no-self. These will be discussed in greater detail in Chapter 5. The selful and no-self scales for women were stable, while the selfish and the selfless were not. For men, only the selfless scale was significantly stable. Nonsignificant correlations were due to the effects of single, very deviant scores from one or two respondents.

More relevant was the difference between means for men and women. On pre-test, undergraduate women tended to score higher on selflessness than men ($df = 32$, $t = 2.50$, $p < .05$), while clinical women seemed to reverse this trend in comparison to men. The no-self dimension was also significantly higher for women than for men ($t = 6.45$, $p <. 01$). On post-test, differences between men and women in selflessness ($t = 3.79$, $p < .01$) and in no-self dimensions ($t = 4.82$, $p < .01$) persisted. To evaluate the concurrent validity of the selfishness scale, it was correlated with the Narcissism Personality Inventory (NPI) using another group of undergraduates. No correlation between these two scales was found, suggesting that selfishness in the intimate realm may be quite different from narcissism as an intrapsychic dimension void of an intimate context.

This approach does suggest that, with PW, tests that still fulfill descriptive as well as predictive functions can also be used for prescriptive purposes, as discussed below.

Evaluation and Workbooks for Families

There are four test-related workbooks related to families: (1) When Parents and Children Argue: From the Eyes of a Child, (2) When Parents Argue: From the Eyes of a Child, (3) Family Functioning, and (4) Family Profile Form (FPF). More information about these tests and workbooks is available in the next chapter.

Here, the relationship between referral question, evaluation, and matching workbooks will be expanded.

Prescriptiveness: A Third Criterion Necessary to Link Test Construction with Workbooks

The goal of linking evaluation with treatment can be accomplished through the creation of *prescriptive* rather than solely *descriptive* or, at best, *predictive* diagnostic instruments (L'Abate, 1990, 1992b, 1994b; L'Abate & Bagarozzi, 1993). In addition to the *descriptive-predictive-prescriptive* distinction, we need to consider two other distinctions of relevance to evaluation using a PW/SCAI approach, and that is: *nomothetic-idiographic* and *direct-indirect.* Through workbooks, as discussed earlier in this chapter, an essentially nomothetic approach can be applied in an idiographic manner. Furthermore, evaluation can be direct, as, for instance, through most psychological test instruments, or indirect, as in the PIRS, where not only dimensions of conflict between partners are measured, but also the personality propensities of each partner.

Consequently, in addition to the two major, traditional requirements for psychological test construction—description and prediction—there is a third criterion necessary to achieve greater control over evaluation's links with workbooks (L'Abate, 1990). How can this third criterion of psychological science, that is, control—equated here with prescriptiveness—be achieved through psychological test construction and through prescription of workbooks? If prescriptiveness determines how tests should be constructed, it becomes possible to satisfy not only the two traditional criteria of description and prediction, but also the third one of control and prescription. How can greater control over test construction and workbooks be achieved? Control over test construction and over certain aspects of psychological interventions can be achieved if we include and assert the crucial importance of its equivalent in test construction, and that is: *prescriptiveness.* This term means the ability of a test to prescribe specific treatments that follow directly from single test scores, test profiles, or referral questions.

Introduction of this third criterion hinges on the difficulty of finding a one-to-one link between diagnosis and treatment, as long as treatment takes place through the verbal medium. The use of manuals (Garfield, 1997) has been an innovation that should have linked evaluation and diagnosis with more uniform treatment. At best, when talk has been recorded, transcribed, and coded, some links between evaluation and treatment can be found on a *post facto* basis, not on the basis of progress notes or patient's reports. However, to date, as far as this writer knows, such a link has not been found easily or economically. In addition to being very expensive to record, transcribe, and code, talk is too infinite and too uncontrollable to allow a specific link between evaluation and treatment (L'Abate, 1999f).

Prescriptiveness, therefore, is equivalent to the establishment and achievement of control that links evaluation with intervention over the course of treatment. Prescriptiveness becomes even more effective when certain aspects of either preventive or psychotherapeutic interventions take place through PW/SCAI rather than through face-to-face talk.

Recent developments in "new rules of measurement" as well as test construction in the 1990s (Embretson, 1996) raise questions about the sound methodological foundations of test creation and construction. In spite of these new developments in test construction and validation, these developments still assume that the two basic and only criteria for test construction are still description (i.e., understanding) and prediction. Clinically, diagnostic labels still remain the best form of understanding for allowing the therapist to predict future behavior. Using the MMPI-2 as an example, if a person achieves a high score on the D scale, the risk and prediction of depression and even suicide are higher than in an individual whose peak score is on the Pd scale. In the latter instance, the prediction would be one of impulsiveness and acting out against others rather than against self. These diagnostic categories supposedly have implications for treatment approaches. But how is the treatment of depression different from treatment for impulsivity? As long as the medium of treatment is talk, it will be difficult if not virtually impossible to answer that question. Through specific workbooks for depression and impulsiveness, for instance, it is now possible to obtain a level of specificity difficult and expensive to achieve verbally.

Recently, Ben-Porath (1997) reviewed the use of personality assessment instruments in empirically guided treatment planning, summarizing a variety of reasons for the need to construct a whole new kind of assessment instrument for prescribing treatment. This viewpoint parallels similar arguments made here about prescriptiveness in relation to PW. This writer has argued (L'Abate, 1990, 1991, 1992b, 1997a, 1997b, 1999f), that as long as psychological treatment is based solely on talk, it will be very expensive to validate what therapists said they did or said and what they think they did or said. One would have to tape-record what was said in the therapy session, transcribe it, and eventually code it for classification. This process, although relevant and important, is limited to a handful of researchers who have the tenacity and motivation, including grant money, to verify the validity of the therapeutic process and link it to assessment and outcome instruments. It is doubtful whether therapists in private practice, for instance, are going to pay attention to replicating such a costly process.

If this is the case, then, how can the process of therapy be connected and related to the initial evaluation? How can one link what is said and done in therapy with what was originally evaluated before therapy started?

Prescriptiveness as Control

If control and regulation are indeed the third goal of a scientific enterprise—in addition to description and prediction—how are they exercised in actual psychological practice? The answer to this question is: "If we prescribe behavior we can also begin to regulate it" (Weeks & L'Abate, 1982). Regulation, however, cannot be total, and it cannot remain solely in the hands of clinicians. If we understand what being in control means, that is, regulation, then we should be able to help those who need it. However, as already argued in Chapter 1, if we do not have a mode of control and regulation, it will be impossible to impart it to anybody. Regulation can be achieved when there are limits to where and when such regulation can be exercised and where and when it cannot be exercised (L'Abate, 1984, 1986b, 1994a). For instance, we have control and regulation whenever we ask respondents to answer questions on a test in our therapy office. We cannot, however, control and regulate how respondents are going to answer these questions, either inside or outside the professional's office. We have control whenever we ask respondents to pay agreed-upon fees. However, we cannot control whether fees will be paid or not, unless we ask to be paid beforehand or as soon as the session is finished. Of course, we cannot control what respondents will do outside of a professional office, even though we may prescribe homework assignments. We still have the problem of compliance and adherence to whatever instructions or prescriptions we administer (Cullari, 1996; Detweiler & Whisman, 1999).

Control, however, may increase whenever we ask respondents to sign an informed consent form regarding completing prescribed homework assignments. Control may increase even more whenever we make completion of written homework assignments a condition for acceptance into therapy. Control may increase even further whenever we ask respondents to complete such assignments at certain times and in certain ways, for example, "for 20 minutes at 9 o'clock PM every other day." Control is exercised any time we ask respondents to start and to end a certain activity, as, for example: "Write for 20 minutes a day for four consecutive days about all the hurts that you have experienced in your life, including those that you have not shared with anyone" (Esterling, L'Abate, Murray, & Pennebaker, 1999; Esterling and Pennebaker, 2001; Pennebaker, 1997).

Whenever homework assignments are completed at pre-set times and on a regular basis, for example, once a week, twice a week, or every other day, we are also teaching respondents how to achieve control over their behavior by regulating it. Determining times of occurrence, frequencies, rates, and intensities of certain behaviors beforehand may increase one's sense of control. If respondents learn to regulate themselves through homework assignments, they might even learn to achieve greater control in other areas of their lives.

What happens when we ask respondents to answer and complete written homework assignments? Through these means we are expanding the notion of control and regulation even further. We ask questions in writing that will be answered in writing in the privacy of the respondent's home, car, or office. Now the medium of communication is no longer just talk. What happens if we make respondents' responsibility for completing written homework assignments a condition for being seen again in the therapist's office? ("This is the way I practice. There are other professionals who do not use homework assignments. Perhaps you should consult them if you are not interested in completing written homework assignments.") The notion of control is expanded even further.

Of course, this possibility must be spelled out clearly in an informed consent form presented and signed as part of a therapeutic contract discussed at the end of the third evaluation session, before a therapeutic contract is made. This procedure implies that the first three sessions serve as reciprocal evaluation. Respondents evaluate therapists, just as the latter evaluate the former.

The issue here is: "What kind of homework assignments? How will this choice be determined?" Hence, prescription of these homework assignments is another way to influence and regulate respondents' behavior and help them achieve greater control over their lives. We do need, however, a model of what is meant by control and regulation (as already discussed in Chapter 1). If we are going to assign written homework as part of the whole treatment process, to make respondents more involved in and more actively responsible for the outcome of that process, then it is crucial that instructions be provided in writing.

In this fashion, we can minimize, if not avoid, distortions ("I did not understand what I was supposed to do. . . . ," "I thought you said. . . ."), avoidance ("I forgot. . . ."), or delay ("I will do it next week"). Consequently, whenever clinical practice progresses along two tracks, through: (1) face-to-face office visits, where talk might be crucial to establish rapport and possibly, if deemed necessary, a therapeutic alliance, and (2) written homework assignments, the control, regulation, and influence of the therapist is at least doubled. Perhaps therapeutic effectiveness might most likely be enhanced when two different approaches are used synergistically. Control and regulation are enhanced whenever a session of face-to-face psychotherapy is matched by one or more hours of written homework assignments.

How and what are therapists going to administer in these written homework assignments? Once the nature of these assignments is determined in its contents (traumatic versus trivial, general versus specific, ad hoc versus systematic, open-ended versus focused, guided versus programmed), then test construction may become prescriptive (L'Abate, 1990, 1992b, 1994a). If there is one-to-one correspondence between a single test score, a test profile, or a referral question with homework assignments, then it would be possible to fulfill the third criterion of prescriptiveness. However, this criterion can only be fulfilled if the domain of treatment is finite and known. Talk is too infinite and indefinite to be controlled and prescribed. There are no boundaries about how one can or should use words (L'Abate, 1999f). Writing is finite because of the very nature of this medium. It is determinable, definite, finite, and, usually, it cannot be forgotten, distorted, or avoided as much as talk. It can be reproduced ad infinitum and it is very inexpensive, certainly much cheaper than seeing a therapist in a face-to-face session. Existing psychological tests cannot control, determine, and prescribe what a psychotherapist says to a respondent and what the respondent will say to the therapist unless they are linked to specific workbooks (as shown in Chapter 4).

Furthermore, psychotherapy is too variable and indeterminate, not only in terms of its various types, theories, and techniques, but also in terms of individual differences among therapists of similar theoretical persuasions, let alone respondents. This variability makes it difficult if not impossible to find or create a specific link between referral problem, symptom, test score, or test profile and treatment. Consequently, one is led to conclude that, as long as psychological interventions are based solely on talk, the link between evaluation and treatment will remain difficult if not impossible to achieve. If and when this link becomes possible, it will be expensive and limited to a handful of researchers rather than to most therapists.

The analogy of this criterion with medical prescribing is relevant here, regardless of whether psychologists should or should not become involved in this process, an issue external to this proposal. The point is that medical prescriptions are usually written for a known domain. There is a finite number of medications that can be prescribed for depression, for instance (Akistal & Cassano, 1997). Given any symptom, there is usually a finite number of medications and procedures that will be relevant and specific to the treatment of that symptom. Most medical prescribing, especially in psychiatry, is an educated guess, hit or miss, trial and error process. If one medication does not work for two or three weeks, another medication is prescribed. Can we mental health professionals do better than writing hit or miss, trial and error prescriptions? Random prescriptions, even within a given realm, for instance, depression, can be avoided once we adopt and use systematically specific written homework assignments matched with that condition, provided that condition is properly and adequately evaluated beforehand.

The systematic use of workbooks becomes prescriptive as a third criterion for test construction when the domain in which this criterion is operationally defined as in writing. If this assumption is correct, it would follow that most traditional tests, which are based on an assumption of verbal communication in psychological interventions, might not fulfill the requirement of a finite domain. Attempts to reduce psychotherapy's variability through the manualization of psychotherapy has produced additional problems (Addis, 1997; Gaston & Gagnon, 1996; Havik & VandenBos, 1997; Strupp & Anderson, 1997). Furthermore, manualized treatment puts restraints on what therapists need to or want to say, but no restraints are put on what respondents will say or do. Apparently, as far as one knows, practicing psychotherapists reject therapy manuals as another attempt to restrict their self-determination, creativity, and responsibility to their respondents. On the other hand, managed care might start to require greater uniformity of treatment and greater accountability in reporting outcome.

By now it should be clear that prescription cannot take place in the infinite domain of talk. Once this contention is accepted, it follows that test construction should take prescriptiveness into consideration, provided that: (1) the domain over which to prescribe is known and finite, and (2) this domain, at least in part, is brought under control through systematically written homework assignments rather than talk.

The rest of this section will illustrate how it is possible to link specific evaluations with specific written homework assignments, once the domain of treatment is written down, known, and available to any clinician who wants to use it.

Workbooks and Prescriptiveness

Once workbooks are used to match treatment with evaluation, it is possible to write those that match either existing evaluation instruments or definite clinical symptoms. For instance, a series of homework assignments for individuals was written to match the 15 content scales of the MMPI-2 (L'Abate, 1992b). Another workbook on Social Learning was written for impulsive individuals who are either incarcerated felons or who score high on the Psychopathic Deviate scale of the MMPI-2. Various depression programs were written for individuals with high scores on either the Depression scale of the MMPI-2 or on the Beck Depression Inventory (L'Abate, Boyce, Fruizer, & Russ, 1992). Other workbooks to match existing tests were written for the NEO-Five-Factor Personality model, the Personality Assessment Inventory (PAI), the Symptom Scale 77, and Hamilton's Depression scale, among others (as shown in Chapter 4).

Conceivably, once characteristics of a specific population are known—for instance, in the case of psychopathic individuals, measured by a simple, single-score, paper-and-pencil, self-report test (Kosson, Steuerwald, Forth, & Kirkhart, 1997)—it is possible to construct a series of homework assignments that match each of those characteristics. Once constructed (nomothetic approach), these assignments can be administered (idiographically) to respondents according to how these characteristics are rated or rank-ordered by each respondent as being most prominent in their test profile. Since the ranking of various descriptive characteristics or descriptive statements is strictly individualized and varies from one respondent to another, it is possible to administer the same workbook to groups of individuals. However, the order of presentation for assignments can vary from one respondent to another within each group. Workbooks as a method of intervention, therefore, are nomothetic in research. Their administration, however, can be idiographic even in research if one so desires, as long as the number of assignments is consistent. Certain characteristics may vary from one individual to another, from one couple to another, and from one family to another.

Workbooks are also related to the referral questions of respondents rather than test profiles. Referral questions focus on problems such as anger, phobias, codependency, loneliness, moodiness, and procrastination for individuals, fighting between partners in couples, and family feelings, among others, that are difficult to evaluate through objective tests if there is no test available to evaluate them. This conclusion does not mean that because there is no test instrument to evaluate it, a condition does not need to be evaluated objectively. On the contrary, an objective evaluation as a way to set up a contextual baseline for the referral question is still necessary.

To match the referral question with treatment in couples, for instance, a workbook was written about arguing and fighting (L'Abate, 1992b). Here, in the first assignment, partners are asked to describe individually the nature and content of the arguing and fighting through rating the frequency, rate, duration, content, and intensity of this behavior. After individual completion of the first assignment, they are to meet to exchange their answers and to discuss similarities and differences in their answers, a practice that applies to all couples and families who are administered this and other programmed homework. In the second assignment, partners rank in order, again individually, 10 "explanations" of arguing and fighting that are all positively reframed, including giving their own explanation, if those given were not satisfactory to them. Again, they have to meet by appointment and discuss their answers. In the third assignment, partners are asked to have an argument or fight according to a series of instructions designed to mimic how couples generally argue/fight (e.g., "really dirty") according to a prescription of the symptom technique (Weeks & L'Abate, 1982).

Couples are instructed to tape-record this session and to bring the tape to the therapy session. Once the tape is brought in (some couples do not because they have quit arguing/fighting and have settled down to calm discussion/negotiation), they are given a rating sheet. They have to listen individually to their tape and score how often each of them has uttered abusive expressions already defined in the previous assignment (You statements/blaming, reading the partner's mind, bringing up the past, finding excuses for self but not for partner, blackmail/bribery, threats and ultimatums, distracting). Once they bring back their scores on these categories, each partner is administered the assignment that matches the highest score achieved. If there are other high scores, each partner is administered the matching assignment in subsequent therapy sessions. Consequently, the use of workbooks is a nomothetic method that can be administered idiographically. As the foregoing example illustrates, the process of prescription between evaluation and written homework assignments can be achieved through links between a symptom, for example, arguing and fighting, and a specific workbook.

In addition to workbooks written to match test scores for individual tests, other couple workbooks that match existing dyadic questionnaires have been written for Marital Satisfaction and Marital Conflict scales, and for families, Kochalka and L'Abate's Family Profile Form (1997). Other family workbooks have been written on the basis of the referral question either for the whole family or for the identified patient. These questions include abuse, lying, overeating, and negativity (Chapter 4).

Conclusion: Do We Need a Criterion for Prescriptiveness?

The search for a one-to-one correspondence between evaluation and treatment has been the Holy Grail of clinical practice since the inception of the mental health professions. This goal has been sought in many ways but not achieved fully because the medium of treatment was talk. Once the medium of intervention is changed in part to PW, the goal of linking a specific diagnosis, for example, understanding, with a specific intervention becomes much more reachable and real. The introduction of novel ways to practice at a distance between professionals and respondents, of course, opens the gate to an array of ethical and professional problems that need further consideration, but that are not insurmountable (as discussed in Chapter 7).

STRUCTURED COMPUTER-ASSISTED INTERVENTIONS (SCAI) AND INTERNET INTERVENTIONS

Through the Internet, PW/SCAI has the potential of becoming the third avenue of delivery for mental health services after medication and psychotherapy (Bracy, 1992; Bradley, Welch, & Skilbeck, 1993; Gould, 2001; Williams, Boles, & Johnson, 1995), in spite of controversy (Kisser & Kraut, 1999; Rierdan 1999; Silverman, 1999; Shapiro, 1999). Thus far, there have been sufficient testimonials as to the potential benefits of SCAI in a variety of settings:

1. Private clinical practice (Gould, 2001; Waterhouse, 1993)
2. Private psychiatric practice (Wolff, 1993)
3. University counseling center (Theye, 1993)
4. Comprehensive community mental health service (Kyle, 1993)
5. Residential treatment facility for adolescents
6. Substance abuse treatment (Kavanaugh, 1993),
7. Correctional institution (Vitelli, 1993)
9. Psychiatric hospital (Pelfry, 1993)

Testimonials as to its widespread usefulness, however, are no substitute for substantive evidence about their usefulness (Marks, Shaw, & Parkin, 1998).

Computers, for instance, are being used to improve memory skills (Ryan, 1994) and the process of play-therapy with children (Aymard, 1999; Kokish,

1994), among many others—too many to cite here. Computerized assessment may be another step in Internet applications. In spite of its critics (Brenneis, 1994), the computer is going to be used more and more in psychiatric and mental health services (Baskin, 1994; L'Abate, 2001a). One can only guess that the number of mental health professionals using computers for direct clinical applications is growing not only in the United States but around the world. More recently, there is evidence (Kobak, Dottl, & Serlin, 1997) that in some circumstances, computers may do a better job than professionals. In the Kobak Dottl, and Serlin study, for instance, it was found that patients were more willing to disclose and admit symptoms of alcoholism and obsessive-compulsive disorder to a computer than to a primary care physician. These results support Bloom's (1992) contention that even disturbed patients respond better to computers than to professionals.

Thus far, SCAI has been found helpful in the treatment of panic disorders, obesity, relaxophobia, test anxiety, phobias, agoraphobias, and depression (Newman, Kenardy, Herman, & Barr-Taylor, 1997). A population that has not been helped by talk therapies but that could profit by PW and SCAI are incarcerated offenders (Reed, McMahan, and L'Abate, 2001; Simon, 1998). Before long, a variety of clinical conditions will be treated through SCAI to determine which clinical conditions are treatable through this medium and which clinical conditions need to be treated by a professional in a face-to-face relationship. SCAI's function, therefore, is to prevent as well as to heal.

Hence, the question is whether computers can fulfill some functions until now reserved for face-to-face interventions. How can PW/SCAI be utilized in the prevention and treatment of mental disorders? In the not too distant future, it will be possible to have networks (i.e., consortia) of clinics, universities, institutional, and public libraries administering workbooks, that is, structured interventions, through computers. These networks could be created especially to help people who are reluctant, unwilling, or unable to seek direct, face-to-face medical, psychiatric, or mental health services. There are people who may not need face-to-face treatment, but who could use PW/SCAI on an instructional and preventive basis. The problem here is one of identifying which people need which levels of intervention (L'Abate, 1990). This is a crucial issue that requires evaluation as standard operating procedure—a requirement for all people who are willing and able to use these new media of intervention at a distance from professionals.

In addition to their many advantages—cost-effectiveness, mass-production, increased involvement of respondents in the helping process, furnishing clear, explicit guidelines for treatment plans, specificity, among others—workbooks fulfill another important function; they are essentially software for computer-assisted interventions (L'Abate, 1992b). With the Internet via computers becoming one of the most efficient avenues of service delivery in mental health practices (L'Abate, 2001a; Williams, Boles, & Johnson, 1995), many professonal helpers will need to offer clear, inexpensive, concrete, and concise homework assignments. In spite of novel ethical and professional issues, however, there is no doubt that computers will fast become an additional way to reach populations that heretofore were impossible or very difficult to reach face-to-face, including vast populations of high school and college students who may need some help but are reluctant to seek it in counseling centers or clinics.

With the advent of computers, it is a skip and a jump to go from workbooks to computers as media of psychological interventions, as pioneered by Gould (2001) and by De Giacomo and De Nigris (2001), among others. The Internet is fast becoming an alternative source of service delivery in the mental health field (Barak, 1999; Gackenbach & Ellerman, 1998; Grohol, 1998; Jones, 1995; King & Moreggi, 1998; Laszlo, Esterman, & Zabko, 1999; Marks, Shaw, & Parkin, 1998; Nickelson, 1998; Reid, 1998; Stamm, 1998). At least in the United States, managed care and insurance companies are pressuring for therapies that are cost-effective and accountable, and SCAI can fulfill these requirements. It also fulfills a need to reach populations that have been either unwilling or unable to seek mental health facilities and interact with mental health professionals in face-to-face relationships (Lauterbach, 1996; Miller, Hammond, & Hile, 1996; Trabin, 1996; Williams, Boles, & Johnson, 1995).

Of course, there is a growing controversy about whether rapport can be achieved on the Internet as well as it can be achieved in face-to-face talk psychotherapy (Kraut, Patterson, Lundmark, Kiesler, Mukopadhyay, & Scherlis, 1998; Parks & Roberts, 1998). Only empirical evidence will provide an answer to this controversy (Rabasca, 1998). Even then, there be sufficient room to help people at a distance through the Internet who cannot be helped through face-to-face talk.

HOW TO WRITE A WORKBOOK AND ASSIGNMENTS

In case readers want to write their own assignments or programmed workbook, general guidelines are available in L'Abate (1992b). There are many ways to organize a workbook or written homework assignments that may be relevant to the professional's theoretical, preventive, or therapeutic predilections. Any topic or subject matter can be broken up into an outline that would contain potential written assignments. Contents, once broken up, need to be divided into parts that will become separate assignments. Assignments should be ordered in a logical and practical sequence, flowing, for instance: (1) from the general to the specific, (2) from the least traumatic to the most traumatic, or (3) from the least confrontive to the most confrontive. The reverse sequence can be followed as well, since there is not yet evidence that would support one sequence over the other.

Some organizing principles may be helpful in preparing an assignment:

Writing a Workbook by Content: What?

One needs to be informed and knowledgeable about the nature of the particular subject matter one wants to address. For instance, if one wants to write a workbook about X, one needs to raise questions about how X is viewed by respondents. The nature of X means asking about various dimensions of X according to its effects on respondents. If one wants to write a workbook about a clinical condition, for instance, one may use outlines given in the DSM-IV manual to divide parts of any condition. Schizophrenia, for example, is described by a variety of symptoms. Each symptom could become one assignment in itself or even a series of assignments. The nature of schizophrenia can be defined by asking respondents to write about its definition, its frequency, its rate, its duration, and its intensity, as well as its specific content. This approach was used in developing workbooks and assignments from a variety of multiple scale tests, such as the MMPI-2 or the PAI. By the same token, one can use items like anxiety and depression in a single-scale test, to ask respondents to define each item and give two examples to make sure the item is defined and understood correctly. The latter approach was used to develop quite a few workbooks presented in the next chapter.

Writing a Workbook by Temporal Perspective: When?

1. Past: Historical background of X. How has X impinged on the respondent's life?
2. Present: Conditions or situations surrounding X
3. Future: What would happen to X in the foreseeable future?

Writing a Workbook by Reasons: Why?

Awareness of how X has affected a respondent's life in terms of rational or even irrational "explanations" about how X originated, persisted, and was reinforced either by the respondent or by external sources.

Writing a Workbook by Style: How?

This question also pertains to how and what the professional wants to elicit in the respondent's answers. How should questions be written to deal with "What" and "How"? These are issues of style that are relevant to what and how questions are going to be asked in a particular assignment.

1. Level of Abstraction: This dimension ranges from abstract to concrete: It may also encompass a dimension of generality-specificity in the same order, that is, the more general the questions (e.g., "Write about the meaning of life."), the greater the level of abstraction implicitly asked of the reader. Asking for specific dates, concrete happenings, and important events lowers the level of abstraction.

2. Goals: Goals of an assignment or workbook have to be decided before formulating the questions. Is the goal to obtain cathartic relief for respondents or is the goal one of prescribing specific behaviors (e.g., "Write for 30 minutes from 7:00 P.M. on Mondays, Wednesdays, and Fridays.")? To achieve the former goal, the stress may be on eliciting emotional release. To attain the latter goal, the prescription may specify what is expected from respondents in the following week or at pre-set time(s), that is, activities in which respondents are expected to become involved.
3. Focused versus Programmed Format: The format of a workbook varies according to its goals.
4. Content: Content ranges from traumatic to trivial and from general to specific. For instance, a focused format may be very general, whereas a programmed format may be more specific.

Writing Workbooks from Single Score Tests

Any single-score test can become the basis for a workbook. All that is necessary is to follow four steps:

1. Definition of items, adjectives, or attributes describing the behavior. For instance, many of the workbooks described in the next chapter require such definition. Respondents can use their own knowledge, use a dictionary, or consult with partners, other family members, friends, or relatives to arrive at a definition. The rationale for this practice is found in a future publication (L'Abate, in press).
2. Provision of at least two examples to show that the respondent has correctly understood the meaning of the term describing the behavior. Thus far the process is nomothetic; it is applied to all respondents.
3. Rank-order of the items according to each individual respondent's personal preferences, needs, and priorities, that is, how applicable the items are to the respondent's self-view, awareness, and goals. This rank-order changes the process from nomothetic to idiographic, since the prescription of all the following, standard format assignments is predicated on the rank-order of the items. The item that is rank-ordered as first in applicability to the respondent becomes the next assignment. The item that is rank-ordered as second in its applicability to the respondent becomes the second assignment, and so on, until all the items viewed as applicable to the respondent are administered.
4. A standard format assignment entitled with the behavior rank-ordered by the respondent in the first assignment is administered in the sequence given by the rank-order. This assignment contains questions about the meaning and nature of the specific behavior, including its historical and developmental origin, its frequency, duration, rate, and intensity as well as its functions. If the behavior is not toxic or lethal, it is prescribed under the principles of control and regulation given in Chapter 1; "If you want to stop it, start it!"

Writing Workbooks from Multiple Score Tests

The same approach used with single-score tests can be used with multiple-score or multidimensional tests. However, the choice of assignments to be administered is determined by the test profile in terms of the scales or dimensions with the most deviant scores. Examples of such workbooks will be given in the next chapter.

CONCLUSIONS

As long as psychotherapy-like, unstructured online interventions possess the same characteristics as traditional, face-to-face talk-based psychotherapy, these interventions will have the same characteristics of:

1. *Immediacy*:
   (a) Rushing in to deal with the respondent's stated needs as soon as possible
   (b) Rushing in without objective evaluation of the respondents' needs
   (c) Therapists need to be immediately available to whomever wants help and who can pay their fees
2. *Generality or nonspecificity*: because this immediacy through talk might fail to provide the specificity and explicitness needed in any intervention
3. *Inefficiency*: because of its nonspecificity, talk, as argued earlier and elsewhere (L'Abate, 1999f), is both cheap and expensive. It is easy to talk about almost anything. However, it is expensive to talk with professionals who charge for their time. It also takes a great deal of time for two parties involved in a verbal transaction to communicate effectively.

Writing, on the other hand, provides the opposite sides of these three characteristics: (1) It takes a little more time to think before writing than before talking—there is an element of delay in writing that is either not present or inadequate in talk; however, (2) through writing one can be much more specific and explicit than through talk, both on the respondent's and therapist's sides; and (3) because of this specificity and explicitness, communication may become more efficient and perhaps more effective. There is little wastage and irrelevance, that is, noise, in the communication.

As argued in this chapter, workbooks are a relatively new phenomenon not yet incorporated into the mainstream of current mental health practices. Workbooks are an affordable, efficient, and controllable avenue and vehicle of psychological interventions for prevention, psychotherapy, and rehabilitation. They represent an intermediate step between nothing and face-to-face talk-based psychotherapy. They present a dynamic way to test theories and models, allowing researchers to intervene above and beyond static and sterile, self-report, paper-and-pencil test instruments and questionnaires. Finally, workbooks can serve as software for structured, computer-assisted interventions on the Internet, increasing the range of populations that could receive help not based on face-to-face, talk-based psychotherapy.

The addition of DW and especially PW as alternative forms of intervention would produce a continuum of care composed of successive sieves or steps in the delivery of mental health services, going from the least to the most expensive:

1. DW in its four different structures alone
2. Traditional primary prevention approaches alone
3. Traditional primary prevention + different structures of DW
4. Secondary prevention approaches (Kaplan, 2000) alone
5. Secondary prevention + DW
6. Tertiary prevention, that is, psychotherapy or crisis intervention alone
7. Psychotherapy + DW
8. Medication + psychotherapy
9. Medication + psychotherapy + DW on an outpatient basis
10. Hospitalization/incarceration + medication + psychotherapy
11. Hospitalization/incarceration + medication + psychotherapy + DW

From only three choices, primary, secondary, or tertiary prevention, which have been historically available to the mental health community (as discussed in Chapter 1), the addition of DW in its four alternative structures expands preventive, psychotherapeutic, and rehabilitative armamentaria to an increasingly more powerful range of choices. This continuum would fit most clinical and nonclinical situations, economic conditions, and managed care plans and restrictions. Hopefully, the synergism that might result from combinations of interventions might increase cost-effectiveness and reduce the length and cost of psychological as well as medical interventions.

4

Specific Applications of Workbooks

The purpose of this chapter is to describe workbooks available on the Internet (*www.mentalhealthhelp.com*) to qualified mental health professionals and researchers. Workbooks are classified by age (children, adolescents, and adults) and composition of respondents (individuals, couples, and families). Within each age range and composition, workbooks are subdivided either by single-score tests, by most deviant peaks or valleys in a test profile, or by referral question or reason. Within categories of either test profile or referral question, workbooks for individuals are subdivided by workbooks for internalization disorders, externalization disorders, or severe dysfunctionalities. The latter, by definition (L'Abate, 1994a, 1997c; Liotti, 1999), include inconsistent and contradictory combinations of extremes of both internalization and externalization. For adult individuals, there is another category of workbooks devoted to normalization of symptoms or to referral questions. For couples and families, workbooks are divided either by test profile or by referral question.

Workbooks should not be administered unless professional helpers or researchers planning to use them in their respective practice or research have read the rationale given in this work. Professionals using these workbooks should keep in mind that these workbooks are all experimental, and not take for granted that they have all been validated. Only a few workbooks contained in this chapter have been subjected to empirical validation (L'Abate, Boyce, Fraizer, & Russ, 1992). Consequently, they should not be administered without a thorough evaluation, both an impressionistic, as in an interview, and an objective evaluation, as in a test battery. Certain workbooks dealing with serious psychopathology must not be administered at all unless an objective evaluation is administered.

Administration and usage of workbooks should be the outcome of a written, contractual agreement between professional helpers and respondents. The agreement should take place from the very outset of the helping process, certainly within the first three evaluation sessions, whether face-to-face or through the Internet. Respondents are to set aside a predetermined, pre-set time to complete these assignments individually, maritally, and familially. Depending on the nature of the referral question and level of functioning of respondents, professionals need to decide whether to respond with a face-to-face relationship or whether to deal with the problem at a distance, through the Internet, or both. This decision, ideally, should be made on the basis of objective evidence rather than professional personal opinion. The decision would involve duration and frequency of contacts plus costs. One copy of the signed contract, consisting of an Informed Consent Form, should be kept by respondents and one by professional helpers.

EVALUATION OF WORKBOOKS OUTCOMES

Evaluation of workbook outcomes can be performed by tests specific to the referral question or symptom as well as by generic test instruments measuring overall, individual, couple, or family base-rate functioning not covered by workbooks. When a direct link between evaluation and intervention is established through workbooks, it is understood that completed homework assignments will be given back to the professional for corrective and supportive feedback. The major problem with this link is the question of whether workbooks will train respondents to answer to the test rather than change behavior for the better. Hence, it is usually preferable to administer another test that measures the same dimension but whose items are different from those contained in the test and its corresponding workbook. For instance, when administering the Hamilton Depression Workbook, it may be useful to administer Beck's Depression Inventory to evaluate whether any improvement has taken place.

Various evaluation instruments have been created (L'Abate, 1992b) to be easily self-administered. Described in greater detail in Chapter 6, they as follows:

1. Social Information Form: This consists of 85 items concerning the general background, interests, and activities of the respondent (L'Abate, 1992b). It can be administered by paraprofessionals in a structured interview format. Many items are reduced to quantifiable, weighted scores for an overall estimate of functionality-dysfunctionality that can be computerized.
2. Adjustment Inventory: This is an individualized, objective assessment of the present level of dissatisfaction in several areas in one's life. It also pinpoints what areas are in need of intervention. It provides a useful baseline for later comparison, after treat-

ment. It is a nomothetic instrument derived from idiographic information obtained by its administration, either as a structured interview or as a self-report test from individuals, couples, or families. Examples of how this inventory was used as a before-after enrichment with couples and families (under Family Adjustment Inventory) can be found in L'Abate and Young (1987).

3. What Kind of Concerns? This instrument was developed from the work of Blatt and his coworkers (1982) on a two-factor model of depression—a matching workbook for each factor is described below. The term "Concerns" is adopted to avoid stigmatization and make the test and workbooks more available to people who are mildly depressed or who deny being "depressed."
4. The Self-Other-Profile Chart (SOPC). The SOPC consists of ratings of self-importance and importance of intimate others in the present, past, and future. It involves subjective ratings on a variety of self-other items.
4. Problems in Relationships Scale (PIRS). This instrument has already been described in Chapter 3 (L'Abate, 1992b). A computer scoring for this test is available from Oliver McMahan (Theological Seminary, Lee College, Cleveland, TN).
5. What Applies to Me That I Agree With? This test is described in Chapter 6. It evaluates a selfhood model of a theory described in Chapter 5 that links the practice of PW/SCAI with theory.

Of these tests, only two, the SOPC (L'Abate, 1997c; L'Abate, De Giacomo, McCarty, De Giacomo, & Verrastro, 2000) and the PIRS have been validated sufficiently (McMahan & L'Abate, 2001) to justify their experimental use. All others are expecting evaluation.

ADMINISTRATION OF WORKBOOK ASSIGNMENTS

In spite of an informed consent form signed by respondents, especially in families, one should expect resistance to the use of workbooks. For instance, parents or care-takers may sign the informed consent form, but a rebellious adolescent member of the family who wants to sabotage treatment may rebel at the use of workbooks. They may decrease the adolescent's perceived or actual power over the whole family.

Limitations of Workbooks

The limitations of workbooks should be kept in mind before administrating them pell-mell, without proper selection, screening, and evaluation.

Resistance to Workbooks

Professionals will meet a great deal of resistance and even withdrawal from treatment if a workbook is suddenly sprung on unsuspecting respondents who have not agreed to it beforehand ("I will give you homework assignments to answer in writing or on your computer as part of the way I work. You should be aware that there are other mental health professionals who do not use this medium. Consequently, you must decide whether you want to work with this type of intervention. I cannot guarantee any better results than other mental health professionals who do not use it. You may want to consult with others if you are not willing to do any written homework.") It is crucial to give an informed consent form contract at the very first session for respondents to read and think about between the first and subsequent two evaluation sessions, and before a treatment plan and a contract are agreed upon at the end of the third evaluation session.

With respondents unwilling to undertake this contract, one may need to discuss and evaluate possible sources of resistance in their many antecedents and correlates. For instance, resistance to working on written homework assignments may represent, among others:

1. Denial to assume responsibility for oneself, often present in spouses and family members who have an investment in considering themselves as not needing any help and externalizing on a partner or family member, the Identified Patient (IP)
2. Unrealistic dependency on the professional to be responsible for the process of change, including
   a. fear of change
   b. fear of the unknown
   c. anxiety about self-disclosure
   d. possibility of hurting self and loved ones, etc.

Whether to make an offer of either verbal psychotherapy or help at a distance conditional on completing homework assignments is an individual decision. Professionals need to make this decision on the basis of their experience and judgment in each individual case, hopefully bolstered by objective evidence.

When and How to Administer Workbooks

Administration of workbooks implies that respondents are in sufficient control to carry out their completion. By assigning workbooks, one can find out very readily whether respondents are ready to work on them. In many cases respondents may be too upset and in crisis to even complete homework assignments. Consequently, one may have to lower the level of stress, crisis, and disturbance before administering them. Some, but not all, workbooks described in this chapter may help professionals evaluate whether the referral question is authentic and substantive or whether it is a distraction from even deeper, unresolved crises and disturbances.

It is important that professional helpers keep an open mind about the inherent usefulness of workbooks, evaluating results on the basis of subjective and objective evidence. Respondents will be the best source of information about the usefulness of these workbooks. The helper should be open to the possibility that not all workbooks will be liked by all respondents. In this writer's experience with workbooks, there is a great deal of variability in consumer satisfaction, regardless of the outcome. Some respondents like workbooks but show little change. Others dislike them a great deal and show a significant improvement in their behaviors. The majority like them and do show improvement in their behavior. Professional helpers, therefore, need to go beyond consumer satisfaction and discover objectively whether workbooks were indeed useful in the process of help-giving and producing change by using a pre-post-intervention evaluation.

Thus, the appropriate administration of workbooks, whether at a distance or in face-to-face contacts, includes at least the following practices: (1) the signing of an Informed Consent Form; (2) an adequate evaluation of historical, situational, personality, and family background surrounding the referral question, including a list of specific symptoms, problems, or complaints, preferably objectively; (3) filling out a battery of short, self-report questionnaires (some examples are described below); (4) assurance that homework assignments have been completed by those who claim that they and no one else are the ones who have completed them.

The sequence of administration of workbook assignments can be ordered in many ways. Where the order is inflexible and already set in the workbook, there is really no choice. In other workbooks, administration would follow rank-orders completed by respondents in the first assignment. Another order of administration follows the test profile. For instance, if depression is the highest score on a personality test, a workbook dealing with this condition would be administered first. In most workbooks produced by Workbooks for Better Living, the first assignment is strictly prescriptive, that is, it serves as a blueprint and treatment plan for the administration of all subsequent assignments according to either objective test results or rank-orders given by respondents (as described in the previous chapter).

The first assignment in many workbooks asks respondents to define each item or behavior making up the disorder. The reasons for asking these definitions are to: (1) confront respondents with the nature of their clinical condition or disorder; (2) enlarge the cognitive repertoire of respondents by giving them a concrete and specific list of all the behaviors involved in their condition; (3) have respondents start using the same terms used by mental health professionals, possibly enlarging their awareness about the nature of the disorder; (4) have respondents learn to communicate with mental health professionals on common semantic grounds; and (5) start respondents thinking about the possibility that by completing workbook assignments, there may be some hope for improvement. These reasons, of course, are strictly hypothetical, because there is little research already reviewed, to document whether workbooks produce the desired results.

Once respondents define items describing behaviors constituting their condition, they are asked to give two examples of the same behavior to show that they have understood the meaning of the items. After giving the examples, they have to rank-order items or behaviors according to their subjective estimate as to how these dimensions are applicable to themselves. For instance, if a depression workbook is based on a list of approximately 20 items from a depression inventory, respondents define and give two examples of behaviors underlying each item. This is the case for anger, anxiety, depression, psychopathy, and other workbooks directly derived from single-score tests based on self-report, paper-and-pencil tests. Subsequent assignments follow the sequence given in the first assignment according to the rank-order of how items or behaviors apply to the respondent. The item or behavior ranked as being the most applicable to the respondent is administered next through a standard format assignment. The item or behavior that is rank-ordered second in applicability is administered next, and so on, until all items or behaviors rank-ordered as applicable to the respondent have been administered. The format of each assignment is the same. However, the title and sequence of the assignment changes with the rank-order given originally by the respondent.

Consequently, in standard format assignments, each item or behavior is written in the title according to whatever criterion, subjective or objective, is followed. The number of assignments is determined by how many items or behaviors are seen as applicable by respondents. They may vary from one respondent to another, unless a research project determines a constant number of assignments for all respondents. When the number of assignments for each workbook is coupled with a + sign, it means that the format of the second assignment can be administered as many times as necessary by changing the title of the assignment but retaining the same format. Usually, there is a final assignment to feed back respondents' opinions and reactions to the whole workbook experience (L'Abate, 1996).

As with most checklists, inventories, or paper-and-pencil self-report tests used to develop many workbooks, professionals will need to reconcile results obtained from a test with rank-orders obtained in the first assignment. If there is a great discrepancy between objective tests results and rankings, it may need to be resolved through discussion and negotiation with respondents themselves. For instance, if Irritability is the highest score on a test profile but is ranked last in the first assignment, both respondent and professional may compromise after negotiating, and administer it somewhere in the middle of a series of assignments. If objective test results are followed, then special care should be given to see that assignments are not completed to produce better "test behavior" but that a genuine change has taken place, as observed by external observers, partners, family members, teachers, and caretakers.

Furthermore, should one start an assignment by confronting the most severe behavior, or start with assignments confronting the least severe? If one were to consider ideal research in an ideal world, it would be possible to administer assignments to two groups of respondents. To evaluate which approach produces better results, one group would receive assignments according to respondents' subjective estimates. The other group would receive assignments according to objective test results. Regardless of approach, however, some workbooks follow an idiographic approach specific to the individual, even though the administration of workbooks as a method of intervention is, in general, nomothetic. Some workbooks are nomothetic, and no individualization is indicated.

It is assumed that it is difficult to administer workbooks to individuals who cannot read or write. However, those who are able—teachers, volunteers, parents, older students, or former respondents who have completed a workbook successfully—could read questions and record respondents' answers. Another approach could consist of audio- or video-tape workbooks with a recorder into which respondents could dictate their answers. Hence, the issue of illiteracy could become a pseudo-issue, since there are many ways to deal with it.

Feedback and support for respondents can be given verbally, if there is a face-to-face relationship with a professional helper. In prevention programs, feedback can be given through fax, mail, or the Internet.

WORKBOOKS FOR INDIVIDUALS

Individual homework assignments recognize the importance of singular characteristics in the overall functioning of a couple, family, or group. With individuals, these assignments can be administered in cases of comorbidity, where one clinical condition is treated through verbal, face-to-face psychotherapy, while the other condition can be treated through a workbook, allowing a more precise, tailor-made approach than would be possible verbally. There should be a synergistic outcome between psychotherapy and workbooks.

WORKBOOKS FOR YOUTH: CHILDREN AND ADOLESCENTS (AGES 8 TO 17)

Workbooks contained in this section are to be administered in residential or nonresidential institutions (clinics, hospitals, jails, or schools), where respondents complete assignments away from their families, entirely on their own, without help or assistance from anyone. The last section in this chapter, on Family Workbooks, contains workbooks for children and youth to be administered by and together with the whole family. Of course, before administration of workbooks to children without including their families, their legal guardians or caretakers will need to give to the professional representing the institution a written, signed Informed Consent Form. Assignments can be administered inside the school, clinic, detention center, or hospital, or at home, provided guardians or caretakers assume responsibility for the youth completing assignments without anybody else's help.

WORKBOOKS FOR INDIVIDUALS BY TEST SCORE OR BY TEST PROFILE: OBJECTIVE, SELF-ADMINISTERED PAPER-AND-PENCIL INVENTORIES

The purpose of this section is to introduce descriptions of workbooks administered either by a single test or by test profile. In the former case, there is an isomorphic relationship between a single-test score, for example, anxiety, depression, etc., and its matching workbook. As described earlier, the first assignment is based on the very items or behaviors making up the test, making the match between evaluation and intervention complete. In the latter case of a multidimensional instrument, such as the MMPI-2 or PAI, each score on its various dimensions is matched by an isomorphic workbook. For instance, if the peak Content Scale on the MMPI-2 is Depression, then a matching workbook is available, either directly derived from that dimension, or from a completely different source, for example, Beck, Hamilton, L'Abate, etc., dealing with the same clinical condition.

An obvious and relevant criticism of test-based workbooks contends that these workbooks would only train respondents to answer assigned homework assignments in a more test-appropriate manner. This possibility would mask any possible improvement independent from test-taking learning. Split-half or odd-even forms of the same test would not counter such a criticism. Another test that is different from the one administered but that measures the same dimension could be administered on a pre-post basis. Otherwise, to assess whether any improvement has taken place independently of the test, ratings from external observers, such as therapists, partners, friends, relatives, or roommates, may be necessary.

In this and other sections, whether by referral question or by test, workbooks are subdivided into three additional categories: (1) externalization, meaning the presence of anger, acting out, impulsivity, noncompliance, psychopathy, rebelliousness, and aggression, (2) internalization, meaning the presence of anxiety, depression, fears, low self-esteem, procrastination, obsessions, and compulsion, and (3) severe psychopathology, where both externalization and internalization are coexisting (L'Abate, 1994a, 1997c), as explained in greater detail in the next chapter.

Externalizations (Anger, Acting Out, Hostility, and Aggression)

With conduct problems, however, two major issues needs to be confronted: (1) dismissive denial ("I do not have this problem") and (2) flat refusal to cooperate. In either case, one may have to make possible consequences very clear to respondents and their caretakers, including signed understanding of what would happen if the child or adolescent refuses to cooperate. If rewards for completion rather then punishments are contemplated, they should be very clear, concrete, and immediate.

Juvenile Psychopathy

This workbook consists of 3+ assignments that are isomorphic, with dimensions evaluated by the *Child Psychopathy Scale* (CPS) (Lynam, 1997). It can be administered either in conjunction with the same self-report, paper-and-pencil test or simply on the basis of persistent acting-out behavior. This workbook can be administered on the basis of either the presenting or referral symptom alone or on the basis of an objective measure of juvenile acting out. Preferably these measures should be administered before and after completion of each workbook, as well as months after termination. This workbook was designed to lower the chances of respondents behaving in destructive fashions toward others, and ultimately to the self. This workbook can be administered on its own or with the CPS, validated by Lynam (1997). Since there is always the danger that the workbook may "train" juveniles to answer the retest in a more acceptable fashion without any real change in behavior, it is recommended that another, different measure of impulsivity or juvenile psychopathy be used, including ratings from external observers. This workbook can be administered in conjunction with other workbooks designed to lower acting out in juveniles: Social Training, anger, and an addendum to Social Training described below.

School Conduct Problems

This workbook consists of 3+ assignments drawn from different sources that cover socially maladjusted and conduct-disordered youngsters, such as the *Behavior Rating Profile* by Brown and Hammill (1978), *Differential of Conduct and Emotional Problems* by Kelly (1990), Kelly and Vitali's (1992) guidelines, and more general sources, such as Hersen and Last (1990) and Mash and Barkley (1996), concerned with conduct disorders in children.

A test instrument like the *Behavior Rating Profile* (Brown & Hammill, 1978) or *Differential of Conduct and Emotional Problems* (Kelly, 1990), or both should be administered before and after completion of the workbook to evaluate results from its administration.

School Social Skills (S^3)

This workbook actually contains four workbooks with 7+ assignments based on the School Social Skills (S^3) scale developed by Brown, Black, and Downs (1984): (1) Adult Relations (2) Peer Relations, (3) School Rules and (4) Classroom Behavior. These workbooks can be administered on the basis of results obtained from that scale, according to which area of school functioning needs the most immediate attention, or in the case of Adult Relations and Classroom Behavior, the rank-order given by the child.

Unusual or Troublesome Behavior

This workbook is composed of 3+ assignments drawn from the Checklist for Aberrant Behavior (ABC) developed by Aman and Singh for residential and community settings.

Internalizations (Anxiety, Depression, Fears)

Anxiety, Depression, and Fears

This workbook is composed of 3+ assignments based on the research by Chorpita, Albano, and Barlow (1998) on the structure of negative emotions. They differentiated among fear, anxiety, and depression according to the presence of different feelings related to each of these three emotions. For a critical discussion of the application of "negative" attributions to feelings and emotions, the reader may consult the next chapter for criticisms about applying "negative" attributions to feelings, affect, and moods. If one distinguishes what feelings we experience, on one hand, from how we express them on the other, then feelings are void of positive or negative valence (as discussed in the next chapter). There is nothing negative about feelings we experience. They may be pleasant or unpleasant, painful or pleasurable, fleeting or permanent, strong or weak. Emotions, on the other hand, are what we express verbally, nonverbally, or in writing. Admittedly, certain emotions, like anger, envy, and hostility, among others, may lead to destructive or hurtful expressions of certain feelings. This issue will be considered in greater detail in Chapter 5.

Even though original research with this workbook was performed with children and adolescents, there is no particular reason why this workbook should not also be administered to adults. For other workbooks on the expression of emotions, the reader may want to consult the workbooks on this topic reviewed below.

Anxiety in Youth

This workbook is composed of 3+ assignments based on the scale of the same name developed by Newcomer, Barenbaum, and Bryant (1994) concerning depression and anxiety in children and adolescents.

Depression and Anxiety in Youth

This workbook is composed of 3+ assignments based on the scale of the same name developed by Newcomer, Barenbaum, and Bryant (1994) concerning depression and anxiety in children and adolescents.

Emotional Problems in Youth

This workbook is composed of 3+ assignments based on a variety of sources, such as Kelly (1990), Kelly and Vitali's guidelines (1992) more general sources, like Hersen and Last (1990) and Mash and Barkley (1996), as well as the Differential Test by Kelly, edited by Vitali, which covers emotional problems in children and adolescents.

WORKBOOKS FOR INDIVIDUALS BY INTERVIEW AND REFERRAL QUESTION

The term "referral question" refers to the reason why people request professional help: why a respondent (an individual, couple, or family), asks for professional help from a mental health practitioner. Questions may range from simple, however trivial, to extremely serious. A respondent may ask for help for himself or herself or for one's partner or a family member. Referral questions or reasons may be for clinical or nonclinical conditions. Yet, the referral question usually concerns very specific behavior that is hurtful to individuals and their caretakers. Regardless of the reason, most referral questions should be corroborated with psychological test profiles or scores, historical documentation, the current situation, and letters of referrals from other nonmental health professionals (lawyers, clergy, physicians, teachers, etc.). In contrast to the next section, where workbooks are administered on the basis of a test profile, the reason may be a diagnosed clinical symptom or behavior that is troublesome to individuals or to those who care for them. In some cases, the reason for referral may also coincide with results from a test profile, a welcome coincidence. The reader should also consult an Annotated Bibliography of Selected Workbooks (L'Abate, submitted for publication, a) to match additional workbooks with specific symptoms.

In spite of workbooks being designed from a referral question rather than a test profile, it would be very helpful if they were administered together with any relevant self-report, paper-and-pencil test that would assess the preexisting level of functionality of respondents. Of course, the same test should be administered on an after-intervention and follow-up basis, to check on whether workbooks have been successful in changing and improving behavior.

Externalizations

Addendum to Social Training

The purpose of this workbook is to add a greater number of supplementary and complementary assignments and, therefore, choices, to the Social Training workbook described below. Both workbooks were designed to teach externalizing, impulsive, and acting-out individuals how to think before acting. These workbooks recognize the need to deal with cognitive skills deficits that are present in acting-out, impulsive individuals on the basis of an epidemiological, public health model (Foglia, 2000; Giancola, 2000; Simon, 1998). There are too many acting-out, impulsive adolescents and adults in jails as well as out of penal institutions to think that talk-based, face-to-face psychotherapy can make a dent in such a population. Through the technology of distance writing in its four structures plus the use of computers we shall be able to make a dent. Even if this approach fails, its relatively inexpensiveness in comparison to existing approaches for these populations merits its serious consideration.

While assignments in the Social Training workbook were freely drawn from clinical practice and pragmatic semantic retraining, those included in this addendum are drawn from a relational theory of personality socialization (summarized in Chapter 5). Assignments in the Social Training workbook were theory-independent, while those included in this addendum are more theory-derived and theory-dependent. In spite of this distinction, assignments from both workbooks can be administered together complementarily. They overlap with each other, including assignments from workbooks on anger, which is a distinctive characteristic of many acting-out impulsive individuals and character disorders (L'Abate, 1994a, 1997c).

In spite of choosing this workbook from symptoms rather than from a test or test profile, it would be very helpful if this choice were also made on the basis of any self-report, paper-and-pencil test. This objective evaluation would assess the pre-existing level of impulsivity and propensity toward acting-out. Of course, the same test should be administered on an after-intervention and follow-up basis to check on whether this workbook has been successful or not.

This workbook consists of 10 assignments. It is written from the viewpoint of how many acting-out individuals think rather than how they should think. The latter approach is the basis for the Social Training workbook reviewed below.

Anger in Children and Teenagers

This workbook is based on the factor analysis of Lahey, Frick, Loeber, Tannenbaum, Van Horn, and Christ (1990) and the work of Feindler (1995).

Social Training

This workbook consists of 20+ assignments about words that control behavior (L'Abate, 1992b). Its simplicity allows administration to adolescents as well as adults, to teach them to think about their behavior before they act. This workbook is based on principles of semantic reconditioning that recognize and stress the power that certain key words (e.g., self, control, law, errors, forgiveness) have over behavior. Each assignment consists of gradually more complicated questions asking respondents to answer sequentially related issues deriving from a self-given answer to the initial question. Each concept is defined, expanded, and elaborated in a personalized fashion. Most assignments end with requirements to demonstrate actual, concrete examples of how respondents applied their answers to everyday behavior. Beginning an assignment is contingent on completing behavioral assignments from the previous assignment. Assignments are programmed in a stepwise sequence that eventually leads respondents to reflect on their behavior.

Supplementary assignments on anger, goals, and reactivity may be included at any point in the process. For instance, each assignment involves having respondents discuss (in writing) their responses in a typical anger-provoking situation. Respondents are encouraged to evaluate the rewards and costs of particular expressions of anger. Verbal alternatives are suggested, for example, "I am angry!" Respondents are required to plan and execute alternative responses to anger-provoking situations. This "floating" assignment on anger may be useful in a variety of other workbooks and be supplemented by completing workbooks dedicated to the same topic.

Preliminary results with incarcerated felons (Reed, McMahan, & L'Abate, 2001) suggest that this workbook may be useful in helping respondents to think in more constructive ways than they have done in the past.

Internalizations

Posttraumatic Stress Disorder in Children

This condition does not necessarily lead to internalizations. Many externalizations may result from the same disorder. Hence, placing this workbook in this section should be considered with a grain of salt. This workbook is based on the extensive confirmatory factor analyses by Anthony, Lonigan, and Hecht (1999) about the structure of posttraumatic stress symptoms in children exposed to disaster. From their confirmatory factor analysis of responses, they extracted three symptom clusters and nine models, from which they derived 16 symptoms.

Self-Other Concerns

This workbook is made up of two distinct and separate workbooks based on the two-factor model of depression developed by Blatt and his coworkers (Blatt et al., 1982). Instead of using a clinical term that could stigmatize respondents, the term "depression" has been changed to "concerns." This change allows administration of this workbook after respondents have answered a simple, 20-item questionnaire called "What Kind of Concerns?" If so desired, self-scoring allows a quick determination of whether concerns are related to self-criticism or to overdependency on others. One workbook is related to the former and another to the latter. The simplicity of the test and of the two workbooks linked to it allows administration to children and adolescents at middle- and high-school levels as well as to adults.

WORKBOOKS FOR BOTH INTERNALIZING AND EXTERNALIZING DISORDERS

Workbooks by Test Profile: Self-Others Profile Charts

These are two theory-derived (L'Abate, 1994a, 1997c) workbooks composed of 6+ assignments based on a brief and easy-to-administer rating scale that allows a quick and focused determination of disturbances in Self, in intimate Others, and in both Self and Others.

Workbooks by Referral Question

See workbooks for adults that could also be applied with a few changes in wording to children and adolescents.

WORKBOOKS FOR ADULTS BASED ON SINGLE-SCORE PSYCHOLOGICAL TESTS

Internalizations

Beck Anxiety

This workbook is based on the research by Joiner, Steer, Beck, Schmidt, Rudd, and Catanzaro (1999) about physiological hyperarousal and anxiety (Wilson, de Beurs, Palmer, & Chambless, 1999). It consists of 3+ assignments. This workbook allows for controlled testing of different views about depression. For instance, a workbook derived from the Hamilton Depression Scale could be compared with another workbook based on Beck's Depression Inventory II, or with a workbook derived from the MMPI-2 (L'Abate, Boyce, Fraizer, & Russ, 1992), or another based on the DSM-IV.

Beck Depression

This workbook is based on the research by Dozois, Dobson, and Ahnberg (1998) and the review by Katz, Katz, and Shaw (1999) of the Beck Depression Inventory-II. It consists of 3+ assignments.

Hamilton Anxiety

This workbook is composed of 3+ assignments and can be used to develop relevant ways to cope with anxiety. It is based on the research by Moras, Di Nardo, & Barlow (1992).

Hamilton Depression

This workbook is composed of 3+ assignments based on the research by Moras, Di Nardo, and Barlow (1992) on the distinction between anxiety and depression in the reconstructed Hamilton Anxiety-Depression Scales (Koback & Reynolds, 1999).

Externalizations

Adult Psychopathy

This workbook consists of 3+ assignments that can be administered in conjunction with a short self-report test for incarcerated felons who want rehabilitation or individuals at high risk for incarceration. It was developed from the research of Kosson, Steuerwald, Forth, and Kirkhart (1997). They validated a

21-item Interpersonal Measure of Psychopathy that furnishes the basis of this workbook. They identified 14 interpersonal dimensions that characterize psychopathic behavior. The assignments are isomorphic with the dimensions of the test.

This workbook could be also compared with the Social Training workbook for dealing with impulsive and acting-out behavior. These workbooks complement and supplement each other. However, they were written from different viewpoints. The present workbook was written about how respondents behave objectively. The Social Training workbook was written about how respondents should think. The Addendum to Social Training was written about how acting-out, impulsive individuals actually think. The comparative effectiveness of these workbooks can and should eventually be evaluated empirically. This comparison would be difficult to obtain if talk were used instead.

Anger Expression

This workbook is composed of 5+ assignments based on the work of Forgays, Forgays, and Spielberger (1997) about the factor-structure of the STAXI-2 (Spielberger, Sydeman, Owen, & Marsh, 1999). It complements at least two other anger-related workbooks.

Anger, Hostility, and Aggression Workbook

This workbook consists of 5+ assignments based on the work of Eckhardt and Deffenbacher (1995) and of Spielberger, Reheiser, and Sydeman (1995). It complements two other anger-related workbooks presented in this chapter.

Gambling I

This workbook is composed of 3+ assignments covering how individuals think about gambling. It was developed from whatever could be gleaned from the relevant literature and clinical experience. Of all the various methods of treating gambling addictions, many with very little success, none mentioned the use of systematic written homework assignments, which such workbooks comprise (Dickerson, Hinchy, & Legg-England, 1990; Wildman, 1992, 1998).

Gambling II

This workbook is composed of 3+ assignments from the recent "Self-Test: Why I Overgamble" developed by Wildman (1999).

Personality Disorders: Form 1992

This workbook is composed of 3+ assignments based on the research by Schroeder, Wormsworth, and Livesley (1992). It is a revision of previous research cited in the workbook below. These investigators found 16 characteristics or symptoms necessary for describing personality disorders.

Personality Disorders: Form 1989

This workbook is based on the research by Livesley, Jackson, & Schroeder (1989). This workbook overlaps a great deal with the preceeding one based on the work by Schroeder, Wormsworth, and Livesley (1992), with the exception that this workbook has a somewhat lengthier list of symptoms.

Personality Disorders: Form 1990

This workbook is based on the research by Clark (1990). It has a much lengthier list of behaviors than the two workbooks described above.

Personality Disorders: Forms SZ, AV, DE, DP, HI, NA, AN, SA, CO, NE, MA, ST, BO, & PA

These workbooks are based on the work of Davis and Millon (1999). These authors list four functional and four structural attributes to define 14 personality disorders, respectively: Schizoid, Avoidant, Depressive, Dependent, Histrionic, Narcissistic, Antisocial, Sadistic, Compulsive, Negativistic, Masochistic, Schizotypal, Borderline, and Paranoid. Each workbook consists of the eight adjectives describing each disorder. There workbooks could be used in conjunction with any assessment tool that would be able to pinpoint each disorder, in addition, of course, to a thorough review of historical background.

Temper

This workbook is composed of 3+ assignments based, in part, on the "Take Your Temper Test" developed by Spielberger and London (1982).

WORKBOOKS FOR ADULTS BASED ON PSYCHOLOGICAL TEST PROFILE

Personality Dimensions I

The purpose of this workbook is to link markers for the Big-Five Factor model structure (FFM) developed by Goldberg (1992, 1999). His factor analysis produced five different workbooks described below, two for dissociative experiences and three workbooks for normalization purposes. This workbook is actually composed of 10 separate workbooks, one workbook for each of the 10 polar dimensions reported by Goldberg. Assignments contained in each workbook can be administered to either clinical or nonclinical individuals who score high or low on the five dimensions of Goldberg's test. In most psychological tests, deviancy is shown in one direction, usually by high scores, as in the Minnesota Multiphasic Personality Inventory-2 (MMPI-2) and the Personality Assessment Inventory (PAI). However, in tests representative of the model, for instance, the NEO Five-Factor Inventory, both low and high scores represent deviations from the norm. Hence, assignments in this workbook take into account both high (excess) and low (deficit) directions of symptoms and problems associated with personality traits.

Even positive scales such as Agreeableness or Conscientiousness were retained as assignments in spite of the relevant objection that very few people who score high on these dimensions will need the related workbook. Nonetheless, they can still be used to control the use of other workbooks, as well as to check further on the nature of these and other dimensions. Furthermore, too much of a good thing may be in some cases deleterious to the individual. Where does one draw the line between high conscentiousness and rigidity or righteousness?

Personality Dimensions II

This workbook was written in conjunction with the first instrument to specifically assess treatment resistance (Perry & Butcher, 1999). It is composed of 3+ assignments. A similar workbook on treatment resistance is also available in the MMPI-2 workbooks described below.

Personality Dimensions III

This workbook is based on one of the most popular research-based, trait-oriented personality inventories. It consists of 12+ assignments. Its purpose is to link the diagnostic Five-Factor Model (FFM) (Anderson, 1998; Costa & Widiger, 1994) with matched, isomorphic homework assignments. According to its proponents, FFM is now one of the most prominent trait-based models of personality in existence. This model of personality, also known as the Big Five Model, is considered by its authors and its advocates as one of the major breakthroughs in personality theory of the last decade (Costa & Widiger, 1994).

Assignments in this workbook take into account both high and low directions of symptoms and problems associated with personality factors (McCrae, 1994, p. 306). The low Neuroticism scale was retained as an assignment in spite of the relevant objection that "it is unlikely that many people will show up for treatment whose major problem is low N" (Robert R. McCrae, personal communication, May 26, 1994). It can still be used as control for other workbooks, as well as to check further on the nature of this trait.

This workbook can be administered to clinical or nonclinical individuals who score high and/or low on the five dimensions. In addition to these assignments, of course, the interested professional could use some other assignments from other workbooks. For instance, assignments for anger, impulsivity, depression, or cynicism, among many other topics, are described below.

Administration of this workbook assumes that, as is the case with all test-driven workbooks: (1) respondents have completed an FFM-derived or related test: (2) the test profile with its peaks and valleys has been thoroughly discussed with respondents: and (3) respondents have agreed in writing, after reading and signing a proper consent form, to participate and, hopefully, complete this workbook, either in addition or as an alternative to face-to-face psychotherapy.

The format of each workbook is the same. In the first assignment, each workbook requires that the respondent define terms that make up the peak or valley of each factor. Supposedly, these definitions will help the respondent become more aware of what component characteristics each peak or valley is composed of. If desired, respondents could be asked to give two examples for each definition. Then, respondents are asked to rank various component characteristics in order of how much they apply to themselves. Through this process respondents begin thinking about these characteristics in a more detailed and, hopefully, differentiated manner than heretofore.

The second assignment is made up by the component characteristic that has been ranked as number 1 by the respondent. This assignment is standard for this and subsequent assignments of all test-driven workbooks. The title of the component for this assignment needs to be written down, either by the professional or the respondent. The third and subsequent assignments use the same standard format, until a component characteristic no longer applies to the respondent's experience. The standard penultimate and last assignments are administered at the end of all assignments to ensure that respondents practice desired behavior as often as possible.

Personality Dimensions IV

This workbook consists of 15 separate workbooks matching the 15 Content Scales of the MMPI-2 (Greene & Clopton, 1999; L'Abate, 1992b): anxiety, fears, obsessiveness, depression, health concerns, unusual thinking, anger, cynicism, antisocial practices, Type A, low self-esteem, social discomfort, family problems, work interference, and negative treatment indicators. Each workbook consists of 4+ assignments.

Personality Dimensions V

This workbook consists of 23+ assignments covering most common psychiatric conditions or syndromes. Administration of this workbook assumes the use of Morey's (1999) professional manual for this test. The Personality Assessment Inventory (PAI) differentiates among three types of anxiety; cognitive, affective, and physiological. Cognitive anxiety consists of prominent worry and concern about current issues to the point that ability to concentrate and attend to relevant life issues are significantly compromised. There is an overconcern about issues or events over which the individual does not feel he or she has any control. Affective anxiety, on the other hand, consists of the experience of a great deal of tension, difficulty in relaxing, and presence of fatigue as a result of high perceived stress. Physiological anxiety consists of experience and expression of stress in somatic form, with overt physical signs of tension and stress, such as sweaty palms, trembling hands, complaints of irregular heartbeats, and shortness of breath, as considered in previous assignments.

The PAI also distinguishes among: (1) cognitive depression, made up of thoughts of worthlessness, hopelessness, and personal failure, where indecisiveness and difficulties in concentrating are likely, (2) affective depression, made up by sadness, loss of interest in normal activities, with loss of pleasure in things that were previously enjoyed, and (3) physiological depression, the experience of depression in somatic form, changing physical functions, activity, and energy, with disturbances in sleep pattern, a decrease in level of sexual interest, loss of appetite and/or weight loss

The PAI describes obsessions and compulsions as character traits. These traits are made up of (a) rigidity and inflexibility in following personal guidelines for conduct, (b) perfectionistic and constricted characteristics, (c) excessive attention to detail, inhibiting decision-making, and (d) an inability to perceive the larger significance of decisions made. Changes in routine, unexpected events, and contradictory information generate untoward stress. The individual is fearful of his or her impulses and doubtful of being able to control them. The workbook is flexible enough to deal with either condition, following completed answers respondents.

To deal with antisocial characteristics and aggression, more than one assignment and more than one workbook will be necessary. The Social Training workbook and its Addendum as well as the Psychopathy workbook could be added together with additional workbooks on anger described in this chapter.

Self-Others Profile Charts

These two theory-derived (L'Abate, 1992b, 1994a, 1997c, 1998a) workbooks consist of 6+ assignments from a rating sheet that allows a quick and focused determination of disturbances in Self, in intimate Others, and in both Self and Others. Externalizations are possible when Self scores are higher than Others scores. Internalizations are possible when Others scores are higher than Self scores. This theory will be summarized in the next chapter to link it with the practice of PW. Its psychometric characteristics and research related to it are reviewed in Chapter 6.

WORKBOOKS FOR ADULTS BASED ON REFERRAL QUESTION

Externalization and Acting-Out Disorders

AA 12 Steps in 4

This workbook consists of 4 assignments. It is a condensation of the well-known approach for alcoholics or addicts who want to work on forgiving themselves and those who love them. It was developed originally by David Russ (L'Abate, 1992b) with guidance from this writer.

Addendum to Anger

This workbook is composed of 7 assignments written to complement and possibly improve on assignments previously published on the same topic (L'Abate, 1992b). This workbook, however, in contrast to those already published, recognizes the multidimentional nature of anger and its multifarious determinants.

Addendum to Social Training

See comments given earlier in this chapter. The simplicity of this workbook allows administration to both youth and adults who act out impulsively and do not think about the consequences of their actions.

Internalization Disorders

Addendum to Phobias

This workbook is composed of 5 assignments designed to help individuals who are controlled by phobias and who need to learn to control them. Additional assignments about phobias are found in the PAI and Anxiety and Depression workbooks. There is no telling how many people are controlled by all the many phobias that are available to choose from. Hence, it is important to develop a set of assignments that will help phobic respondents learn to control phobias that, at their extremes, can make them feel completely miserable and helpless. This workbook was developed from the works of Levinson (1986) and Henley (1987), which were complementary with each other.

Anxiety

This workbook is composed of 6 assignments based on the DSM-IV definition of this condition. This workbook does not have a concluding assignment. If one is necessary, concluding assignments can be found in other workbooks, or the professional could write one to fit the needs of respondents and professionals (L'Abate, Boyce, Fraizer, & Russ, 1992).

Codependency

This workbook is composed of 13 assignments based on a model developed by L'Abate (Jordan & L'Abate, 1999; L'Abate, 1994a, 1997c; L'Abate & Harrison, 1992). Its purpose is to help people who are codependent, that is, addicted to other individuals who themselves are addicted to substances, alcohol, gambling, etc., including physical and verbal abuse. More specifically, the purpose of this workbook is to help individuals who are presently living in a codependent relationship, that is, usually married or living with an abusive or addicted individual. So-called codependent individuals are addicted to: 1. Receiving abuse (physical, sexual, verbal), or 2. A substance (alcohol, drugs, food), or 3. Driven by an activity (excessive sports, excessive spending, excessive TV watching, excessive work), or 4. Blindly fanatical in a mission (e.g., excessive religion, extreme patriotism to the point of paranoia).

This workbook, therefore, can be administered in conjunction with individual, group, couple, or family therapy, either prior to or during the therapy process or after it has been completed. In addition, the workbook can be administered in conjunction with prevention programs focused on individual, marital, or parental skills training.

Dependent Personality Characteristics

This workbook is composed of 3+ assignments based on research by Hartlage, Arduino, and Alloy (1998) on depressive personality characteristics. This workbook can be administered by itself or in conjunction with other depression workbooks or depression assignments contained in other personality tests, MMPI-2 or PAI, for instance.

Dissociative Experiences (Form BA)

This is one of five workbooks composed of 3+ assignments based on the research by Goldberg (1999) using a scale of the same name. The five workbooks are; one composed of scales from the International Personality Item Pool (IPIP); a second, made up from a variety of personality scales correlated with the Curious Experiences Survey (PSC), a third, consisting of items from the Internationally Personality Item Pool that were most highly correlated with total dissociative experiences (TDE), a fourth, based on the highest scale correlates of the Abridged Big Five-dimensional Circumplex (AB5C) model, which classifies personality traits into 10 subsets, and a fifth based on behavioral acts (BA). These subscales are more highly correlated with total dissociative experiences. BA and TDE workbooks are designed specifically for individuals with dissociative experiences. The IPIP, PSC, and AB5C workbooks, because of their generic, normative, and neutral nature, can be administered either after completion of the BA or the TDE workbooks, or independently of those two workbooks, to relatively well-functioning individuals without dissociative experiences.

Dissociative Experiences (Form TDE)

Like all the five workbooks based on the research by Goldberg (1999) this one is also made up of 3+ assignments, as described above.

Loneliness

This workbook consists of 6 assignments based on edited volumes by many contributors in Hurtug, Audy, and Cohen (1998) and Peplau and Perlman (1982). This workbook is also an example of how research findings, as contained in both volumes, can be used to develop workbooks. A questionnaire about loneliness that could be used as a pre-post-workbook administration measure is contained in Peplau and Perlman's volume.

Procrastination

Procrastination is an extremely pervasive problem not only in college populations, but also in the population at large. It may be more apparent, however, in a college milieu, where deadlines are of the essence. Procrastination is due to a variety of personological or characteriological characteristics, like depression, anxiety, low self-esteem, and poor study habits, among others (Ferrari,

Johnson, & McCown, 1995). It is an extremely hurtful condition for many people, bringing untold suffering to those who are affected by it, either in school, at work, or at home. This workbook, therefore, should be administered on a pre-post intervention basis, in conjunction with any paper-and-pencil, self-report instruments available in Ferrari, Johnson, and McCown.

Sexual Abuse

This workbook is based on the author's clinical experience. He is indebted to Doris Hewitt, Ph.D. and her survivors' group for constructive feedback about an early draft. This workbook is designed to be administered on a one-to-one basis in addition to group therapy, including couple and, under certain conditions, family therapy.

PSYCHOPATHOLOGY: INTERNALIZATION AND EXTERNALIZATION DISORDERS

As discussed at great length elsewhere (L'Abate, 1994a, 1997c) and briefly in Chapter 5, psychopathology is defined as the contradictory and inconsistent combination of extremes in both internalization and externalization disorders.

Brief Psychiatric Rating Scale (BPRS)

This workbook permits a very quick confrontation of most symptoms of psychiatric disturbance (3+ assignments). It is based on the research on its factor structure by Mueser, Curran, and McHugo (1997). They found that 18 dimensions of psychiatric disorder could be condensed into five factors: (1) thought disturbance, (2) anergia, (3) affect (anxiety-depression), (4) activation-disorganization, and (5) hostility-suspiciousness.

Posttraumatic Stress Disorder (PTSD)

This workbook is based on the latest factor-analytic study of the scale by the same name (3+ assignments) and research by King, Leskin, King, and Weathers (1998) about a confimatory factor analysis scale.

Posttraumatic Stress Symptoms (PTSS)

This workbook is designed to help respondents who still suffer from painful experiences from their pasts (3+ assignments). It is based on the research by Taylor, Kuch, Koch, Crockett, and Passey (1998) into the structure of posttraumatic stress symptoms. From their factor analysis of responses to two questionnaires on which the assignments of this workbook are based, they extracted two factors: (1) Intrusions/Avoidance, and (2) Hyperarousal/Numbing. The first factor supports the position enunciated in the next chapter that psychopathology may result, in part, from the avoidance of hurt feelings and fears of being hurt.

Social Growth

This is an all-purpose workbook for generalized anxiety that can be used with a variety of clinical and borderline conditions (14 assignments). This workbook could be applied to individuals who desire a therapeutic experience but who do not show a pattern of acting out, requiring and requesting a more general approach based on awareness and experiential learning. This workbook, by exclusion, does not apply specifically to either the treatment of depression or of impulsivity. Its specific usefulness needs to be assessed much more carefully than it has been heretofore. Thus far, results interpreted impressionistically from college students who have completed this workbook on an experimental basis have not shown any specific pattern of improvement. Of comparable workbooks available at the time, more than a decade ago, Social Growth seemed to produce more nonspecific effects than other workbooks. This nonspecific outcome suggested that this workbook can be used before or in addition to psychotherapy, but not as a sole alternative to psychotherapy or primary prevention. It certainly could be used as a structured interview. More research will be needed to specify the conditions under which this workbook is maximally effective and the conditions under which it is not.

Symptom Scale 77 (SS-77)

This workbook covers most severe psychiatric conditions, many already covered by the PAI (2+ assignments). The scale on which this workbook is based was developed and validated for the purpose of finding valuable information about respondents (clients/patients/subjects) "with a minimum of professional time expenditure and at very low cost" (Johnson, 1994, p. 11). It is a measure of major affective problems identified in the clinical and scientific literature on psychiatric and medical patients. It can be used to assess baseline functioning and to document the need for psychotherapy or other forms of therapy. Its coauthor did not consider this a psychological test and was of the opinion that many nonlicensed mental health professionals, other than psychologists, could use it. Indeed, its coauthor hopes that this instrument will assist "those non-psychologists who are at a disadvantage in justifying their services since they are not allowed to use psychological testing to establish baseline and outcome" (William McCown, personal communication, November 16, 1994).

The SS-77 is a 77-item paper-and-pencil, self-administered instrument with scales that were developed through rational, theoretical, and statistical procedures. These items produced 9 symptom scales concerning: (1) Somatic complaints, (2) Depression, (3) Alcohol and other drug abuse, (4) Anxiety (Rapee, 1997), (5) Obsessive-Compulsive symptoms, (6) Panic disorder and Agoraphobia, (7) Traumatic stress, (8) Minimization of symptoms, (9) Amplification of symptoms. The professional who would like to receive more detailed information about the validity and reliability of this instrument—information contained in a manual (Johnson, 1994)—should contact the author directly. There is a great deal of overlap between the assignments of this workbook and the PAI workbook. Thus, many assignments of both workbooks are interchangeable.

NORMATIVE EXPERIENCES

Under this rubric are workbooks that could be administered to either functioning individuals or respondents who have completed a course of talk psychotherapy and need another approach to learn more about themselves.

Development of Emotional Competence

This workbook is composed of 11 assignments based, in part, on the work by Saarni (1999) as well as others (Averill, 1997; Bradley, 2000; Cacioppo & Gardner, 1999; Gottman, Fainsilber, & Hooven, 1997; Kennedy-Moore & Watson, 1999; L'Abate, 1994a, 1997c; Mascolo & Griffin, 1998), on how to become a more emotionally competent individual. It aims at filling and fulfilling the great need to help people learn to cope with and express their emotions in more constructive ways than they have done heretofore. Of course, some terms and concepts have been simplified to make sure that this workbook can be administered to the widest possible audience. As noted earlier (and as will be repeated below and often in Chapter 5), the differentiation between feelings, affect, and mood—the subjective, receptive and internal side of experiencing, and emotions, the observable, external side of expressing them—is made from the very outset. Feelings need to be discriminated from emotions, lest respondents become confused about the whole topic. Furthermore, the content of Assignment 7 has been influenced by Pennebaker's (1997) model as well as by the notion that intimacy consists of the sharing of hurts and the fears of being hurt (L'Abate, 1994a, 1997c, 1999a, 1999c; Prager, 1995).

This writer disagrees strongly (L'Abate, 1997c) with Saarni's differentiation between positive and negative emotions (made in Chapter 11). Feelings are what happen to us (Averill, 1997). Emotions are what and how we chose to act on our feelings. We have no choice over events that happen to us and how we experience them. However, we do have a choice about how we outwardly express their subjective, internal experience.

Emotionality, of course, is now in the forefront of current psychological "hot" topics (Averill, 1997; Bradley, 2000; Cacioppo & Gardner, 1999; Kennedy-Moore & Watson, 1999; L'Abate, 1994a, 1997c; Mascolo & Griffin, 1998). As such, this workbook can be administered to functional as well as semifunctional and dysfunctional respondents.

This workbook is complementary with many other workbooks about feelings and emotions reviewed here, such as Anxiety, Anger, Depression, Loneliness, Moodiness, Sadness, and especially Emotional Expression. In fact, the latter workbook could be used in tandem with or as a supplement to the present one.

Emotional Expression

This workbook is composed of 3+ assignments based on the list of feelings developed by Bonanno and Keltner (1997). Even though each assignment can be used independently of their work, one can add as many other feelings not contained in this workbook as one desires. A much longer list of feelings is available in the Family Interviews workbook, while specific workbooks on anger and depression are available.

Self-Awareness

This workbook is composed of 12 assignments developed originally by De Giacomo and his collaborators in Italy (De Giacomo and De Nigris, 2001), and translated and adapted into English by this writer.

The theoretical background for this workbook can be found in cognitive theory as well as in a systemic-relational theory (De Giacomo, 1993; L'Abate, 1994b). The contents of this workbook, in terms of tragedies, comedies, triumphs, things to do, and aspirations for the future, have a loose connection with Pennebaker's work (1997). For instance (as already reviewed in Chapter 2), he requests respondents to write down all of their traumas, including those that were never heretofore shared with or disclosed to anyone. Pennebaker, however, did not differentiate among the nature, intensity, and importance of traumas in general. Hence, it would be difficult from his research to differentiate among the effects of traumas differing in intensity and content, even though he has developed ingenious ways and means to measure emotionality and rationality in narratives (Esterling & Pennebaker, 2001; Pennebaker, 2001).

This workbook, instead, does differentiate among three levels of "tragedies," ranging from extremely painful to less painful ones. Furthermore, it does give room to the possible influence of funny and pleasant events, that is, comedies, in one's life. In addition, rather than concentrating on past events, there is at least one assignment devoted to forward rather than backward thinking, that is, dreams, daydreams, aspirations, and hopes for the future.

The hypothesis of this workbook, therefore, is that greater awareness of one's painful and pleasurable events may produce a change in the dysphoric nature of thoughts themselves. Respondents start to think also about possible comedies, switching from being passive recipients of a "sickness" to active "observers" and "reporters" of their own awareness. This switch may make the difference between being "sick" and being "healthy." Greater awareness of one's thought processes as well as their expression would help one's functioning, as already noted in supporting guidelines of control summarized in Chapter 1 (Table 1.7). Approaching (rather than avoiding) and expressing (rather than avoiding and repressing) painful and even buried emotionally charged events and experiences, especially in writing, may have a salutary effect on one's functioning (Esterling, L'Abate, Murray, & Pennebaker, 1999).

This workbook is composed of 12 assignments including an introductory and a final one. The first assignment guides respondents to choose specific times to work on each assignment and the sequence of assignments to work on. The sequence of the 10 assignments that constitute the bulk of this workbook is dictated by the respondent's wishes and priorities. Assignments are composed of:

1. Three tragedies, ranging from extremely painful, moderate, and somewhat painful
2. Three comedies, ranging from extremely funny to moderately and somewhat funny
3. One assignment on realistic tasks or chores to be completed
4. One assignment on triumphs to be proud of
5. One assignment on neutral happenings that still occupy one's mind
6. One assignment on dreams, daydreams, aspirations, and hopes for the future

The last (12th) assignment asks for feedback by having respondents rank-order assignments in order of liking and usefulness, closing with an open-ended request for ways to improve the workbook. This is really an "all-purpose" workbook because it can be administered to clinical and nonclinical individuals. For research purposes the first assignment could be changed from a flexible (idiographic) to a nonflexible format, in which the order of administration of assignments remains constant for all respondents (nomothetic). Respondents would not have a choice about the order or assignment administrations.

From the viewpoint of the classification of workbooks made in Ch. 2, this workbook: (1) has a *precriptive* goal, to improve self-awareness of respondents, (2) deals with the whole range of positive and negative experiences in *content*, (3) is available to a whole gamut of functional and dysfunctional individuals, (4) is focused on specific topics, making it semistructured, and (5) at least in the English translation, has a lowered level of abstraction. Clearly, this workbook—even though creative and original—needs empirical validation with both clinical and nonclinical populations, using better controls than a no-treatment control group (De Giacomo & De Nigris, 2001). For instance, the control group should spend as much time answering in writing questions on innocuous and neutral topics as the experimental group, as in the case of Pennebaker's research.

In conclusion, this workbook can be administered to a wide range of individuals. After all, who would not profit from a workbook that would or should improved one's awareness? Its largely untested nature (De Giacomo & De Nigris, 2001) makes it ideal for controlled clinical and research application. Consequently, if used by clinicians, it should be administered with "awareness" inventories rather than "symptom"-oriented ones to avoid stigmatization. Available symptom-oriented inventories could be changed to "awareness inventories" or "concerns" to allow applications to a wide range of clinical and non-clinical individuals. Researchers should use pre-post testing with the same "awareness-oriented" inventories, but also use controls who are administered homework assignments dealing with neutral topics like one's closet, house, wardrobe, car, books, and so on.

Emotional Intelligence

This workbook is based on the User's Manual developed by Bar-On (1997). It should be administered in conjunction with the test instrument of the same name as well as with other paper-and-pencil self-report tests measuring level of emotionality and personality functioning. It can be administered to well or semi-functioning respondents provided an Informed Consent Form is signed.

The first assignment is prescriptive in the sense that all subsequent assignments follow either from the objective rank-order obtained from the test profile or from the rank-order given by respondents in the first assignment. Any discrepancy between the objective order from the profile obtained from test results and the subjective rank-order given in the first assignment needs to be reconciled through discussion and negotiation between professionals and respondents.

This discrepancy would be an indication of how aware a respondent is of his or her emotional behaviors. The greater the discrepancy, the more restricted awareness might be. The concluding assignment can be administered when all the assignments concerning emotional behaviors of relevance to each respondent have been completed satisfactorily.

Multiple Abilities

This workbook, consisting of 15 assignments, is the combined product of three theories of intelligence, one by Gardner (1983, 1995, 1998, 1999) about multiple intelligences, a second by Mayer and Salovey (1995), as popularized by Goleman (1995) and Bodine and Crawford (1999), about emotional intelligence, and a third by Sternberg (1996) about successful intelligence as composed of at least three components: practical, analytical, and creative. For a review about the status of these and other theories of intelligence, the reader is referred to Campbell, Campbell, and Dickinson (1999), Fogarty and Bellanca (1998), and Sternberg and Kaufman (1998).

The sensual-sexual ability was added because it is an important ability that may well be specific, as suggested also by the work of Orbach and Mikulincer (1998) on body investment. Even though it may be a combination of other abilities, in its "pure" form, the sensual-sexual ability may account for some individuals specializing in it to the point of mastery and obsessive deviance, just like all the other abilities. Mastery and deviance are some of the criteria developed by Gardner to qualify as separate "intelligences." Of course, there is overlap among many abilities. Nonetheless, in spite of this overlap, there are sufficient prototypes for these abilities to justify its inclusion rather than its exclusion.

Of course, terms like "intelligences," "abilities," or "skills" are not free from controversy. For instance, Gardner argues that there should be a distinction made between "intelligence" and "domain." "One cannot see an intelligence in operation directly; one can only look at skills and progress in domains which putatively involve the intelligence. I would personally prefer a workbook that honored this distinction, and that probed the extent to which individuals were confortable with, and gained mastery of domains that are valued by a society" (Howard Gardner, personal communication, November 30, 1998). His argument for taking this position derives from his definition of domain:

a *domain* is an organized set of activities within a culture, one typically characterized by a specific symbol system and its attendant operations. Any cultural activity in which individuals participate on more than a casual basis, and in which the degree of expertise can be identified and nurtured, should be considered a domain. . . . Any domain can be realized through the use of several intelligences; thus, the domain of musical performance involves bodily kinesthetic and personal as well as musical intelligences. By the same token, a particular intelligence, like spatial intelligence, can be put to work in a myriad of domains, ranging from sculpture to sailing to neuroanatomical investigations. (Gardner, 1995, p. 202)

As much as one would like to agree with Gardner's definition, the reason for sticking to using the term "ability" in the title of this workbook relies on communicating directly with respondents who might otherwise be confused by the rather esoteric term "domain." Ability, to most laypersons, denotes a group of skills focused on a specific subject matter. Indeed, even Gardner (1999, p. 33) agrees that this term is a popular one. Most "lay" respondents would understand what abilities are once they read their individual definitions. By the same token, the term "intelligence" is even more controversial, confusing, and possibly misleading. Hence, of all the possible choices available, it seems that the term "ability" may be less controversial and confusing than any other possible term, if not to scholars, to nonprofessional respondents (with apologies to Dr. Gardner).

Normative Experiences (Form PSC)

This workbook, developed from research by Goldberg (1999), is generic and neutral enough to be administered to relatively well-functioning individuals, perhaps on a postpsychotherapy basis (3+ assignments).

Normative Experiences (Form IPIP)

This workbook, developed from research by Goldberg (1999), is generic and neutral enough to be administered to relatively well-functioning individuals, perhaps on a postpsychotherapy basis (3+ assignments).

Normative Experiences (Form AB5C)

This workbook, developed from research by Goldberg (1999), is generic and neutral enough to be administered to relatively well-functioning individuals, perhaps on a postpsychotherapy basis (3+ assignments).

Social Skills

This workbook, consisting of 3+ assignments based on the Inventory of the same name, was developed by Lorr, Youniss, and Stefic (1991). The field of social skills (see Chapter 1 for an introduction to this field) covers a veritable plethora of publications that cannot be reviewed here but that attests to the importance of this field in primary, secondary, and tertiary prevention.

WORKBOOKS FOR COUPLES

This section contains descriptions of workbooks devoted to improving the relationships of couples involved in long-term and intimate commitments. It is assumed that professionals administering these workbooks are experienced in working with couples. As in the case of workbooks for individuals, those for couples can be divided by test profile and by referral question. Of course, administration of each workbook should be coupled with the administration of an Informed Consent Form.

Workbooks Based on Test Profiles

Assignments from the Relationship Conflict or Marital Satisfaction workbooks need to be assigned after the administration of self-report, paper-and-pencil inventories, which are the basis for each workbook. The profile obtained from each inventory indicates for which area or dimension of the couple relationship assignments should be administered first. The administration of each homework assignment from one session to another should follow sequentially from the most deviant to the least deviant area or dimension as indicated by test profile. The more deviant from the norm an area or dimension is in comparison to all the other areas or dimensions in the profile, the greater the need to administer its matched assignment. Even though there may be just one assignment for each area or dimension, the assignment could be used for further discussion in the professional's office. A discussion of the test results should, of course, proceed administration of matching assignments.

Improving Relationships

This program was written by Brenda Whaley, Ph.D., with revisions from the first author. (A program is defined as a combination of an evaluation instrument with matching assignments in a workbook). The purpose of this program is to recognize unrealistic ideas or personality flaws that prevent couples from developing and maintaining good relationships. These assignments will attempt to help partners change directions so that their relationship can incorporate more helpful aspects. Clarification of personal values can build the foundations of relationships, where most of these values, even though latent, are neither expressed nor explored. If alternatives are available, each partner can decide what is important for himself/herself, and can develop a model of free choice rather than coercion.

Even the most stable relationships have some conflict because couples disagree on issues, become annoyed at something done, and sometimes have negative moods. Since it is expected that couples will argue, it becomes very important to find more appropriate ways of dealing with anger. Very often partners give up the freedom of seeking personal goals, feeling forced into situations or activities that they despise, but that are valued by the other partner. Couples and families function best when each member feels important and able to share decision-making. Unequal relationships lead to instability. In many relationships, sex becomes routine and boring, with little caring and concern involved. Sex alone does not provide the intimacy that many of us desire. When a relationship is under stress, some couples attempt to ease the tension by having more sex because that is easier than admitting that they have a problem that needs to be worked out, or they avoid sex altogether.

The assessment and consequent assignments presented in this workbook attempt to locate both strong and weak areas of a relationship so that couples can become more understanding of themselves, and develop better ways of dealing with stressful situations when they arise.

Marital Satisfaction

This workbook is based on the Marital Satisfaction Inventory—Revised, one of the most frequently administered inventories available commercially. It was developed empirically to cover major dimensions of marital satisfaction. Most of the characteristics, research, and psychometric properties of this instrument can be found in Snyder and Aikman (1999). This test yields 13 scales using gender-specific norms.

The first assignment is strictly prescriptive, that is, its purpose is to find how each partner views the dimensions covered by the instrument and how each partner prioritizes the various dimensions in relationship to the other partner. The scales of this Inventory indicate greater distress with higher scores on the profile. Hence, administration of homework assignments based on these scales can proceed in a variety of ways:

1. Assignments could proceed from the scale on which partners jointly indicate the greatest discrepancy between their individual profiles, or an equal amount of distress.
2. Assignments could proceed from the dimension where partners jointly indicate the smallest degree of discrepancy between their individual profiles. Of course, there would not be any need to administer any assignment in nonconflictual areas, that is, similar and/or equal scores, with little or no discrepancy between partners, unless one wanted to start with low-conflict assignments, increasing gradually to more conflictual assignments.
3. Instead of using objective individual profile scores, assignments could be administered according to the joint subjective rankings given by partners in the first assignment.
4. Given a large discrepancy between objective individual profiles and subjective rank-orders given by each partner in the first assignment, a compromise to reconcile discrepancies between couple rank-orders and test results should be reached with the professional who administers this workbook, perhaps merging both objective and subjective rankings.

Note: The creation of artificial conflict situations between partners over their rank-orders of the dimensions taken from the inventory in the first assignment should be expected by the professional. By the same token, one should consider and reconcile their subjective rank-orders from the first assignment with their test profiles, to everybody's satisfaction.

If there is little or no overlap between partner scores, then the choice of the second assignment should be based on a coin toss. The partner who wins the coin toss determines the first choice of assignment for both partners. The partner who loses the toss determines the second and third choices of assignments for both partners, with the winning (of the coin toss) partner determining the fourth choice of the assignment according to his or her ranking. The partner who loses (the coin toss) determines the choice of the fifth assignment while the other partner (who won the original coin toss) determines choices sixth and seventh, with the choice of assignment going to the "losing" partner. In other words the partner who wins the coin toss determines choices 1, 4, 6, and 7. The partner who loses the coin toss determines choices 2, 3, 5, and 8.

The length of the workbook can be determined through negotiation with the couple, ranging from a minimum of 6 to a maximum of 12 assignments. If the couple needs more help after completion of this workbook, they may need an additional workbook or may need to be referred elsewhere for psychotherapy, if it is not available from the professional administering this workbook.

Another possibility may lie in the individual determinants of the relationship. For instance, if one partner is depressed, or the other partner is too impulsive, each may need to receive specific workbooks to deal with individual conditions. If an objective evaluation was made at the very outset of the premarital workbook, these individual determinants should have been dealt with from that time on.

Problems in Relationships

This program, as described earlier (Chapter 3), includes a workbook and a 240-item computer-scored Problems in Relationship Scale (PIRS), to pinpoint major discrepancies among 20 scales of potentially conflictual areas. Once most conflictual dimensions are located, they can be coupled with matching assignments for each of the 20 areas (22 assignments + scale). The first and last assignments function respectively as introduction and follow-up (L'Abate, 1992b).

Relationship Conflict

This workbook covers the most stressful areas of conflict, including abuse and fighting (14 assignments). It was written to parallel the Relationship Conflict Inventory developed by Bodin (1996), who is continuing to research its psychometric properties and clinical applicability. Copies of this inventory can be obtained directly from its author. In addition to questions concerning demographic and background factors, this inventory covers three major areas of conflict: (1) *processes*, that is, forms or styles of conflict, (2) *contents*, or topics of conflict, and (3) *abuse*, a characteristic of this inventory that makes it preferable to many other marital inventories that do not confront or deal with this very relevant area of intimate relationships.

The choice of assignments, that is, which assignment to administer first, which second, etc., should be sequential. Assignments can be administrated according to severity, starting with assignment of the most conflictual area, according to the professional helper's best judgment, in agreement with the couple. Of course, this inventory should be readministered to the couple at termination of this workbook to evaluate whether any progress in the relationship took place.

Workbooks Based on Referral Question

Arguing and Fighting

Fighting and/or arguing are the most frequent, pervasive, and intense of symptoms, especially in couples. They are also some of the most difficult to control and to turn into constructive discussions and negotiation. Unless definite steps are taken at the outset of therapy to decrease them, these patterns may derail and defeat the process of treatment. This workbook consists of description, positive reframing, and prescription of 7 different aspects of abusive behavior (10 + assignments). This workbook is designed to deal with the referral question in a way that is also followed in most of the workbooks for families listed below, and that is: Right after the first assignment, when the referral question has been established as being excessive arguing or fighting, the couple is administered individual evaluation forms asking them to describe the frequency, duration, intensity, and content of the symptomatic behavior. They are required to discuss their answers with each other and to return for the next session with notes of their discussion as well as their completed forms. The next assignment for couples is to rank-order a list of 10 positively framed explanations of the problem. Partners are expected to discuss with each other how these explanations apply to them. They are given space to include their own explanation if they do not like the 10 explanations given. Their answers are then discussed in the next session. The third assignment consists of a detailed prescription for arguing and fighting "dirty." This prescription includes specific guidelines on how to use blaming, accusing, name-calling, giving ultimatums, bringing up the past, mind-reading, threatening, blackmailing, and bribery. The three initial sessions serve to establish rapport, trust, and confidence in the therapist and his or her procedures. Once this initial confidence is established, the couple is ready to deal with whatever underlying maladaptive patterns (if any) may have been responsible for arguing and fighting ("It may take three months to have you two quit arguing and fighting. It may take more than a year to find out why you argue and fight. Which will it be?")

Before administering this workbook to a couple, it is crucial that both partners sign an Informed Consent Form that also contains a written commitment to work on homework assignments at predetermined, prearranged times (for example, every Monday at 7 P.M., every Tuesday at 9 P.M., etc.). These times should be considered "sacred" and should supersede any other obligation or commitment unless there is an emergency. A contract to the frequency (usually once a week), length (usually 1 hour), and duration (for at least 6 months, depending on the number of assignments they want to complete) should be signed by both partners, with individual copies retained by each partner and the professional helping them. The rationale for holding individuals, couples, and families to predetermined appointment times is found in the section about control in Chapter 1. (L'Abate, 1986b, 1994a, 1997c). It is important that professionals hold couples responsible for completing assignments at these appointed, agreed-upon times, lest couples lose control of their relationship and professionals lose control of their relationship with couples.

The rationale for the prescription of symptomatic behaviors is found in the fact that they mimic what most couples have been doing for years. Prescriptions are derived from a paradoxical (i.e., circular) approach to therapy of resistant patterns (Weeks & L'Abate, 1982). Couples are further instructed to argue by appointment and to make a tape of the argument. After they bring a tape, they are given it back with a sheet of instructions on how to make a content-analysis of their individual contributions to the argument. They have to classify and tally their individual responses according to categories given to them in the previous assignment (blaming, mind-reading, etc.). Once they bring back their tallied, individual content analyses, each partner is given an assignment that matches the pattern with the highest frequency count. For instance, if one partner has the highest frequency of blaming responses, he or she is given the assignment on Blaming. If the other partner has the highest frequency of Bring Up the Past, he or she is given the matching assignment. During the next therapy session they are administered the assignment that fits the pattern with the second highest frequency count. It has been found that by this time, couples usually do not need any more assignments in this area (L'Abate, 1999c, 1999e).

If these guidelines do work, that is, if the couple is no longer arguing or fighting, the therapist may need to express surprise and disbelief: "I really don't understand how this assignment worked for you. We better continuing arguing and fighting for the next couple of weeks, because I am pretty sure there is going to be a relapse."

Depression in Couples

This workbook (L'Abate, 1986b) teaches partners to become aware of how depression develops from past family patterns that produce deadly triangles. It consists of eight assignments. The first one deals with the Deadly Drama Triangle, composed of three major pathogenic roles, the Victim, the Persecutor, and the Savior. For each of these roles there are additional variations. For instance, for the Victim role there is also the Martyr, Poor Me, etc. For the Persecutor role, there is also the Judge, Jury, Inquisitor, etc. For the Savior role, there is the Advice Giver, the Caretaker, etc. The second assignment deals with

Distance Regulation, composed of the Pursuer (approach), the Distancer (avoidance), and the Regulator (approach-avoidance). The third assignment consists of definitions of depression according to 10 positive reframings ("explanations") of depression. The rest of the workbook focuses on the prescription of depression to help couples achieve some control over it as a relational process.

Intimacy

This workbook consists of six assignments (L'Abate, 1986b) to teach couples and families to care, see the good, forgive, and to share joys, hurts, and fears of being hurt, qualities that are the essence of love.

Couple Violence

Couple violence has reached epidemic proportions in the United States and other parts of the world. It is an ever-present problem in couples as well as in parent-child relationships. Consequently, it is important to make a workbook available that will allow the training of partners at risk for violence on a preventive as well as on a psychotherapeutic basis. This workbook teaches couples to control their violence through cognitive processing of their actions. It can be used complementarily with the Partner Violence workbook.

This workbook (3+ assignments) is based on the research of Eckhardt, Barbour, and Davison (1998). Its purpose is to help partners at risk for violence learn to confront and possibly control their tendencies. The first assignment can be administered to both partners to evaluate agreement or disagreements concerning the seriousness and severity of violence in their relationship. If couple violence is present with criminal behavior, it may be helpful to use the Psychopathy workbook, or the Social Training workbook, or its addendum for impulsive individuals. If abuse is present, it may perhaps be more practical to have partners complete assignments separately and come together to discuss them in front of a professional.

Negotiation

This workbook (L'Abate, 1986b) teaches couples negotiation step-by-step because few couples learned it from their families of origin (9 assignments). The rationale for this workbook will be discussed in the next chapter.

Partner Violence

This workbook (3+ assignments) teaches partners to control their violence and learn to express their feelings in more helpful ways than in the past. This workbook is based on the research of Magdol, Moffitt, Caspi, Fagan, and Silva (1997). Its purpose is to help partners at risk for violence learn to confront and possibly control their tendencies toward violence. It should be administered with an Informed Consent Form as well as paper-and-pencil self-report instruments documenting the level and type of violence present before and after completion of this workbook.

Premarital Preparation

The purpose of this workbook (3+ assignments) is to help couples prepare for marriage in better ways than they would without any direction or support. The major emphasis of this workbook is for couples who plan to marry to learn more about reasons for wanting to get married. There are, of course, other premarital workbooks available on the market. Other workbooks can be used instead of or in addition to this particular workbook, for instance, Negotiation, and Intimacy (L'Abate, 1986b). Another workbook that could be used in tandem with this one is "Stand UP for Yourself!" It teaches partners to speak in a more constructive and helpful way rather than in a destructive and hurtful fashion. In couples with a great deal of conflict and who have been together for a long time or cohabited before marriage, it may be useful to administer either the Marriage Conflict or Marriage Satisfaction workbooks.

All subsequent assignments (after the first) are administered on the basis of the combined rank orders given by both partners. The title of the second assignment consists of the "Reason" that is ranked highest by the combined score of the two rankings. For instance, if the male partner ranks "We are expecting a child" as the primary reason for getting married while the female partner ranks it as fifth ranking, instead, "To fulfill a promise" as number 1, the combined score would consist of the sum of the two rankings (1 + 5 = 6). If the male partner ranks "To fulfill a promise" as number 20, the combined ranking would be (5 + 20 = 25). Hence, both partners must receive assignments in the order of the two combined rankings to assure that both receive the same assignment at the same time and in the same order.

Stand UP for Yourself

The purpose of this workbook (5 assignments) is to help partners learn how to speak up for themselves instead of speaking down to self or others. To communicate helpfully, partners need to become more aware of errors (and horrors!) of hurtful, abusive communication by increasing their sensitivity to errors and leaving them behind. When partners become fully aware of how painful and hurtful these errors are, they might be able to give them up. These errors should be replaced by the secrets of successful, helpful communication, by behaving proactively rather than reactively.

To communicate better, partners need to become aware of the hurts they have accumulated in their lives to share them, reciprocally, with those they love and who love them. Sharing hurts is another skill that can facilitate successful communication and emotional intimacy. Couples or families must meet at home at prearranged, preset times to exchange and discuss their assignment completions. Without full sharing of hurts, there cannot be full sharing of joys, as discussed in the next chapter. Once they become aware of these hurts and are able to share them, partners can learn to communicate in more helpful ways and give up hurtful, defensive patterns. Helpful and successful communication is based on the use of three small, simple core words that are critical and most difficult to use to stand up for oneself: "I," "It," and "We."

WORKBOOKS FOR FAMILIES

There are many repetitive, often strongly and rigidly resistant, patterns in families that need to be addressed before therapy can be initiated. These patterns are negativity, violence, binge eating, sibling rivalry, stealing, physical and verbal abuse, lying, and temper tantrums. These patterns come to the attention of therapists after long and arduous attempts by parents to control the child using straight-forward punishments or erratic and contradictory parental practices. These resistant patterns are dealt with using the same format described above for arguing and fighting. The first assignment requires a detailed *description* of the pattern. The second assignment frames it positively in at least 10 ways (*explanation*). The third assignment gives specific guidelines on how to repeat the same pattern at home (*prescription*).

As with all test-derived workbooks developed by this writer for either individuals, couples, or families, one can assign homework according to the objective test profile, or one can follow the individual rank-order of assignments according to the preferences of family members. Even when the referral question is stated qualitatively, it is strongly suggested that some self-report, paper-and-pencil questionnaire or rating sheet be administered to family members before administration and after completion of any workbook. However, no interpretation of test results should take place until after the post-test. Premature interpretation of test profiles might lead to the possibility that family members answer for the test answers rather than because of behavior change. If they do not know what the dimensions of the test are to begin with, there is less danger that changes will be made to conform to the test.

As part of the Informed Consent form, the family should agree in writing that they will work individually on the workbook's assignments on a weekly, biweekly, or monthly basis before completing any objective measure. They should agree beforehand as to when they are going to meet as a family to discuss (compare and contrast) their individual answers to their assignments. They have to agree that family meetings are to be held consistently at a predetermined time and place. In a way, it could be said that these assignments serve as a pretext for the family to learn to come together to talk and be together in ways they have not been heretofore.

Family members should be encouraged to give their individual answers to each assignment. After individual completion, they can and should compare and contrast their answers during prearranged, pre-set, predetermined family meetings. If a family is not able to conduct these meetings, it is an indication of a greater disfunctionality than it may be willing to acknowledge. During these family meetings, no one should attempt to change anybody else's mind. The goal here is to learn about each other rather than to change anybody's feelings, opinions, or behaviors. Whether the process of learning about each other's views leads to any behavior change remains to be seen.

Workbooks Based on Test Profiles

When Parents and Children Argue

This workbook allows pinpointing of specific patterns of arguing that lead to stress and breakdown in family relationships (3+ assignments). It is based on research by Weston, Boxer, and Heatherington (1998) on how children view their parents' arguments. Both parents and children could benefit by the Stand Up for Yourself workbook, which would teach them how to communicate with each other in a nonabusive fashion.

When Parents Argue: From the Eyes of a Child

This workbook allows pinpointing of sources of disagreement between parents and how to solve these disagreements (3+ assignments). It is based on research by Weston, Boxer, and Heatherington (1998) on how children view their parents' arguments. Partners wanting to communicate with each other in more helpful ways could benefit by working on the Stand Up for Yourself, Negotiation and Intimacy workbooks.

Self-Report Measures of Family Functioning

This workbook is derived from the factor analysis of self-report measures of family functioning by Bloom (1985) (3+ assignments). The workbook is devoted to dimensions of family structure that could be thought of as complementary to another workbook developed from the Family Profile Form, where significant correlations were found between these two instruments and the Dyadic Adjustment Scale (Kochalka & L'Abate, 1997).

Like all test-derived workbooks developed by Workbooks for Better Living for either individuals, couples, or families, one can assign homework according to an objective test profile or follow the individual rank-order of assignments according to the averaged preferences of family members. It is suggested that this workbook be administered to family members after completion of an objective self-report scale. However, no interpretation of test results should take place until after the post-test. Premature interpretation of the test profile might lead to family members answering for the test dimensions rather than for behavior change. If they do not know what the dimensions of the test are to begin with, there is less danger that changes will be due to conforming to the test.

As part of the Informed Consent Form, the family should agree in writing that they will work individually on the workbook's assignments on a weekly, bi-weekly, or monthly basis before completing this workbook. They should agree beforehand about when they are going to meet as a family to discuss (compare and contrast) their answers. They should agree to hold family meetings at a pre-determined time and place consistently. In a way, these assignments are a pretext for the family to learn to come together to talk and be together in ways that they have not before.

During the family meetings to discuss individual's answers to each assignment, no one should attempt to change anyone else's mind. The goal here is to learn about each other rather than to change each other's feelings, opinions, or behaviors. Whether the process of learning about each other's views leads to any behavior change remains to be seen.

The number of assignments for this workbook is 17. Included in this total are two assignments from the first and final assignments plus the 15 dimensions covered by each assignment. The format for assignments after the first one is standard for each person. However, the order of administration for all assignments after the first should follow from averaging all family members' rank-orders to reach a "family rank-order," unless the professional administering this workbook has a responsible and well thought out rationale for doing otherwise.

Family Profile Form (FPF)

The purpose of this workbook is to help family members learn to communicate better than they have done in the past. This workbook (3+ assignments) contains nine dimensions of family living derived from an instrument developed by L'Abate and Weinstein (1987) and validated by Kochalka and L'Abate (1997). This workbook can be administered together with the test of the same name (L'Abate & Weinstein, 1987) or with another family measure that is independent from the workbook. This workbook deals with dimensions of family processes and could be conceivably thought as complementary to the Family Functioning workbook. Kochalka and L'Abate (1997) found high and significant correlations among both the Family Profile Form, the Family Environment Scale (FES), and the Dyadic Adjustment Scale, indicating some relationships between process and structure in family dimensions. Process and structure will be defined below.

There are eleven assignments in this workbook, that is, the first prescriptive, and final follow-up assignments plus the nine dimensions covered by each assignment. The format for the assignments after the first one is standard for everybody. However, the order of administration for all assignments after the first should follow the same route suggested for other family workbooks, and that is: combine (add) all the rank-orders from all family members and from this overall profile to develop the sequence of assignments. This will lead to all family members completing and discussing the same assignments.

Workbooks Based on the Referral Question

Binge Eating

This workbook consists of three assignments focused on description, positive reframing, and prescription for this symptom in children and teenagers. This workbook was written in collaboration with Monique Gray (L'Abate, 1992b).

Divorce Adjustment for Children

This workbook was developed by Karin B. Jordan, Ph.D., on the basis of her clinical experience with elementary school-aged children whose parents are divorcing (7 assignments). It should be used in conjunction with either group or family therapy.

Domestic Violence and Child Abuse

This workbook consists of three assignments focused on description, positive reframing, and prescription for this symptom. It was written in collaboration with Fran Greenfield (L'Abate, 1992b).

Feelings in the Family

This workbook was developed with the help of Doris M. Hewitt, Ph.D. It does not have a definite number of assignments because quite a few assignments can be administered to families on an ongoing basis. The rationale for this workbook is found in the next chapter. However, it is argued here, as earlier regarding two other "emotion" workbooks, that feelings are neutral—neither "good" or "bad," "positive" or "negative." How we express our feelings makes them "good" or "bad," "constructive" or "destructive," "helpful" or "hurtful." What we feel, how we experience feelings, is one thing we cannot control. What we express and how we express them is another matter completely, which we can control. Because one is angry, it does not mean that one should take a gun and shoot whoever is made responsible for the anger. Given the same feeling, let us say, anger, there are an almost infinite number of ways of expressing it and justifying its expression, good or bad. Between feeling and emotions we need to introduce thinking; how we proceed from experiencing a feeling to how we express it. Without the introduction of thinking in between feelings and emotions, it would not be possible to establish any controls.

We are more likely to be in charge of how we express our feelings when we: (1) become aware of them, (2) can identify or label them, (3) can identify what has caused or is causing them, and (4) can express these feelings in appropriate, constructive and helpful ways, using the "I" pronoun instead of the accusatory "You" pronoun. It is important that verbal expressions of feelings take place appropriately. This means that individuals make "I" statements, accepting responsibility for their feelings and emotional reactions and not blaming someone else for them.

Foster/Adoptive Family Care

This workbook (8 assignments) was originally written by Professor Mario Cusinato with revisions from this author. The purpose of this workbook is to help instructors teach potential foster or adoptive family parents how to cope with their often novel and difficult responsibilities. However, with some revisions, parts of this workbook could be also used with parents of natural children.

Foster or adoptive care is an important and serious responsibility, because it allows a child to have a concrete experience of positive family relations at the very moment when his/her family might be in chaos or the child might be forced to live in an institutionalized situation. Nevertheless, foster or adoptive family care is not without problems. This workbook begins by clearing these troublesome aspects. In fact, most would-be caretakers dealing with foster/adoptive care, directly or indirectly, ask themselves many questions about the process contained in this workbook.

Initial Family Interview and Feelings

The purpose of this workbook (5 assignments) is to help families confront feelings and emotions that many families do not know how to express, eliciting as much information as possible from a family. The issue here is: "What kind of information?" The focus of this initial family interview is directed toward how family members feel about themselves and about each other. Questions asked in this interview can be administered in writing to individual family members, or they can be asked verbally by the interviewer. If the answers are in writing, then each family member can share the answers of other family member by reading them. If the answers are given verbally, it will be up to the interviewer to ask each family member about how he or she feels about what other family members have written.

Lying

This workbook consists of 3 assignments focused on description, positive reframing, and prescription for this symptom in children. This workbook was written in collaboration with Maureen O'Toole (L'Abate, 1992b).

Negativity

This workbook for families consists of 3 assignments focused on description, positive reframing, and prescription of a behavior that permeates many dysfunctional families (Greene & Anderson, 1999; L'Abate, 1986b). This workbook was written in collaboration with Tricia Jones (L'Abate, 1992b).

Relationship Styles

This workbook is based on 16 relationship styles derived from the elementary pragmatic model of De Giacomo (1993; L'Abate, 1994b; L'Abate, De Giacomo; McCarty, De Giacomo, & Verrastro, 2000).

Revised Temper Tantrums

The purpose of this workbook is to helps parents of children from pre-school to adulthood deal with sudden and unprovoked explosive tantrums (4 assignments). This is a vastly revised version of the original workbook published earlier (L'Abate, 1992b). However, the basic format of (1) description, (2) explanations, and (3) prescription remains, with one extra follow-up assignment.

Shyness in Children

Consists of three assignments focused on description, positive reframing, and prescription of this symptom. This workbook was written in collaboration with Sue Matthews (L'Abate, 1992b).

Sibling Rivalry

This workbook consists of 3 assignments focused on description, positive reframing, and prescription of this symptom.

Stealing

This workbook consists of 3 assignments focused on description, positive reframing, and prescription of this symptom. This workbook was written with the collaboration of Ernestine Williams (L'Abate, 1992b).

Time-Out Procedures

This workbook is designed to help parents of preschool and elementary school children (4 assignments). The purpose of these guidelines is to help parents learn to decrease misbehavior in their children without resorting to physical punishment or verbal abuse. The basic issue in parenting is whether the parent should react negatively to the child's misbehavior or whether the parent should be in charge and able to control misbehaviors without losing his/her temper and resorting to immediate negative *reactions*. Parents who react usually explode. Time-out procedures should help parents learn *proactive parenting*—being in charge of the child without physical punishment or verbal abuse. Proactive parenting means having a positive plan; reacting means having no plan. These guidelines, therefore, give parents a positive plan that allows them to become proactive rather than reactive parents.

Verbal Abuse

This workbook consists of three assignments focused on description, positive reframing, and prescription for this symptom (L'Abate, 1992b).

CONCLUSION

This chapter has presented workbooks available for purchase from the Internet (L'Abate, 1996). They represent a whole range of possible clinical and nonclinical test scores, test profiles, referral questions, problems, symptoms, and syndromes. They need to be administered and evaluated by professionals and researchers who are external to their development. Hopefully and ideally, they should be administered under controlled conditions of objective and multidimensional pre-post evaluation. Those workbooks that have been developed from factor-analytic studies or from already validated tests are as good as the tests on which they are based. Supposedly, the link between a test and a workbook derived from it should attest to the validity of that workbook. Nonetheless, this link is no sinecure for a direct evaluation of the workbook itself. A workbook could be developed from a psychometrically well-validated test. Yet, this linkage does not automatically guarantee a successful outcome from its administration.

5

Linking Workbooks with Theory in Psychotherapy: Possible If You Have the "Right" Theory

> Personality has never truly coalesced as a subject matter in psychology.... There has never been an overarching theory or even a thoroughly acceptable definition as to what personality is.
>
> (*Psychological Monitor*, December 1999, p. 22)

> Suffering is a basic characteristic of human life.... It hurts to tell about hurts.
>
> (Hayes, Strosahl, & Wilson, 1999, p. 58)

> I believe there is an emerging consensus that therapy promotes affect regulation.... The need for individuals to find ways of exposing themselves to previously avoided situations—such as discussing painful affects—appears as a consistent theme.
>
> (Bradley, 2000, p. 146)

The purpose of this chapter is to introduce a theory of personality socialization in the family and other settings that can be related to a systematic administration of workbooks. This theory has also been called "developmental competence theory." Linking theory and evaluation with specific workbook interventions is difficult if not impossible to achieve when interventions take place verbally. This link is much easier to achieve when workbooks are derived directly from theory itself, especially if the theory and workbooks are evaluated with test instruments also derived directly from the theory (L'Abate, 1990, 1994a, 1997c, 1998a, in preparation) as well as by test instruments independent of the theory. The empirical bases for this link will be presented in Chapter 6.

In addition to linking theory directly with workbooks, the latter can also be linked to the theory indirectly, or can be linked with theories, models, or empirical evidence completely independent of the theory, a point to be elaborated below. Except for behavioral and cognitive psychotherapy schools, which have attempted to link one with the other (as mentioned in Chapter 1), links between theory and practice have existed mostly in the minds of theoretical beholders.

Recently, however, a series of important papers on the role of theory in the practice of child clinical psychology has highlighted how important theory is for the practice of psychotherapy, and not just child clinical psychology. Kadzin (1999), for instance, decried the neglect of theory in psychotherapy research and the need to understand how interventions produce therapeutic change. Goldfried (1999), on the other hand, warned about the dangers of potential biases that theory may pose for practice, becoming a straight jacket rather than a map and compass. He suggested that practice principles be based on the convergence of clinical observations and research findings. Orvaschel (1999) noted that theory has not occupied an essential place in clinical practice, but that theory should have the purpose of providing a coherent framework for clinical interventions. She asserted that theory should provide a foundation for understanding presenting pathologies, factors that affect them, the patient's and therapist's roles within the context of treatment, and the specific intervention strategies to be utilized (p. 548). Finally, Jensen (1999) stressed that "explicit links" among clinical theory, research, and practice are necessary if a clinical discipline is to survive in the current managed care marketplace. Robust links among theory, research, and practice would enable elaboration of a treatment body of clinical knowledge that is practical in its development, effective in its methods, and compelling in its rationale. All of the above is quite consistent with the aims and thesis of this work, except the repeated skepticism that any changes will occur between a theory and its application as long as interventions are based on talk.

Hence, this and the next chapter will show how it is possible to link theory with practice not just in psychotherapy but also in the laboratory and primary and secondary prevention. To achieve this goal, we will need to summarize a theory of developmental, relational competence that has been attempted for the purpose of developing this link. This chapter is a summary of past and future elaborations. A more extended work is in preparation.

Before beginning with the theory proper, however, it is important to consider the current status of personality theories, at least in the United States, to introduce a conceptual background that will allow comparing and contrasting this relatively new theory with existing personality theories.

BACKGROUND FOR A THEORY OF PERSONALITY SOCIALIZATION IN THE FAMILY AND OTHER SETTINGS

Considerations about the status of personality theories are important for helping distinguish this theory from existing ones. This writer has argued repeatedly

(L'Abate, 1994a, 1997c, 1998a) about the chasm that exists between systems thinking—stressing the importance of the family context in personality socialization—and monadic psychology, as exemplified by existing personality theories. Monadic psychology has traditionally stressed something inside the individual, be it genes, temperament, a *deus ex machina*, or hereditary dispositions. These factors propel the individual to action from the inside, seemingly without any influences from the outside. Therefore, behavior in general, and personality in particular exist, develop, and are socialized in a vacuum, away from immediate, external factors and forces that impinge on and influence that socialization practically every single day. Personality develops without any anyone feeding, nurturing, loving, touching, or abusing, punishing, or even killing it—without the help or hindrance of anyone around it. There are no children or older parents to care for, no siblings to contend with, no relatives to rely upon, no friends to socialize with, no partners or lovers to become intimate or fight with, no neighbors to interact with, let alone schoolmates, coworkers, and leisure-time associates.

In case the reader finds this conclusion too contentiously overstated, extreme, and possibly unsupported by evidence, let us briefly review the sources for this possible overstatement. An early survey (L'Abate & Dunne, 1978) of textbooks on personality, exceptional children, and developmental psychology found that only 1% of the total pages were devoted to family-related topics (family, father, marriage, mother, parents, siblings) in personality textbooks. The only exception was developmental psychology textbooks, where this percentage rose to 15 %. This survey was repeated (L'Abate, 1994a) strictly with theories of personality textbooks, showing that only .05 % of all references were devoted to family-related topics. Most personality textbooks also have few if any references to criminality and/or psychopathology (L'Abate, 1997c), as if personality were always normal and did not show any dysfunctionalities. This is another indication of how acontextual current personality theories are. To make this point even stronger, let us consider four representative, edited personality textbooks.

Contributors to Derlega, Winstead, and Jones' edited work (1991), a very select group of personality theorists, as is the case with the other three textbooks, devoted one page to marital satisfaction and two pages to maternal separation out of 535 pages of text. In an encyclopedic treatise (Hogan, Johnson, & Briggs, 1997), to the editors' credit, one chapter (Halverson & Wampler, 1997) out of 36 was devoted to family influences on personality development. It consisted of 28 pages out of 967 pages of text, equivalent to 3.2 % of the total. An advanced personality textbook (Barone, Hersen, and Van Hasselt, 1998) contained 12 out of 408 pages devoted to family therapy, but no other references were made to family-related topics. In a more recent handbook of personality theory and research (Pervin & John, 1999), there were two pages devoted to marriage, two to parental relationships, and two to parental motivation out of 704 pages of text. It was acknowledged by two contributors (Winter & Barenbaum, 1999, p. 19) that future developments in personality psychology should ascertain the importance of family influences, among many other influences not otherwise acknowledged in that work.

Does one need to go on to conclude that, as a whole, systemic, that is, family-oriented, thinking has been missing from personality theories, and that most existing personality theories are still dealing with personality in vacuum? No wonder that there is no agreement about what personality is! One representative textbook on theories of personality (Ewen, 1988) does not contain one single reference to family-related items except for less than a page for the "only child." The same conclusion applies to another comparative analysis of personality theories (Maddi, 1989). QED?

If the above arguments are not sufficient to support the thesis of nonrelationality and acontextuality in personality theories, let us add more evidence to support them. For instance, personality arises and develops *ipso facto*, by fiat, or by some mysterious forces, usually internal rather than external (Sauding & Plomin, 1996). A recent series of articles on personality failed to mention the family as the primary context in which personality arises, develops, and is socialized (Baumeister & Tice, 1996; Carver, 1996; Diener, 1996; Dweck, 1996; McAdams, 1996; Pervin, 1996). In their commentary on this series, Shoda and Mischel (1996) called for an "intra-individual" emphasis in personality research, mainly on college sophomores while among the contributors cited above, only Carver called for an unspecified "social" emphasis in personality research.

In an editorial in the same issue, Sarason, Sarason, and Pierce (1996) concluded that: "We can add significantly to our knowledge base by taking two steps: (1) arranging laboratory research so that it more closely resembles aspects of life, and (2) actually conducting research in the real world" (pp. 452–453). In the only reference to the family that this writer could find in the whole series, Sarason et al. added:

> These steps will contribute to the enhancement of external validity and lessen reliance on only one methodological approach, be it experimental, observational, or clinical. For example, Freud was well aware of *the family as a determinant of personality dysfunction*. Unfortunately, he explored the family unit mainly through the eyes of individual patients. Because of the errors—both systematic and unsystematic—caused by this reliance on patients' reports and also because of schemata that guided his own thinking, Freud's conceptualization of the family leaves out a number of important phenomena and overemphasis on others. A variety of valuable methodological approaches to the study of the family are now available and it is possible to explore what goes on when family members interact, either in the laboratory or in their living room in ways more sophisticated than those of which Freud was aware. (p. 453, italics added)

If the family is a determinant of personality dysfunction, would it not follow that the family is also a determinant of personality functioning? Should a theory of personality include both functional and dysfunctional aspects? Current personality theories are not only acontextual, they do not go far enough in reaching outside the immediate context of the individual. They fail to stress the family as the most important context of socialization, lasting throughout the life cycle. They also fail to recognize settings, such as schools, work, and leisure-time activities, as important aspects of a life-long socialization process. For instance, none of these topics appeared in any of the sources cited above. Paradoxically, these theories also do not go deep enough inside the individual to deal with the most important aspects of his/her intrapsychic development, and those are, hurt feelings and fears of being hurt.

These feelings are avoided, repressed, and suppressed, producing life-long consequences for personality development and socialization. Little if any references were made in the sources already cited about affect, feelings, and moods, which, as discussed below, are at the bottom of human existence and experience. One important belief shared by the theory presented here and the personality theories cited above is *verifiability*. This writer agrees wholeheartedly with most personality theorists that however personality is thought of, it should be verifiable.

There is another source of difference between the present theory and past personality theories that is relevant to the purposes of this chapter. The acontextuality of the past theories is shown further by their having little if any connection with psychological interventions used in prevention or psychotherapy. In Chapter 1, it was indicated how humanistic and behavioral viewpoints had contributed a fair amount to primary prevention programs (L'Abate, 1990). That is not the case with personality theories. They are completely free of connections with preventive or psychotherapeutic interventions, precluding their dynamic application and evaluation in settings other than the laboratory—nowhere else. As shown in Chapters 3 and 4, however, it has been possible to develop workbooks based on many different empirical and theoretical sources. Among others, for example, the Big Five Model of personality traits (John & Srivastava, 1999) is just one of the many workbooks showing that it is indeed possible to link evaluation with workbook interventions. Therefore, through workbooks, it is possible to link theory with practice, and, as we shall see below, personality functioning with workbooks.

On the other hand, systems thinking, as currently interpreted by most couple and family therapists, is appealing and seductive but remains untestable. It is a paradigm or a metatheory at best rather than a theory (L'Abate & Colondier, 1985; L'Abate & Jurkovic, 1987). It focuses on the family as a group rather than on individual personalities within the family. Even though, as early as 1927, Burgess, a sociologist, defined the family as a "unity of interacting personalities" (Loukas, Twitchell, Piejak, Fitzgerald, & Zucker, 1998), systems thinking did not provide a definition of personality that would suggest, let alone indicate, connections between individual socialization and its immediate family influences.

The sizable gap between monadic personality theories and family systems lead to the creation and existence of family psychology as a discipline dedicated to studying relationships among individuals within their families, rather than studying families *qua* families as in sociology, or as individuals *qua* individuals as in monadic psychology, or intervening with them in family therapy (L'Abate, 1976, 1983a, 1985a, 1987, 1992a, 1994a, 1997c, 1998a, 1998b). No other references to past works related to this discipline will be made in this chapter unless they are relevant to the theory itself and necessary for its fullest possible explication, given the constraints of just one chapter.

WHY A THEORY?

Should one have a theory? Why? Theories are necessary because they describe functions that need spelling out from the very outset, lest we forget why a theory should be developed and even evaluated. Theories furnish a map of a territory to be explored and mastered. For instance, this theory is specifically oriented toward relationships among intimates. It is not concerned with temporary, short-lived, artificial, and contrived relationships established within the narrow confines of a laboratory. In that setting, links with real life in real relationships are questionable, as they are even with short-lived public relationships in a grocery store or the like. That reality is furnished by the family and not by vague, general, and all-encompassing terms such as "culture, "environment," and, even worse, "situation," which pervade many personality textbooks. These statements do not mean that laboratory research should not be undertaken. On the contrary, it is an important aspect of evaluating this as well as other theories. However, laboratory research is not enough. We also need to evaluate this theory in applied, clinical, and nonclinical settings, through its applications—where it matters.

It would be an extra dividend if one were able to link this theory with other monadic theories to demonstrate that, perhaps, the same map is being used by different people, like the often-quoted allegory about six blind persons and an elephant. These people were looking at different parts of the same animal. An example of how to relate "internal" characteristics, shared by both attachment and circumplex models, to relational and multirelational models, is found in Table 5.1. The selfhood model, to be described in detail later on in this chapter, stands in the very middle of a continuum defined by internality on one hand and externality on the other. It acknowledges the relevance of internal feelings and cognitions as well as underlying external, intimate, interpersonal, and intergenerational relationships.

Theories also function as compasses used to direct, understand, predict, and prescribe behavior. For instance, once a territory like "intimate family relationships" is staked out as being part of the theory, compasses in the form of probe bodies or test instruments allow one to consider whether the map covers the territory adequately, or whether one is going in the wrong direction and being misled into a territory outside the map. It would be an extra bonus if this theory also applied to maps of similar territories. Test instruments calibrated in the

Table 5.1
Theoretical Integration of Six Relational Models Along a Continuum of Internality-Externality

Internality←——————————————————————→Externality

Models					
	Individual		Dyads	Families	
Attachment	Interpersonal Circumplex	Developmental Competence Selfhood	Elementary Pragmatic	Paradigms	Typology
secure	friendly	selful	sharing	environmental/ balanced	balanced
dismissing	dominant	selfish	maintaining	achieving/distancing/limiting	disconnected
preoccupied	submissive	selfless	accepting	consensus/preoccupied	traditional
fearful	hostile	no-self	antifunction		emotionally strained

Source: L'Abate (1998a).

laboratory can be validated on their own, in terms of concurrent and criterion validities, but now they can also be validated prescriptively through workbooks (as shown in previous chapters).

This theory serves also as a clothes-hanger, in which parts and pieces of this and similar annexed theories, theorettes, and models have been hung according to some systematic order. For instance, there are parts of the theory that relate to and are similar to other theories. By the same token, a theory may also become a straight-jacket. Not allowing one to look outside of it, restricting one's vision to just one theory and that one alone, without paying attention to other theories, as in the case of psychoanalysis. This is the reason for always comparing a theory with others, lest one becomes enamored with a theory to the point of making it into a religion rather than a fallible map, vulnerable to faulty compasses. There is no perfect theory, just as there are no perfect maps. Even maps, as Korzybski (1949) was fond of reminding us, are not the territory. They are just condensed approximations awaiting improvements. They are never the territory itself. There is no way they can ever be.

Requirements for a Theory of Personality Socialization in the Family

In constructing this theory, various criteria were kept in the foreground, lest one forget the limits of the theory and go outside its boundaries, making it into something more than it claims to be. In the first place, this theory must be *verifiable* in the laboratory, through paper-and-pencil, self-report test instruments (that is, compasses). Individuals in families can also be evaluated through visual and verbal tests (L'Abate & Wagner, 1985, 1988). In addition, a theory must be verifiable in primary prevention, through structured enrichment programs, in secondary prevention through workbooks, and in psychotherapy with tasks derived directly from the theory. Explanation of this verification will take place in the next chapter, after the theory is explained here, albeit briefly.

The major characteristic of all these operations, whether in the laboratory or in applied, clinical, and nonclinical settings, is *replicability*. The same operations (tests, programs, workbooks, and tasks) can be repeated from one professional to another and from one applied or clinical setting to another. This is why talk is so difficult to verify. It varies too much from one professional to another and from one setting to another. It is difficult and expensive to control and to replicate. Given the same score and the same instrument, music is repeatable, but is it science? What makes music different from science? After all, workbooks are scripts equivalent to musical scores, but workbooks are played with different methods and with human beings rather than with musical instruments. However, the criterion of replicability is common to both music and science. In science, as in music, however, interpretations of the same score, script, or evidence vary from one scientist to another, the dialectic aspect of demonstrability.

Furthermore, a theory can be evaluated by comparing it conceptually with other theories whose major constructs are similar but entirely *independent* from this theory. For instance, the ability to love and the ability to negotiate are two basic tenets of the present theory. However, there are countless theories about the ability to love and the ability to negotiate. The issue here is whether conceptual comparisons among theories can be accomplished at the empirical level and not just at the conceptual level. For instance, L'Abate, De Giacomo, McCarty, De Giacomo, and Verrastro (2000) evaluated the comparative validity of three models of intimate relationships: attachment, elementary pragmatic, and selfhood. These models were drawn from completely different and independent theoretical origins, object relations, systems thinking, and resource exchange, respectively. They also varied along a continuum of internality to externality, as shown in Table 5.1. For instance, traits drawn from the circumplex model of personality (Plutchik & Conte, 1997) at one extreme of this continuum are internal characteristics inferred from paper-and-pencil self-report tests. Relationships, at the other extreme, are external and observable. Once significant correlations among the measures of the three models were found (as shown in the next chapter), these models ceased being independent of each other. Their similarities became greater than their differences. They seem to measure four enduring characteristics of intimate relationships, to be reviewed below.

A theory can also be evaluated *indirectly* when some of its constructs are derived from another theory very similar to it. For instance, selfhood, a major model of the theory, is derived from resource exchange theory (Foa, Converse, Tornblom, & Foa, 1993). Hence, any evaluation of the validity of resource exchange theory would indirectly enhance the validity of the selfhood model.

A third way to test a theory is *directly*, that is, through test instruments, workbooks, therapeutic tasks, and operations derived directly from the theory. For instance, the selfhood model has been evaluated in its psychometric properties through the Self-Other Profile Chart (SOPC) (L'Abate, 1992b, 1997b) and other tests. Additional supporting evidence will be presented in the next chapter, after the theory is explained.

In short, a theory can be evaluated: (1) conceptually, through comparisons with other similar theories completely *independent* from the theory itself, (2) *indirectly*, when another theory or model forms the basis for the development of a model of the theory itself, that is, resource exchange theory, and (3) *directly*, when tests, structured enrichment programs in primary prevention, workbooks in secondary prevention, and therapeutic tasks in tertiary prevention, are derived from the theory itself or from models of the theory.

In the second place, the theory must be *relational*, stressing the nature of intimate relations as functions of individual characteristics in transactions with demand characteristics of intimate others and of various settings (Gergen, 1994). One cannot have a theory about how individuals behave separate from how they behave with their partners, parents, children, siblings, relatives, friends, neighbors, coworkers, and occasional salespersons. By the same token, neither can one have a theory of couples without considering their families. This theory stresses relationships between and among intimate others, rather than positing separate theories for individuals, separate theories for couples, or separate theories for families. Individuals are products and producers of the very relationships they live in, in a process of continuous and reciprocal exchange, give and take. What is exchanged? This is the crucial question attempted in vain by systems theories, but never satisfactorily answered.

In the third place, the theory must be *contextual-ecological*, relating to events within each setting and relationships among the various settings: residence, school/work, and surplus-time settings. We take our families of origin and of procreation along with us and keep them inside everywhere we go in how we behave toward nonintimates. Nonetheless, other settings do influence personality socialization. Normatively speaking, family may be primary, with other settings being secondary. However, in some individuals, secondary settings may become primary, as in case of workaholics, for instance, who are consumed by their work, or athletes who are consumed by their sport.

In the fourth place, this theory must be *developmental*. It must be applicable to all major stages of the life cycle: (1) dependence in early childhood, (2) denial of dependence in adolescence, (3) interdependence-autonomy in adulthood, and (4) return to dependence in old age. Developmental is also meant to include various stages of the individual-family life cycle, that is, getting married, having children, seeing children leave to produce their own families, retirement, death, and death's aftermath on the family.

This theory acknowledges the importance of specific developmental competencies as a function of interactions with specific settings. Acquisition of personal and interpersonal competence is a socialization process that acknowledges the importance of specificities peculiar to a given setting. These personal specificities are abilities and skills particular to the interaction between specific task characteristics and specific demands of settings and other individuals. Given a grocery store, for instance, one needs to know rules of entrance, lay-out of goods, their nature in comparison to similar goods, prices, and exit rules relating to checkout and payments. Each setting has its own task demands that change from one setting to another. By the same token, each family has its own explicit, spoken rules and rituals, and implicit, unspoken ones. These rules and rituals may well be transferred to the next generation without any awareness on the part of those who practice them.

In the fifth place, this theory must be applicable to a continuum of care (presented in Chapter 1) using all three media of communication—nonverbal and written as well as the verbal. Included in this continuum, in addition to the laboratory, would be clinical (clinics, hospitals), criminal (jails, penitentiaries), and nonclinical educational institutions (schools, colleges, universities). What one learns and how one learns to behave in the family tends to generalize to other settings. This link between family and other settings is especially visible in explanatory styles of optimism vs. pessimism (Buchanan & Seligman, 1995; Seligman & Csikszentmihalyi, 2000). Functional families are optimistic. Dysfunctional families are pessimistic, producing individuals who think pessimistically (L'Abate, 1976, 1986b).

In the sixth place, this theory must be sufficiently wide to encompass functional and dysfunctional aspects of personality socialization (L'Abate, 1994a, 1997c, 1998b), including behaviors more appropriate for the administration of workbooks, that is, functionality, externalizations, internalizations, and psychopathology. Psychopathologies consist of inconsistent and contradictorily extreme combinations of internalizations and externalizations (L'Abate, 1994a, 1997c; Liotti, 1999). For instance, Krueger (1999) found two factors basic to mental disorders:

1. Externalizing, reflecting alcohol, drug dependence, and antisocial personality disorders
2. Internalizing, including two components:
   a. Anxious misery, reflecting major depression, dysthymia, and generalized anxiety disorders
   b. Fear component comprising social and simple phobia, agoraphobia, and panic disorders.

Bradley (2000) also differentiated among internalizations, externalization, and psychopathologies.

What theory or model of personality will describe, "explain," or predict these four factors, functionality, on one hand, and three different types and severities of internalizations, externalizations, and psychopathologies, on the other hand? As introduced earlier, there are two other models, namely, attachment and elementary pragmatic (Table 5.1), which come close to describing the same territory covered by this theory (L'Abate, De Giacomo, McCarty, De Giacomo, Verrastro, 2000). This is why it was important to see whether there were more commonalties than differences among the three models. If these characteristics, functionalities, and dysfunctionalities are not predicted by a theory above and beyond what is claimed rather than what is verified, what kind of specificity is then achieved? Without such specificity how can we intervene effectively? This writer prefers that the theory or any of its models be specific and run the risk of being found empirically "wrong," rather than being general and claiming to be "right." Specificity can be evaluated. Vague generalities of the kind proffered by systems thinking or psychoanalysis are difficult if not impossible to verify.

This theory, therefore, attempts to meet at least three requirements, to (1) redefine personality according to relational, ecological, developmental, and contextual concepts, including functionalities and dysfunctionalities, (2) reduce these concepts to known and accepted psychological constructs and (3) verify these concepts empirically as well as applicatively. From the viewpoint of comprehensiveness and integration, this theory is admittedly quite ambitious in attempting to integrate earlier theories as well as the full range of functionalities and dysfunctionalities. However, it is quite simple in its structure and concrete in its stress on visible and measurable constructs.

This theory stresses individual characteristics that are developed from the family of origin. Two individuals start a family by conceiving children and, hopefully, living under the same roof. Both individuals are the products of their respective families of origin. Both partners carry influences, positive and negative, from their families of origin into their new families of procreation. Individual characteristics must adapt to and adopt new demands from different settings, which in turn influence the functioning of their offspring.

This theory, therefore, straddles individual and family perspectives by viewing individual socialization in the context of the family. This link between the individual and the family requires keeping the importance of the family context primary, relating individual determinants to family functioning, and using relational rather than intrapsychic or systems language. If the family is a unit(y) of interacting personalities, as Burgess wrote long ago, then we need to define personality within its various contexts in various settings. Thus, this theory defines socialization and functioning in the family as a set of competencies in diverse settings. Personality socialization and psychological theory have been strongly influenced by what has been called "interactionism" (Magnusson, 1999), with personality being the product of outcome of a "personality × situation" interaction. Since both terms are quite vague and are usually left unspecified, it is useful to break down a definition of personality into specific "competencies × settings" interactions.

Hurt Feelings and Personality Socialization in the Family

The thesis of this theory is that underlying personality socialization in whatever setting, there are hurt feelings and fears of being hurt at the bottom of that process (Leary, Springer, Negel, Ansell, & Evans, 1998). This thesis is supported strongly by the work of Bradley (2000) on affect regulation, Hayes, Strosahl, and Wilson (1999) on affect avoidance, Pennebaker (2001) on traumas and expressed emotions, and Watson (2000) on mood regulation. Hence, personality (as defined at the end of this chapter) is like an artichoke. Underneath the external leaves and below them, after passing through its prickly choke of anger, at the very bottom, there are hurt feelings, sometimes referred vaguely in the extant literature as "distress." These feelings are sometimes solved and resolved in functional relationships. However, they linger on and influence dysfunctionalities throughout the individual and family life-cycle. Before getting to those feelings, however, one must deal with the many leaves that cover and protect them, also overcoming the prickly choke of anger that makes it difficult, and, in some cases, impossible, to get to those feelings.

This theory includes (1) assumptions of *processes* in space and time, (2) postulates about *contents* in resources and modalities of exchange, leading to the ability to love and to negotiate, (3) *settings*, (4) *models*. These parts go from the general to the specific and from the abstract to the concrete, going from the left to the right of Figure 5.1. The rest of this chapter is devoted to expanding and explaining Figure 5.1.

Personality socialization assumes space and time as two basic processes. Space and time subsume, respectively, distance among, between, and within individuals and control henceforth, regulation among, between, and within individuals. Distance subsumes a dimension defined by extremes of approach-avoidance. Extreme of approach-attachment produce symbiotic conditions (Johnson, 1991), which end up in internal (against self rather than others) self-abuse and apathy. They produce abandonment and neglect. Somewhere in the middle of this dimension lies the proper balance of distance, ultimately culminating in closeness and intimacy. The latter characteristics, closeness and intimacy, are frequent in functional relationships and defective if not absent in dysfunctional ones.

Time subsumes a dimension of regulation, used here as synonymous with control, defined by extremes in discharge (fast/strong in responding) at one extreme and delay (slow/weak in responding) at the other. Corresponding terms in the literature have been dysregulation or dysinhibition and inhibition, respectively (Bradley, 2000; Watson, 2000). Extremes in discharge (dysregulation, dysinhibition) tend to produce hyperactivity, impulsivity, and acting-out behavior. Extremes in delay (inhibition) tend to produce obsessive, ruminative thinking and compulsive behavior as well as nonreactivity. Functionality is found in a balance and regulation of discharge-delay processes.

Petronio (2000) attributed three meanings to the construct of balance that are

Figure 5.1
A Developmental Theory of Interpersonal Competence

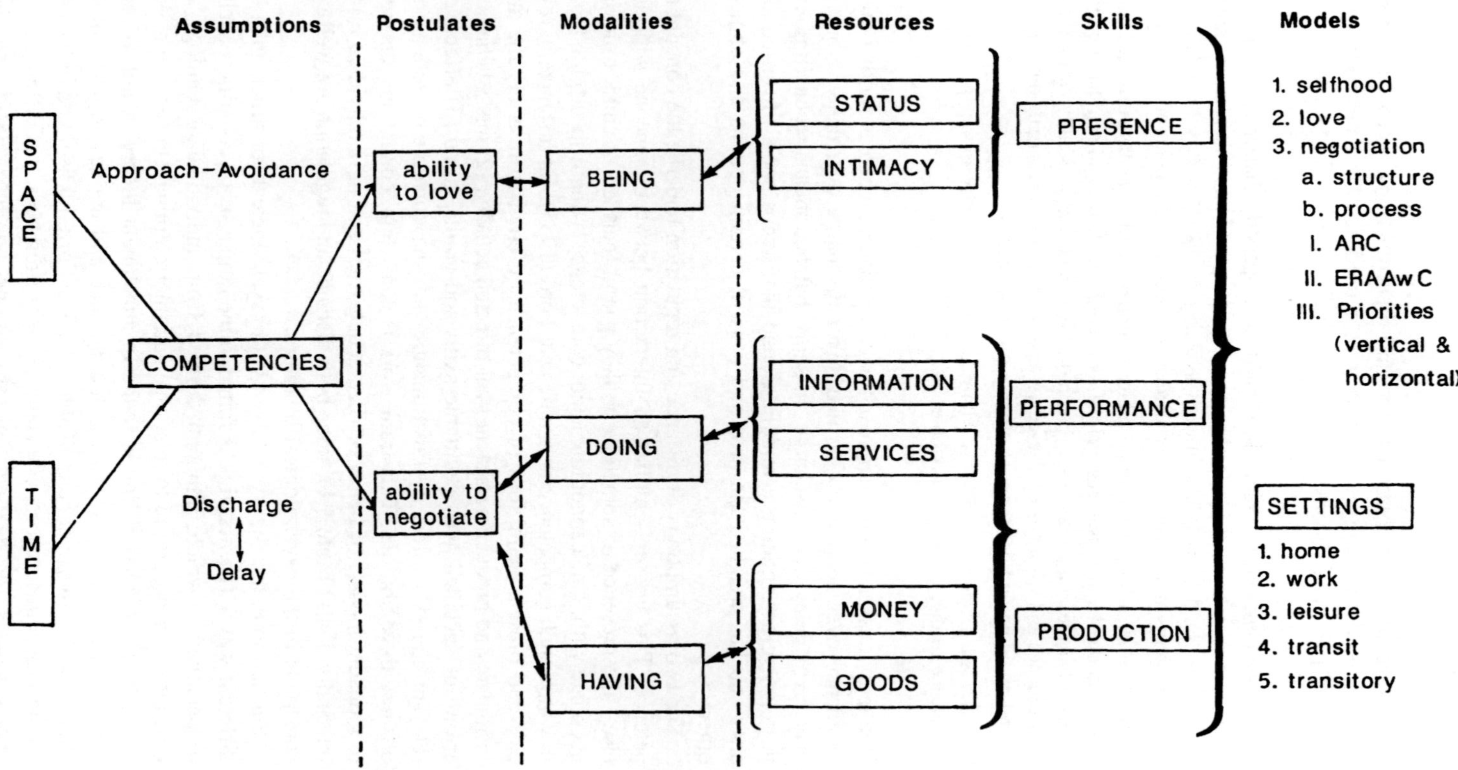

Source: L'Abate (1994a).

basic to regulation of both distance and time functions. According to her, and in agreement with the way this construct is used here, "balance is not a unitary concept" (pp. xiv). It consists of:

1. *Polarizations*, which, within this context, encompass the dialectical dimension of balance versus inbalance. For instance, one may be polarized in approaching others while another would be polarized toward avoiding others. One may be polarized toward discharging immediately, while another may delay to the point of nonacting
2. *Equilibrium*, which, within this context, implies oscillations between stasis and status quo on one hand versus change and even conflict, chaos, and confusion on the other. For instance, one may vary contradictorily and inconsistently within approach-avoidance and within discharge-delay, approaching and discharging on some occations and avoiding and delaying on other, similar occasions
3. *Weighted proportions*, which, within this context, imply giving greater value and valence to one choice over another

One individual may value approach over avoidance, whereas another may value avoidance over approach. One may favor discharge over delay, while another may favor delay over discharge. In short, balance means reconciling extremes in polarizations, finding a middle ground that keeps one's life in equilibrium, after one has weighed the pros and cons of certain options and choices over others.

The two assumptions of distance and regulation underlie the concept of competence. This concept implies an interaction between someone with someone else—the presence of someone, be they parent, partner, or child, to love and to negotiate with. One cannot talk about competence without specifying the context in which such competence is manifested. Ford (1985), for instance, in reviewing past and present definitions of competence, referred to it as (1) the ability to formulate and produce persistent goal-directed activity, (2) one's behavioral repertoire of specified and specifiable skills and abilities, and (3) effectiveness in relevant contexts. Most dysfunctionalities are the outcome of deficits in either of these three abilities. This framework is consistent, continuous, and reducible to monadic models of behavior (i.e., acontextual and intraindividual rather than interindividual) (Table 5.1), since both distance and regulation are well-accepted constructs in the psychological literature.

Furthermore, this theory is linked with psychological constructs in at least six different ways. The first link is found in the emphasis on constructs such as self or personality, which, although derived from individual psychology, will be redefined here according to relational and interrelational concepts (e.g., love and negotiation). A second link is found in attachment theory, which is related to the spatial assumption of approach-avoidance and the development of dependencies and interdependencies (Table 5.1). The third link is found in the emphasis on individual differences, especially gender differences, that differentiate at least two strategies for dealing with stress, one presence-related and the other performance-related, as explained later. The fifth link is found in reordering and applying resource exchange theory in social psychology (Foa, Converse, Tornblom, & Foa, 1993; Foa & Foa, 1974) to a selfhood model of relationships, also to be explained later. Finally, a sixth link is found in sex and sexuality, which are two of the biologically evolutionary and social bases for the formation and development of the family.

The two assumptions of space and time lead to two postulates about two respective sets of abilities: the ability to love and the ability to negotiate.

The First Assumption: Ability to Love

Love is expressed through attributing, asserting, and affirming the importance of self and loved ones, and through the ability to be intimate. This ability is shown by concern for self and intimate other and being available emotionally to oneself and to intimate others through sharing hurts and fears of being hurt. This process means being together unconditionally, without demands for performance, perfection, production, or problem-solving. The ability to love, therefore, even though it may possess a cognitive component, is based on the ability to experience and accept a wide spectrum of feelings. Hence, Emotionality (E) is at the very bottom of our existence—feelings of love between partners, between parents and children, among intimates, family, and friends. E is the primary component of a crucial model in the theory. It is in E, in its passive, receptive aspects, that feelings of hurt and fears of being hurt develop. These feelings are shared in functional relationships. They are avoided, either through internalizations, externalizations, or psychopathologies, in dysfuntional ones (Bradley, 2000). E is the basic context of socialization. Infants are born in an emotional context, the marriage or its absence, and are socialized in an emotional network of family relationships. E is followed developmentally by Rationality (R). Both E and R are the basis for Activity. Awareness, and Context. The five components of the ERAAwC model are expanded below.

The Second Assumption: Ability to Negotiate

The ability to negotiate, problem-solve, brain-storm, and bargain develops from the ability to regulate self in relationship with intimate others (Bazerman, Curhan, Moore, & Velley, 2000). This ability, based on a balance of discharge-delay processes, is present in functional relationships but defective or even absent in dysfunctional ones (Bradley, 2000; Shapiro, 2000). It means being able to regulate oneself and, in so doing, allow others to express themselves, giving them the freedom to discharge, that is, express themselves and be heard. This ability is shown in helpful and creative ways, without delays, distractions, and procrastinations. If there is no balance in regulation, then severe, abusive, neglectful, and hurtful discharge would bring about similar extremes, either in rebellion and retaliation, or in extreme delays and withdrawals.

Negotiations and problem-solving take place within functional democratic relationships where the singular importance of all participants is not only acknowledged but valued. In dysfunctional relationships there is either immediate discharge (name-calling, blaming, etc.) reaching abusive proportions, on one hand, or procrastinating delays on the other. There is no possibility of reaching an agreement and consensus about how to solve even the smallest, most irrelevant issue.

The process of negotiation is composed of: (1) task assignments, consisting of decisions concerning orchestrational (big tasks, such as moving or buying a house or a car) and instrumental (small, routine, everyday) tasks, (2) power sharing and division of labor, consisting of authority (who makes the decisions) and responsibility (who carries them out), and (3) contents (information, services, goods, and money). Negotiation potential is a multiplicative function of functionality (*ill*), ability to negotiate (*skill*), and motivation to negotiate (*will*). While the process of Being Present is based mostly on Emotionality, the process of Negotiation requires access, acknowledgment of, and reliance on E first, followed by Rationality and Regulation. Both E and R determine subsequent *Activities, Awareness*, and *Context*. These constructs will be elaborated below.

Postulates and Modalities of Exchange: Contents of a Life Triangle

Processes of loving and negotiating are related to six resource classes defining the contents of these processes: importance or *status*, intimacy or *love*, services and information, and possessions and money. These classes are derived from resource exchange theory (Foa, Converse, Tornblom, & Foa, 1993; Foa & Foa, 1974) and reduced to three modalities that form the Triangle of Living (Figure 5.2). The three modalities through which we exchange resources are: (1) being or presence, which means being available emotionally to ourselves and to loved ones through attribution of importance, concern, and intimacy, defined as the sharing of hurts and fears of being hurt—the combination of attribution of importance and intimacy define the ability to love, (2) doing or performance, combining information with services, and (3) having or production, combining goods with money. The combination of Doing and Having defines power and the ability to negotiate. Thus, the two fundamental competencies exchanged for individual, marital, and family living are the ability to love and the ability to negotiate.

Presence is not negotiable because it is based on feelings and attributions that are impossible to negotiate. One does not negotiate over how much one loves intimate others. One may negotiate about how to show and share love in ways that are most reciprocally acceptable with intimate others. Presence, in the sense of emotional availability to oneself and to significant others, can only be shared. In functionalities, presence is kept separate from performance and production. In dysfunctionalities, of course, power and presence become confused, diffused,

Figure 5.2
The Triangle of Living

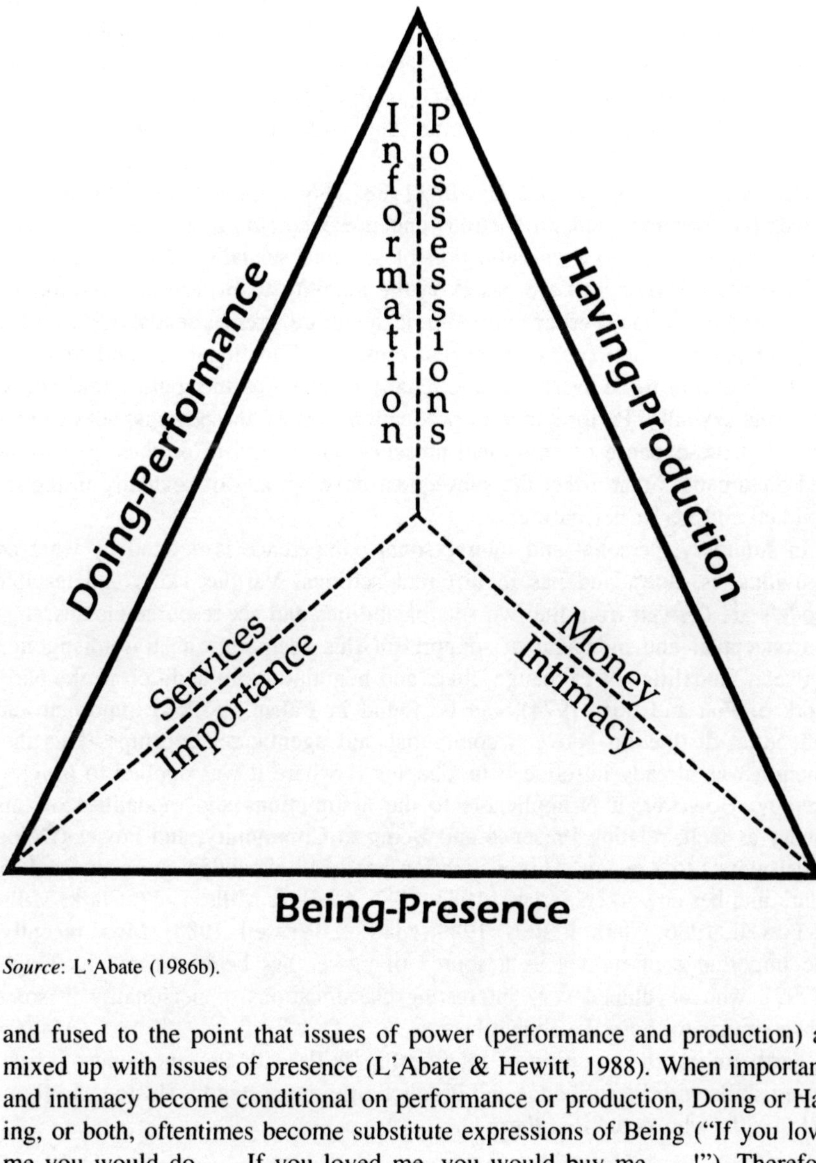

Source: L'Abate (1986b).

and fused to the point that issues of power (performance and production) are mixed up with issues of presence (L'Abate & Hewitt, 1988). When importance and intimacy become conditional on performance or production, Doing or Having, or both, oftentimes become substitute expressions of Being ("If you loved me you would do. . . . If you loved me, you would buy me . . . !"). Therefore, Being deals with the ability to attribute importance to self (status) and to others (partners, family members, or friends), and the ability to be intimate—sharing hurts and fears of being hurt.

The ability to negotiate also requires the skill to separate Being from Doing and Having in five different settings (residence, work, surplus time, transit, and transitory). Power is negotiated effectively and successfully in functional relationships but is negotiated ineffectively or unsuccessfully, or not negotiated at all, in dysfunctional ones. The greater the level of competence, the greater the possibility of successful negotiation. Unwillingness or inadequate ability to negotiate power is the basis for conflicts and struggles. We negotiate about what kind of information should be allowed in the home, who will provide which services within and without the home, and what should be bought with the money earned.

For instance, L'Abate and Hewitt (1988, 1989) applied the distinction of power (performance and production) and presence (importance and intimacy, i.e., Being Present) to a classification of sex and sexuality. They argued that most sexual dysfunctions are based on the inability to Be Present emotionally to self and to partner. Perhaps our American culture stresses sexual performance or production at the expense of sexual presence. Functional sex and sexuality imply an ability to be available emotionally to one's partner before one can be available sexually. Performance or production, that is, the physical act of intercourse at the expense of emotional presence, are bound to produce deviations and disturbances that affect the subsequent development of sexuality in the individual and his or her partners.

In summary, personal and interpersonal competence is defined by what an individual is, does, and has in different settings. Various skills and testable models are derived from the two sets of abilities and six resource classes.

Conceptual and independent support for this seemingly abstract distinction between modalities of exchange, love, and negotiation, in addition to the early work of Foa and Foa (1974), can be found in Bakan's (1968) important and influential distinction between communal and agentic relationships. This distinction was already introduced in Chapter 1, where it was applied to psychotherapy. However, it is applicable to the assumptions and modalities of this theory as well, relating Presence and Being to Community, and Power (Doing and Having) to Agency. This distinction has been expanded and supported by Clark and her coworkers (Clark, 1983, 1986; Clark & Mills, 1979; Clark, Mills, & Powell, 1986; Clark & Reis, 1988; Clark & Wassell, 1985). More recently, the importance of money as a source of power has been stressed by Doyle (1999), who developed very interesting classifications of personality in some ways similar to those developed here.

Furthermore, the equation of relationship skills with Presence and of structuring skills with Performance and Production is supported by Huston and Rempel (1989), who noted that there are:

> Two almost separate literatures . . . about family and other close relationships. One focuses on general interpersonal attitudes and dispositions such as love, commitment, and trust; the other centers on the analysis of behavioral exchanges, usually concentrating on the detailed examination of behaviors that take place during face-to-face interaction. (p. 177)

Huston and Rempel distinguished between the two literatures by referring to them as attitudinal/dispositional and behavioral, respectively. In relation to a developmental theory of interpersonal competence, the attitudinal/dispositional view would tend to support the postulate about the ability to love. The behavioral view would tend to support the postulate about the ability to negotiate. Both abilities are the two most fundamental processes for individual, dyadic, and family living. This distinction allows one to relate this developmental theory of interpersonal competence to communal psychotherapeutic practice—being emotionally available to respondents, that is, relationship skills—and to agentic practice—structuring therapy through workbooks (Chapter 1). However, as discussed in previous chapters, this context does not need to be face-to-face and verbal to be helpful.

Settings

Settings are necessary to evaluate and understand personality and psychological functioning in its totality, not just in a vacuum or in the abstraction of a laboratory, but in the very settings that occupy our lives. One could be extremely successful in one setting and a failure in another. A marvelous employee at work could be a failure at home. Without settings, psychological functioning would be evaluated and understood piecemeal. Furthermore, settings are necessary to evaluate and understand an individual's relationships with intimate and nonintimate others. The latter, like one's boss, may be responsible for one's economical and physical well-being. However, bosses would not be responsible for one's emotional well-being.

The nature of settings needs specification to detail the interaction of settings with the competencies, abilities, and skills that are manifested and used. As mentioned earlier, competence can be specified, even assessed, in a specific setting much more easily than can personality. Although personality seems to encompass a wide range of traits and states, most of them internal and difficult to measure, competence is limited to a definite number of settings. Competence may be a more restricted term than personality. However, it may also be easier to define and measure because, as suggested earlier, the interaction is more specific than person × situation. Of course, there is a resource class × setting interaction to the extent that money is negotiated in banks, information in schools, libraries and now on the Internet, services are provided in stores like hospitals and clinics (and now on the Internet), goods are sold in stores (and now on the Internet!), and so on. Only in the family do all resource classes coalesce and differentiate.

The importance of settings in determining behavior and interactions has been stressed by ecological psychologists (Moen, Elder, & Luscher, 1995). Each setting has its own peculiar, explicit or implicit rules, predictable or unpredictable regulations, peculiar requirements or task demands that are setting-specific and that differ from one setting to another. The three major settings where exchanges take place are: (a) residence; (b) school/work; and (c) surplus time. Surplus time is divided into survival and leisure-time activities, that is survival vs. enjoyment. All three settings interact and overlap with two other settings, transit and transitory. Transit settings are used for transportation to move from one setting to another, such as cars, buses, planes, trains, roads, highways, parking lots, airports, buses, or train stations. Transitory refers to settings that change over one's life cycle, such as schools, grocery stores, banks, barber shops, beauty salons, shopping malls, restaurants, churches, retail stores, sport arenas, and hotels. In some settings both dimensions overlap, for instance, in the residence. Some people have fun at work. Others work very hard in settings that are supposed to produce enjoyment, like gyms, parks, and recreational facilities.

Competencies and abilities vary according to the task requirements of each setting. The number of settings is finite and objectively defined. In order of functional importance, they are: residence, school/work, surplus time (survival & enjoyment), transit, and transitory. Of course, there may be overlaps among all five settings. For instance, leisure activities may take place in the home or, in some instances, in work settings as, for example, fitness rooms in workplaces. Competence in one setting does not necessarily predict and transfer to competence in another setting. One could be a terrific parent but a mediocre employee. By the same token, one could be a strong athlete during leisure hours but not function as well at work or at home.

Competence in various settings defines the level of functioning of an individual. Superior functioning, for instance, means being a caring and effective partner and parent, who excels in school or at work, enjoying leisure time activities after successfully completing survival tasks. By the same token, settings can be used to discriminate adequate from mediocre and/or inadequate functioning. Below are competencies relevant to each setting.

Residence

A residence, where one or more people live, is not necessarily a home. It is also the most private of all settings. One could live in a one-bedroom apartment all week to be close to work but leave on the weekend for what is called "home." A house or a dwelling does not make a home. Thus, residence is understood as a place where one lives most of the time. It may be called "home" if there are feelings attached to it, especially if loved ones live there also. This setting has task requirements that are related to the maintenance of a family as an emotional unit and to the home as a physical entity. Most responsibilities can be broken down into four specific roles: caretaker, provider, partner, and parent. Each role demands specific skills. For instance, the responsibilities of the *caretaking* role are of two kinds. One refers to the nurturing qualities that deal with love—being present and emotionally available. The other refers to instrumental qualities that deal with the physical and material well-being of the home, such as cooking, cleaning, purchasing, repairing. The role of *provider* deals with the economic aspects of family living. Salary, income, credit rating, and mortgages are aspects of this role. How much money comes into the home and how is it spent? Both caretaker and provider roles depend a great deal on the kind of person one is. How well one functions as a *partner* depends on a variety of personality competencies that will be summarized in the selfhood model to be presented below. In this role, abilities to love and to negotiate are necessary.

The fourth role—*parent*—is probably one of the most difficult and demanding in our lives, and is not without stress (Deater-Deckard, 1998). Often, this is the role for which we have received little if any training except for what we learned by watching our parents. Most of us perpetuate their errors and forget their assets because the task requirements of today are different from those of preceding generations. The ability to love and to negotiate become crucial at this stage. Consequently, an appropriate developmental sequence requires first of all the development of personhood as being basic to partnership. Both personhood and partnership are basic to parenthood. Being able to be a partner is basic to being a parent. Unfortunately, very few are lucky enough to develop in such an orderly sequence.

School/Work

Both settings require two separate but intertwined sets of skills. The first set consists of specific educational/occupational skills that are necessary to perform a job, such as reading, writing, arithmetic, filing, typing, drawing, writing, ditch digging, decision-making, delegating, and so on. The second set of skills is extra-job, consisting of interpersonal skills for getting along with schoolmates, peers, coworkers, superiors, clients, or customers. This set of skills may require interpersonal sensitivity, political gamesmanship, and contextual awareness. It may have little to do with the substantive job skills necessary for success. Yet, these skills may make the difference between promotion stagnation on the job, or being laid off!

In the Western culture, many people identify themselves according to their occupational roles. In fact, this role may often provide the main source of gratification. Therefore, it may require an investment of energy that would take away from other roles. We tend to identify ourselves by what we do or what we have instead of who we are as persons. What happens to us when we lose our jobs or retire? Do we have any self left? How does this role (unemployed or retired) interfere with other roles? The importance of the home and work settings for healthy functioning has been supported by, among many others, McCubbin, Thompson, Kretzschmar, Smith, Snow, McEwen, Elver, and McCubbin (1992). On the basis of a discriminant analysis of responses from 117 women and 39 men to a health risk inventory, they found six family and eight work factors in women that predicted health risk with 86.3% accuracy. They found six family and four work factors that predicted health risk for men with 87.2% accuracy.

Below are leftover skills that are neither home- nor school/work-related. Making fewer demands and having fewer requirements, these skills may be considered more discretionary than obligatory.

Surplus Time

These activities are divided into survival (paying bills, grocery shopping, buying clothes) and discretionary, or enjoyment-related. Survival skills are part of the roles reviewed under residence. Leisure activities, on the other hand, are discretionary, chosen freely by individuals who decide on how to spend time after survival responsibilities have been fulfilled. This time is sometimes spent at home, sometimes in other settings. Leisure time takes place in the company of others, or it can be solitary. It can be active or sedentary, indoor or outdoor, oriented toward people or toward things. Working in one's basement on a hobby, participating in the Elks Club, watching TV, going to church, or running a marathon—all are examples of activities in this setting. Leisure activities are important for one's enjoyment of life and for personality socialization. They are an integral part of how we function as individuals. These activities specify the value we put on friends and relationships. Leisure settings require skills that are specific to the activity being performed in a particular setting as well as skills used to develop and maintain relationships that are formed within each setting, whether partners, family members, relatives, friends, or just playmates.

Transit

These settings may have not been as important in the past as they are today, given our capacity to travel long distances in short periods of time. This capacity increases the number and variety of transit settings within which we interact each day (highways, airports, cars, buses). As perceptions about distance and time allotment change, the time and the activities spent in these settings may take on their own identity. Increased commuting time requires the acquisition of the skills to commute and to make the best of it. But the ease of commuting within settings may also increase the chance of overlap among settings. For instance, having an office in one's home may reduce commuting time. However, it may produce conflicts in fulfilling responsibilities one might not be required to fulfill if one had an office away from home.

Transitory

These settings are temporary and vary in importance from one person to another and from one family to another. Purchasing goods and services, shopping in a mall, going to a beauty salon, or attending a bar, may require different time and energy requirements, depending on how important one considers that activity. There are purchasing geniuses who spend a great deal of time plotting how to use coupons to get a better bargain and comparing costs for the same merchandise sold in different stores. Getting the oil changed at the corner garage, waiting in an unemployment line, completing the requirements for automobile registration, buying a bottle of aspirin—each takes us to a different setting. Each setting has peculiar role demands and codes. Transitory settings may seem less important than other settings, yet our ability to transact in these settings allows us to survive in the most important setting, the home.

To conclude, it should be stressed that settings are qualitatively and quantitatively different from contexts. Contexts are subjectively perceived by multiple observers—self and others within a given setting. Settings are objectively observable and measurable. For instance, one can measure how long one spends on household chores, how long one spends in leisure activities, and so on. The meaning of these activities represents the context as viewed by self and observers. While one observer may discount the importance of housework, for instance, another may value it as an importance contribution to the family's well-being and functioning. By the same token, one may spend a great deal of time at work, but not consider it as important as other family activities. Settings are objectively measured. Contexts are perceived and less easily measured than settings. Settings function at the macrolevel. Contexts function at the microlevel of observation. This distinction, as well as the use of Context in the ERAAwC model, should not be confused with being part of or similar to the many schools of thought that advocate various brands of "contextualism" (Capaldi & Proctor, 1999). By now the allegiances of this writer to traditional empiricism as active manipulation of variables should be clear.

Models

This theory is composed by one not-yet tested and nine testable models. A model is a simplified, usually visual, summary simplification, and representation of more complex concepts or patterns derived from the assumptions and postulates of the theory. For instance, the two assumptions of the theory, space and time (Figure 5.1), become more concrete and visible when distance and regulation with their respective polarities are visualized as two hortogonal dimensions, making them into a first model. By the same token, the three modalities of Being, Doing, and Having can be visualized as an equilateral triangle with Presence at the bottom, Performance on the left, and Production on the right (Figure 5.2), making them also into a second model.

A Not-yet Tested, Metatheoretical Model

This model has not been tested and is called metatheoretical because it goes above and beyond the theory itself. Furthermore, it belongs to various theories, independent from this one, all reviewed in previous works. This model pertains to levels of observation and interpretation, how to look at relationships and how to make sense of them. While relationships may be considered in their extensionality from internal to external (Table 5.1), this model pertains more to the deep, multilayered or multileveled dimension of relationships. It discriminates between two major levels, descriptive and explanatory. Each level is subdivided into two other levels.

The first descriptive level means the presentational level: what is visible and immediate, to the point of being photographed, audio-taped, or video-recorded. Description can either be public, including how a relationship is presented to outside observers ("I am a nice person with a nice marriage and nice children."), or more private, involving phenotypic aspects that may be hidden from the self, from intimate others, and from public observation and even measurement. What really happens in the secrecy and privacy of one's residence? The publicly "nice" person may phenotypically be actually a nasty partner, and a nasty parent with nasty children inside the home. The most hidden parts and the most difficult to access, confront, face, express, and share in relationships are hurt feelings and fears of being hurt.

The connection between presentational and phenotypic levels can be minimal or completely reversed. What is presented outwardly in public may be fairly consistent with what happens inside. Or, it can be extremely inconsistent, for instance, nice on the outside and nasty on the inside. By the same token, this connection, conceivably, could be reversed the other way—nasty on the outside and nice on the inside, with all possible consistencies and inconsistencies in between the public and the private. For instance, Activity (A) (doing and saying), in the ERAAwC model, is visible at the public level, while E is present but not always acsessible at the private level.

The public/presentational vs. private/phenotypical distinction is supported in part from Hussong's (2000) peer control model. She distinguished between overt vs. covert behavioral and verbal controls. Additional evidence to support this distinction has already been reviewed (L'Abate, 1994a, 1997c) and will be reviewed elsewhere (L'Abate, in preparation).

The explanatory level is what is used to make sense of both descriptive, presentational levels and phenotypical levels, by stressing determinants of A. It is subdivided into genotypic and historical levels. The former includes hypothetical (ego, superego) ascribed needs (drive, motivation), or inferred traits (extraversion, open-mindedness, etc.). The latter are constructs dear to theorists who stress the importance of specific traits inferred from self-report, paper-and-pencil instruments, such as the Big Five Factors model (reviewed in Chapter 4). These traits are used to "explain" why someone behaves or relates the way he or she did ("She is liberal because she is extroverted, open-minded, etc."). At this level function E, R, and Awareness (Aw) (in the ERAAwC model). They are the determinants, sometimes inferred, sometimes hypothetical, and sometimes elicited, of A.

The historical level consists of intergenerational, generational, and developmental events underlying a particular relationship, including the present situation in the family of procreation. This level "explains" all three levels better than any observable relationship or inferred trait. Here is where past traumas, illnesses, painful and joyful events help to understand how one relates with intimate others. Here is where Context (C), in the ERAAwC model, is omnipresent, as perceived and interpreted internally by respondents and externally by observers.

TESTABLE MODELS OF THE THEORY

Nine models are derived from the assumptions and postulates of the theory. The first two models—distance/regulation and presence, production, and performance—have already been introduced.

A Circular, Comprehensive Model

The third model, already introduced but needing expansion, is the circular Emotionality, Rationality, Activity, Awareness, and Context (ERAAwC) shown in Figure 5.3. As this figure shows, these five components vary in: (1) size, (2) strength of boundaries, and (3) amount of overlap. They produce completely different outcomes in behavior and intimate relationships.

This model fulfills at least three functions. First, it serves as a basis for an understanding of socialization from E to C. It would take too much space to expand on this function, already explained in previous works. Second, this model serves to describe an almost invariant sequence of steps in the process of negotiation. One ideally should start from E, expression and sharing feelings, progressing to R, discussing or brain-storming about possible courses of actions—their pros and cons—with agreement or consensus about following one particular course of Action. After trying A for a chosen period of time, ideally, there should be feedback in Aw about whatever has been learned during this course of Action. This feedback loop would return to E, starting the process all over again. This circular process takes place within the overarching Aw (feedback, acknowledgment, denial, or ignorance) of C. This process, of course, could take place internally, as a dialogue, as well as between and among individuals.

Third, this model serves as a basis for a classification of theories of personality and therapy. For instance, E has been stressed by humanistic schools. R has been stressed by psychodynamic, reality, cognitive-behavioral, and rational-emotive schools. A has been stressed by behavioral schools. Aw has been stressed by Gestalt or Gestalt-like schools or Eastern philosophies. C has been stressed by family therapies. The latter, as well as primary prevention programs, can be classified, in turn, according to the ERAAw components of the model (Hanson & L'Abate, 1982; L'Abate, 1981b; L'Abate & Frey, 1981; L'Abate, Frey, & Wagner, 1982; L'Abate, Ulrici, & Wagner, 1983).

Personality Differentiation According to a Continuum of Likeness in Close Relationships

The fourth model of this theory consists of a developmental continuum of likeness that underlies close relationships. The purpose of this continuum is to

Figure 5.3
Functional and Dysfunctional Aspects of E-R-A Model

A. Rigid Boundaries

1. Denial of context
2. Minimum Overlap Among Parts

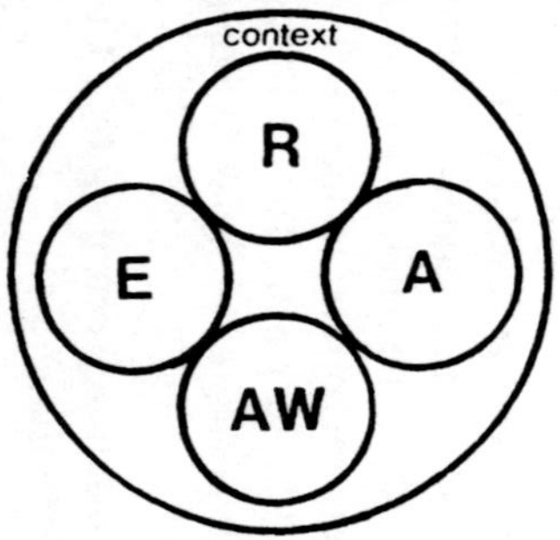

3. Maximum Separation of Parts

B. Balanced Boundaries

1. Awareness of context
2. Adequate Differentiation of Parts

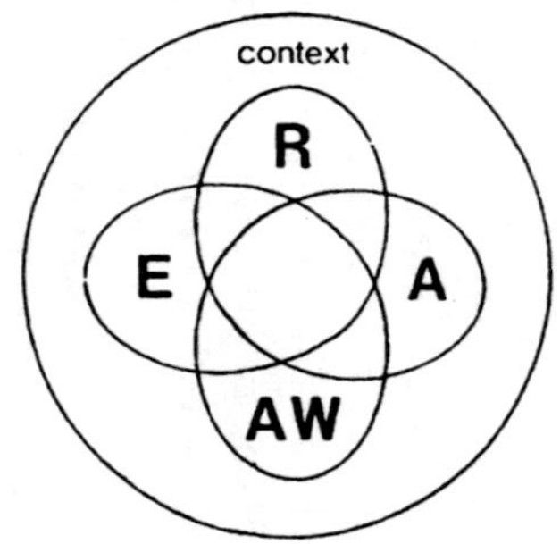

3. Appropriate Separation of Parts

C. Permeable Boundaries

1. Overintrusion of context
2. Maximum Overlap Among Parts

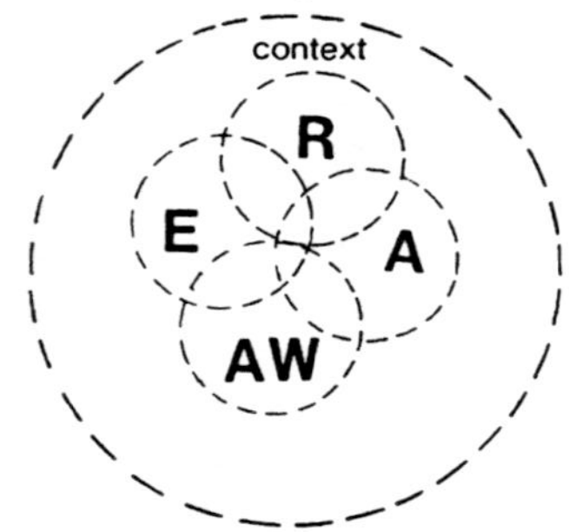

3. Minimum Separation of Parts

describe how people relate to each other in intimate and nonintimate relationships, an aspect not covered by previous models. This continuum was originally postulated as a bell-shaped, dialectical distribution consisting of six ranges: Symbiosis (Johnson, 1991), Sameness, Similarity, Differentness, Oppositeness, and Alienation (Figure 5.4; L'Abate, 1976, p. 79). No single range can conceivably describe behavior in intimate relationships by itself, isolated from other ranges. Each range needs a counterpart to define itself according to a combination of two ranges dialectically related to each other. For instance, the combination of the two extremes of the distribution, Symbiosis with Alienation, would lead toward an Abusive-Apathetic (Neglectful) interpersonal style (AA) and individual-relational pathology in close relationships. The combination of Sameness with Oppositeness, at the intermediate level in the distribution, would lead toward a Reactive-Repetitive, conflictful and competitive style (RR), intra- and inter-personally. The combination of Similarity and Differentness, in the center of the distribution, would lead toward a positively collaborative Conductive-Creative style (CC). These three styles serve as a basis for the fifth ARC model (Figure 5.4), which has two dysfunctional interpersonal styles, AA and RR, and a functional style CC.

Hence, in Figure 5.4, a dimension of psychopathology lies vertically at the bottom and two extremes of the distribution, while emotional and mental health are intermediate in the middle. Creativity lies in the center of the distribution. Creativity here means interacting and relating with intimate others in extremely positive ways, according to the CC style. It does not mean creativity in artistic, scientific, or professional endeavors. In the middle of the distribution (Similarity-Differentness) the likelihood of functionality in most relationships would be high, where differences (Aiken, 1999) are reconciled with a minimum of conflict. By the same token, in the two intermediate ranges (Sameness-Oppositeness) an intermediate level of functionality would be predicted. In the two extremes of the distribution (Symbiosis-Alienation), dysfunctionality would be highest.

How Did this Continuum Develop Theoretically?

The theoretical origins of this continuum have been explained in previous publications. Conceptually, its predecessors are found in: (1) social comparison theory, (2) concepts of imitation, identity, and identification in developmental and personality theories, and (3) self-differentiation theory (Barone, Hersen, & Van Hasselt, 1998; Cate & Loyd, 1988; Duck & Pittman, 1994; Ewen, 1988). Briefly, a child develops a sense of self-identity and becomes socialized, at least in part, by comparing itself with major caretakers, modeling, mimicking, and imitating how they relate to each other and to the child. For instance, the child may learn positive or negative behavior, relating positively to both caretakers, or positively to one caretaker and negatively to the other, or negatively to both.

Figure 5.4
Continuum of Likeness, Hurt Feelings, and Styles in Intimate Relationships

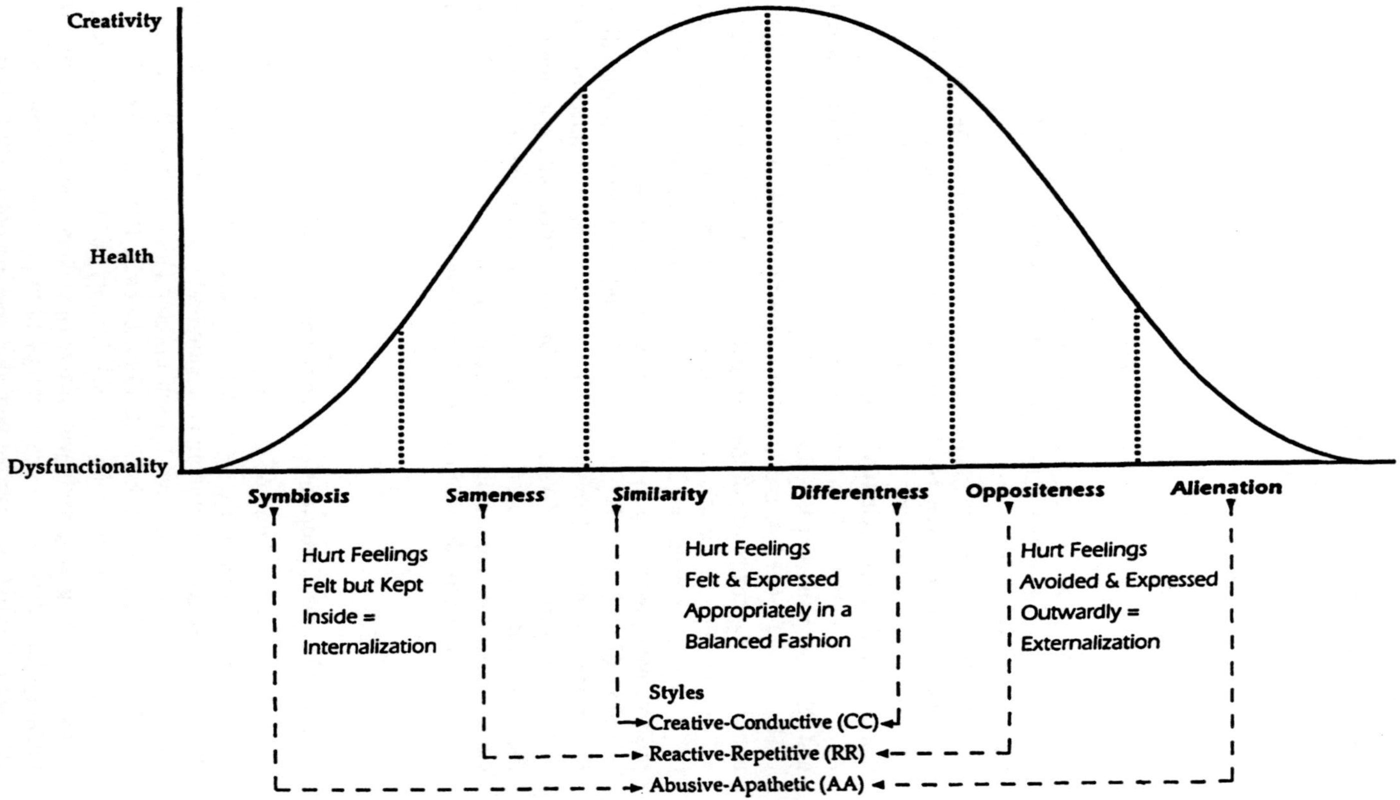

Whether the behavior is positive or negative depends, of course, on the behavior of the caretakers.

The three developmental processes, social comparison, identification, and self-differentiation are explained in the extant literature through a single dichotomy of similarity-dissimilarity, a process that also takes place within couples and between parents and children. Early theories describing these processes, however, were usually acontextual, nonrelational, and rather vague in terms of their interpersonal origins. Social comparison, identification, and self-differentiation seemed to develop in a vacuum, without specific relationships with intimate others (as discussed earlier). Furthermore, since similarity was conceptualized according to a simple dichotomy of similar-dissimilar, no other possibilities on a continuum were considered. Consequently, this relational continuum was deemed necessary to "describe" or even "explain" self-differentiation in close relationships. It meant going well beyond a simple-minded dichotomy of similarity-dissimilarity and extending it to a continuum of six ranges.

The Need for a Continuum of Likeness

The need to describe self-differentiation from a developmental viewpoint, at least in part, according to a continuum of likeness, has been highlighted by three recent contributions to the literature. In the first, Hojjat (1997) reviewed research on similarity. This term has been used in the literature to describe one side of a dichotomy, as noted earlier, rather than to denote just one specific range of a continuum, as used here. In this regard, Hojjat noted that:

> Few studies, if any, have dealt with the topic of similarity from a theoretical point of view . . . the importance of similarity appears to extend to all phases of a relationship, from early attraction to the later stages, where partners may construct their own reality. (p. 115)

For Hojjat, similarity is nothing less than a "shared philosophy of life" (p. 115), covering a multitude of topics, such as "political attitudes, privacy preferences, moral standards and sex," and "even food preferences" (p. 115). If Hojjat's conclusion is valid, then similarity would seem fundamental to a process of self-differentiation in close relationships, not just attraction. She concluded her review with this statement: "Similarity literature dating back to the 1960s has mostly been concerned with the role of similarity in attraction rather than satisfaction. *No theoretical model has presented an integrated and detailed account of satisfaction based on similarity*" (p. 121, italics added). If that is the case, it would be relatively easy to predict satisfaction in intimate relationships from a viewpoint of a continuum of likeness. In Symbiosis-Alienation (Abuse-Apathy), there would be extremes in emotionally close relationships, hence, there could not be satisfaction of practically any sort. If there were satisfaction, it would be either at its lowest or it would consist of dissatisfaction. In Sameness-

Oppositeness (Reactivity-Repetitiveness), satisfaction would be sporadic, conflictual, and rather low or intermediate at best. In Similarity-Differentness (Creativity-Conductiveness), the level of satisfaction would be at its highest.

In the second contribution, Felmlee (1998) used questionnaire data from 301 terminated romantic relationships to investigate whether a quality that was initially appealing to respondents was disliked later, as the relationship was dissolving ("fatal attraction"):

> Individuals are expected to be prone to fatal attractions when they are attracted to a quality in a romantic partner that is "different" in any of three ways: (1) different from the individual's own qualities (i.e., dissimilar); (2) different from average (i.e., extreme, or unique); or (3) different from normative expectations (i.e., gender atypical). Such attractions are less likely, however, when individuals are drawn to similarity in another. (p. 235)

From her data, using a logistic regression analysis, Felmlee found that:

> Fatal attractions are significantly more likely when an individual is drawn to partner characteristics seen either as "dissimilar" from his or her own, as "unique" or as "extreme" in nature. When these characteristics are viewed as "similar," disenchantment is less likely. (p. 235)

In discussing the implications of her findings, Felmlee concluded:

> My results have implications for several theories, including those that address the issue of whether "oppositeness attract". . . . at least in some cases, "opposites" do attract. Nevertheless, such attractions are more apt to be "fatal" than when dissimilarity is not the source of allure. In other words, "opposites" may attract, but they also repel. . . . Dissimilarity within a couple can play a crucial role in relationship dissolution. On the other hand, as some degree of variation between partners is unavoidable, it is obvious that diversity is not inevitably linked to breakups. . . . Dissimilarity may be particularly troublesome, however, when it is the source of initial attraction . . . *Theoretical work on the role of differences in intimate pairings has been quite limited.* . . . Much more attention has been devoted to the function of similarity. *The research reported herein implies that dissimilarity is deserving of at least as much attention.* (pp. 249–50, italics added)

The third contribution (Chappell & Davis, 1998) illustrated how important similarity is for the attachment-security process in romantic relationships. Unfortunately, once similarity is accepted as a dimension, without further distinction among different levels of similarity, it is rather difficult to make more specific predictions about behavior in close relationships.

Nonetheless, all three contributions, at least indirectly, suggest the importance of considering a continuum of likeness rather than a simple similar-dissimilar dichotomy. At the same time, these contributions appear rather limited conceptually by the absence of a theoretical model. For instance, Felmlee's interpretations of her results are hampered by the difficulty of distinguishing "differentness" from "oppositeness" at the conceptual as well as at the empirical level. By the same token, her qualification of differentness according to three criteria—dissimilarity, uniqueness, and nonnormativeness—is a distinct conceptual contribution to an amplification of this range. An additional distinction about differentness would consist of its being "unusual" behavior that is not encountered often and may be unconventional, creative, and even rebellious. All three contributions validate the need for a theoretical elaboration of a continuum rather than just a simple dichotomy. Of course, this continuum is relevant to theories of close relationships, integrating both complementarity and similarity theories (Chappell & Davis, 1998). Complementarity, for instance, may be positive when similarity and differentness are combined, but it would be negative when sameness and oppositeness are combined.

Applications of a Continuum of Likeness

Applications of this continuum to various intra-inter-personal situations are many. Very briefly, as summarized in Table 5.2, starting developmentally with two processes of Approach-Avoidance in distance (space) and Discharge-Delay in regulation (time), it is possible to expand this continuum and apply it to various intrapersonal and interpersonal situations. Not all situations can describe all individuals. For instance, one individual could conceivably be in the middle of the distribution in one situation, let us say, parental practices, and be at one extreme in another situation, let us say, personality propensities. Being in one range in one situation does not necessarily predict where one would be in the range of another situation, even though the likelihood of being in the same range over a variety of situations would be high. Of course, the more situations describe an individual or a relationship between individuals, the greater the chances of functionality or dysfunctionality.

Likeness and Hurt Feelings

Feelings—how one perceives and experiences emotionally tinged situations—and how these feelings are expressed as emotions develop along a continuum of likeness. Feelings can be kept inside or can be expressed outwardly verbally, motorically, or manually. How feelings are experienced and expressed is a process related to how differentiated an individual is, as defined by the Likeness Continuum. The direction of these feelings can be internalized and kept inside in symbiosis and sameness, or it can be externalized and directed outwardly in oppositeness and alienation (Figure 5.4). These two processes reach maximum dysfunctionality when they coexist, as shown dialectically by this continuum, producing extreme, inconsistent, and contradictory expressions shown in severe psychopathology. The inward or outward direction of how feelings are expressed will be elaborated in the next model.

Table 5.2
Developmental Applications of a Likeness Continuum

Functions	Symbiosis	Sameness	Similarity/Differentness	Oppositeness	Alienation
Distance	Extremes in Ap/Av	Ap < Av*	Balance in Ap/Av	Ap > Av ***	Extremes in Ap/Av
Control	Extremes in Di/De	De > Di	Balance in Di/De	Di > De	Extremes in Di/De
Positivity/Negativity	−−	−+	++	+−	−−
Interaction Outcomes	−/− Split**	O Repetition Status Quo	X Growth Change	O Repetition Revolution	−/− Split
Characteristics	Folie à deaux	Blind & uncritical Conformity	Enlightened creativity and conformity	Rebelliousness Defiance of norms	Criminalities
Personality Propensities	No-Self	Selfless	Selful	Selfish	No-self
Parental Styles	Abusive Permissive	Reactive Authoritarian	Conductive Authoritative	Reactive Oppositional	Abusive Violent
Parental Practices	"I cannot live without you. Live for me."	"Be and do exactly like I do"	"Follow my example but use your head" "Be and do whatever you like to achieve what you want"	"I will do the opposite of what I was told to do by my parents."	"You will be severely punished regardless of how you behave."

Identification	"I am you"	"I am like you"	"I am somewhat like you" "I am different from you"	"I am the opposite of you"	"I am not" or "I am tough and mean"
Directionality	Internalization ← Extremes	Balanced directions			→ Externalization Extremes
Dependencies	Extreme dependence	Dependence	Autonomous interdependence	Denial of dependence	Extremes between dependence and its denial
Ability to Love	Almost nonexistent	Inadequate	Adequate to superior	Inadequate	Almost nonexistent
Ability to Negotiate	Almost nonexistent	Inadequate	Adequate to superior	Inadequate	Almost nonexistent
Power Orientation	Anarchic	Dominant-dictatorial to blindly submissive	Democratic	Autocratic	Anarchic
Identity Formation and Sexual Orientation	Fused Confused	Traditional Conventional Passive	Active-creative	Unconventional Nontraditional Active Opportunistic	Rigid Extreme Diffused
Appearance	Disheveled to conventional	Conventional	Individualized	Nonconforming	Uncaring to conforming
Level of Adjustment	Very poor	Borderline to questionable	Adequate to superior	Borderline to questionable	Very poor

Table 5.2 *(continued)*

Most Likely Psychiatric Diagnoses	Psychoses	Affective disorders Anxieties Dependencies Depressions	None to mild adjustment disorders	Impulse and character disorders	Criminalities
Marital or Intimate Relationships	Extremely variable	Conflictful to very conflictful	Relatively harmonious	Conflictful to very conflictful	Extremely variable
Academic Achievement	Very inadequate	Adequate	Adequate to superior	Inadequate	Very inadequate
Resistance to Change	High to very high	Moderate	Little to none	High	High to very high

*Av = Avoidance; Ap = Approach; De = Delay; Di = Discharge.

**A split may be intrapersonal, like suicide or mental illness on the symbiotic side, or murder and incarceration on the alienation side.

***Interpersonal Ap high but internal Ap to hurts low

The Selfhood Model

In addition to using an underlying Likeness Continuum to describe the subtle and not so subtle or not so obvious development of functionality, internalizations-externalizations, and psychopathology in relationships, it was necessary to introduce a sixth model. This one deals with how intimates interact with each other in a fairly visible fashion. Here is where the metatheoretical model of levels of observation and interpretation comes into being. People behave in different ways in different settings and at different levels of observation and interpretation. How one relates privately at home does not necessarily predict how one is going to relate in other public settings. Furthermore, the resource class of importance needs expansion into a full-fledged model. How does the Self manifest itself to describe, if not explain, personality propensities that predict how individuals relate with each other? Hence, this Selfhood model assumes that attribution, ascription, and assertion of importance is the primary, fundamental resource exchanged among intimates and nonintimates, verbally, nonverbally, and in writing.

Once the assumptions of approach-avoidance and discharge-delay are brought to bear on how one relates in intimate relationships, four possibilities come to the fore (Figure 5.5). When there is an appropriate balance of distance and regulation processes, there is the development of functional relationships, seen in a personality propensity called Selfulness. When approach is greater than avoidance and discharge is greater than delay, there is the development of a personality development called Selfishness. When avoidance is greater then approach and delay greater than discharge, there is the development of a personality propensity called Selflessness. When there are extreme and contradictory imbalances in distance and regulation processes, there is the development of a personality propensity called No-self.

These four propensities derive from the two assumptions of distance and regulation, coupled with the attribution of importance. This model is called Selfhood because it makes self-importance, as conceived and observed by self and others, the centerpiece of exchanges between and among intimates (partners, parent-child, sibling-sibling). The self is shown by how one relates with intimates in close, prolonged, and committed relationships. This process takes place away from the scrutiny of occasional outsiders in the privacy of one's home, where self-presentational facades cannot last very long.

1. *Selfulness* represents the positive attribution of importance to and concern for self and intimate others, resulting in a positive outcome and synergistic growth in the relationship ("We both win."). Selfulness tends to balance distance (the ability to love) and regulation (the ability to negotiate) processes appropriately. In this personality propensity, issues of presence, that is, being emotionally available to self and intimate others, are kept separate from issues of power, that is, negotiation and problem-solving. From this propensity develop mostly functional relationships.

Figure 5.5
A Selfhood Model Derived from a Developmental Theory of Interpersonal Competence

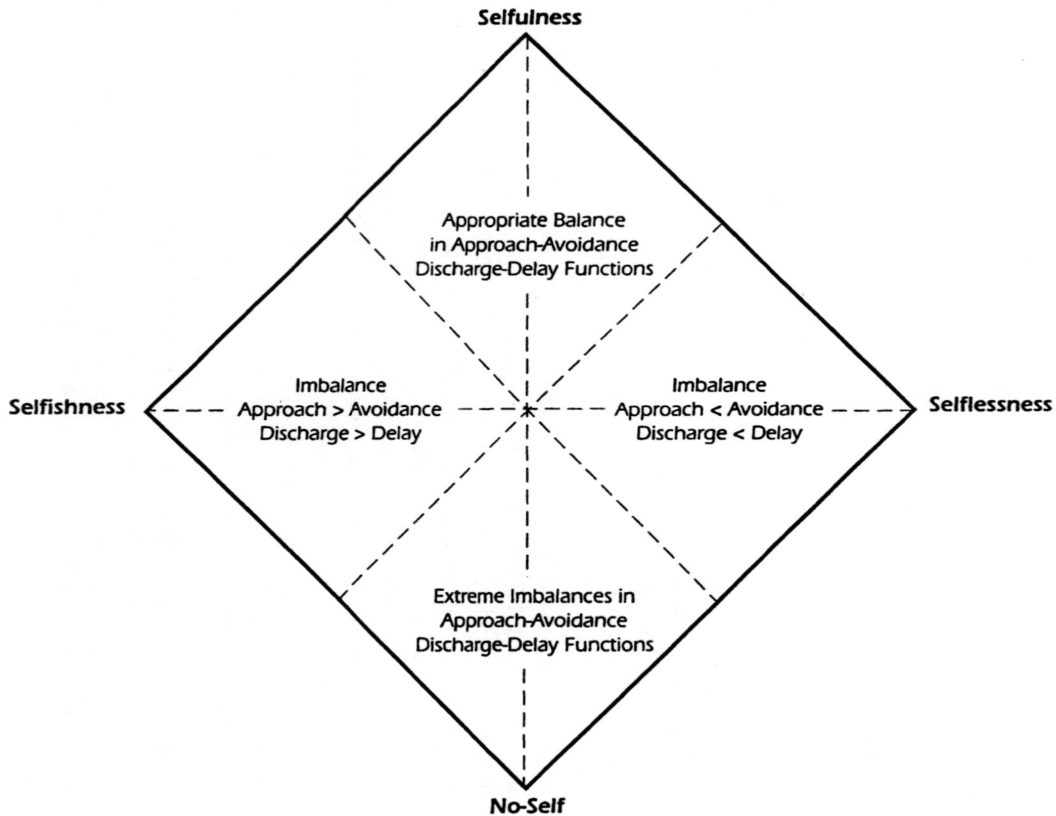

Source: L'Abate (1994a).

2. *Selfishness* represents the positive attribution of importance to and concern for self and the negative attribution of importance to and little if no concern for intimate others, resulting in a conflictful outcome and no growth in the relationship ("I win, you lose"). Selfishness tends to rely more on approach than on avoidance, and more on discharge than on delay. Individuals characterized by this propensity tend to push limits (do and take as much as they can get away with) on their partners, authorities, and anybody else who lets them, as seen in the pathological extremes of this propensity, like addictions and criminalities (Fishbein, 2000). Extremes in selfishness are represented, therefore, in *externalizations*, where the self is asserted at the expense of others, as in assault, theft, rape, and murder. Of course, there are various degrees of selfishness, from self-centered egoism to narcissistic self-absorption, and semifunctional selfish behaviors that take place at no cost to anyone else. In this context, there are positive and negative expressions of selfishness that will be detailed in future work (L'Abate, in preparation).
3. *Selflessness* represents the negative attribution of importance to and little or no concern for the self, and positive attribution of importance to and concern for others, not necessarily intimates. This results in a conflictual stasis in the relationship ("You win, I lose"). Selflessness tends to rely more on avoidance than on approach and on delay more than on discharge. Individuals characterized by this propensity are unable to draw lines to protect themselves and their bodies ("the condom line"), as in the case of so-called codependent individuals, usually spouses of addicts and criminals. Selfless individuals tend to be gullible, loyal, and responsible, trying to make up complementary qualities not found in selfish individuals. They are attracted to selfish individuals just as the latter are attracted by the former, producing in the long run antagonistic and conflictual relationships, in which divorce may be one of the ultimate outcomes. Of course, there are various degrees of selflessness, ranging from functional to dysfunctional, positive or negative.

   The main characteristic of relationships polarized along the selfish-selfless dimension is the selfless individuals' unrealistic optimism, hoping that somehow selfish partners will eventually, by some miracle, change for the better. Selfless individuals are defective in drawing lines and setting definite limits to protect themselves and their bodies from selfish partners (L'Abate & Harrison, 1992). This selfish-selfless dimension has been subjected to a great many theories and theorettes in psychology as well as other disciplines (Sober & Wilson, 1998). Extremes in selflessness consist of *internalizations* found in depressions, anxiety, panic, and affective disorders, which lead to suicide, either slow and prolonged, real or metaphoric, as in some addictions, or sudden, unexpected explosions.
4. *No-self* represents the negative attribution of importance to self and other, with little if no concern for either, resulting in a negatively nihilistic, chaotic, and ultimately destructively deteriorating breakdown in relationships ("We both lose. Neither you nor I are going to win."). No-self relies on contradictory and inconsistent extremes in both distance and regulation processes. Extremes of No-self are represented by severe *psychopathology*, as in paranoias, schizoid, and schizophrenic type disorders, combining both ruthlessness and attack with apathy, passivity, and submission.

These four personality propensities are related to the three styles of intimate relationships derived from a continuum of likeness: Abusive-Apathetic for No-self, Reactive-Repetitive for Selfishness and Selflessness, and Conductive-Creative for Selfulness. Intimacy and negotiation are possible in Selfulness, chancy and conflictual in Selfishness and Selfless, and impossible in No-self. As shown in Figure 5.6, relationships with the attachment model, concurrently equated with Selfhood, are in parenthesis. As promised, this model discriminates among one higher level of functionality, two levels intermediate in dysfunctionality—externalization and internalization—and a lower level of dysfunctionality.

From this model it is possible to derive an integrative classification of personality, criminality, and psychopathology, as shown in Figure 5.7. Instead of a series of ordinal categories without any relationship among themselves, as found in the *Diagnostic and Statistical Manual of Mental Disorders* (DSM-IV), this model sees functionality, dysfunctionality, and personality disorders as being contiguous and continuous with each other in an integrated whole. This model of psychopathology was evaluated with the MMPI-2 as well as the Doverspike Rating Sheets (L'Abate, Lambert, & Schenk, 2001), using four algorithms with more than 800 clinical respondents whose data were made available by 75 clinical psychologists in Georgia. The results of this study tended to support a relationship between measures of externalization with ratings of externalization, measures of internalization with ratings of internalization, and measures of psychopathology with severe psychopathology. Since this was a sample of clinical respondents, there was no way to measure functionality.

This selfhood model has been related conceptually to and compared with similar models (L'Abate, 1994a), among them: self-esteem (p. 123), attachment patterns (p. 137), dependency (p. 138), emotions (p. 139), thinking patterns (p. 141), temporal perspective (p. 143), and personality, affective disorders, and psychopathology (p. 144). More recently (L'Abate, 1997c), this model has been related with ego defenses (p. 181), De Giacomo's (1993; L'Abate, 1994b) elementary pragmatic model (pp. 183–187), family defense mechanisms (p. 187), an analytical model of family paradigms (pp. 187–189), Olson's (1993) circumplex model of family relationships (pp. 188–191), and McCubbin, Thompson, Kretzschmar, Smith, Snow, McEwen, Elver, and McCubbin's (1992) model of family types and strengths (pp. 190–191). Comparisons among all these models were made on the basis of the two assumptions of approach-avoidance and discharge-delay (pp. 193–196).

The relationship of the selfhood model with another model developed by Benenson (1996) is illustrated in Figure 5.8. Further comparisons of this model with classifications of feelings and emotions will be made below.

From the four personality propensities relevant to the Selfhood model (Table 5.3), it is now clear how these propensities are related to workbooks independent of the theory itself as well as to workbooks derived directly from the theory. Regardless of theory, however, this foursome classification allows for a more specific administration of workbooks than would be possible otherwise.

Figure 5.6
Personality Propensities: Psychopathology, Internalization-Externalization, and Attachment Styles

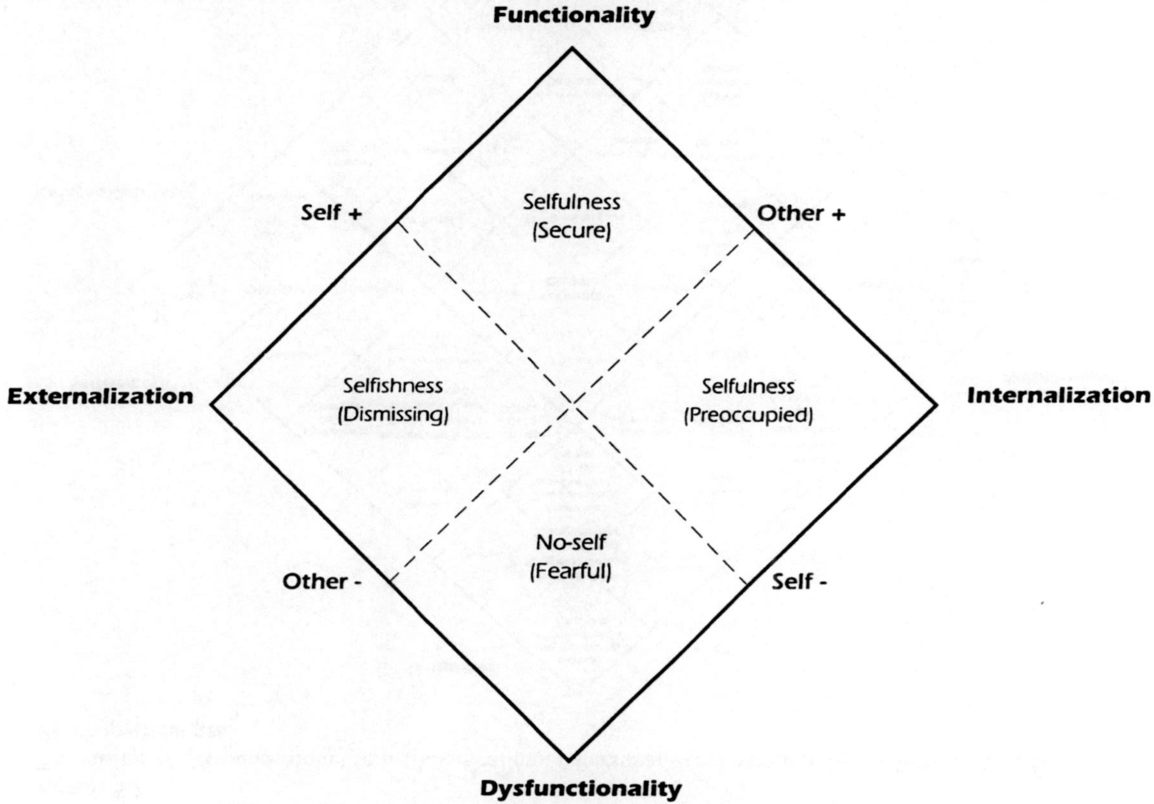

Figure 5.7
Expansion of Selfhood Model to a Classification of Personalities, Criminalities, Affective Disorders, and Psychopathologies

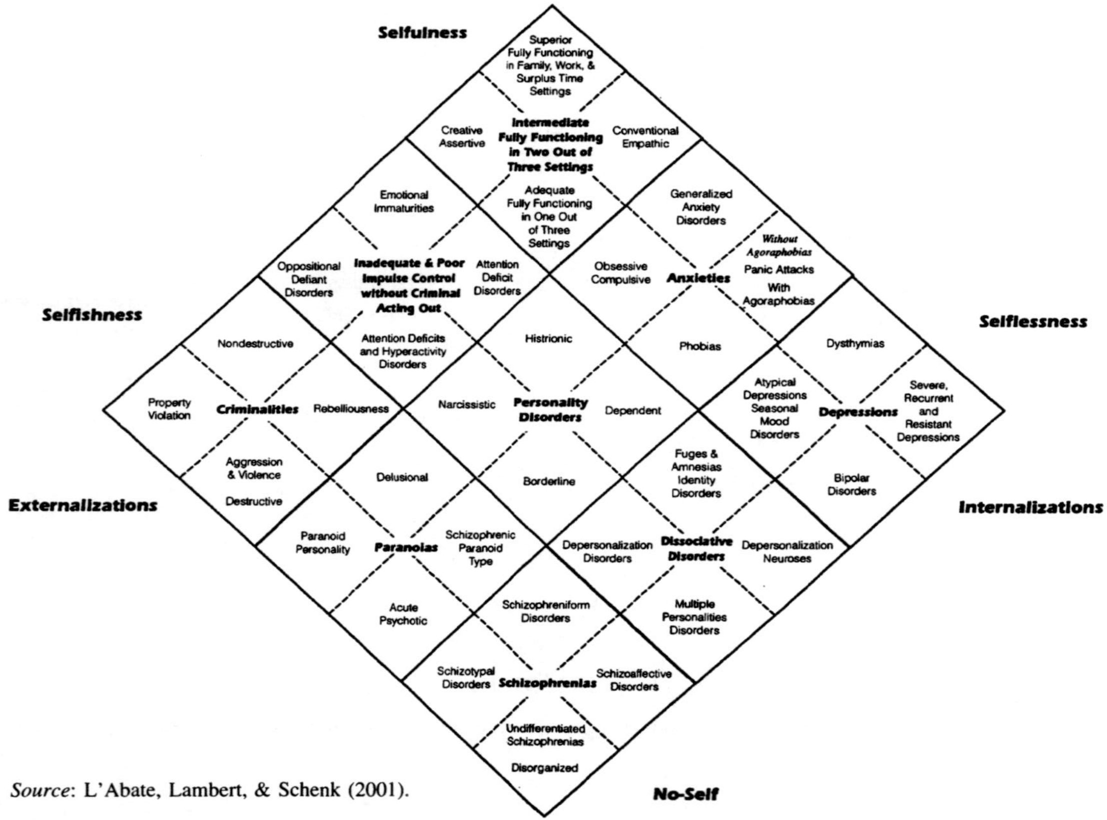

Source: L'Abate, Lambert, & Schenk (2001).

Figure 5.8
Expansion of Selfhood Model to Include Benenson's (1996) Model and Other Character Types

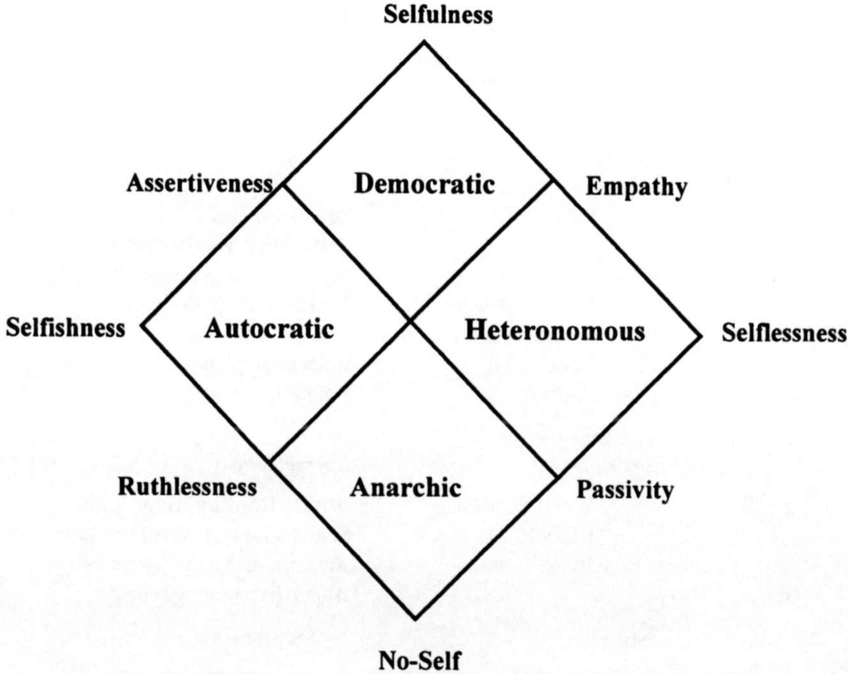

Priorities

To understand how we allocate time and energy within each setting and from one setting to another, we need to invoke a seventh model of priorities. This model is motivational in nature and similar to "goals" in the work of other theorists (Carver & Scheier, 1999). Priorities pertain to choices we make about who and what is important in our lives. How important is a person, an object, or an activity? How important is one's self in relationship to other selves? In a way, the Selfhood model is another way to look at Priorities. However, the Priorities model goes beyond Selfhood. It also includes settings and contexts within each setting. One setting can be enhanced or reduced in importance by increasing or decreasing the importance of other settings. For example, pleasurable activities in the leisure area can become direct antidotes for the negative effects of stresses at work or at home. How one juggles and counterbalances demands and difficulties in maintaining balance in one's life reflects one's priorities. Priorities motivate people to negotiate important issues in their lives with themselves and with significant others. By the same token, narrow and confused or dysfunctional priorities may motivate avoidance of any intimacy and nego-

Table 5.3
Classification of Representative Workbooks for Individuals According to the Selfhood Model

	Selflessness	Selfulness
	Internalizations	*Balance in Externalization and Internalization*
Importance of Other		
High		
O	Depression	Self-Awareness
	Anxiety	Self–Other workbooks*
	Fears	Normative experiences
T	Codependency*	Social skills
	Procrastination	Multiple abilities
	Loneliness	Relationship styles
H	Phobias	Emotional intelligence
	Extremes in Internalizations and Externalizations	*Externalizations*
E	Social Growth	Anger, Hostility, Aggression
	PTSS/PTSD	Social Training & Addendum*
	BPRS	Juvenile & Adult Psychopathy
R		Anger Expression/Temper
	No-self	Selfishness

Low —————————————————————— High
1 2 3 4 5
Self-importance

*Workbooks developed from the Selfhood Model of the theory.

tiation. Sober and Wilson (1998), in addition to their distinct contribution to the whole dimension of altruism-egotism, distinguished between instrumental and ultimate desires. Instrumental desires here are equated with survival priorities, while ultimate desires are equated with enjoyment priorities (Table 5.4).

These priorities can be measured easily by time analysis. How much time does one spend in each setting? What modality of expression for Being, Doing, or Having is being used in a primary, secondary, and tertiary manner? Of course, Being is much more relevant to the home setting than Doing and Having at work. The latter modalities are more relevant and primary at work and in leisure settings. How important are Being, Doing, and Having? How are these priorities evaluated? Are other selves more important than ours? If this is the case, why and how are they important? As shown in the Selfhood model, individuals choose how self relates with other selves. However, the Selfhood model needs to be expanded and specified further. At this point, one can see that, thus far,

Table 5.4
Toward a Hierarchy of Priorities: At What Level of Observation and Interpretation?

1. Processes
   Survival .... Enjoyment
   Instrumental .... / .... *Ultimate**
   Discharge-Delay .... / .... Approach-Avoidance
2. Contents — Experiencing
   Money/Goods/Services/Information — Importance/Intimacy
   Having .... Doing .... / .... Being
   Horizontal (Settings) .... / .... Vertical (Self-Other)
   Power .... Presence
   Negotiation .... Being together
3. *Components* (RAC) — (EAwC)
4. Differentiation: *Continuum of Likeness and Its Applications*
5. Selfhood: *Personality Propensities*

Source: *Sober & Wilson (1998).

all models in this theory are sequential expansions of previously presented models. One model builds on a previous one. The leaves of the artichoke are being peeled off.

Priorities can be divided into *vertical* and *horizontal*. Vertical priorities can be differentiated into the three modalities of Being, Doing, and Having. Personal, family, and interpersonal priorities are ranked according to the relative importance given to self and significant others. Vertical priorities are developmental, horizontal priorities are structural. The latter exist regardless of a person's level of development. One may value Doing more than Having or Being, stressing the work setting at the expense of the home and leisure settings. This emphasis, for instance, could define the great American workaholic man or woman. By the same stereotypic token, of course, a woman may be described by her stress on Being present emotionally in the home. Work and leisure settings may be considered secondary to her emotional availability. In other words, vertical and horizontal priorities intersect and interact with each other to produce different outcomes.

How successful one is in any of these settings depends a great deal on one's priorities. If one defines oneself primarily in occupational terms, obtaining a sense of importance from one's job ("I am an engineer") rather than domestically ("I am a partner and a parent"), it follows that that person may spend more time and energy at work than at home. By the same token, avocational pursuits may overshadow domestic and occupational roles. There is a need to balance modalities and settings so that no one modality or setting is stressed at the expense of the others.

Priorities and Awareness (Aw): A Hierarchy of Priorities

Some priorities are automatic, outside the realm of Aw. Other priorities are completely conscious and within the realm of Aw, including pleasant and unpleasant memories (Bargh & Chartrand, 1999; Cleyman, 1992; Gollwitzer, 1999; Kirsch & Lynn, 1999; Wegner & Wheatley, 1999). Within this dimension, defined by automatic/nonconscious Aw at one end and by intentional/conscious Aw at the other end, there is a whole hierarchy of possible choices or priorities. The choices we make are based on how important the content or process of that choice is to us. The salience and satisfaction derived from each modality and setting remain an individual prerogative that determines how each modality and setting is ranked in respect to how important other modalities and settings are.

Primary priorities are automatic and outside of the realm of individual Aw. They are called primary because they develop earlier in the life-cycle than secondary ones. Consequently, they are more difficult to change, like one's ability to be close or distant and the ability to negotiate or not to negotiate. Secondary priorities are semiautomatic and somewhat within the realm of individual Aw, depending, of course, on how wide and deep Aw is, varying a great deal from one individual to another. Tertiary priorities are within the realm of Aw and within the conscious regulation of the individual. They become voluntary and intentional. Quartic priorities consist of routine, everyday behaviors that are taken for granted as a matter of course, like brushing one's teeth, taking a shower, etc. This hierarchy of priorities is similar to the one proposed by Carver and Scheier (1999) in regard to goals, a notion that is conceptually similar to priorities but more difficult to evaluate.

Ease of change is greater with quartic realities and decreases going up this hierarchy. It is easier to change how one brushes one's teeth or takes a shower than to change developmentally produced, life-long habits that have been established automatically since early age, as in the case of approach versus avoidance and discharge versus delay processes. Secondary, semiautomatic priorities include the modalities of Being, Doing or Having, where, normatively speaking, Being is balanced with Doing and Having. Dysfunctionalties develop when Doing > Having or Being, or Having > Doing or Being. If economic survival is the major priority, Doing and Having would be the only necessary modalities. However, if enjoyment is an added goal, then Being emotionally present to self and other needs to be added as an additional priority.

Voluntary, intentional, tertiary priorities include the ERAAawC model. Normatively, there are various choices available, each with its pros and cons, as, for instance, in E > R or A; R > E or A; A > R or E; R > A or E. For instance, emphasis on R at the expense of E may lead toward obsessive-compulsive disorders. Emphasis on A at the expense of E or R may lead toward impulsive or driven behavior. Emphasis on E at the expense of R or Aw may lead toward hysteric moods and episodes. Additionally, within each component of this model, there are choices to be made according to which priority is relevant. For instance, within E one must chose between disclosure versus nondisclosure, expression versus nonexpression, sharing versus nonsharing, positive versus negative expression. Within R, one can chose whether to use versus nonuse, privacy versus nonprivacy in relationship to E and A. Within A one must choose whether to be destructive vs. nondestructive, helpful versus hurtful. Within Aw one needs to choose whether to allow Aw to vary in reference to intrusion versus rejection, acceptance versus refusal, and overuse versus underuse or disuse. Within C one can choose between its denial versus acknowledgment and awareness of C valuing versus dismissing it. Of course, many individuals do not feel they have choices concerning these components. Again, it depends on what is most important to them in terms of their level of differentiation in likeness, interpersonal style, and personality propensity.

Within this level of tertiary conscious choices are *vertical* priorities pertaining to the self, others, parents, partner, children, relatives, friends, and neighbors, and *horizontal* priorities relevant to settings, pertaining to home, school/work, leisure time activities, These priorities are related to the Likeness Continuum by being differentiated and functional within the middle (Figure 5.4), and undifferentiated and dysfunctional toward the two sides of the distribution.

Quartic priorities consist of everyday, routine habits necessary for self-preservation, self-presentation, and self-survival. Attainment of priorities at a higher level begins with completion of priorities at lower levels going on up the hierarchy. For instance, if the major priority is to advance at work and work is more important than family, then brushing one's teeth, taking a shower, and presenting oneself in acceptable clothes fitting the setting and tasks to be accomplished at work could be the beginning preparation even before going to work. One may not devote too much time and energy to self-presentation if home and family have a different priority. At work, getting along with coworkers and fulfilling supraordinates' requests well would be another level of attainment. Asking for extra assignments could be another way to enhance oneself. If too much time and energy is expended at work, there may not be sufficient time and energy to devote to one's family, home, and leisure time activities. A tentative classification of a hierarchy of priorities is summarized in Table 5.4.

The issue of priorities is involved in the next and last model, where one needs to chose whether E is more important than R or other components of the ERAAwC model, and whether reliance on E is made at the expense of the other four components of the model. Functionality is present when there is a balance of all five components. Dysfunctionality is present when just one component is used at the expense of the others.

Intimacy: Hurt Feelings and Fears of Being Hurt

A specific and concrete definition of intimacy as the sharing of joys, hurts, and fears of being hurt has been productive, if not successful, in creating distance programmed writing, that is, workbooks, with face-to-face approaches to improve intimacy (Cusinato & L'Abate, 1995; L'Abate, 1999a, 1999c). Once intimacy is defined this way (Leary, Springer, Negel, Ansell, & Evans, 1998), it brings in the realm of E which is differentiated between the internal experience of people or events on the passive, receptive, input side, that is, feelings, and their active, external expression on the output side (A), that is, expressed emotions, as noted repeatedly in previous chapters (Hussong, 2000). Two synonyms for feelings are moods and affect (Watson, 2000). Hurt feelings and fears of being hurt are what is at the bottom of our socialization. These feelings are fiercely avoided at all costs in most semifunctional (RR) interpersonal styles, including selfish and selfless personality propensities, and in dysfunctional (AA), no-self ones. Only in selful, CC styles it is possible to achieve intimacy (Firestone & Catlett, 1999).

This position is supported conceptually by Bradley (2000), who brings an array of empirical evidence to support it:

> My thesis is that emotional arousal and the failure to regulate this arousal constitute a general factor in the development, recurrence, and maintenance of various forms of psychopathology. In so-called "internalizing" disorders, such dysregulation occurs most typically when an individual with heightened stress reactivity becomes stressed. In the "externalizing" disorders, stress reactivity may be less central to the affect dysregulation; a genetic vulnerability to anger and aggressive behavior may instead play the pivotal role. (p. vi).

Furthermore, a major area of continuing debate in the study of emotions is the differentiation between experiencing emotional stimuli or events on the receptive, input side versus expression of these stimuli or events on the output side. L'Abate (1997c, 1999c) has stressed the importance of clearly separating between emotional stimuli on the receptive side, as feelings, affect, or moods, versus the output of such feelings on the expressive side, as emotions. Between the experiencing of such feelings and their expression lies the importance of cognition (R) in the reception, processing, and expressing of emotionally tinged stimuli, including self-awareness (Aw) and awareness of external, interpersonal, and intimate context (C).

A further differentiation relates to developmentally primary or simple feelings (anger, sadness, joy, and fear) on the receptive side and more complex or secondary feelings, like contentment, arrogance, humility, misery, guilt, shame, envy, embarassment. These complex secondary feelings require a sense of self (Johnson-Laird & Oatley, 2000) if a person is to become aware and process them cognitively.

When experience, management, and regulation of emotions is used as a criterion for functionality-dysfunctionality, functionality is defined as the ability to experience a wide range of differentiated feelings and to express them helpfully without blaming, criticism, or attacks on others. In functionality, rationality plays a significant role in how feelings are expressed. Dysfunctionality in the expression of felt feelings is defined as overreliance on experience and consequent expression of a restricted emotional repertoire limited at best to one single, two, or few feelings, with a subsequent hurtful expression toward self or against others. Indeed, a limited repertoire of expressed, mostly negative, emotions is one of the marker variables in the etiology of schizophrenia (Nicholson, 1998). Hence, the purpose of most emotion-oriented workbooks, like most other workbooks, is parapreventive as well as paratherapeutic. There are many workbooks specifically targeted for the externalization of emotions such as anger, hostility, and aggression. Other workbooks have been targeted toward the internalization of emotions such as anxiety, fears, intimacy, and depression (L'Abate & Kern, in press).

A much more comprehensive and original model of experiencing has been proposed by two economists (Pine & Gilmore, 1999), as summarized by McLellan (2000). These authors argued that we are globally switching from a service to an experience economy. They propose a model of passive vs. active participation and external vs. internal involvement, producing four types of experiencing: entertainment (movies, theater), education (books), esthetics (art, music), and escapisms (addictions). Hence, in their own original way, these authors support the importance of experiencing dear to the heart of humanistic theorists as well as to recent affect and emotionality researchers (Bradley, 2000; L'Abate & Kern, in press; Watson, 2000).

Stress on subjective experience is basic to this theory in relation to avoiding painful experiences and approaching pleasurable ones instead. Pine and Gilmore's model, however, is too detailed and important to be summarized briefly. It will be explained and expanded in a future publication (L'Abate, in preparation). A distinct advance could be made when various models of experiencing feelings, proposed by Bradley, Watson, and other mood researchers, are related to Pine and Gilmore's model. The former are abstract models constructed in an interpersonal vacuum. No one knows empirically what feelings or moods are associated with particular external events (Gergen, 1994).

Pine and Gilmore's model, on the other hand, is interactional in nature because it classifies different types of experiencing on the basis of external events. It begs that question about what kind of feelings are elicited by the four classes of experiences classified by Pine and Gilmore. For instance, while most legitimate educational, entertainment, and esthetic experiences are pleasurable, what kind of feelings are elicited during escapist experiences, like drinking alcohol or taking addictive drugs? One could argue that the temporary and artificial high obtained during those experiences is an avoidance of hurt feeling and of fears of being hurt (L'Abate, 1997c, 1999a).

Why is E so important to this theory and what is its connection with workbooks? In the first place, E, in the passive-receptive sense of just plain experiencing, is at the very bottom of our ability to be moved by external events and to remember those that are either very pleasurable or very painful. In this sense, E is basic to personality development. The inability to feel is deleterious to personality development and lies at the beginning to psychopathology, as seen, for instance, in alexithymia and in other psychopathological conditions (Bradley, 2000). Hence, no theory of personality socialization is complete without a statement about the functions and processes of E. In the second place, E is important to the development of intimacy. Most close, committed, and prolonged relationships have to rely on experiencing, that is, being together, for their existence. The greater the sharing of E, especially hurt feelings, the greater will be the chances of a positive and constructive relationship. In the third place, it is important to help people learn to share their hurts and become intimate with those who are bound to them by ties of love, caring, and concern. Given the immense number of people in need of learning how to share feelings, it becomes crucial to have a variety of workbooks devoted to this topic, as reviewed in the previous chapter, and as stressed elsewhere (L'Abate & Kern, in press). Using talk and face-to-face contacts alone, there are not sufficient personnel, professional or paraprofessional, to teach all those who need to learn to express feelings in positive and constructive ways.

Both distinctions, feelings vs. emotions, positive vs. negative emotions, therefore, bring about the need to review the nature of emotions (Gergen, 1994; L'Abate & Kern, in press), a topic too vast and too important to consider here. It is introduced briefly here to locate feelings and emotions within the Selfhood model and show their relationship to relevant workbooks. This introduction necessitates a discussion about "list" theories of emotions, which have proliferated in the extant literature. The numbering of primary and secondary emotions is another competitive attempt to add to the continuing and seemingly futile controversy about how many emotions we are endowed with—4, 8, 10, 12, 15?

This controversy can go on forever as long as the battle is fought in the arena of numbers. It is seemingly without a solution because there is no solution. How can these different theories be evaluated comparatively? If there is no criterion with which to evaluate them, there is no way to find out which theory is "better" than the others, certainly not by the number of emotions. Dividing them into primary and secondary emotions has usually bypassed the distinction between feelings and emotions, lumping them together without distinguishing between the two processes.

The purpose of this conclusion is to suggest an alternative way to evaluate feelings as well as emotions according to their placement in two nomological networks—one receptive and the other expressive—rather than just listing them and comparing numbers in their respective lists. Drawing on both networks, it is possible to administer feelings- and emotions-related workbooks in a more specific way than it would be otherwise.

Why is it theoretically relevant to stress the importance of receptive experiences and not just expressive ones? From the viewpoint of the Selfhood model, a model-driven classification of feelings, affect, and moods might show some relationship with a classification of expressed emotions, demonstrating that receptive (E) and expressive processes in A have some lawful relationship with each other. Furthermore, receptive experiences, when positive, like happiness, joy, contentment, and satisfaction, lead to better psychological functioning and even improved negotiation and problem-solving skills (Isen, 2000, pp. 417–435). If this conclusion is valid, then these positive emotions would be more likely to be present in Selful personalities rather than in the other three, less functional personality propensities. Functional, that is, Selful individuals would negotiate and problem-solve more efficiently and effectively than dysfunctional ones, as predicted earlier in this chapter.

Consequently, through the Selfhood model it is possible to link *E* with personal and interpersonal behavior in a more specific way than would be possible with an equivalent theoretical model, including attachment. As Isen concluded, "people in the positive affect condition who bargained face-to-face were significantly less likely to break off negotiation, and more likely to reach agreement, and to reach the original agreement possible in the situation than were face-to-face bargainers in the control condition" (p. 421).

More to the point of the Selfulness propensity, Isen added, "more positive affect in general promotes not selfishness (sic), but a tendency to be kind to both self and others, social connectedness, responsibility, and the ability to see situations from another's person perspective" (p. 424).

The marketplace of emotion theories, as reviewed in Salzen (1995), is composed of what has been called "list" theories (L'Abate, 1997c) of emotions. These theories consist essentially of various lists of emotions, anywhere from 4 to 15. One reason these lists cannot be tested comparatively is due to their very nature. These lists are not theories in the sense of what is understood here as theory, that is, a list does not a theory make. If a theory consists of a hierarchical structure made up of assumptions, postulates, models, and ways to evaluate the models, then these lists do not qualify as theories. They qualify eminently for what they are—lists, but not theories. This is one of the reasons for not being able to find a criterion for these lists that will allow their comparable evaluation among themselves. Whether there are 4 or 15 emotions, the issue is not how many emotions there are, but how these lists can be evaluated, especially when the commonalties among them are greater then their differences.

It is not the number of emotions that counts, but how emotions are located in a nomological network. What is meant by a "nomological network"? The term means a model that will allow the location of emotions in some kind of order or classification (Bashfield & Livesley, 1999). The Selfhood model will be used to illustrate what is meant by a nomological network. This model allows one to place and locate emotions according to some semblance of order and classification. In differentiating between feelings at the receptive end from emotions at the expressive end, it is possible to obtain a framework of feelings around hurt, as shown in Figure 5.9, and from emotions, as shown in Figure 5.10. As seen in these figures, the Selfhood model allows one to integrate feelings at the receptive side and emotions at the expressive side of E. In these, as well as in proceeding figures, hurt is central but, in most cases, avoided, or

Figure 5.9
Organization of Feeling Terms, Hurts on the Receptive Side, and the Selfhood Model

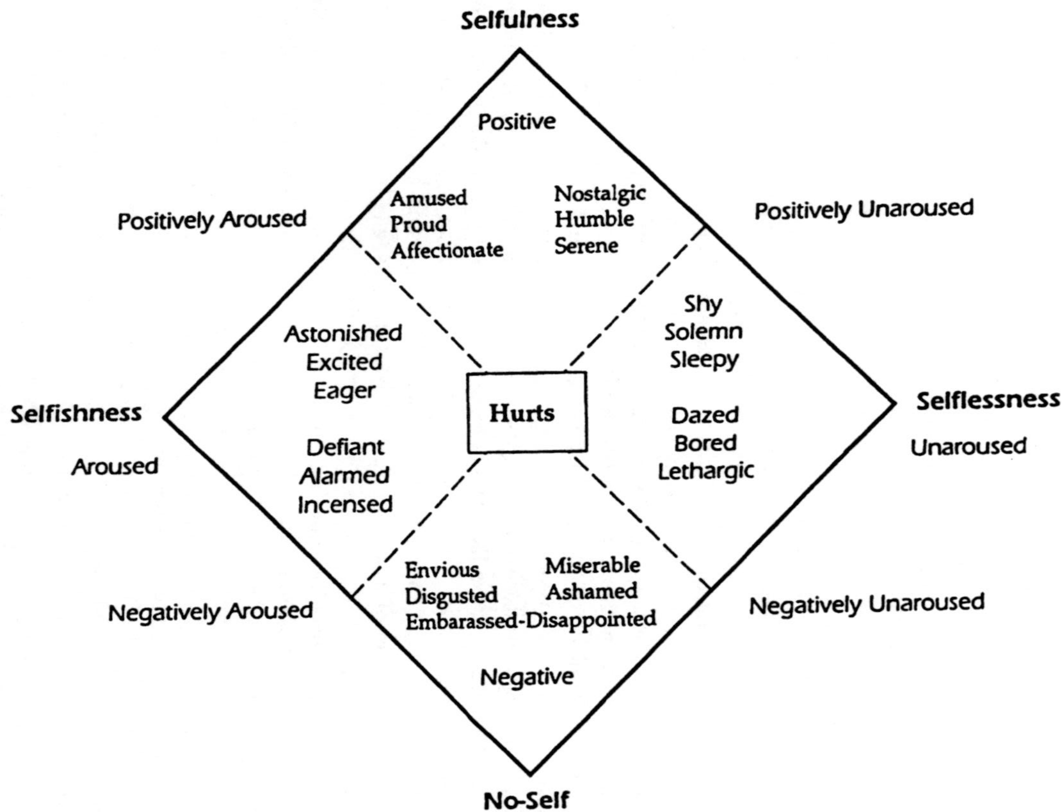

Source: Adapted from Averill (1977, p. 518).

Figure 5.10
A Taxonomic Tree of Emotions on the Expressive Side, Hurts, and the Selfhood Model

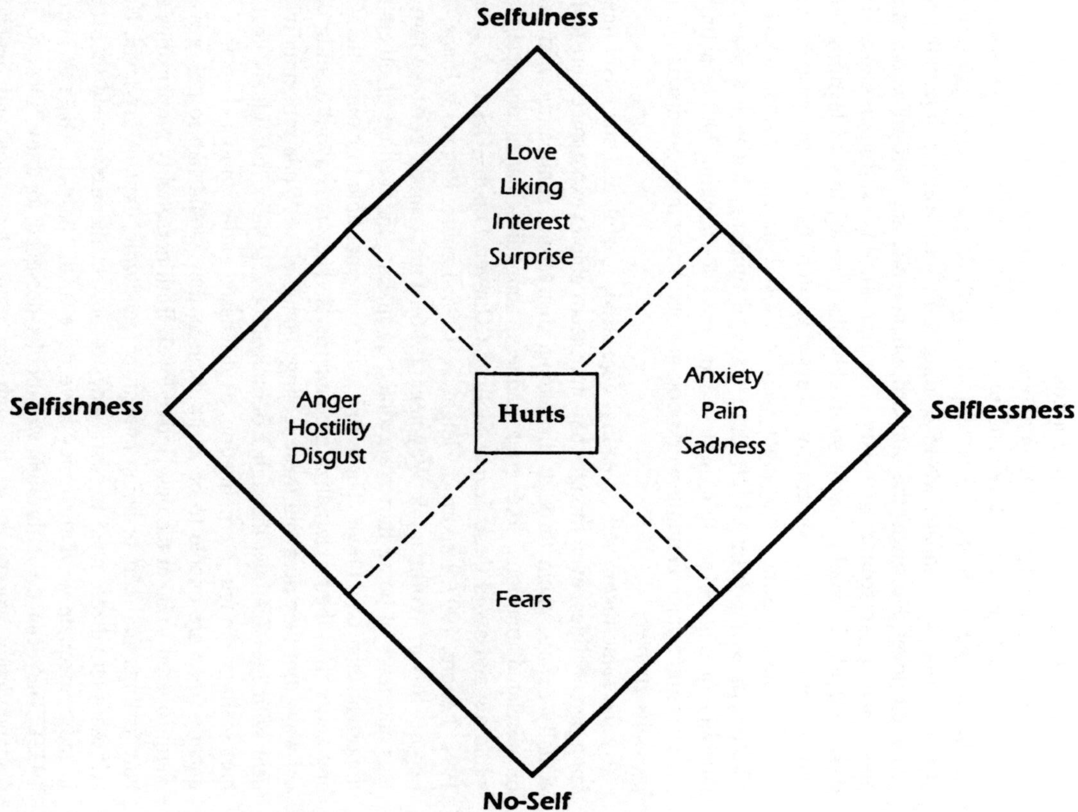

Source: Adapted from Storm & Storm (1987).

handled inadequately or destructively, especially in externalizations, internalizations, and psychopathologies. Excellent reviews of how hurt feelings are avoided are available (Bradley, 2000; Firestone & Catlett, 1999; Hayes, Strosahl, & Wilson, 1999).

At this juncture, however, one needs to invoke the metatheoretical model of levels of observation and interpretation to expand on how hurt feelings are avoided at the genotypic level and expressed outwardly at self-presentational and phenotypic levels. For instance, people with acting-out character disorders, that is, selfish individuals, avoid dealing with hurt feelings internally at the genotypic level. However, the outward, phenotypic, and self-presentational expression of these feelings consists of anger, hostility, and aggression. Hence, these individuals would benefit by workbooks directed toward learning how to express anger in more constructive ways than they have in the past. A variety of workbooks dealing with anger were reviewed in the previous chapter. In addition, it is important to introduce ways of thinking that would reduce impulsivity (acting before thinking) and increase *R* (thinking before acting), as found in the Social Training workbook and its Addendum (as discussed in the previous chapter).

By the same token, self-defeating, depressed, fearful, and anxiously internalizing personalities, even though they may seem able to experience hurt feelings, actually express them through distancing, distracting, ruminating, and relying on unrelated emotions, like grief, sadness, and guilt, maneuvers designed to withdraw and avoid these deeper feelings (Kliewer, Lepore, Oskin, & Johnson, 1998; Lepore, 1997; Lepore & Helgeson, 1998; Lepore, Ragan, & Jones, 2000; Lepore, Silver, Wortman, & Wayment, 1996). Furthermore, personal hurt feelings and fears of being hurt are avoided by making the feelings of others more important than one's own. These individuals are not able to express their hurts any better than their externalizing counterparts. They may avoid them in different ways, but they do avoid these feelings nonetheless. While selfish individuals deal with hurt feelings through externalizations, selfless individuals deal with hurt feelings though internalization, as discussed earlier in this chapter. Consequently, they are unable to be as intimate as they would like to be, or as they claim to want to be at the descriptive level. Both personality propensities avoid hurt feelings and fears of being hurt at the genotypic, explanatory level. Hence, selfless internalizers need to learn ways to protect themselves and their bodies in more adequate ways than they have done in the past (L'Abate & Harrison, 1992). They can do it through workbooks designed to draw lines, as in the Codependency workbook, or through the many depression and dependency workbooks available (Chapter 4).

In No-self psychopathologies, the problem is even more complex because it is practically very difficult to access hurt feelings and fears of being hurt without provoking a great deal of agitation and distress, including a psychotic break. Feelings in general, let alone hurts, are almost completely avoided to the point that a resulting psychosis may well be the outcome of any attempt to access and express them. Hence, a workbook approach may be coupled with medication and with crisis intervention. Clearly, this is still an unexplored area for workbook applications.

The Nonlinearity of Emotionality and Activity

In spite of some theoretical attempts (Plutchik, 1993) to relate feelings (E) with emotions and external behavior (A), the gap between these two aspects of behavior is too wide to expect that given any feeling, there is a corresponding, matching emotion. As argued elsewhere (L'Abate, 1994a, 1997c), given the same feeling, hostility or anger, for example, there are myriad ways in which one can express that very same feeling. Hence, one needs to consider the many factors involved in this nonlinearity between E and A. They can be outlined here before expansion elsewhere (L'Abate, in preparation):

1. Intensity of E
2. Strength of boundaries between E with R, A, Aw, and C, as described in Figure 5.3
3. Amount of overlap among components of the model (Fig. 5.3)
4. Strength of *R* as interposed between E and A
5. Strength of Aw intervening after A as a circular change loop to revert to E
6. Aw of C, as an overarching factor in bridging the gap between E and A

In spite of this nonlinearity between E and A, it is possible to make sense and show through a Selfhood model that there is still a linear relationship between E and Aw, when Aw is low and defined as unexpressed emotions. One can feel and be aware of one's anger and hostility. However, as long as R is present and functioning, there are various ways, some constructive and some destructive, of expressing this Aw outwardly. However, if Aw is restricted, then feedback to E may be limited, inadequate, faulty, and possibly distorted, short-circuiting even more the circularity of E to R and to A.

Intimacy and Selfhood

There are two implications for personality development within the context of intimacy and selfhood. One aspect of intimacy and selfhood relates to how we deal with our hurts at the receptive level: (1) we are all hurt human beings, in some way or another, (2) some are more hurt than others, (3) some are able to deal with their hurts more constructively than others, (4) some are completely unable to deal with their hurts because they are unable to face this fundamental human condition. Hurt feelings are at the bottom of our existence (L'Abate, 1999a). Once we accept the importance of these feelings, three different possibilities come to mind: (1) our *neediness* in wanting to be close to someone who will share hurt feelings reciprocally with us, because without this reciprocity there is little if any potential for an harmonious relationship, (2) our *vulnerability* to being hurt by the very ones we love and who love us—we are not vulnerable to slights from strangers—we are vulnerable to people who are important to us, because we are more liable to be hurt "unintentionally" from those we love and who love us, (3) our *fallibility* in hurting "unintentionally" the very ones we love. Acceptance of these existential conditions and forgiveness (Fincham, 2000; L'Abate, 1986b; McCullough, Pargament, & Thorensen, 2000) may go a long way toward achieving selfulness in personality socialization.

A second aspect of the relationship between intimacy and selfhood at the expressive level is the differentiation among three roles in intimate relationships. They have been called the Eternal Triangle basic to the development of psychopathology (Karpman, 1968; L'Abate, 1986b; Liotti, 1999), as explained in the Depression in Couples workbook described in the previous chapter. Given that Triangle, there are four possible interpersonal roles to play in dealing with hurt feelings:

1. *Rescuer or Savior*, trying to make things better for those who are hurting, often at one's own expense, by not valuing one's own feelings, and valuing others' feelings more than one's own instead, leading to *Selflessness*
2. *Persecutor*, inflicting hurts on others, making things worse for them, whether intimates or not intimates, to protect one's feelings and avoid being hurt, leading to *Selfishness*
3. *Martyr, Saint*, or *Victim*, keeping hurt feelings inside without ever expressing them, or, at the other extreme, exploding in a destructive manner, assuming three roles all at the same time, that is, stoic Victim, hateful Persecutor, and noble, compassionate Savior, leading to *No-self*. A workbook for depression in couples (L'Abate, 1986b) was developed to help couples and families learn from these triangles (Chapter 4).

All three roles are played out in dysfunctional relationships, with each individual switching from one role to another. The fourth alternative is played out in functional relationships. This is the normalizing role of *Selfulness—sharing* hurt feelings with loved ones though crying, hugging, and cuddling together, that is, being together physically and emotionally (L'Abate, 2001b) without demands for perfection in production, performance, or problem-solving. Sharing hurts means not playing these destructive roles and becoming sane and intimate, a process that happens sometimes between individual respondents and therapists when partners or family members are not included in the therapeutic process.

An additional model in the form of a triangle is relevant to *distance regulation* in intimate relationships. In this model three roles are played out: the Pursuer, who wants closeness; the Distancer who avoids it; and the Regulator, who oscillates between the other two roles ("Come close, I need help. You did not help.").

CONCLUSION

The quote at the beginning of this chapter questioned whether personality could be defined satisfactorily. A multileveled, integrative theory of personality socialization stresses the crucial roles of the ability to love, as expressed in Presence, and the ability to negotiate performance and production, as expressed in Doing and Having. This chapter produced an artichoke definition of personality composed of 10 models (Table 5.3), one probably nontestable and 9 testable and, in some cases, tested:

1. Levels of observation and interpretation, including self-presentation in public and in private settings, with genotypic and historical explanation
2. Distance and regulation
3. Modalities of Being, Doing, and Having, leading to the distinction between Presence and Power
4. Expressing oneself through Emotionality, Rationality, Activity, Awareness, and Context
5. Self-definition along a Continuum of Likeness made of by six ranges in relationship to intimate others
6. Three styles of intimate and nonintimate relationships, Abusive-Apathetic (AA), Reactive-Repetitive (RR), and Conductive-Creative (CC)
7. Attribution of importance to self and intimate others, leading to four personality propensities, Selfulness, Selfishness, Selflessness, and No-self—these personality propensities were then related to a classification of workbooks, linking theory with the practice of PW/SCAI
8. Balancing Priorities along the life cycle
9. Intimacy or sharing hurts and fears of being hurt with intimate others

Two subsidiary models, the Drama Triangle and Distance Regulation, could be added to this list.

It will be shown in the next chapter how this theory can be evaluated in the laboratory and in primary, secondary, and tertiary prevention approaches through replicable operations.

6

Verifiability: Linking Theory with Research and Practice

> What is needed is a focused attention on the evidence for theories, not on the psychological quirks of theorists.
>
> (Sober & Wilson, 1998, p. 9)

> Throughout the sciences and other domains laying claim to objective reports, there is a pervasive attempt to establish conditions of *public replicability*.
>
> (Gergen, 1994, p. 170)

The purpose of this chapter is to illustrate how a theory of personality socialization in the family and other settings (summarized in the previous chapter) can be evaluated in four settings: (1) laboratory, (2) primary, (3) secondary, and (4) tertiary prevention, or psychotherapy (Table 6.1).

One of the major issues facing any theory, but especially this theory, is whether and how it can be evaluated. Evaluation, verification, or testing are here used synonymously, meaning any intersubjectively repeatable method that allows one to study the empirical or experiential validity of a theoretical statement evaluated by someone else who is extraneous to that statement. For instance, there are many theories of personality and psychotherapy as well as family theories and family therapy that vary in degrees of verifiability, ranging from verifiable and verified to unverifiable and unverified (Gurman & Kniskern, 1991; Hansen & L'Abate, 1982; Mikesell, Lusterman, & McDaniel, 1995). Verifiability, therefore, means the condition of being evaluated, verified, or tested, implying an observer/examiner external to the theory.

A theory could be verifiable in the laboratory but unverifiable in the clinic.

Table 6.1
Validation of a Theory of Personality Socialization in the Family

Models	Tests	Enrichment	Workbooks	Tasks
Distance/Regulation	What applies to me that I agree with?			
Modalities			Assignment in negotiation	
ERAAwC	Cusinato's star model (Figure 6.1)	Negotiation potential	Assignment in negotiation	
Likeness Continuum	Likeness scale Likeness grid What applies to me that I agree with? Likeness profile			
Styles in Interpersonal Relationships (ARC)	PIRS	Negotiation potential		
Selfhood	PIRS SOPC TRD		Self-Other Codependency	Drawing lines
Priorities	Grid Inventory	Negotiation potential	Assignments in negotiation Codependency	Drawing lines
Hurt Feelings & Intimacy	SOHF	Helpfulness	Intimacy	Sharing hurts Hugging, holding, huddling, and cuddling (3HC)
Drama Triangle			Depression	
Distance Regulation			Depression	

Another theory could be evaluated clinically in terms of results produced, but remain untestable in the laboratory. Another theory could be tested in primary prevention settings but not in therapy (tertiary prevention) or laboratory settings. Some theories are very appealing therapeutically but are either unverifiable or have not been verified as yet, as is the case with systems theory (Gurman, Kniskern, & Pinsoff, 1986, p. 569). For instance, Satir's (1964) theory, like many pioneering theories in family therapy, is a prime example of a very influential theory that appears unverifiable. At least, as far as this writer knows, no one has as yet attempted to verify it.

On the other hand, one needs to consider recent theoretical advances that are couched in ways that make them more amenable to verification (Alexander & Barton, 1995). Very appealing and seductive theories, like systems theory, may be very difficult or impossible to verify, because, as mentioned in the previous chapter, they are metatheories or paradigms that cannot be verified directly. Theories that are verifiable may not be very appealing to some professionals.

Some verifiable theories can be expanded to clinical applications and some cannot. For instance, Olson's circumplex model (Gorall & Olson, 1995) has led to the creation of preventive and therapeutic applications. Attachment theory (Atkinson & Zucker, 1997; Feeney & Noller, 1996; Goldberg, Muis, & Kerr, 1995; Sanford, 1997), on the other hand, through its Strange Situation, the Attachment Story Completion Task (ASCI) (Bretherton, Ridgeway, & Cassidy, 1990), and structured interviews semistructured interviews, and rating scales, has been verified in laboratories around the globe. In spite of its indirect therapeutic implications (Cassidy & Shaver, 1999), it has not produced, as far as this writer knows, any direct (i.e., theory-derived) clinical application or therapeutic task that is verifiable or that could be verified. The Strange Situation is applicable to early childhood, the ASCT to older children. Its structured and semistructured interviews and rating scales are applicable to adults. However, these are all diagnostic tools and not therapeutic tasks.

Furthermore, what information would these procedures add to a clinical population? When people ask for professional help, it is assumed that they are "insecure," because if they were secure they would not ask for help. Does being diagnosed as "insecure-dismissing" lead to different therapeutic practices than those applied to individuals diagnosed as "insecure-preoccupied"? If this is the case, what and where are these different practices to be found? As far as this writer knows, this specificity has not been observable in the vast attachment literature (L'Abate, De Giacomo, McCarty, De Giacomo, & Verrastro, 2000).

In addition to *verifiability*, however, for application to clinical or preventive settings, a theory of personality socialization in the family should produce results in clinical practice in both prevention and therapy, thus fulfilling a second criterion of *accountability* (as concluded in Chapter 1). As Stricker (1997) suggested: "For science and practice to be commensurable, the same theoretical matrix must generate both science and practice activities" (p. 442). Accountability and verifiability, however, are criteria independent of each other. We need verifiability in theory-building as well as in therapy. The criterion of accountability is more relevant to preventive and therapeutic outcomes than to theory construction and testing (L'Abate, 1986b).

Producing results, however, is no longer a sufficient criterion for either prevention or psychotherapy, especially in family therapy. If a theory or a technique is useful to a practicing clinician, is that all that is necessary? For instance, some very appealing theories of therapy may produce impressionistic results in spite of their inherent unverifiability, as used to be (in part) the case with psychoanalysis and, more recently, with family therapy. At least in psychotherapy, a theory could conceivably account for a positive outcome but remain unverifiable otherwise. To take into account both criteria, verifiability and accountability, therefore, a theory of personality socialization in the family needs to be verifiable as well accountable. Accountability may be necessary in therapy but insufficient in theory, just as verifiability may be necessary in theory but insufficient in therapy. Both criteria, verifiability and accountability, are necessary and sufficient to verify a theory in the laboratory if that theory is then to be applied also in clinical or preventive settings (Beutler, Williams, Wakefield, & Entwistle, 1995).

Hence, there are two aspects of this theory of personality socialization in the family that are relevant to its evaluation: (1) dialectical, so that it may be verifiable qualitatively/impressionistically, and (2) demonstrative, so that it may be verifiable quantitatively/empirically. Both aspects, dialectics (rhetoric and qualification) and demonstrability (data, evidence, and quantification), are necessary for scientific and applied enterprises, as discussed in Chapter 1 (L'Abate, 1986b, 1994b). Dialectics is hypothesis-generating, while demonstrability is hypothesis-testing (McGuire, 1997). Preliminary evidence to support one model of this theory has already been published elsewhere (L'Abate, 1997c, 1998a; L'Abate, De Giacomo, McCarty, De Giacomo, & Verrastro, 2000). However, this evidence was related to specific models and specific instruments and not to methods of intervention. The latter will be added here.

This evidence is still preliminary, selective, and piecemeal. Once cannot really verify a theory directly. It can be verified through its models. Models, in turn, are verified though instruments or interventions, task assignments, or exercises, derived directly from the models themselves. Thus, a theory is as valid as the instruments or interventions developed to test its models. How is the theory just reviewed in the previous chapter linked with workbooks? First, we need to see whether the theory or its models are valid in the laboratory and in primary, secondary, and tertiary prevention practices. Then, we can see whether and how this theory is linked with workbooks. These links are summarized in Table 6.1, connecting theoretical models with research and practice.

LABORATORY

Over the years, this writer, with the help of his students and collaborators (Cusinato, Aceti, & L'Abate, 1998; L'Abate, 1997c, 1998a; L'Abate & Wagner, 1985, 1988; Stevens & L'Abate, 1989), has developed self-report, paper-and-pencil tests derived directly from models of the theory. Not all tests have been validated as yet (as indicated already in Chapter 4).

Social Information Form

This 85-item questionnaire can be administered in writing or as a structured interview. Its major advantage lies in its having objective weights related to functionality-dysfunctionality and divisions into subparts related to self, partner, and family relationships. These weights produce subscores in the three areas just mentioned, with a total functionality score. Its relationship to personality and marital adjustment is presently being researched (McMahan & L'Abate, in preparation). In this way, it will be possible to relate historical, developmental factors, which would be "explanatory." This point was discussed in the nontested model of levels of observation and interpretation summarized in the previous chapter. This level, historical-developmental, will be linked to genotypical (personality traits) and phenotypical (marital adjustment) factors. Presentational level factors in a particular sample of seminarian couples have already been considered in McMahan and L'Abate (2001).

What Applies to Me (that I agree with)?

This is a 200-item multipurpose test still in the experimental stage that covers all of the major models of the theory, as summarized in Table 5.2. Its translation in Italy is presently being subjected to empirical validation (Mario Cusinato, personal communication, February 22, 2000).

Modalities

No tests have been developed to evaluate the Modalities model as yet, except indirectly through the instruments and methods developed by Foa, Converse, Tornblom, and Foa (1993). Our assignment in the Negotiation workbook deals with Modalities.

ERAAwC

Mario Cusinato (personal communication, April 6, 2000) has developed a five-scale, 47-item questionnaire to evaluate each component of this model and its statistical properties, validity, and reliability. Unfortunately these scales are available only in the Italian language. However, they can be translated into English with no difficulty. Cusinato has also developed a visual, star-shaped model (shown in Figure 6.1), where scores from the five scales can be embedded.

Likeness Continuum

Three paper-and-pencil, self-report instruments were developed originally to evaluate this continuum's original formulation (L'Abate, 1976), as part of a theory-derived test battery (L'Abate & Wagner, 1985, 1988).

Likeness Scale

This is a global, nonspecific measure used to compare oneself with intimate others. It is composed of 20 true-false items and part of a Marital Questionnaire designed to evaluate two additional postulates of the theory, Priorities and Congruence (L'Abate & Wagner, 1985, 1988).

Figure 6.1
ERAAWC Questionnaire

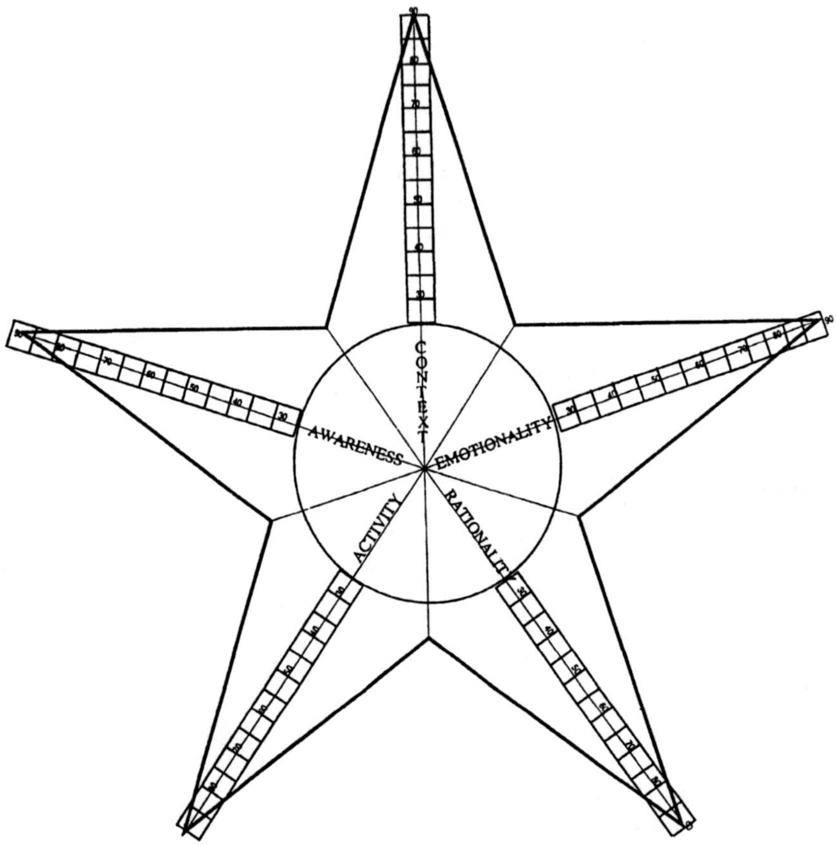

Source: Personal communication, Mario Cusinato, February 16, 1999.

Likeness Grid

This test was developed as another measure of self-differentiation in the format suggested originally by Kelly's (1955) personal constructs theory. It consists of a list of 24 persons related in some way to the respondent (family members, friends, teachers, etc.). For each person, respondents rate themselves as "completely the same as," "the same as," "similar to," or "different from," "opposite from," or "completely opposite from" the particular person being rated. In keeping with the dialectical aspects of the continuum of likeness, ratings of being "completely the same" (symbiosis), and "completely the opposite" (alienation), are considered equivalent from the viewpoint of dysfunctionality and scored one point. Ratings of "same" or "opposite" are scored two points, and ratings of "similar" and "different" are scored three points. These points are added together to provide a total differentiation score.

The first evaluation of test-retest reliability for both instruments in 138 undergraduate respondents (L'Abate & Wagner, 1988) produced an alpha coefficient of .74 for the Likeness Scale and one of .79 for the Likeness Grid. Both instruments correlated with each other ($r = .27$, $p < .05$).

Predictions from the present elaboration of this continuum are very specific to the point that they can be falsified, while general predictions from just a simple dichotomy of similar-dissimilar would be more difficult to falsify. It would be necessary to find a variety of measures, tasks, and manipulations that would allow empirical evaluation of this continuum within each specific dimension outlined in Table 5.2. There are quite a few measures available in the literature for evaluation of many dimensions predicted by this continuum. However, each measure would need to be paired with the "What Applies to Me That I Agree With?" scale developed to test this and other models.

Hence, this continuum can be evaluated through an experimental paper-and-pencil self-report that together with a measure of the specific situation being evaluated, as well as through an external criterion of functionality, either by self-report or by external observations or diagnoses (criterion validity). As Felmlee's (1998) research indicated, open-ended self-report measures might be quite sensitive to disclosure, even though many individuals, especially in the two extreme ranges of the distribution, may either be completely unaware of their behaviors, or, if they are aware, be unwilling to disclose them. Chappell and Davis' methodology (1998), with some refinements about their measure of similarity, may be another way to test this continuum.

Likeness Profile

This is another paper-and-pencil, self-report instrument still at the experimental stage. It is only available in the Italian language. It has been administered to 200 undergraduate students in a major Italian university and, together with the SOPC, to 150 respondents of various social and educational backgrounds in the island of Malta (Mario Cusinato, personal communication, April 6, 2000). Results are not yet available.

Problems in Interpersonal Relationships Scale (PIRS)

This is a 240-item scale developed to measure Abusive-Apathetic, Reactive-Repetitive, and Conductive-Creative styles, as well as the four personality propensities of the Selfhood model (L'Abate, 1992b). It was validated by McMahan with seminarian couples (McMahan & L'Abate, 2001). Its total discrepancy score for partners, a measure of marital adjustment, correlated significantly and negatively with the Spanier Dyadic Adjustment Scale. In addition to diagnostic functions, this test is prescriptive in the sense that written homework assignments are isomorphic with the very same 20 conflict areas covered by test items.

Selfhood

In addition to the PIRS, this model has been evaluated with the Self-Other Profile Chart (SOPC) already introduced in previous chapters. Its Italian translation has been subjected to various studies relating it concurrently with attachment measures (L'Abate, De Giacomo, McCarty, De Giacomo, & Verrastro, 2000).

Self-Other Profile Chart (SOPC)

This measure has been subjected to many evaluation studies reviewed elsewhere (L'Abate, 1997c). Table 6.2 summarizes correlations among the SOPC and two other measures of attachment and relationship styles (L'Abate, De Giacomo, McCarty, De Giacomo, & Verrastro, 2000), demonstrating sufficient concurrent validity with two other tests. Lindaver (1998) used the SOPC as an independent variable to determine its relationship to the Italian version of Olson's FACES and the Italian version of an Attachment measure (Table 6.3). As Lindaver's results show, there were statistically significant relationships among the three measures. These results are supported by the work by L'Abate et al., presented in Table 6.2. These and other results support the usefulness of this test theoretically as well as clinically, since it takes two minutes to administer and less than a minute to score.

Cusinato and Pastore (2001) administered this Profile to 1438 respondents from age 14 to 60 years at different stages of the life cycle, of which 50% were between 14 and 20 years of age. The respondents lived in in different regions of Italy. Using exploratory factor analysis, two factors were identified for Self—external, presentational variables, like physical appearance, and internal, genotypical variables, like morality and self-esteem. Two factors were identified for Others, restricted family members versus friends and acquaintances. These two factors for each scale were validated with confirmatory factor analyses.

Eleonora Maino and Donatella Fara (personal communication, June 22, 2000) administered the SOPC to 405 respondents in an experimental group of families of handicapped children and 824 respondents in a control group of families drawn from the same classes attended by the handicapped children. The SOPC administered the Optimism-Pessimism Scale, six scales of the Family Environment Scale (FES), four scales of the Family Crisis Oriented Personal Evaluation Scale, and three scales of the Short Form of the Questionnaire on Resources and Stress.

The results of the correlations matrix among all these measures are shown in Table 6.4.

This matrix shows significant correlations of the SOPC with most measures, with the exception of FC3 for both Self and Others, FC4 for Self, and QRS2 for Others. These significant correlations and results from research summarized above tend to support the concurrent validity of this instrument. These results also indicate how attribution of importance to self and intimate others cannot

Table 6.2
Correlation Matrix for Adult Attachment Questionnaire (AAQ), Self View Questionnaire (SVQ), and Self-Other Profile Chart (SOPC)

	AAQ				SVQ Factors				SOPC-RAF	
	Secure	*Preoccupied*	*Dismissing*	*Fearful*	*1*	*2*	*3*	*4*	*Self*	*Other*
AAQ										
Secure	1.00									
Preoccupied	−.23**	1.00								
Dismissing	−.13	.41**	1.00							
Fearful	−.45**	.60**	.59**	1.00						
SVQ Factors										
1	.15	−.15	−.34**	−.28**	1.00					
2	−.27**	.08	.09	.21*	.07	1.00				
3	.30**	−.35**	−.18*	−.40**	.44**	−.10	1.00			
4	.25**	−.16	−.13	−.26*	.43**	.08	.34**	1.00		
SOPC										
Self	.22**	−.20*	−.11	−.18*	.04	−.27**	.26**	.16	1.00	
Other	.18*	−.19*	−.29**	−.26**	.14	−.28**	.22*	.16	.42**	1.00

$^*p < .05$; $^{**}p < .01$.

Source: L'Abate, De Giacomo, McCarty, De Giacomo, & Verrastro (2000).

Table 6.3
ANOVA for FACES and AAQ Measures as Dependent Variables of SOPC as Independent Variable

Propensities						
Selfhood:	Selful	Selfish	Selfless	No-self	ANOVA	
	$n = 44$	$n = 13$	$n = 29$	$n = 56$	F(3,129)	
Dimensions FACES III: Means					**F**	**p**
Cohesion*	39.38	36.50	31.92	27.76	17.26	<.001
Adaptability*	30.04	30.25	27.00	23.30	9.28	<.001
Dimensions AAQ: Means						
Secure	48.25	48.95	48.69	41.83	10.73	<.001
Avoidant	28.40	29.00	33.84	36.76	7.17	<.001
Fearful	26.75	23.45	27.00	31.46	4.16	<.007
Preoccupied	28.41	25.92	28.20	30.09		n.s.

Source: Lindaver (1998).

be independent of positivity or optimism and negativity or pessimism. Positivity is the hallmark of functionality, while negativity is the hallmark of dysfunctionality (L'Abate, 1986b). Furthermore, one cannot separate this attribution from other family characteristics and, by extension, from how one relates to problematic issues and relationships with the community at large. One cannot conceive of the self and a sense of importance without relating them to their most immediate context, the family, as well as to the most distal but relevant context, the community.

Dyadic Relationships Test (TRD, for Test di Relazione Diadica)

This test was developed by Cusinato (1997) to measure the four personality propensities of the Selfhood model through 12 comic-type visual-verbal vignettes for seven stages of the life-cycle:

1. Close to wedding
2. Young married couple without children
3. Couple with small (pre-school) children
4. Couple with school-age children
5. Couple with teenagers
6. Couple with adult children
7. Empty nest couples

For example, one vignette visually shows a situation described verbally—a change of plans for a couple that was going to spend the weekend with friends. At the last minute, the parents of one partner report that a long-lost uncle is

Table 6.4
Correlation Matrix of Self-Others Profile Chart (SOPC) and Other Measures

(N = 1229) N = 824 in control group and N = 405 in experimental group

	Self	Others	Optimism	Pessimism
Self	1.000	.48**	.17**	−.14**
Other	.48**	1.000	.19**	−.10**

	FES 1	FES 2	FES 3	FES 4	FES 5	FES 6
Self	.14**	.19**	−.12**	.16**	.17**	−.10**
Others	.21**	.23**	−.20**	.17**	.21**	−.12**

	F-C1	F-C2	F-C3	F-C4	QRS 1	QRS2	QRS3
Self	.16**	.08*	−.01	−.04	−.08*	−.09*	−.09*
Others	.17**	.20**	.01	−.11**	−.07*	−.07	−.08*

*$p < .05$; **$p < .001$
SOPC, Self-Others Profile Chart (L'Abate, 1997c; Cusinato, 1997)
FES 1 = Family Cohesion Scale
FES 2 = Ease of Expression Scale
FES 3 = Manifest Conflict Scale
FES 4 = Personal Autonomy Scale
FES 5 = Locus of Family Control Scale
FES 6 = Family Control Scale
F-C = Family Crisis Oriented Personal Evaluation Scale
F-C 1 = Redefinition of the problem
F-C 2 = Obtaining community support
F-C 3 = Advocacy to obtain help from social services
F-C 4 = Passive acceptance of problematic issues
QRS = Short-Form of the Questionnaire on Resources and Stress. Please note that this scale has been administered only to the experimental group.
QRS 1 = Parental and family problems in relation to the handicapped child
QRS 2 = Pessimism in relation to the characteristics of handicapped child
QRS 3 = Characteristics of handicapped child.

Source: Family Psychology Service of the Research Institute "Eugeneo Medea" in the Association "La Nostra Famiglia," Bosisio Parini (Lecco), Italy.

coming to visit and that the couple is invited to a party to celebrate his return. The four possible answers to this conflict represent the four personality propensities:

Selful: "Let's see how we can combine both parties."
Selfish: "I have no intention of changing my program!"
Selfless: "If you like, we can let go of our friends."
No-self: "We will end up arguing again."

Seventeen studies were conducted to refine the statistical properties of this test and establish its concurrent and criterion validities and reliability. In six different studies with 60 couples each, between the ages of 25 and 45, the internal consistency (Cronbach's alpha) of this test ranged from .53 to .75. Its scores correlated at a significant level of confidence ($p < .01$). with the Italian translation of a Locus of Control Scale, a measure of couple negotiation, a measure of couple communication, Beck's Depression Inventory, and a measure of intimacy derived from Cusinato and L'Abate's (1995) model. Internal correlations among the various scales measuring the four personality propensities attested to the homogeneity of the items (Cusinato & L'Abate, submitted for publication).

Their results established the concurrent and discriminant validity of this measure as one way to evaluate the Selfhood model. This test is worthy of a translation into English, just like all the other tests developed by Professor Mario Cusinato and his collaborators in the Department of General Psychology at the University of Padova in Italy.

Priorities

Priorities have been evaluated by the Priorities Grid and the Priorities Scale. Results from evaluative studies have been reported by L'Abate and Wagner (1985) and by L'Abate (1994a).

Sharing of Hurts and Intimacy

A sharing of Hurts Scale was developed and evaluated in its psychometric properties—validity and reliability (Stevens & L'Abate, 1989). It was revised to fit more closely with a more complex, circular model of intimacy proposed by Cusinato and L'Abate (1995). It was revised further by Cusinato, Aceti, and L'Abate (1998) to evaluate the effects of asking undergraduate students to share in writing their hurts with friends or partners.

Primary Prevention: Structured Enrichment Programs

This approach consists of written-down exercises to be administered by semiprofessional trainers under the supervision of a professional (L'Abate & Weinstein, 1987; L'Abate & Young, 1987). These exercises are administered verbatim from the text to couples and families (L'Abate, 1990; L'Abate, 1999d).

ERAAwC

This model can be evaluated by administering an enrichment program isomorphic with this model (L'Abate & Weinstein, 1987, pp. 376–383). L'Abate and Young (1987) present seven different case studies in which this program was successfully administered.

One enrichment assignment for the evaluation of Distance Regulation, divided into Pursuer, Distancer, and Regulator, is found in the Depression in Couples workbook. The Modalities model is available in one assignment of the negotiation program (L'Abate, 1986b).

Styles

The ARC model can be evaluated by an assignment in the Negotiation workbook containing a series of questions isomorphic with the model (L'Abate & Weinstein, 1987, pp. 317–375).

Priorities

This model can be evaluated through the administration of a program of the same title (L'Abate & Weinstein, 1987, pp. 384–391).

Intimacy

An early version of an Intimacy Enrichment program was published verbatim (L'Abate & McHenry, 1983, pp. 357–362). In another collection with hundreds of exercises and questions on a variety of topics (L'Abate & Weinstein, 1987), one exercise addresses avoidance of intimacy (p. 162), and a complete program (No. 29) on helpfulness (pp. 300–309) contains lessons on:

1. Establishing levels of caring, hurts, and strengths
2. Seeing the good
3. Caring
4. Sharing of hurt feelings
5. Forgiveness
6. Protectiveness
7. Responsibility
8. Enjoyment

Two case studies (L'Abate & Young, 1987), illustrate specific applications of this program to issues of parentification (pp. 134–153) and to a psychosomatic family (pp. 163–179). Both studies describe how this program was applied with pre- and post-enrichment test batteries.

SECONDARY PREVENTION: WORKBOOKS

Here is where theory and theory-testing become relevant—by linking both with applied and clinical practice. The same three-level criteria used to evaluate a theory (presented in Chapter 5) can be used to evaluate the effectiveness of workbooks. For instance, *independent evidence* about the overall use of DW, and especially focused DW, is represented by the research summarized by Esterling et al. (1999), Pennebaker (1997), and Smyth (1998). *Indirect evidence* about the use of workbooks and homework assignments in general is represented by meta analyses presented by Kazantzis (2000), Kazantzis, Deane, and Ronan (2000), and Smyth and L'Abate (2001). *Direct evidence* about workbooks specifically developed by this writer is summarized by L'Abate (submitted for publication, b). Preliminary direct evidence is available in L'Abate et al. (1992), McMahan and L'Abate (2001), and Reed, McMahan, and L'Abate (2001). Of course, more evidence will be necessary to evaluate the whole enterprise. The term "preliminary" is used in the sense that any evidence presented by the proponent of any method is suspicious at best. Consequently, no matter how much evidence this writer and his collaborators were able to accumulate, it would never be enough. It is much more important for such evidence to be found by researchers independent to this approach (L'Abate, submitted for publication, b).

Workbooks, of course, are used primarily to help people, secondarily to test competing theories or models. In regard to both uses, the criterion becomes: "Which workbook (representing which theory or model) will produce the best results in the shortest number of assignments?" This is a new rephrasing of the old psychotherapy dictum: "Who will be helped by which intervention and by which helper (at what price)?" For instance, given two different workbooks to deal with two dimensions of the Selfhood model, Self and Other, is it possible to compare each workbook with workbooks designed to deal with the same two dimensions based on different theoretical viewpoints?

Both workbooks could be compared with the two workbooks about Self-Other Concerns developed on the basis of Blatt et al.'s (1982) two-factor model of depression, self-criticism, and overdependency. How well does the Selfhood model compare with workbooks derived from other models about the same two dimensions of Self and Other? If no competing workbooks are available, it is possible to compare either the Negotiation or Intimacy workbooks (both derived from the theory) with workbooks on the same topic. In another instance, two assignments idiographic with two subsidiary models of depression (L'Abate, 1986b), the Drama Triangle and Distance Regulation, are found in two respective assignments in the workbook of the same name (Table 6.1). Through workbooks a wide range of nonclinical, semiclinical, and clinical populations can be helped, while at the same time testing different theoretical models from which the workbooks were derived.

TERTIARY PREVENTION: PRESCRIBED TASKS

In initial as well as subsequent interviews with clinical respondents, it is possible to ascertain the validity of the theory directly but qualitatively by evaluating the assumptions of distance and regulation, the ability to love and to negotiate, whether presence is mixed with power, how individuals compare with each other according to a continuum of likeness, what interpersonal style they are using, what personality propensities are prevalent, what priorities are present and influential, and whether there is any sharing of hurts and of fears of being hurt. In psychotherapy, after a thorough history and the administration of objective tests, it has been found useful to administer the following tasks in the author's office, and, in many cases, to prescribe them as homework assignments.

Interpersonal Styles

Through face-to-face interviews and direct observation of couples and families, especially in clinical, critical, or criminal relationships, it is possible to discern relatively easily whether their styles are Abusive-Apathetic (AA), Reactive-Repetitive (RR), or Conductive-Creative (CC), as in the ARC model. The latter style is not usually visible in clinical relationships, unless used to present a positive facade. However, this facade usually crumbles after a few interviews. Once they are observed, these styles can be prescribed paradoxically, to see whether they can be changed (Weeks & L'Abate, 1982). Many assignments, like Time Out, Sibling Rivalry, etc. (described in Chapter 4), were derived from clinical practice, where repetition of the same instructions was found to be more useful if administered in writing.

Drawing Lines

This is a task administered in therapy as well as in homework assignment in the Codependency workbook (Chapter 4). This task is drawn from the Selfhood model and is to be administered to so-called "codependent" individuals (addicted to the addict) or couples involved in symbiotic relationships (Jordan & L'Abate, 1995; L'Abate & Harrison, 1992).

Intimacy

This model is evaluated in therapy with two tasks: (1) Sharing of Hurts and (2) Hugging, Holding, Huddling, and Cuddling (3HC).

Sharing of Hurts

On the basis of Pennebaker's work and research (1997) (reviewed in Chapter 2), this author routinely asked all respondents, whether individuals, couples, or families, to write about their hurts for 20 minutes a day for 4 consecutive days from the very outset of therapy. In couples and families, respondents had to make an appointment with each other to share, compare, and discuss what they had written about their hurts. Variations on this assignment consist of listing "hurts given" and "hurt received," also including targets of given hurts and sources of received hurts.

On the basis of these homework assignments with clinical couples, it could be seen readily that the process of intellectualization and other defenses—the leaves of the artichoke—were still present. Often, even though they may be cognizant of the inflicted hurts, partners were not yet ready to share them in an affective fashion. Hence, when couples brought their lists of hurts to the therapist, this homework assignment was very informative from the outset of therapy. However, most couples were not yet ready to share their mutually inflicted hurts in a cathartic fashion, at least not in front of the therapist and not at the beginning of therapy. This area of sharing hurts through writing is completely open to clinical and preventive applications (Esterling et al., 1999; L'Abate, 1997a, 1999a; L'Abate & Kern, in press; Riordan, 1996).

The Sharing of Hurts exercise (L'Abate, 1986b, p. 235, 1997c, pp. 320–321, 1999a, 1999c, 1999e, 1999f) requires partners to face each other on a sofa or two chairs, closing their eyes and holding each other's hands. They are asked to concentrate on their physical sensations first, such as those elicited and expressed by holding each other's hands, before concentrating on their hurts. Once the request to concentrate on their hurt is given, the professional is to wait for the outcome. One may repeat the request for a second time, but no more than twice altogether. Once they are in touch with the hurts that are dwelling inside their bodies, partners are asked to acknowledge and, if possible, share them ("I hurt, I am hurting"). This task has also a diagnostic function—to evaluate whether partners can share their hurts or are defending against disclosing them (the leaves of the artichoke!).

Hugging, Holding, Huddling, and Cuddling

The second task consists of partners or families hugging, holding, huddling and cuddling (3HC) each other for a predetermined length of time, without any erotic moves (L'Abate, 1999f, 2001b). It requires nothing more than being together without any demands for perfection, production, performance, or problem-solving. Traditional treatment approaches, whether behavioral or otherwise, are directed usually toward "doing something" or "performing," requiring problem-solving ability and activity either on the part of the therapist, the identified patient (IP), or a child's caretakers. Why not teach respondents how to enjoy "doing nothing together" as the Italians call *dolce far niente* (sweet doing nothing)? Instead of action or the activities that are part of the American culture, why not use tasks that require no solution or activity, but that instead allow family members to learn about being available to each other nonverbally without doing anything?

Such a therapeutic orientation, systemic in nature, derives directly from the modality of "Being" or "Presence." Loving someone means being physically together in a way that allows direct, frequent, and consistent physical contact, that is, affection rather than just sex. This contact is necessary to feel emotionally available to and close with another intimate in a nonverbal fashion. The close physical presence of family members, offering and sharing "unconditional love," defines "presence" as the major glue that holds families together and makes them function well. Inadequacies in Presence brings about mixed priorities, with emphasis on Performance and Production. Under these circumstances it is possible to see an increase in symptomatic behavior in any one member of the family. Doing and Having characterize some aspects of the American culture, while Presence or Being characterize some Mediterranean and Latin cultures (Spiegel, 1971).

CONCLUSION

This chapter has reviewed preliminary evidence to support a developmental, contextual theory of intimate relationships. Its validity is necessary to establish a nexus between theory and practice, whether in the laboratory or in primary, secondary, or tertiary prevention. The administration of workbooks, then, can be guided by theory and not by a random, hit-or-miss process. There is no way that this writer by himself can validate the theory or the usefulness of workbooks that have been developed. This task will fall on larger and broader shoulders than this writer's.

7

Psychotherapy in the Twenty-First Century: What Is Going to Happen?

The purpose of this chapter is to relate the theory reviewed in Chapter 5 and partly validated in Chapter 6 to psychological interventions, first psychotherapy and then PW/SCAI. Diagnostic considerations deriving from the theory will be discussed from theoretical as well as clinical viewpoints. Within these applications, one needs to consider the impact of managed care in the delivery of mental health services, including, of course, psychotherapy. Ethical and professional issues and their implications for psychological interventions at a distance from respondents will be viewed within the context of a continuum of care. Lastly, some suggestions for a hierarchical organization of mental health personnel and training of psychotherapists for the future will be presented.

WHERE THEORY MEETS PRACTICE

Why do people ask for professional help? Heretofore, specifics of the referral question or symptoms as reasons for seeking professional help, have by necessity been largely expressed in negative terms, that is, in terms of distressful and hurtful behavior, either to self or intimate others (Weeks & L'Abate, 1982). It is much more relevant, in keeping with developmental competence theory, to assert from the very outset of a professional contact that people ask for help because they love themselves and intimate others. Only people who care for self and intimate others seek professional help. Those who do not know how to love self and others are unable or unwilling to seek that very same help. From this viewpoint, then, it follows that concern for self and concern for intimate others is the main motivation for seeking professional help and motivation for change.

Thus, the purpose of any psychological intervention is to help people improve their concerns for themselves and for loved ones and learn to negotiate internally within themselves and externally with intimate and nonintimate others.

Consequently, the aim of psychological interventions is to empower and enable people to function in more rewarding ways toward themselves and close others than they have done in the past (Diunst, Trivelle, & Deal, 1988). Whether it is done directly or indirectly, psychological intervention must have that effect to improve respondents' sense of importance and worth. Some therapists might be inclined to improve feelings of empowerment, helping to increase self-importance in respondents seeking help. Other therapists might tend to improve competencies and skills, enabling people to deal successfully with negotiating difficult or stressful life situations. Improved skills may or may not lead to increased feelings of empowerment, which, in turn, may or may not lead to greater ability to negotiate. Either way, psychological interventions, indirectly or directly, tend to improve the ability to love and the ability to negotiate in people who cannot do either well. Both *empowerment* and *enablement* match the two basic concepts of this theory: the ability to love (importance and intimacy) related to empowerment, and the ability to negotiate power issues (performance and production), related to enablement (L'Abate, 1990). Within these purposes are included the major priorities of survival and enjoyment.

Relationship skills, that is, empowerment, must be integrated with structuring skills, that is, enablement, because both sets of skills are necessary for successful outcome in any type of psychological intervention. The qualifying verb "may" is used here advisedly. Both skills may not be necessary with all people. While relationships skills may be necessary for starting and maintaining a therapeutic relationship, they are insufficient, and in some cases, counterproductive, in producing change for the better in character disorders, severe psychopathology, and especially in couples and families. While structuring skills may be insufficient and sometimes counterproductive in starting and maintaining a relationship, they are necessary to produce changes in individuals as well as couples and families. Relationship skills (as reviewed in Chapter 1) relate to the modality of Being, that is:

1. Being able to be present and available emotionally to oneself and to another verbally and nonverbally without demands for performance, production, perfection, or problem solving
2. Asserting the inherent importance and worth of respondents as autonomous, self-determining human beings
3. Expressing unconditional regard, warmth, and empathy
4. Reframing negative behaviors in positive terms
5. Showing concern for self and loved ones by asking for help: "Only strong people ask for help, because weak ones do not."

Being present is not negotiable. It can be experienced, expressed, and ultimately shared with respondents. This is the aspect of psychotherapy that is considered important by most humanistically oriented therapists (Bohart & Tallman, 1999). This aspect of therapy, however, may be useful with certain type of anxious or depressed, internalizing disorders, that is, those of selfless individuals. However, it becomes questionable when dealing with externalizing, acting-out, selfish, or no-self individuals.

Structuring skills and administration of workbooks, on the other hand, are basic to a mechanistic approach to symptoms and problems through repeatable methods such as manuals (Nathan & Gorman, 1998). Stepwise interventions are found in a more expressively active, even intrusively directive mode of intervention based on prescriptions, task assignments, and written homework assignments away from the therapist's office. This approach is favored by behaviorally oriented therapists (Kazantzis, Deane, & Ronan, 2000) and, possibly, by certain marital and family therapists. In terms of the theory, this approach favors Doing and Having, asking respondents to perform and produce (*service*) any time they are asked to process and complete homework assignments (*information*). If they want to save money and time, the more they perform and produce, that is, service themselves, in the area of homework assignments, the more money they may be able to save to use to buy other goods. Homework assignments administered on a collaborative basis are subject to negotiation (confrontation, bargaining, and problem solving) between therapists and respondents. This structuring stance favors explicitness and specificity in the differential treatment of disordered conditions.

Relationship and structuring skills can be integrated as two sides of the same coin, one side stressing subjective experiencing (*E*), the other side stressing objective activities (*A*). Psychodynamic, rational, and behavior-cognitive approaches represent the core, processing middle-point (*R*) that bridges the gap between between receiving input (*E*) to expressing output (*A*). By being aware of *C* and, hopefully, changing *Aw*, the circular process from its beginning to the end may be changed.

There are many ways to help hurt people if they want help. The process of change may take place within Rogers' *sine qua non* requirements (1957) of warmth, empathy, and unconditional regards for certain (depressed and anxious) individuals. However, these requirements are severely questionable with character disorders, severe psychopathology, couples, and families. Since Rogers, the psychotherapy literature has become replete with explanations about the basic conditions for therapeutic change. None of them, as far as this writer knows, deal with the content-free, structural factors that are repeated implicitly in the therapeutic process (L'Abate, 1997b). These factors are:

1. *Novelty* in meeting someone who is concerned and interested in the respondent's plight

2. *Positivity* in attending to and reframing respondent's negative attributions to self and others by reframing them positively
3. *Intensity* in accepting the depth, strength, and range of expressed emotions, validating them rather than dismissing and devaluing them as was done in the past, perhaps by intimate others
4. *Predictability*, in the consistent duration, repeated rate, and expected frequency of appointments
5. *Direction*, giving a sense of purpose in how the process of change needs to proceed

Of course, the latter factor is even clearer whenever a particular workbook is administered to deal specifically with the referral question.

DIAGNOSTIC CONSIDERATIONS

One important diagnostic consideration at the very outset of evaluation is to determine which component of the ERAAwC model dominates relationships. Should one then match a prevalent or dominant component with specific interventions, or follow a generic treatment format? For instance, should respondents marked by excessive E be matched with E-focused treatment? Should R-dominated relationships be matched with R-oriented approaches? Should an A-dominated system be matched with A-oriented treatment? Should one follow areas of strength or areas of weakness? Answers to these questions depend on the theoretical proclivities of therapists, their experience and knowledge bases, and their skills in relying on both relationship and structuring skills.

For instance, following Karasu's (1996) classification (summarized in Chapter 1) E-based interventions would consist of fantasy trips, awareness exercises, hurt-sharing, empathy-training, and body work, among many others. R-oriented interventions would consist, among many others, of relabeling and positively reframing the reason for referral (Weeks & L'Abate, 1982), cognitive reconstruction, interpretation of "irrational" beliefs, positive "explanations," and reliance on written homework assignments. A-oriented interventions, among many others, would consist of task assignments, paradoxical prescriptions of symptoms, prescriptive (vs. cathartic) homework assignments, straightforward directions, and paradoxical ordeal-oriented directives to deal with symptoms. This very brief catalogue of treatment approaches is given to illustrate how comprehensive one model of the theory, ERAAwC, is and how it can be used in treatment planning, in addition to its usefulness as a workbook (L'Abate, 1986b) and as a classification of major treatment approaches.

In considering the three modalities of exchange, Being, Doing, and Having, therapists will have a chance to evaluate whether the main point about psychopathology consists of deficits in Being rather that just Doing or Having. Furthermore, they will be able to evaluate whether misguided emphasis on Doing and Having derive from disturbances along the Continuum of Likeness and confused Priorities about self, intimate others, and settings. Ultimately, one needs to evaluate the presence or absence of intimacy. Are respondents able to cry together with loved ones? Did they ever see their parents share their hurts through crying, hugging, holding, huddling, and cuddling (L'Abate, 1999a, 1999f, 2001)? As indicated in the previous chapter, definite tasks assignments can be prescribed to deal specifically with these issues.

Polarizations in Self-definition

After dealing with the list of hurts, with stress on catharsis of the most traumatic ones, there are a variety of directions that can be followed through FW, depending on respondents' immediate needs and the therapist's theoretical and therapeutic predilections. One direction that can be taken is to concentrate on self-definition (Chapter 2). As explained in Chapter 5, at the genotypical bottom of our existence, in addition to hurts and fears of being hurt, there is a basic definition of how we choose to see ourselves, the genotype. This definition may be called the self-concept. It lies at the bottom of how important we think we are and how we act accordingly, oftentimes without awareness of the connection between internal self-definition and external behavior. In dysfunctional relationships this definition is usually: (a) *dichotomous* (either-or), (b) *defensive* (to make up for perceived inadequacies), (c) *incomplete* (based on a one-sided and limited view of the self with just one or two attributes—it takes more than one attribute to make up a self), therefore, (d) *negative* ("bad" rather than "good"), and (e) *reactive* (to the individual's past and present experiences). This type of self-definition is bound to isolate individuals and produce a great deal of conflict in their intimate relationships.

Most dysfunctional dyads meet, match, and sometimes marry on a complementary basis to fit into and satisfy their perceived definitions—selfulness with selfulness, selflessness with selfishness, or no-self with no-self (as discussed in Chapter 5). Eventually, they are bound to clash over how they perceive themselves and each other. These self-other perceptions of importance deteriorate into conflict and all of its possible negative outcomes. Partial and negative self-definitions, of course, represent the outcome of generational and developmental deficits in past parenting and socialization experiences. These experiences leave individuals with a partial, negative, and incomplete sense of self-importance or no sense of self-importance at all. As a result of this partial and negative self-definition, individuals may develop behavior that might allow for minimal survival skills and, (if any) some occasional enjoyment.

Briefly, because this rationale was expanded in Chapters 2 and 5, these definitions are at the bottom of the selfish-selfless polarities in marital relationships, characterized by repetitive, manipulative, and coercive patterns. These characteristics are also found in many abusive-apathetic or neglectful family relationships, or addictions and psychiatric conditions. Once the marital relationship is polarized, the same kind of polarization is likely to take place repetitively between parent and child, since the child will have to contend with and react to a caretaker whose self-definition is lacking and who, most likely, will use the child to achieve what is perceived as an adequate sense of self-importance.

Consequently, by concentrating on partners' or caretakers' self-concepts, one can undercut a variety of projections and externalizations. For instance, the two most frequent self-definitions that lie at the bottom of a great many destructive conflicts in intimate relationships (between partners and between parent-child) are the "good-bad" and the "right-wrong" dichotomies. Usually partners or parent-child (adolescent) dyads are polarized around one of these two dichotomies. Or else, there is a cross-over between individuals who want to be thought as "right" (in marriage or parenting) to individuals who want to be thought as "good." Either way, individuals with these self-definitions cannot win with each other. There is either an "I win, you lose" outcome in the selfish position, or a "You win, I lose" in the selfless position. In the no-self position, both partners or parent-child lose and no one in the family wins. Of course, one could argue that if one partner or parent wins at the expense of the other, both partners or parent-child will lose. However, these defeats may not be perceived as such from the viewpoint of partners-parents themselves. The one who wants to be right or "correct" finds the other (partner or child) always (or most of the time!) "wrong," while the one who conceived themself as being "good" finds the other "bad." The worst outcome takes place when one partner or parent is both "right" and "good," since there is no room left for the partner or the child to be himself or herself. Under these conditions only, oppositeness is possible.

The choice is to stay the same or find a more acceptable and less destructive self-definition. The major decision to be made at this point is whether to retain the same label (right versus wrong and good versus bad) or consider other labels (helpful, effective, competent) to define oneself. Here is where the Drama Triangle and Distance Regulation come into play. The therapist should not accept any spur of the moment decision. Instead, he or she should encourage thinking and reflection on whether to retain or discard old definitions and limiting, destructive roles ("Why don't you think about it and let me know what your decision is next time we meet?"). Once the decision is made in favor of a more helpful and effective self-definition ("I would have found it hard to help you in retaining the old labels. You could have kept them without my help."), the therapist can assign relevant, focused homework assignments for whoever is involved (Chapter 2). Oftentimes, this confrontation brings a change in respondents' attitudes concerning themselves. However, if this initial assignment is insufficient to bring about any change in self-definition, additional assignments may be necessary.

Treatment Considerations

Depending on the severity and type of dysfunction or referral question, the successive sieves modes of treatment indicate using the least expensive approaches first, moving on to more expensive modes of treatment when earlier treatment fails or is inadequate in producing results (Chapter 3). If early approaches do not work or work insufficiently, then one can move to more expensive approaches. For instance, one could start with primary prevention using groups of individuals, couples, and families structured around a common topic, the least expensive approach. This approach can be used when functionality is greater than dysfunctionality, as defined in the continuum of care presented in Chapter 1. If administered on a before-after basis, plus observations during the process, these evaluations will yield respondents who have not improved. They will furnish the bulk of secondary and tertiary prevention, as well as medication.

Successive sieves, of course, could be reversed when dysfunctionality is greater than functionality, starting with verbal, face-to-face crisis intervention and psychotherapy, adding workbooks, and ending with enrichment. The expense of treatment, however, could be decreased if, in addition to verbal and personal contacts, respondents were required to follow secondary prevention approaches, that is, working at a distance from therapists through focused and programmed distance writing, through the mail and or Internet between therapy sessions. While the goal of psychotherapy is to reduce crises and symptoms, the goal of secondary prevention is to improve relationship, negotiation, and problem-solving skills through workbooks. After the crisis has lessened, and greater skills have been learned, enrichment can be added at the end (Scheel, Forsythe, Kristjansson, Pranata, Packard, & Packard, 2000).

The Impact of Managed Care in the Delivery of Mental Health Services

In the last decade managed care has had a distinct impact on mental health practices in general and on the field of psychotherapy in particular. Depending on one's viewpoint, the impact can be conceived as negative or positive. Many mental health professionals see managed care as another bureaucracy superimposed in an authoritarian fashion over their professions, robbing them of initiative and creativity. Someone unknown, who represents the managed care company that pays for the therapy, phones from outside of the provider's state. This person proceeds to ask the therapist personal questions about the patient under care. Then, this stranger—whose professional qualifications are usually also unknown—in a few minutes and on the basis of the information given, proceeds to tell the therapist in how many more therapy sessions the patient should be "cured."

This process robs the responsible therapist of self-determination and initiative. Instead of a verbal process, the therapist is asked to complete a variety of forms that will determine how many therapy sessions will be necessary to complete the treatment process. Either way, control of the therapeutic process takes place long-distance. This unknown manager never sees the patient and, on the basis of the information received, makes extremely serious decisions that may, in some cases, mean life or death for the patient. This process leaves therapists with little or no input for the treatment but with responsibility for the outcome. Essentially, this stranger is practicing psychotherapy without a license outside the state in which the practice is taking place.

The other, more positive side of the managed care coin lies in its stress on two important criteria for mental health practices that are relevant to the practice of PW/SCAI. They are *cost-effectiveness* and *accountability*. Sky-rocketing costs of mental health services and the easy abandon with which psychotherapy has been practiced—with, in some cases, little concern for its costs or cost-containment—and stress instead on cost-effectiveness may be a corrective boundary that perhaps needed to be drawn. Furthermore, given the conservative and, seemingly, secretive way in which mental health procedures were practiced, perhaps the mental health community needed to reevaluate the costs of its services. Cost-effectiveness was really never considered until managed care made its entrance and started to establish some controls and some limits.

In addition to cost-effectiveness, managed care attempted to establish another criterion, perhaps vaguely addressed by the psychotherapeutic community, and that is, *accountability*—accounting for documentation and examination of its methods of treatment procedures. This criterion forced "private" practices to become more open to the eyes and judgment of external referees. Consequently, (1) accounting for treatment selection, (2) detailing the process of treatment, and (3) justifying results to external judges rather than remaining unaccountable to anyone, except, perhaps its patients, produced another monumental change in the whole mental health and psychotherapy communities. Now psychotherapists are asked to report on the outcome of their treatments, an unheard-of demand that was unthinkable to require a decade or so ago. Consequently, especially for those who rode on the coat-tails of the psychotherapeutic enterprise with a minimum of personal and professional preparation and responsibility, managed care came as a cold shower. It started to make demands that the least experienced and prepared psychotherapists were neither ready nor inclined to fulfill. For years, some members of this profession ignored or gave little weight to the very criteria set presently by managed care: cost-effectiveness and accountability. What are the ways to satisfy both criteria? One way is to keep written records of interventions taking place. The second way is a pre-post-intervention evaluation, especially when working at a distance. It is here that workbooks and SCAI can make their major contributions.

Why Interventions Rather than Therapy?

Many hours and quite a few dollars in legal advice and discussion were spent in advocating the use of "intervention" rather than "therapy" in the practice of PW/SCAI. First of all, therapy is commonly understood as a professional relationship that implies face-to-face verbal contact between a patient and a professional helper-therapist. A professional duly credentialed in any state of the Union can practice within the geographical confines of that state and in no other state. Hence, the purpose of licensing or certification is to safeguard the public from charlatans who could hang shingles proclaiming themselves to be what they are not.

What happens when a professional starts practicing PW or SCAI across state lines, outside of the confines of his or her license or certificate? If the word therapy is used and the intervention is taking place outside of the state of certification, the professional is liable to charges of practicing outside the confines of the license. Hence, under these conditions, the professional could be subjected to all kinds of legal challenges, not only from out-of-state respondents, but also from authorities within the state in which the license is operational. Consequently, it would be dangerous and foolhardy for any professional to call communications away from face-to-face relationships, via PW or SCAI, "therapy." This label raises more questions than can be answered.

Professionals who want to use either DW or SCAI or both should be extremely careful, therefore, in using the term "therapy." Its use in this context would bring about legal and professional challenges. One must consider the ire of colleagues who see these two media as threats to their practice and livelihood rather than novel ways to help people in trouble. There is nothing more satisfying for envious and threatened colleagues than to see someone practicing though PW or SCAI fall into legal or professional trouble. When using PW or SCAI, professionals must define this practice as "assistance," "education," "training," or use more neutral terms like "distance intervention," but never, never "therapy" or "treatment." In PW or SCAI we do not "treat patients." We educate, and train "respondents," never "patients," unless we also see them directly in face-to-face contact. Perhaps, in the not too distant future, it will be possible to call respondents through PW/SCAI "patients." However, many laws will have to change for this term to be used in this context. In the meantime, responsible professionals need to check state laws covering the practice of psychotherapy in their specific disciplines in which they have been licensed or certified.

By the same token, no matter what significant results one obtains through either PW or SCAI, a professional should never claim these results as "therapeutic" unless there is credible, objective evidence to substantiate that claim. We do know that education and training can reach many more people than face-to-face psychotherapy. It would help, as it would help in any context, for professionals to administer pre-post evaluations, not only to determine whether PW/SCAI has been helpful in and by itself, but also to document any results in case at any time this practice is or might be challenged.

PW/SCAI

Thus, PW/SCAI has the potential to decrease costs, increase efficiency, and reach a much greater number of people in need of help than current mental health practices can do when based on spoken, face-to-face interactions with professional helpers. Whether PW/SCAI approaches are as effective as verbal, face-to-face ones remains to be seen. The research by Segal and Murray (2000), and the work by Esterling, Antoni, Fletcher, Margulies, and Schneiderman (1994), as well as Szell (1994), suggest that the verbal medium still remains the most desired and desirable approach to helping people. However, when one considers costs for unit of professional time spent on listening to and resolving people's problems, PW/SCAI still remains a much cheaper and much more mass-oriented medium than talk.

SCAI

Gould (2001) should be considered the pioneer of SCAI. He has administered one generic interactive program called "Therapeutic Learning Program" (TLP) over the last 15 years to more than 18,000 patients. Each patient receives computer-generated feedback after 1 of 10 assignments is administered through a computer. Patients bring a feedback printout from computers to a group-therapy session immediately after completing each assignment. This self-administering program is now available on the Internet at *<www.masteringstress.com>*. In a variety of studies, Gould claims extremely high rates (up to 100%) of consumer's satisfaction. Therapists' ratings of patients' improvement ranged from 69% for "improved interpersonal satisfaction" to 83% for "improved personal satisfaction." This level of satisfaction remained high even after a three-year follow-up. A psychometric study suggested that as a result of this program, patients "became much more active in confronting problems and finding solutions." Results from a doctoral dissertation (Vosen, 1991), in which participation in TLP was evaluated, indicated a statistically significant reduction in medical costs for inpatient and outpatient services. There was no comparison group. In a study of 236 outpatients who received TLP compared with 13,233 patients from other therapists who did not receive TLP, Gould claimed that: (1) 53% of his patients were "improved" versus 32% for the other therapists, (2) 41% of his patients maintained some gains, while 58% of the others did not, (3) 6% of his patients regressed versus 10% in the others.

Most studies summarized by Gould suffer from a variety of methodological weaknesses. For instance, no demographic information about the characteristics of his patients or their diagnoses are given. Hence, it is difficult to compare his groups with any other group according to age, sex, socioeconomic level, religion, or ethnic group. Practically no study is cited in which a comparison group, matched in all variables except treatment, is described. Most of the ratings are subjective estimates by either patients or therapists. If and when pre-post tests or questionnaires are used, the sample is very small and no control group is present. Furthermore, as long as computer training is paired with group-therapy sessions, it is almost impossible to separate the effects of one treatment from the other.

In spite of these questionable results, Gould's work remains the pioneer effort in the area of SCAI. Better controls and more sophisticated research designs in the future should allow a more objective answer to the age-old question, "Who will profit by PW or SCAI? Who will profit by talking to a therapist? Who will profit by talking to a microphone? What synergistic effects will result from pairing two or more supposedly therapeutic media?"

Expansion to New and Different Settings

In addition to mental health clinics, mental hospitals, and penal institutions, PW/SCAI can be expanded to many more settings, such as high schools and colleges, and public and university libraries through computer terminals. However, these terminals should not be free-standing but should be connected with or linked to existing mental health facilities. Whoever logs in on these stations should know that a caring professional will be looking into what is written. Whoever logs in cannot be left disconnected but should know that someone at the other end of the computer link cares about how the computer is used, even if it is not in real time. On the other hand, it is conceivable that some workbooks, like those written for normative purposes (Chapter 4), could be administered to anyone who wants this experience.

Expansion to New and Different Populations

What kind of populations can be reached though PW/SCAI that cannot be reached through face-to-face contact? A great many people in rural areas as well many isolated people in urban settings have little access to mental health help. Military and missionary families, as well as Peace Corps volunteers who are under extreme stress, could be populations that may be difficult to reach through face-to-face contact. High school and college students who may be reluctant to visit local counselors or mental health facilities may find that logging in on a computer is easier than seeing someone face-to-face. Juveniles and adult inmates in many institutions may be reluctant to write using a pen or pencil. However, they may not be as reluctant to write if the medium is a computer. Older people without transportation (although some are computer literate), and handicapped people who are home-bound, are other populations lacking ready access to face-to-face services. Indigent populations who might be able to use public terminals in libraries, clinics, and hospitals, might profit by this approach. One is mindful of blood pressure machines being available in groceries and drugstores. Why not computer terminals?

Of course, expansion to new and heretofore diverse settings and populations is bound to create a whole host of new ethical and professional problems. These problems will come up as both PW and SCAI are applied to new settings and populations. Fear of new problems arising cannot be the basis for avoiding innovation. With the danger of possibly new ethical and professional issues, there is also the challenge of opening completely new vistas in the delivery of mental health services to heretofore underserved populations. These new populations, even though they may not be in current crisis, may need help that might forestall future crises. PW/SCAI, when administered responsibly and caringly, has the potential to reach populations that may not be reachable through traditional, verbal, face-to-face professional interventions.

ETHICAL AND PROFESSIONAL ISSUES IN PW/SCAI

Of course, the approach advocated here, working at a distance from respondents, is chock-full of ethical and professional issues. Some issues can be resolved with a thorough interview, a test battery, and a detailed informed consent form that specifies all the dangers and benefits that may derive from an approach that is not yet in the mainstream of clinical practice. Therapists desiring to use PW/SCAI should be conversant with state laws defining the practice of psychotherapy as well as the many new regulations defining this practice by many professional and scientific associations.

As long as psychotherapeutic interventions are limited to just "talk," there is no specific effect to be expected because of the very nature of this medium. Once we switch to DW and specifically PW, as in workbooks, such specificity can be achieved to a much greater degree of cost-effectiveness degree than is possible verbally. For instance (as already discussed in Chapter 4), there are different types of depression and there are different workbooks on the market that deal with depression. Comparing workbooks that claim to treat depression will allow us to evaluate and compare: (1) which kind of depression can be treated by which workbook, synergistically, (2) with which medication, (3) with or without face-to-face, talk-based psychotherapy, and (4) which combination or amalgam of which approaches does work rather than single-shot interventions. As long as talk is the only medium of communication, such specificity will be difficult and expensive to achieve. We need talk plus action.

The introduction of new and different media of intervention like PW/SCAI inevitably brings about a host of novel and diverse ethical and professional issues (Maheu, 2000; Maheu, Allen, & Whitten, 2001). Some of these issues may not be listed here because this is still *terra incognita* for many professional helpers, including this writer, as well as for many potential respondents. Hence, no matter how thoroughly one may want to report on these issues, there is no doubt that we are just skimming the surface. With time and usage of PW/SCAI, many more ethical and professional issues will arise.

The purpose of this section is to forestall a few of these problems. In spite of this proviso, it is assumed that mental health professionals using PW/SCAI are already knowledgeable about overall ethical and professional issues specific to their discipline, including issues of copyrights that are specific to the use of materials purchased from Workbooks For Better Living (WFBL, LLC). For those who want to pursue this area in greater depth, the works by Gackenbach

(Gackenbach & Ellerman, 1998) and by Maheu et al., (2001) are highly recommended. Since publication of this work, a host of additional papers and Internet communications about ethical and professional issues in the practice of PW/SCAI have become available in print and on the web.

How can these dangers be minimized? They will not go away. Many professional associations are setting up guidelines, if not restrictions, about the use of cyberspace therapy with respondents. For instance, one must restrict distance practice to the state in which one is licensed or certified. Consequently, if licensed in Georgia, one can work at a distance with someone in Gainesville, Georgia, but not in Gainesville, Florida. These restrictions also come from a helping model that conceives of psychotherapy as the sole mode of psychological treatment, taking place only through face-to-face contact and contract. This and many other restrictions about working at a distance from patients derive from a private practice, fee-for-service model. This model restricts access to professional help, in contrast to a public health model that makes access to professional help universal, to whoever wants it when need or desire is present.

Vicarious Liability

The major issue that is peculiar to the practice of PW/SCAI is "vicarious liability," a legal concept in which the responsibility for a harm caused by one person is imputed to a second party or person (Robert Henley Woody, Ph.D., Attorney at Law, Omaha, NE, personal communication, December 9, 1997). For example, if a complaint is filed against a professional based on a workbook sold by Workbooks for Better Living (WFBL), this business may be held accountable for any damages suffered by the complainant, even though the professional was the person who supposedly caused the alleged injury in the first place. Even more explicitly, this writer could be held legally liable for what another professional may have done to produce the damage. This is the reason why this writer insists that the use of workbooks be defined as interventions based on "assistance," "training," "education," "prevention," or any other term that does not imply "therapy," as explained earlier.

There are other precautions that should be followed by any responsible and caring mental health practitioner, as repeated throughout this work. Those are:

1. Conducting pre-post evaluations using objective self-report, paper-and-pencil tests before and after PW/CAT interventions
2. Use of the Informed Consent Form that was developed with legal counsel and that is mailed free of charge together with a Licensing Agreement to anyone ordering workbooks published by WFBL
3. Use of exclusionary rules, included in the Informed Consent Form
4. Appropriately matching a clinical condition or tests results with an isomorphic workbook

5. Continuous monitoring of the process, demanding that homework assignments be completed and feedback about each completed assignment given before assigning additional ones. This feedback, of course, can be given verbally in face-to-face therapy or in writing, through a fax or e-mail, in PW/SCAI.

In spite of all these precautions, there is still room for irresponsible practice, that is, the inappropriate administration of workbooks to individuals, couples, or families who should not have received them, especially if inordinate claims were made about the magical qualities of workbooks that do not and will never exist.

PW/SCAI and Confidentiality

A second issue in the practice of PW/SCAI is confidentiality. How can we safeguard our respondents' confidentiality? At first blush, one could answer that this issue is the same whether the medium is verbal, nonverbal, or written. As long as the medium is PW, confidentiality might not be an issue different from the other two media. If mail or e-mail is used to transmit PW assignments, it would be always wise to keep copies of everything that is written from both the professionals' or respondents' point of view. The major problem, however, arises when the medium of communication and intervention is web SCAI. How do we know that what respondents write to us and what we feed back to them through computers is going to be kept confidential, with no one except professional and respondent being privy to it? Is e-mail really confidential? How confidential is it? Can anyone who is familiar with computers break into these communications?

Certainly, no professional helper who is willing to use this medium to intervene should take it for granted that confidentiality is automatically granted, even through e-mail. Consequently, professionals who want to use this medium should ascertain from the very outset how confidential their communications will be. They may need to consult with a more knowledgeable colleague or Internet specialists to safeguard the absolute confidentiality of their communications. They may also need to consult with their respective professional associations at the state and national levels. Best of all, all of the communications with other colleagues, professional associations, and computer experts should be recorded (with back-up records kept on the computer), with copies kept, in case questions are raised about their confidentiality at any future time.

PW/SCAI and Certainty: How Do We Know Whether Respondents Wrote What They Claim They Wrote?

This is assuredly a question that critics of both media are asking. Whether PW or SCAI is used, this question should not be sloughed off lightly. There is always a nagging doubt, when using either PW or SCAI, about whether the answers do indeed belong to the one specific person with whom the professional is corresponding or interacting. In DW one can rely on the comparison between samples of handwriting obtained in face-to-face sessions and handwriting obtained when one switches to PW. However, the same is not true for SCAI. How can a professional be sure? The answer to this question is: "No one can be sure. If an individual wants to fool the professional and use someone else's name to respond to written homework assignments, it can be done." A professional can be fooled in face-to-face sessions as well as in DW and SCAI, if this is what the respondent wants to do. In the long run, of course, the one who loses is that respondent. However, there are some people, we must admit, who like to win by making others lose, making fools (seemingly in their eyes) of them, including psychotherapists. Certain paranoid personalities and some with character disorders, especially some types of felons, for instance, might get a kick out of "fooling" the professional. This possible manipulation underlines the critical importance of pre-intervention evaluation, not only in traditional verbal therapies, but especially in PW and SCAI.

Certain safeguards may be necessary, if not crucial, to ensure that whoever is communicating with the professional is indeed the very one who: (1) completed pre-intervention testing, (2) signed an Informed Consent Form, (3) paid a fee for the intervention, and (4) continued completing homework as assigned. Here, one is reminded of the situation in which the hero, Dr. Ryan (Clancy, 1991) was attempting to communicate via computers with the President of the Soviet Union during an international crisis. Opponents of Dr. Ryan raised the question about whether he was indeed communicating with the very person he claimed to be communicating with. Opponents of the President were raising the same question in the Soviet Union. Consequently, there followed a sequence of messages with content known only to Dr. Ryan and that President. These cryptic messages ensured that both communicants were actually dealing with the correct person. These safeguards are often followed by many credit card companies, which from the outset of signing new clients, register personal information only known to their clients and to no one else. Beyond these safeguards, one needs to be clear that what is communicated though either PW or SCAI is not therapy, but, as explained above, training or intervention. One should consult state laws to determine how the term "psychotherapy" is defined locally. Countless ways to assure privacy and assured direct links are available on the Internet (i.e., passwords, encryptions, etc.).

However, how is one to know whether tests and assignments have been answered by the intended "respondent"? One can ascertain through phone calls and by a statement signed below each test or assignment administered that the person signing it is indeed the same one who took the test or completed the assignment. When in doubt, the professional helper might decide to ask the person being evaluated for permission (in writing!) to use local intermediaries such as clergy, lawyers, and teachers to ascertain that the tests were administered to the same person who signed the Informed Consent Form and paid the bill for the workbook. However, if professionals need to use these safeguards, they may also want to consider that the respondent needs face-to-face interaction because of the need to monitor the respondent more closely. Ultimately, as already stated, if one wants to fool a professional, we can all be fooled, as in the completed case of the first treated felon reported in detail (L'Abate, 1992b). However, this is not an excuse. Professionals have the responsibility to make sure that they have taken as many precautions as are humanly possible to ensure that test results apply to the very individual, couple, or family who has been helped through PW or SCAI.

On the basis of the foregoing considerations, the Web Counseling Task Force for National Board for Certified Counselors recently set up standards that should be followed carefully by any professional who wants to practice, at least in part, through PW/SCAI. Even though these standards apply to "counseling" in cyberspace, listing them may help professionals understand what needs to be done to avoid doing any harm to anyone:

1. Review pertinent legal and ethical codes for possible violations emanating from the practice of Web counseling and supervision.
2. Inform WebClients of encryption methods being used to help ensure the security of client/counselor/supervisor communications.
3. Inform clients if, how, and how long session data are being preserved. *Note: For PW/SCAI, it is advisable to make sure that copies of completed homework assignments be kept by both the professional and the respondent, including, of course, copies of any written feedback given to the respondent.* Usually these copies should retained for as long as the professional is practicing.
4. In situations where it is difficult to verity the identity of the WebCounselor or WebClient, take steps to address impostor concerns, such as using code words, passwords, numbers, or graphics.
5. When parent/guardian consent is required to provide WebCounseling to minors, verify the identity of the consenting person. *Note: This criterion may apply if homework assignments are administered to adolescents below 18 years of age, since anyone older than 18 must be considered a consenting adult.*
6. Follow appropriate procedures regarding the release of information for sharing WebClient information with other electronic sources. *Note: No information about a client should be shared with anyone without the expressed, written consent of that client.*
7. Carefully consider the extent of self-disclosure presented to the WebClient and provide rationale for WebCounselor's level of disclosure.
8. Provide links to websites of all appropriate certification bodies and licensure boards to facilitate consumer protection.
9. Contact national, regional, or state licensing boards to obtain the name of at least one Counselor-On-Call within the WebClient's geographical region. *Note: The professional practicing PW/SCAI should be on call for any emergencies arising from this practice and have a substitute professional available on call in case of sickness*

or vacation. However, if respondents have been screened properly, there should not be emergencies of this kind because respondents should know from the very outset, from signing the Informed Consent Form, that in PW/SCAI there is little room for crises and emergencies that would require direct face-to-face contact with a professional.

10. If necessary, discuss with respondent procedures for contacting the professional when he or she is off-line. *Note: All respondents should know the address and phone number of the professional from the very outset of the intervention. The same applies to professionals, especially in the payment of fees.*
11. Mention in the websites those presenting problems they believe to be inappropriate for WebCounseling, that is, PW/SCAI. *Note: Exclusionary rules are part of the Informed Consent Form furnished by WFBL with any workbook.*
12. Explain to clients the possibility of technological failures.
13. Explain to clients how to cope with potential misunderstandings arising from the lack of visual cues from WebCounselor or WebClient. For example, suggest the other person simply say: "Because I couldn't see your face or hear your tone of voice in your e-mail message, I'm not sure how to interpret that last message."

There is another restriction recently set up by the Association of State and Provincial Psychology Boards (ASPPC), and that is:

An individual licensed to practice psychology in another jurisdiction may practice psychology by electronic or telephonic means in this jurisdiction no more than 30 days per year without applying for a license, as long as the requirements for a license in the former jurisdiction are equal to, or exceed, the requirements for licensure in this jurisdiction, or if the owner is the holder of an ASPPC CPQ.

This statement makes one wonder whether whoever drafted this statement knew what they were doing or understood the implications of what they wrote. This statement means that a professional can work at a distance only with respondents who live in the same state as the professional. A professional cannot work outside the confines of his or her state license. Can one not consult across state lines, especially if SCAI is not defined as psychotherapy? These limitations show a complete lack of awareness about prevention and preventive efforts that would allow reaching underserved populations that are and will remain unreachable unless PW/SCAI is used across state lines. What about military and missionary families and their members (DeLeon, 1998)? What about home-bound shut-ins? How about Americans living abroad? What about incarcerated felons?

These jurisdictional restrictions were written from the viewpoint of safeguarding traditional psychotherapeutic practices and pay no attention to functional and semi functional populations who may not need face-to-face verbal psychotherapy but could benefit by PW/SCAI. Hence, the restrictions set by the foregoing statement deprive professionals who follow a public health model from extending their usefulness outside the confines of a proprietary, private practice model.

A more specific criticism of the ASPPC statement pertains to the definition of "30 days per year." How is a day to be defined? If one communicates in minutes and hours, does this mean that "30 days per year," means the total sum of hours spent on the Internet? That would mean that one could confortably practice at a distance for 720 (30 days times 24) hours without applying for license in any state. That is an amount that many professionals practicing through PW/SCAI could probably live with. However, who is going to check for how long one has practiced in another state, and how? By calendar days? By computer hours? It can be readily seen that a great deal of thinking needs to be done before arriving at guidelines that would be realistic and appropriate to the practice of PW/SCAI.

In the meantime, professionals practicing PW/SCAI or planning to practice through these media need to be mindful of the supplement to ethical guidelines given by the American Psychological Association:

> The Ethics Code is not specific with regard to telephone therapy or teleconferencing or any electronically provided services as such and *has no rules prohibiting such services.* Complaints regarding such matters would be addressed on a case by case basis.
>
> Delivery of services by such media as telephone, teleconferencing and Internet is a rapidly evolving area. This will be the subject of APA task forces and will be considered in future revision of the Ethics Code. Until such time as a more definitive judgment is available, the Ethics Committee recommends that psychologists follow Standard 1.04c, Boundaries of Competence, which indicates that "In those emerging areas in which generally recognized standards for preparatory training do not yet exist, psychologists nevertheless take responsible steps to insure the competence of their work and to protect patients, clients, students, research participants, and others from harm." Other relevant standards include Assessment (Standards 2.01–2.10), Therapy (4.01–4.09, especially 4.01 Structuring the Relationship and 4.02 Informed Consent to Therapy), and Confidentiality (5.01–5.11). Within the General Standards section, standards with particular relevance are 1.03, Professional and Scientific Relationship: 1.04 (a, b, and c), Boundaries of Competence; 1.06, Basis for Scientific and Professional Judgments; 1.07a, and c). Describing the Nature and Results of Psychological Services; 1.14, Avoiding Harm; and 1.25, Fees and Financial Arrangements, Standards under Advertising, particularly 3.01–3.03 are also relevant.
>
> Psychologists considering such services must review the characteristics of services, the service delivery method, and the provisions of confidentiality. Psychologists must then consider the relevant ethical standards and other requirements, such as licensure board rules. (italics added)

This is certainly not the last word on the use of PW/SCAI. However, for the time being, until and unless new guidelines come about, it will have to suffice.

Professional Issues: The Importance of Feedback

The major issue with both PW and SCAI is feedback. How is the professional to respond to whatever is received as a completed homework assignment from a respondent? How should this feedback be worded? WFBL makes available on request a list of possible "canned" replies of a general nature, with space for specific replies. The nature of the feedback, or course, depends on the nature of the relationship established, the theoretical and personal predispositions of the professional, and the nature of completed homework assignments. First of all, was the assignment completed? If it was not completed, it should be sent back to the respondent with a note that no future assignments will be sent unless the homework is completed satisfactorily. Secondly, if the homework is completed, how was it completed? Sloppily? Minimally? Irrelevantly? Superficially? The professional should be attentive to all these nuances of quality before accepting completed homework. Some feedback should be given about the way the homework appeared to the professional, for example, "Perhaps you may not be aware of it. However, your response appeared to me to have been answered too quickly, without much thought of your own behind the answers. I may be wrong. However, I would like to see you respond to the same assignment in a more thorough and thoughtful fashion. I am sure you can do it."

This feedback is to assure respondents that they are not dealing with someone who is going to accept anything they write without corrective feedback. A great deal of attention by the professional must be given to the completed homework. Positive feedback should be given where it is rightfully deserved: "I liked the way you answered this question. Especially, I appreciated what you wrote in addition about. . . ."

Feedback might not be limited to the specific content of the answers. This is an extremely crucial issue. Where does one draw a line between corrective feedback and "therapeutic interpretation"? This writer wishes he could give readers clear, concise, and concrete guidelines here. Unfortunately, he cannot. Within this context of ignorance, the writer is willing to suggest some possibilities. First, before giving corrective feedback that borders on "therapeutic interpretation," the professional should ask for more information on the subject. For instance, often times respondents reveal new, traumatic, and relevant information that is not and cannot be contained within the strict limits of the assignment just administered. Hence, it is imperative that extra information be considered charitably and compassionately: "I was really surprised to hear about XYZ happening to you years ago. I appreciate your revealing it to me. What was the outcome of this event on the future course of your life?" Second, what seems to be strictly programmed may expand to a wide range of topics that may be addressed directly. If this feedback cannot be given, and if the event is definitely too traumatic to be dealt with through PW/SCAI, one of the recommendations to be made at the end of the workbook would pertain to getting direct professional help, if this help has not yet been considered. Third, PW/SCAI can be used to overcome whatever fears, defenses, or resistance may exist to obtaining face-to-face help, by using the workbook based on Butcher's Treatment Planning Inventory (BTPI), for instance (Chapter 4).

Recommendation for face-to-face psychotherapy would carry greater weight if no improvement is found on the basis of pre-post-test results: "I am sorry to report that test results fail to indicate any improvement in your condition. On the basis of these results, as well as on everything that has been written during the course of this approach, it would seem that direct professional help should be the treatment of choice at this time. Please keep in mind that everything that you have written to me in the workbook is strictly confidential. It can be released to any professional you choose, but only with your expressed written consent. Have you ever thought about asking for professional help? You know, it takes a lot of strength to ask for help. There are a great many people who are so weak that they are unable to ask for help. I think that you are strong enough to ask for such help at this time. I strongly recommend it because the approach we have used here did not produce the results we were hoping for. What do you think?"

Who Cannot or Should Not Receive PW or SCAI?

Once this practice is labeled as "training" or "education," or, at best, "prevention," is important to limit it from the very outset to individuals, couples, or families who can benefit from it. This important process of selecting appropriate respondents is accomplished through a complete history, a full description of the referral questions, and the administration of pre-post objective test instruments. Who can benefit by either PW or SCAI? We really do not know, at this juncture, who can and who cannot be helped. We can only guess that people who are seriously addicted, intellectually handicapped, brain-damaged, psychotic, or under extreme stress and in crisis will not be able to concentrate enough to answer and to learn from written homework assignments (L'Abate, 1990, 1992b, 1994a). Abusive couples and families, especially those who hide the abuse from mental health personnel, should be carefully screened. How can one determine these conditions without face-to-face contact? No matter how self-selecting some individuals, couples, or families, that is, respondents, will be, there will be some who will fall into the cracks. Hence, the importance of objective evaluation on a pre-post-intervention basis cannot be stressed enough.

If this approach is labeled "training," "education," or "prevention," it very likely might not fall into the category of payable remuneration, as defined by managed care or insurance companies. These companies do not pay, as yet, for preventive or paratherapeutic approaches like PW/SCAI. Professionals who practice PW/SCAI will need to demonstrate, as shown in the review by Esterling et al. (1999), that DW does indeed produce beneficial physical and mental results. By the same token, one should be aware and cognizant of seemingly negative, unexpected, and paradoxical results, reported in this work, found with undergraduates and seminarians. These results perhaps demonstrated that DW, whether focused or programmed, may be as powerful and as confrontive, or even more so, than talk and produce unforeseen results, not always beneficial (L'Abate, submitted for publication, b).

The fees charged for PW or SCAI, however, may be smaller than those charged in face-to-face professional interventions. Some people may be willing to pay smaller fees from their own pocket. Furthermore, in PW/SCAI, charges should be made for the administration of a whole workbook rather than for single assignments, even though the cost of a workbook may depend on the number of assignments it contains. The cost of a workbook should also include pre-post evaluation, as spelled out in a written informed consent form.

Solution: Written Informed Consent?

A considerable amount of time and effort was spent in developing an appropriate informed consent form (ICF). Unfortunately, to cover all the possible legal and professional bases, such a form became unyielding, too complex to give to anyone who might use this form of intervention. Thus, an abbreviated form is available to administer when using either PW or SCAI. The professional, however, should consult the "long form" and check on the way each possible source of contention has been approached by legal counsel. Even if it is labeled "training," this term should not imply that the professional is free from moral, ethical, and professional responsibilities, the first one being, "Do no harm." Hence, informed consent is one solution to possible issues that may arise from the practice of DW and SCAI, but it is not, by any means, the only solution.

Implications of a Continuum of Care for a Hierarchy of Mental Health Personnel

A continuum of care asks the question, "Who is going to perform all these services?" There are not sufficient doctorate level personnel to perform all of the various services deemed necessary to help all the people at risk, in need, and in crisis. Consequently, we will need to start differentiating among different types and levels of personnel according to a hierarchical perspective, a ladder or a lattice of human services, as summarized in Table 7.1. As this table shows, a classification of methods of intervention will allow a parallel differentiation among different types of personnel, from professional to clerical. Whether this proposal will be implemented is a matter of policies outside the realm of this work.

Training Psychotherapists for the Past or for the Future?

The complex classification of psychotherapies according to traditional and more recent categories or dimensions presented in Chapter 1 allows us to see

Table 7.1
Toward a Hierarchy of Mental Health Personnel

Educational Level	Skills and Responsibilities
Board Diplomate	Supervision and support of doctorate level professionals
	Research leadership
Doctorate	Crisis intervention
	Treatment plans based on conclusions from evaluation (history, interview, objective tests, and diagnosis)
	Decision making and delegation of therapeutic responsibilities: matching of treatment with helpers or matching problem with solution; assumption of therapeutic responsibilities with more difficult cases
	Supervision and support of master level personnel
	Quality control, maintenance of ethical, professional, and scientific standards
Master or equivalent	Carrying out most therapeutic, paratherapeutic, and pretherapeutic responsibilities: prolonged face-to-face contact before, during, and after crisis
	Support and supervision of bachelor level personnel
Bachelor or equivalent	Administration and scoring of standard tests
	Administration of primary and secondary preventive activities, including review, and feedback of written homework assignments with selected cases.

what we need to learn to help people in trouble. In addition to the verbal modality, training programs in psychotherapy may need to develop additional courses in nonverbal and written modalities of intervention. Once a vast armamentarium of different intervention methods is learned, we should be able to find out how to use them synergistically, to improve chances of positive outcome.

Long gone are the days when we could draw conclusions about the effectiveness of any treatment approach on a dichotomous black-and-white, true-false, applicable-nonapplicable basis. One cannot dismiss any legitimate and professionally available form of treatment on grounds of fruitfulness or popularity alone. There are other criteria to be considered, such as empirical grounds, cost-effectiveness, specificity in client-treatment matching, and personal and interpersonal relevance. With so many treatment approaches available, we can no longer base our choice and selection of treatment(s) on an all-or-none basis. Instead, we need to choose one or more treatment approaches matched with specific problems. We may need to rely on other professions and on a hierarchy of personnel for whatever their particular contribution may be. If a respondent is extremely upset, he or she may need medical as well as nonmedical approaches, like a massage or a hot tub. Extratherapeutic approaches may be prescribed, provided it is understood that they are temporary crutches that cannot be used for life, unless, of course, that is what respondents want—another form, albeit legitimate, of addiction! An appropriate and effective course of treatment for any dysfunctionality would involve multiple treatment media and modalities used synergistically—rather than on an exclusionary basis—with a variety of specialized personnel.

As long as talk remains the major if not the only medium of exchange between respondents and therapists, the education and personality of therapists is stressed at the expense of treatment methods (Bickman, 1999). However, thus far, it has been very difficult to find which sets or types of competencies are necessary to make up a competent therapist (L'Abate, 1983b). Once we introduce the other two media of exchange (nonverbal and written), and we enlarge the therapeutic repertoire to include primary and secondary prevention strategies, we need to deal with the practical problem that no one single professional, no matter how bright or well trained, can learn and apply all three media.

Yet, there are not enough professionals to take care of the many mental health problems existing in the United States today. The inefficiency, costs, and impracticality of the single face-to-face client-therapist practice used initially by psychiatrists was paralleled in and enlarged by the creation of many other therapeutic professions. Members of these professions assumed the roles of frontline therapists, taking over the roles originally allocated to psychiatrists. In spite of their growth in numbers, from a public health viewpoint, there will never be a sufficient number of professional personnel to deal with the many mental health problems facing us. We need to think in terms of a lattice and ladder of professional and subprofessional personnel, as suggested above (Table 7.1).

We need to learn to work at a distance from people in need of help. To work at a distance we need to rely on less trained and experienced personnel and more on nonverbal and written media than we have done heretofore. In the first place, we need to distinguish between professional and technical skills. For instance, one may need a bachelor degree to administer and score an intelligence test. Both administration and scoring are technical skills that can be learned from reading a manual and practicing both administration and scoring, at least initially, under the supervision of a doctorate-level professional. Interpretation and reporting of test results, on the other hand, require professional skills. These skills are based on an understanding of statistics, knowledge of the psychometric properties of the particular intelligence test being used, awareness of the relationship of an intelligence test profile to cultural, developmental, and organic conditions, as well as the background of the professions one is reporting to. One needs to know the limits of knowledge of other professions or clients one is reporting to. This knowledge requires graduate training and supervised clinical experience at the doctorate level. Conclusions arrived at professionally may take a few minutes, but the background behind them took years.

By the same token, when this differentiation is applied to therapeutic interventions, we can distinguish primary and secondary prevention from tertiary prevention. Crisis intervention, treatment planning, and supervision of paraprofessional personnel are all professional skills. Administration of primary and secondary prevention approaches, however, are technical skills. They definitely require some human sensitivity and warmth, but, from the viewpoint of educational experience, a bachelor-level degree would be sufficient, provided, of course, that personnel at this level were supervised and supported by a doctorate-level professional. Crisis intervention, at the beginning of therapy, could be administered by a professional. However, once the crisis or the symptom has been taken care of, further psychoeducational social skills and enrichment programs, that is, primary and secondary prevention approaches, could be administered by less trained personnel.

A second issue with current mental health and psychotherapeutic practices is cost. In the United States there is now a spiralling increase in physical and mental health costs that, with the advent of AIDS, has reached catastrophic proportions. Insurance companies which up to now have footed the bill for most mental health problems to the tune of several billion dollars a year, are decreasing most benefits in this area. Many companies are restricting mental health benefits for their employees because of these ever-increasing costs. Most cuts have been made in the mental health field. Psychotherapy sessions have been limited to the point that most insurance companies, unless there is a need for hospitalization, severely limit the number of psychotherapy sessions available within a year. Up to the present, the psychotherapy and family therapy professions, because of their undeniable success, seemed oblivious to financial considerations. However, the many restraints being exercised presently will eventually force a change in how therapists are going to practice. We may need to keep professional functions for a doctorate and rely on paraprofessional personnel to perform technical functions.

Thus, doctorate-level professionals, to be maximally effective, would need to work with clients at a distance through less trained and experienced personnel, using all three media of communication and modalities of exchange. The time and training of a doctorate-level professional cost more than the time and training of a bachelor- or master-level paraprofessional. A ladder and lattice of different levels in professional and paraprofessional training would realistically confront overwhelming social problems facing us (Table 7.1).

Working at a distance from people in need through less trained personnel would require greater reliance on structured written materials and on group work using the nonverbal medium, as administered by paraprofessional personnel. While most primary prevention programs deal with groups of individuals, couples, or families, secondary prevention programs rely mostly on the written medium (Chapter 1). We need to give less trained personnel a structure to follow that would limit their responsibilities and, therefore, decrease their anxiety about working with people in need. For instance, structured enrichment programs for couples and families contain verbatim instructions that can be followed by any sensitive and conscientious individual without professional training but working under the supervision of a professional. Workbooks do not even require a less trained paraprofessional. They can be administered directly by the professional. This division of labor leaves little if any room for individual initiative or intuition at the technical level, but leaves most responsibilities in the hands of the professional.

CONCLUSION: THE FUTURE OF PROGRAMMED WRITING/STRUCTURED COMPUTER-ASSISTED INTERVENTIONS

The future of PW/SCAI is wide open for innovation and expansion. The possibilities arising from both media are immense in terms of the number and type of people that can be reached and the kinds of settings where both can be applied. As shown in the various workbooks reviewed in Chapter 4, PW/SCAI may be two cost-effective, mass-oriented ways to deliver alternative or additional mental health services, either in conjunction with existing mental health practices or separately from them. The latter possibility should be more relevant to prevention than to crisis intervention. It will be critical to find out: (1) who will be helped through these media, and (2) who will not be. Unless both PW/SCAI are applied, however, it will be virtually impossible to find an answer to these questions. There will be a day when institutions, schools, hospitals, clinics, and public libraries will be interconnected to allow as many people as are at risk and in need to access and accept mental health help at a distance, without seeing anybody face-to-face.

Psychological interventions could follow what this writer (L'Abate, 1990; L'Abate & Rupp, 1981; L'Abate & Thaxton, 1981) has called a "successive sieves" approach, going from the least expensive to the most expensive, as followed in appropriate medical practice. He and his collaborators identified and differentiated among six successive sieves in mental health delivery systems: (1) prevention, including (2) mutual self-help groups, and (3) skill training programs, (4) the psychotherapies, (5) environmental modifications, and (6) community efforts (L'Abate & Rupp, pp. 121–125).

The approach without a specification of a continuum of care presented in chapter 1 has recently been called the "Stepped Care" model. It is based on individual differences rather then on clinical labels alone (Davison, 2000; Haaga, 2000; Newman, 2000; Otto, Pollack, & Maki, 2000; Sobell & Sobell, 2000; Wilson, Vitousek, & Loeb, 2000). At the core of this model is careful evaluation and screening to determine which respondent needs which approach, as advocated in the present work. To quote the introductory abstract to the foregoing contributions:

> Not all patients need the same type and intensity of intervention. Some may be helped greatly by reading a self-help book, watching an instructional video, using a computer program. Others could benefit from a brief psychoeducational group conducted by a paraprofessional, and still others may require long individual treatment from a highly trained professional therapist with specialized expertise. Accordingly, we need to be

Table 7.2
Successive Sieves and Stepped Treatment in the Continuum of Care* and the Selfhood Model of Personality Propensities in Workbook Administration**

1. *Primary Prevention*: Proactive, Pre- or Post-therapeutic and Universal:
Sieve No. 1. Distance Writing in Its Four Structures:
a. Open-ended, as in journals and diaries
b. Focused, as in autobiographies and expressive writing about one's hurts
c. Guided, as in questions deriving from open-ended or focused writing
d. Programmed, as in nontargeted workbooks used for screening and selection purposes, as described in Chapter 4:

• For Youth, the following workbooks would be appropriate for screening and evaluation purposes with general (middle and high school) populations: Social Skills (S^3), Anxiety, Depression, and Fears, Emotional Problems in Youth, Emotional Intelligence, and Social Training.

• For Adults, the following workbooks would be appropriate for screening and evaluation purposes: Self-Awareness, Social Training, Multiple Abilities, Normative Experiences in the three forms (PSC, IPIP, AB5C), Social Skills, Emotional Expression, Emotional Intelligence, and Social Growth.

• For Couples, the following workbooks would be appropriate for screening and evaluation purposes; Premarital Preparation, Stand UP for Yourself, and Improving Relationships.

• For Families, the following workbooks would be appropriate for screening and evaluation purposes: Initial Family Interview, Feelings in the Family, Family Profile Form, and Relationship Styles.

Sieve No. 2. Traditional Primary Prevention Programs alone requiring a trainer and verbal, face-to-face contacts

Sieve No. 3. Combination of Sieves 1 and 2

2. *Secondary Prevention*: Para-active, Para- or Pre- or Post-therapeutic and Selectively Labeled:

Sieve No. 4. Targeted workbooks for externalizing and internalizing conditions, either through referral question or single-test scores or test-profiles, as discussed in Chapters 3 and 4

Sieve No. 5. Traditional Secondary Prevention Approaches alone

Sieve No. 6. Combination of Sieves 4 and 5

3. *Tertiary Prevention*: Reactively therapeutic, Necessary or Indicated

Sieve No. 7. Psychotherapy and Crisis Intervention alone

Sieve No. 8. Medication alone

Sieve No. 9. Combination of Sieve 4 with either Sieve 8 or 9 or a combination of all three (4 + 7 + 8) sieves, including workbooks for psychopathological conditions, comprising both internalizing and externalizing conditions (Chapter 4)

Sieve No. 10. Hospitalization or Incarceration alone

Sieve No. 11. Combination of Sieve 10 with selected sieves below 10

*See Table 1.1.
*See Table 5.3.

Source: L'Abate (1994a).

concerned with how to manage our scarce resources efficiently so as to deliver beneficial interventions to as many people who need them as possible. (Haaga, 2000, p. 547)

If this is the case, distance writing and especially workbooks can be added to the stepped treatment model and the continuum of care reviewed in chapter 1 (Table 1.1), with the classification of workbooks to be administered according to the selfhood model given in Chapter 5 (Table 5.3). By starting with the cheapest form of mass, that is, "universal" intervention, using distance writing in its four structures, and adding traditional approaches alone or in combination with other approaches, one obtains a vast and all-encompassing classification of successive sieves (Table 7.2), as the need arises. Instead of subjective evaluation and decisions made on the basis of test responses, screening and evaluation could also be reached on how: (1) respondents complete assignments, (2) they react to feedback from professional helpers, and (3) they react to information concerning their performance in completing both baseline test evaluations and workbooks.

Failure to complete one sieve satisfatorily would automatically mean the introduction of a more expensive sieve. Satisfactory completion would be defined by the nature of responses given by respondents as well as by pre-post-intervention rating sheets from external observers, self-report paper-and-pencil tests, and comparisons with responses and results from similar respondents. Instead of traditional primary, secondary, and tertiary prevention choices, as in psychotherapy, medication, or hospitalization/incarceration, distance writing and workbooks, either alone or in combination with traditional approaches, have the potential to access and help a much greater number of people in distress than heretofore. The summary of this model, as presented in Table 7.2, epitomizes and summarizes what has been presented in all the preceding pages and chapters of this work.

References

Abt, L. E., & Stuart, I. R. (Eds.) (1982). *The newer therapies: A sourcebook.* New York: Van Nostrand Reinhold.

Addis, M. E. (1997). Evaluating the treatment manual as a means of disseminating empirically validated psychotherapies. *Clinical Psychology: Science and Practice, 4,* 1–11.

Aiken, L. R. (1999). *Human differences.* Mahwah, NJ: Earlbaum.

Akistal, H. S., & Cassano, G. B. (Eds.) (1997). *Dysthymia and the spectrum of chronic depression.* New York: Guilford.

Albee, G. W., & Guillotta, T. P. (Eds.) (1997). *Primary prevention works.* Thousand Oaks, CA: Sage.

Alexander, J., & Barton, C. (1995). Family therapy research. In R. H. Mikesell, D. D. Lusterman, & S. H. McDaniel (Eds.), *Integrating family therapy: Handbook of family psychology and systems theory* (pp. 199–115). Washington, DC: American Psychological Association.

Allman, L. (1982a). The aesthetic preference: Overcoming the pragmatic error. *Family Process, 21,* 43–56.

Allman, L. (1982b). The poetic mind: Further thoughts on an "aesthetic preference." *Family Process, 21,* 415–428.

Alloy, L. B., Abramson, L. Y., Whitehouse, W. G., Hogan, M. E., Tashman, N. A., Steinberg, D. L., & Donovan, P. (1999). Depressogenic cognitive styles: Predictive validity, information processing and personality characteristics, and developmental origins. *Behavior Research and Therapy, 37,* 503–531.

Aman, M. G., & Singh, N. N. (n.d.). *Aberrant behavior checklist (ABC): Residential and community version.* East Aurora, NY: Slosson Educational Publications.

Ammerman, R. T., Last, C. G., & Hersen, M. (Eds.) (1993). *Handbook of prescriptive treatments for children and adolescents.* Boston, MA: Allyn & Bacon.

Anastasi, A. (1992). A century of psychological science. *American Psychologist, 47*, 842–842.

Anderson, C. M., Reiss, D. J., & Hogarty, G. E. (1986). *Schizophrenia and the family: A practitioner's guide to psychoeducation and management.* New York: Guilford.

Anderson, K. W. (1998). Utility of the Five-Factor model of personality in psychotherapy aptitude-treatment interaction research. *Psychotherapy Research, 8*, 54–70.

Andrews, D. A., Bonta, J., & Hoge, R. D. (1990). Classification for effective rehabilitation: Rediscovering psychology. *Criminal Justice and Behavior, 17*, 19–52.

Anthony, J. L., Lonigan, C. J., & Hecht, S. A. (1999). Dimensionality of posttraumatic stress disorder symptoms in children exposed to disaster: Results from confirmatory factor analysis. *Journal of Abnormal Psychology, 108*, 326–336.

Atkinson, L., & Zucker, K. J. (Eds.) (1997). *Attachment and psychopathology.* New York: Guilford.

Austad, C. S. (1998). *Is long term psychotherapy unethical?* San Francisco, CA: Jossey-Bass.

Averill, J. R. (1997). The emotions: An integrative approach. In R. Hogan, J. Johnson, & S. Briggs (Eds.), *Handbook of personality psychology.* San Diego, CA: Academic Press.

Aymard, L. L. (1999). Therapeutic applications of computers with children. In C. Schaefer (Ed.), *Innovative psychotherapy techniques in child and adolescent therapy* (pp. 271–314). New York: Wiley.

Baggett, M. S. (1980). *The auditory-visual-oral-manual test as a screening device for behavior disordered and learning disabled children on the basis of socioeconomic background.* Unpublished Ph.D. dissertation. School of Education, Georgia State University, Atlanta, GA.

Bakan, D. (1968). *Disease, pain, and sacrifice: Toward a psychology of suffering.* Boston, MA: Beacon Press.

Bandura, A. (1989). Human agency in social cognitive theory. *American Psychologist, 44*, 1175–1184.

Bonanno, G. A., & Keltner, D. (1997). Facial expression of emotions and the course of bereavement. *Journal of Abnormal Psychology, 106*, 126–137.

Barak, A. (1999). Psychological applications on the Internet: A discipline on the threshold of the new millennium. *Applied & Preventive Psychology, 8*, 231–245.

Bargh, J. A., & Chartrand, T. L. (1999). The unbearable automaticity of being. *American Psychologist, 54*, 462–479.

Barkham, M., Shapiro, D. A., & Firth-Cozens, J. (1989). Personal questionnaire changes in prescriptive vs. exploratory psychotherapy. *British Journal of Clinical Psychology, 28*, 97–107.

Barlow, D. H., & Craske, M. G. (1994). *Client workbook: Mastery of your anxiety and panic II.* San Antonio, TX: Psychological Corporation.

Bar-On, R. (1997). *Bar-On Emotional Quotient Inventory: User's Manual.* Toronto, ON: Multi-Health Systems.

Barone, D. F., Hersen, M., & Van Hasselt, V. B. (Eds.) (1998). *Advanced personality.* New York: Plenum.

Baskin, D. (1994). Administrative uses for computer database in psychiatry. *Psychiatric Annals, 24*, 30–32.

Bastien, S., & Jacobs, A. (1974). Dear Sheila: An experimental study of the effectiveness of written communication as a form of psychotherapy. *Journal of Consulting and Clinical Psychology, 42*, 151.

Baucom, D. H., Shoham, V., Mueser, K. T., Daiuto, A. D., & Stikle, T. R. (1998). Empirically supported coupled and family interventions for marital distress and adult mental health problems. *Journal of Consulting & Clinical Psychology, 66*, 53–88.

Baumeister, R. F., & Tice, D. M. (1996). Rethinking and reclaiming the interdisciplinary role of personality psychology: The science of human nature should be the center of social sciences and humanities. *Journal of Personality Research, 30*, 363–373.

Bazerman, M. H., Curhan, J. R., Moore, D. A., & Velley, K. L. (2000). Negotiation. *Annual Review of Psychology, 51*, 279–314.

Beck, A. (1976). *Cognitive therapy and the emotional disorders*. New York: Meridian Press.

Bellack, A. S., & Hersen, M. (Eds.) (1979). *Research and practice in social skills training*. New York: Plenum.

Bell-Pringle, V. J. (2000). *Contextual theory and writing about upsetting events: An outcome study*. Unpublished doctoral dissertation. Department of Psychology, Georgia State University, Atlanta, GA.

Benenson, J. F. (1996). Gender differences in the development of relationships. In G. G. Noam & K. W. Fischer (Eds.), *Development and vulnerability in close relationships* (pp. 263–286). Mahwah, NJ: Earlbaum.

Ben-Porath, Y. S. (1997). Use of personality assessment instruments in empirically guided treatment planning. *Psychological Assessment, 9*, 361–367.

Berger, R., & Hannah, M. T. (Eds.) (1999). *Handbook of preventative approaches to couples therapy*. Bristol, PA: Brunner/Mazel.

Bergin, A. E., & Garfield, S. L. (1994). *Handbook of psychotherapy and behavior change*. New York: Wiley.

Beutler, L. E. (1979). Toward specific psychological therapies for specific conditions. *Journal of Consulting and Clinical Psychology, 47*, 882–897.

Beutler, L. E. (1989). Differential treatment selection: The role of diagnosis in psychotherapy. *Psychotherapy, 26*, 271–281.

Beutler, L. E. (1991). Have all won and must all have prizes? Revisiting Luborsky et al.'s verdict. *Journal of Consulting and Clinical Psychology, 59*, 1–7.

Beutler, L. E., & Clarkin, J. F. (1990). *Systematic treatment selection: Toward targeted therapeutic interventions*. New York: Brunner/Mazel.

Beutler, L. E., Williams, R. E., Wakefield, P. J., & Entwistle, S. R. (1995). Bridging scientist and practitioner perspectives in clinical psychology. *American Psychologist, 50*, 984–994.

Bickman, L. (1999). Practice makes perfect and other myths about mental health services. *American Psychologist, 54*, 965–978.

Bird, G. (1992). *Programmed writing as a method for increasing self-esteem, self-disclosure, and coping skills*. Department of Counseling and Psychological Services, Georgia State University, Atlanta, GA.

Blashfield, R. K., & Liveley, W. J. (1999). Classification. In T. Millon, P. H. Blaney, & R. D. Davis (Eds.), *Oxford Textbook of psychopathology* (pp. 3–28). New York: Oxford University Press.

Blatt, S. J., Quinlan, D. M., Chevron, E. S., McDonald, C., & Zuroff, D. (1982). Dependency and criticism: Psychological dimensions of depression. *Journal of Consulting and Clinical Psychology, 50*, 113–124.

Bloom, B. L. (1985). A factor analysis of self-report measures of family functioning. *Family Process, 24*, 225–239.

Bloom, B. L. (1992). Computer-assisted psychological intervention: A review and commentary. *Clinical Psychology Review, 12*, 169–197.

Bloom, M. (1996). *Primary prevention practices*. Thosand Oaks, CA: Sage.

Bodin, A. M. (1996). Relationship conflict—verbal and physical: Conceptualizing an inventory for assessing process and content. In F. W. Kaslow (Ed.), *Handbook of relational diagnosis and dysfunctional family patterns* (pp. 371–393). New York: Wiley.

Bodin, A. M., & Ferber, A. M. (1972). How to go beyond the use of language. In A. A. Ferber, Mendelsohn, M., & Napier, A. (Eds.), *Book of family therapy* (pp. 272–317). New York: Science House.

Bodine, R., J., & Crawford, D. K. (1999). *Developing emotional intelligence: A guide to behavior management and conflict resolution in schools*. Champlain, IL: Research Press.

Bohart, A. C., & Tallman, K. (1999). *How clients make therapy work: The process of active self-healing*. Washington, DC: American Psychological Association.

Bolter, J. D. (1991). *Writing space: The computer, hypertext, and the history of writing*. Hillsdale, NJ: Earlbaum.

Bonanno, G. A., & Keltner, D. (1997). Facial expression of emotion and the course of conjugal bereavement. *Journal of Abnomal Psychology, 106*, 126–137.

Bond, L. A., & Rosen, J. C. (Eds.) (1980). *Competence & coping during adulthood*. Hanover, NH: University Press of New England.

Bond, L. A., & Wagner, B. M. (1988). *Families in transition: Primary prevention programs that work*. Newbury Park, CA: Sage.

Boyd, C. P., Gullone, E., Needleman, G. L., & Burt, T. (1997). The Family Environment Scale: Reliability and normative data for an adolescent sample. *Family Process, 36*, 369–373.

Bracy, O. L. (1992). Q & A. *Computer Assisted Rehabilitation Therapy, 1*, 2.

Bradley, S. J. (2000). *Affect regulation and the development of psychopathology*. New York: Guilford.

Bradley, V. A., Welch, J. L., & Skilbeck, C. E. (1993). *Cognitive retraining using microcomputers*. Hillsdale, NJ: Earlbaum.

Breggin, P. R. (1991). *Toxic psychiatry: Why therapy, empathy, and love must replace drugs, electroshock, and biochemical theories of the "new psychiatry."* New York: St. Martin's Press.

Brenneis, C. B. (1994). The skewing of psychiatry. *Academic Psychiatry, 18*, 71–80.

Bretherton, I., Ridgeway, D., & Cassidy, J. (1990). Assessing internal working models of the attachment relationship: An Attachment Story Completion Task for 3-year-olds. In D. Cicchetti, M. Greenberg, & E. M. Cummings (Eds.), *Attachment during the preschool years: Theory, research, and intervention* (pp. 272–308). Chicago: University of Chicago Press.

Brewin, C. R., & Lennard, H. (1999). Effects of mode of writing on emotional narratives. *Journal of Traumatic Stress, 12*, 355–361.

Brickman, P., Rabinowitz, V. C., Karuza, J., Coates, D., Cohen, E., & Kidder, L. (1982). Models of helping and coping. *American Psychologist, 37*, 368–384.

Brown, E. C., & L'Abate, L. (1969). An appraisal of teaching machines and programmed instruction. In C. M. Franks (Ed.), *Behavior therapy: Appraisal and status* (pp. 396–414). New York: McGraw-Hill.

Brown, L., Black, D., & Downs, J. (1984). *School social skills (S^3).* East Aurora, NY: Slosson Educational Publications.

Brown, L., & Hammill, D. D. (1978). *Behavior rating profile (BRP-2).* East Aurora, NY: Slosson Educational Publications.

Bruner, J. S. (1990). *Acts of meaning.* Cambridge, MA: Harvard University Press.

Bryant, M. J., Simons, A. D., & Thase, M. E. (1999). Therapist skill and patient variables in homework compliance: Controlling an uncontrollable variable in cognitive therapy outcome research. *Cognitive Therapy & Research, 23*, 381–399.

Buchanan, G. M., & Seligman, M.E.P. (Eds.) (1995). *Explanatory style.* Hillsdale, NJ: Earlbaum.

Burns, B. J., Hoagwood, K., & Mrazek, P. J. (1999). Effective treatment for mental disorders in children and adolescents. *Clinical Child and Family Psychology Review 2*, 199–254.

Burns, D. D., & Nolen-Hoeksema, S. (1992). Therapeutic empathy and recovery from depression in cognitive-behavior therapy: A structural equation model. *Journal of Consulting and Clinical Psychology, 60*, 441–449.

Burns, D. D., & Spangler, D. L. (2000). Does psychotherapy homework lead to improvements in depression in cognitive-behavioral therapy or does improvement lead to increased homework compliance? *Journal of Consulting and Clinical Psychology, 68*, 46–56.

Butcher, J. M. (1998). *Psychological Treatment Planning Inventory: Test manual and interpretative guide.* San Antonio, TX: Psychological Corporation.

Cacioppo, J. T., & Gardner, W. L. (1999). Emotion. *Annual Review of Psychology, 50*, 191–214.

Cahalan, D. (1991). *An ounce of prevention: Strategies for solving tobacco, alcohol, and drug problems.* San Francisco, CA: Jossey-Bass.

Campbell, L., Campbell, B., & Dickinson, D. (1999). *Teaching and learning through multiple intelligences.* Boston, MA: Allyn & Bacon.

Capaldi, E. J., & Proctor, R. W. (1999). *Contextualism in psychological research? A critical review.* Thousand Oaks, CA: Sage.

Carver, C. S. (1996). Emergent integration in contemporary personality theory. *Journal of Personality Research, 30*, 319–334.

Carver, C. S., & Scheier, M. E. (1999). Stress, coping, and self-regulatory processes. In L. A. Pervin & O. P. John (Eds.), *Handbook of personality: Theory and research* (pp. 553–575). New York: Guilford.

Cassidy, J., & Shaver, P. R. (1999). *Handbook of attachment: Theory, research, and clinical applications.* New York: Guilford.

Cate, R. M., & Lloyd, S. A. (1988). Courtship. In S. Duck (Ed.), *Handbook of personal relationships* (pp. 409–427). New York: Wiley.

Caudill, O. B. (2000). Long distance liability: Let your fingers do the walking in the courthouse. *Family Therapy News, 31*, 10–12.

Cellini, H, R., Hinze, T., Speaker, T., & Wood, R. M. (2000). The treatment and management of severe personality disordered offendents. *Offender Programs Report, 3*, 83–84, 92–94.

Chambless, D. L. (1997). In defense of dissemination of empirically supported psychological interventions. *Clinical Psychology: Science and Practice, 4*, 230–235.

Chappell, K. D., & Davis, K. E. (1998). Attachment, partner choice, and perception of romantic partners. *Personal Relationships, 5*, 327–342.

Chorpita, B. F., Albano, A. M., & Barlow, D. H. (1998). The structure of negative emotions in a clinical sample of children and adolescents. *Journal of Abnormal Psychology, 107*, 74–85.

Cicchetti, D., & Toth, S. L. (1991). *Internalizing and externalizing expressions in dysfunction.* Hillsdale, NJ: Earlbaum.

Clancy, T. (1991). *The sum of all fears.* New York: G. P. Putnam's Sons.

Clark, L. A. (1990). Toward a consensual set of symptom clusters for assessment of personality disoders. In J. H. Butcher & C. D. Splielberger (Eds.), *Advances in personality assessment* (pp. 243–266). Hillsdale, NJ: Earlbaum.

Clark, M. S. (1983). Some implications of close social bonds for help-seeking. In B. M. DiPaulo, A. Nadler, & J. D. Fisher (Eds.), *New directions in helping. Vol. 2: Help-seeking* (pp. 205–229). Orlando, FL: Academic Press.

Clark, M. S. (1986). Evidence for the effectiveness of manipulations of communal and exchange relationships. *Personality and Social Psychology Bulletin, 12*, 414–425.

Clark, M. S. (Ed.) (1992a). *Emotion.* Newbury Park, CA: Sage.

Clark, M. S. (Ed.) (1992b). *Emotion and social behavior.* Newbury Park, CA: Sage.

Clark, M. S., & Mills, J. (1979). Interpersonal attraction in exchange and communal relationships. *Journal of Personality and Social Psychology, 17*, 12–24.

Clark, M. S., Mills, J., & Powell, M. (1986). Keeping track of needs in communal and exchange relationships. *Journal of Personality and Social Psychology, 51*, 333–338.

Clark, M. S., Pataki, S. P., & Carver, V. H. (1996). Some thoughts and findings on self-presentation of emotions in relationships. In G.J.O. Fletcher & J. Fitness (Eds.), *Knowledge structures in close relationships: A social psychological approach* (pp. 247–324). New York: Guilford.

Clark, M. S., & Reis, H. T. (1988). Interpersonal processes in close relationships. *Annual Review of Psychology, 39*, 609–672.

Clark, M. S., & Wassell, B. (1985). Perceptions of exploitation in communal and exchange relationships. *Journal of Social and Personal Relationships, 2*, 403–418.

Clarke, B., & Schoech, D. (1994). A computer-assisted therapeutic game for adolescents: Initial development and comments. *Computers in Human Behavior, 11*, 121–140.

Clay, R. A. (2000). Psychotherapy *is* cost-effective. *Monitor on Psychology, 31*, 40–41.

Cleyman, R. B. (1992). The procedural organization of emotions: A contribution from cognitive science to the psychoanalytic theory of therapeutic action. In T. Shapiro & R. N. Emde (Eds.), *Affect: Psychoanalytic perspectives* (pp. 349–382). Madison, CT: International Universities Press.

Cobb, C.L.H. (1996). Adolescent-parent attachments and family problem solving. *Family Process, 35*, 57–82.

Corrigan, P. W. (1995). Wanted: Champions of psychiatric rehabilitation. *American Psychologist, 50*, 514–521.

Corsini, R. J. (Ed.) (1984). *Current psychotherapies.* Itasca, IL: F. E. Peacock.

Costa, P. T., Jr., & Widiger, T. A. (Eds.) (1994). *Personality disorders and the five factor model of personality.* Washington, DC: American Psychological Association.

Cullari, S. (1996). *Treatment resistance: A guide for practitioners.* Boston, MA: Allyn & Bacon.

Cummings, N. A. (1987). The future of psychotherapy: One psychologist's perspective. *American Journal of Psychotherapy, 41*, 349–360.

Cummings, N. A. (1999). Comment on L'Abate: Psychotherapist future shock. *The Family Journal: Counseling and Therapy for Couples and Families, 7*, 221–223.

Cusinato, M. (1997). *TRD: Test di relazione diadica: Manuale di istruzione.* Treviso, Italy: Edizioni Centro della Famiglia.

Cusinato, M., Aceti, G., & L'Abate, L. (1998). Condivisione del dolore e-di intimita' di coppia. *Famigla, Interdisciplinarita', Ricerca: Rivista di Studi Familiari, 2*, 31–49.

Cusinato, M., & L'Abate, L. (1995). A spiral model of intimacy. In S. M. Johnson & L. S. Greenberg (Eds.), *The heart of the matter: Perspectives on emotion in marital therapy* (pp. 108–123). New York: Brunner/Mazel.

Cusinato, M., & L'Abate, L. (submitted for publication). The Dyadic Relations Test: A decade of research.

Cusinato, M., & Pastore, M. (2001). Analisi delle strutture tassonomiche in prospettive evolutiva del "Self-Other Profile Chart." *Eta' Evolutiva, 69*, 5–10.

Darken, R. P., Bernatovich, D., Lawson, J. P., & Person, B. (1999). Quantitative measures of presence in virtual environments: The roles of attention and spatial comprehension. *CyberPsychology & Behavior, 2*, 337–347.

Davis, M., & Hadiks, D. (1990). Nonverbal behavior and client state: Changes during psychotherapy. *Journal of Clinical Psychology, 46*, 340–351.

Davis, R. D., & Millon, T. (1999). Models of personality and its disorders. In T. Millon, T. H. Blaney, & R. D. Davis (Eds.), *Oxford textbook of psychopathology* (pp. 485–522). New York: Oxford University Press.

Davison, G. C. (2000). Stepped care: Doing more with less? *Journal of Consulting and Clinical Psychology, 68*, 580–585.

Dawes, R. M. (1994). *House of cards: Psychology and psychotherapy built on myth.* New York: Free Press.

Deater-Deckard, K. (1998). Parenting stress and child adjustment: Some old hypotheses and new questions. *Clinical Psychology: Science and Practice, 5*, 315–332.

De Giacomo, P. (1993). *Finite systems and infinite interactions: The logic of human interaction and its application to psychotherapy.* Norfork, CT: Bramble Books.

De Giacomo, P., & De Nigris, S. (2001). Computer workbooks in psychotherapy with psychiatric patients. In L. L'Abate (Ed.), *Distance writing and computer assisted interventions in psychiatry and mental health* (pp. 113–133). Stamford, CT: Ablex.

De Giacomo, P., L'Abate, L., & De Giacomo, A. (1997). Integrating models of human interaction: Three models, one reality? *Italian Journal of Psychiatry and Behavioral Science, 7*, 18–23.

De Giacomo, P., Pierri, G., Lefons, E., & Mich, L. (1990). A technique to simulate human interactions: Relational styles leading to a schizophrenic communication pattern and back to normal. *Acta Psychiatrica Scandinavica, 82*, 413–419.

Derlega, V. J., Hendrick, S. S., Winstead, B. A., & Berg, J. H. (1991). *Psyhotherapy as a personal relationship.* New York: Guilford.

Derlega, V. J., Winstead, B. A., & Jones, W. H. (Eds.) (1991). *Personality: Conteporary theory and research.* Chicago, IL: Nelson-Hall.

DeRubeis, R. J., & Crits-Christoph, P. (1998). Empirically supported individual and group psychological treatments for adult mental disorders. *Journal of Consulting & Clinical Psychology, 66*, 37–52.

DeRubeis, R. J., & Feeley, M. (1990). Determining of change in cognitive therapy for depression. *Cognitive Therapy and Research, 14*, 469–482.

Detweiler, J. B., & Whisman, M. A. (1999). The role of homework assignments in cognitive therapy for depression: Potential methods for enhancing adherence. *Clinical Psychology: Science & Practice, 6*, 267–282.

de Vries, B., Birren, J. E., & Deutchman, D. E. (1990). Adult development through guided autobiography: The family context. *Family Relations, 39*, 3–7.

Dickerson, M., Hinchy, J., & Legg-England, S. (1990). Minimal treatments and problem gamblers: A preliminary investigation. *Journal of Gambling Studies, 6*, 87–102.

Diener, E. (1996). Traits can be powerful, but are not enough: Lessons from subjective well-being. *Journal of Personality Research, 30*, 309–318.

Dobson, K. S., & Craig, K. D. (Eds.) (1998). *Empirically supported therapies: Best practice in professional psychology*. Thousand Oaks, CA: Sage.

Dobson, K. S., & Shaw, B. F. (1993). The training of cognitive therapists: What we have learned from treatment manuals. *Psychotherapy, 30*, 573–577.

Donnelly, D. A., & Murray, E. J. (1991). Cognitive and emotional changes in written essays and therapy interviews. *Journal of Social and Clinical Psychology, 10*, 334–350.

Doyle, K. O. (1999). *The social meanings of money and property: In search of a talisman*. Thousand Oaks, CA: Sage.

Dozois, D.J.A., Dobson, K. S., & Ahnberg, J. L. (1998). A psychometric evaluation of the Beck Depression Inventory-II. *Psychological Assessment, 10*, 83–89.

Draper, J. V., Kaber, D. B., & Usher, J. M. (1999). Speculations on the value of telepresence. *Cyberpsychology & Behavior, 2*, 349–362.

Duck, S. W., & Pittman, G. (1994). Social and personal relationships. In M. L. Knapp & G. R. Miller (Eds.), *Handbook of interpersonal communication* (pp. 676–695). Thousand Oaks, CA: Sage.

Dunst, C., Trivette, C., & Deal, A. (1988). *Enabling and empowering families: Principles and guidelines for practice*. Cambridge, MA: Brookline Books.

Dweck, C. S. (1996). Capturing the dynamic nature of personality. *Journal of Personality Research, 30*, 389–399.

Eckhardt, C. I., Barbour, K. A., & Davison, G. C. (1998). Articulated thoughts of marital violence and nonviolent men during anger arousal. *Journal of Consulting and Clinical Psychology, 66*, 259–269.

Eckhardt, C. I., & Deffenbacher, J. L. (1995) Diagnosis of anger disorders. In H. Kassinove (Ed.), *Anger disorders: Definition, diagnosis, and treament* (pp. 27–47). Philadelphia, PA: Taylor & Francis.

Ehrenwald, J. (Ed.) (1991). *The history of psychotherapy*. Northvale, NJ: Aronson.

Ekman, P., & Davidson, R. J. (Eds.) (1994). *The nature of emotion: Fundamental questions*. New York: Oxford University Press.

Elliott, R., & Greenberg, L. S. (1995). Experiential therapy in practice: The process-experiential approach. In B. Bongar & L. E. Beutler (Eds.), *Comprehensive textbook of psychotherapy: Theory and practice* (pp. 123–139). New York: Oxford University Press.

Embretson, S. E. (1996). The new rules of measurement. *Psychological Assessment, 6*, 341–349.

Emery, R. E., & Laumann-Billings, L. (1998). An overview of the nature, causes, and consequences of abusive family relationships: Toward differentiating maltreatment and violence. *American Psychologist, 53*, 121–135.

Enos, R. L. (Ed.) (1990). *Oral and written communication: Historical approaches*. Newbury Park, CA: Sage.

Epstein, S. (1994). Integration of the cognitive and psychodynamic unconscious. *American Psychologist, 49*, 709–724.

Epstein, S. (1998). *Constructive thinking: The key to emotional intelligence*. Westport, CT: Praeger.

Esterling, B. A., Antoni, M. H., Fletcher, M. A., Margulies, S., & Schneiderman, N. (1994). Emotional disclosure through writing or speaking modulates latent. Epstein-Barr virus antibody titers. *Journal of Consulting and Clinical Psychology, 62*, 130–140.

Esterling, B. A., L'Abate, L., Murray, E., & Pennebaker, J. M. (1999). Empirical foundations for writing in prevention and psychotherapy: Mental and physical outcomes. *Clinical Psychology Review, 19*, 79–96.

Esterling, B. A., & Pennebaker, J. W. (2001). Focused expressive writing, immune functions, and physical health. In L. L'Abate (Ed.), *Distance writing and computer-assisted interventions in psychiatry and mental health* (pp. 47–60). Westport, CT: Ablex.

Ewen, R. B. (1988). *An introduction to theories of personality*. Hillsdale, NJ: Earlbaum.

Eysenck, H. J. (1952). The effects of psychotherapy: A evaluation. *Journal of Consulting Psychology, 16*, 319–324.

Faustman, W. O., & Overall, J. E. (1999). Brief psychiatric rating scale. In M. E. Maruish (Ed.), *The use of psychological testing for treatment planning and outcomes assessment* (pp. 791–830). Mahwah, NJ: Earlbaum.

Feeney, J., & Noller, P. (1996). *Adult attachment*. Thousand Oaks, CA: Sage.

Feindler, E. L. (1995). Ideal treatment package for children and adolescents with anger disorders. In H. Kassinove (Ed.), *Anger disorders: Definition, diagnosis, and treament* (pp. 173–195). Philadelphia, PA: Taylor & Francis.

Felmlee, D. H. (1998). "Be careful what you wish for . . .": A quantitative and qualitative investigation of "fatal attraction." *Personal Relationships, 5*, 235–253.

Fennell, M., & Teasdale, J. (1987). Cognitive therapy: Individual differences and the process of change. *Cognitive Therapy and Research, 11*, 253–271.

Ferrari, J. R., Johnson, J. L., & McCown, W. G. (1995). *Procrastination and task avoidance: Theory, research and treatment*. New York: Plenum.

Fincham, F. E. (2000). The kiss of the porcupines: From attributing responsibility to forgiving. *Personal Relationships, 7*, 1–23.

Firestone, R. W., & Catlett, J. (1999). *Fear of intimacy*. Washington, DC: American Psychological Association.

Fishbein, D. H. (Ed.) (2000). *The science, treatment, and prevention of antisocial behaviors: Application to the criminal justice system*. Kingston, NJ: Civic Research Institute.

Fisher, L., & Ransom, D. C. (1995). An empirically derived typology of families: Relationships with adult health. *Family Process, 34*, 161–182.

Fishman, D. B. (1999). *The case for pragmatic psychology*. New York: New York University Press.

Foa, E. B., & Kozak, M. J. (1986). Emotional processing of fear: Exposure to corrective information. *Psychological Bulletin, 99*, 20–35.

Foa, U. G., Converse, J. Jr. Tornblom K. J., & Foa, E. B. (Eds.) (1993). *Resource exchange theory: Explorations and applications*. San Diego, CA: Academic Press.

Foa, U. G., & Foa, E. B. (1974). *Societal structures of the mind*. Springfield, IL: Charles C. Thomas.

Fogarty, R., & Bellanca, J. (1998). *Multiple intelligences: A collection*. Boston, MA: Allyn & Bacon.

Foglia, W. D. (2000). Adding an explicit focus on cognition to criminological theory. In D. H. Fishbein (Ed.), *The science, treatment, and prevention of antisocial behaviors: Application to the criminal justice system* (pp. 10-1–10-25). Kingston, NJ: Civic Research Institute.

Fonagy, P., & Target, M. (1997). Should we allow psychotherapy research to determine clinical practice? *Clinical Psychology: Science and Practice, 4*, 245–250.

Ford, M. E. (1985). The concept of competence: Themes and variations. In H. A. Marlowe, Jr., & R. B. Weinberg (Eds.), *Competence development: Theory and practice in special populations* (pp. 3–39). Springfield, IL: Charles C. Thomas.

Forgays, D. G., Forgays, D. K., & Spielberger, C. D. (1997). Factor structure of the State-Trait Anger Expression Inventory. *Journal of Personality Assessment, 69*, 497–507.

Fox, R., Rotatori, A. F., Macklin, F., Green, M., & Fox, T. (1983). Socially maladjusted adolescents' perceptions of their families. *Psychological Reports, 52*, 831–834.

Frank, J. D. (1973). *Persuasion and healing: A comparative study of psychotherapy*. Baltimore, MD: Johns Hopkins University Press.

Frank, R. G., Gluck, J. P., & Buckelew, S. P. (1990). Rehabilitation: Psychology's greatest opportunity? *American Psychologist, 45*, 757–761.

Freedheim, D. K. (Ed.) (1992). *History of psychotherapy: A century of change*. Washington, DC: American Psychological Association.

Freeman, A., Simon, K. M., Beutler, L. E., & Arkowitz, H. (1989). *Comprehensive handbook of cognitive therapy*. New York: Plenum.

Friedman, P. H. (1985). The use of computers in marital and family therapy. *Journal of Psychotherapy and the Family, 1*, 37–48.

Fuhr, R. A., Moos, R. H., & Dishotsky, N. (1981). The use of family assessment as feedback in ongoing family therapy. *American Journal of Family Therapy, 9*, 24–36.

Furth, H. G. (1966). *Thinking without language: Psychological implications of deafness*. New York: The Free Press.

Gackenbach, J., & Ellerman, E. (1998). Introduction to psychological aspects of internet use. In J. Gackenbach (Ed.), *Psychology and the Internet: Intrapersonal, interpersonal, and transpersonal implications* (pp. 1–26). San Diego, CA: Academic Press.

Gardner, H. (1983). *Frames of mind: The theory of multiple intelligences*. New York: Basic Books.

Gardner, H. (1995). Reflections on multiple intelligences: Myths and messages. *Phi Delta Kappan*, November Issue, 200–209.

Gardner, H. (1998). Are there additional intelligences? The case for naturalistic, spiritual, and existential intelligences. In J. Kane (Ed.), *Education, Information and transformation* (pp. 53–85). Englewood Cliffs, NJ: Prentice-Hall.

Gardner, H. (1999). *Intelligence reframed: Multiple intelligences for the 21st century*. New York: Basic Books.

Garfield, S. L. (1997). Some problems associated with "validated" forms of psychotherapy. *Clinical Psychology: Science and Practice, 4*, 218–229.

Gaston, L., & Gagnon, R. (1996). The role of process research in manual development. *Clinical Psychology: Science and Practice, 3*, 13–24.

Gergen, K. J. (1994). *Realities and relationships: Soundings in social construction*. Cambridge, MA: Harvard University Press.

Gerris, J.R.M., Van As, N.M.C., Wels, P.M.A., & Janssens, J.M.A.M. (1998). From parent education to family empowerment programs. In L. L'Abate (Ed.), *Family psychopathology: The relational roots of dysfunctional behavior* (pp. 401–426). New York: Guilford.

Giacomo, P., & Weissmark, M. (1987). Toward a generative theory of the therapeutic field. *Family Process, 26*, 437–459.

Giancola, P. R. (2000). Neuropsychological functioning and antisocial behavior—implications for etiology and prevention. In D. H. Fisbein (Ed.), *The science, treatment, and prevention of antisocial behaviors: Application to the criminal justice system* (pp. 11-1–11-16). Kingston, NJ: Civic Research Institute.

Gibbs, J. P. (1989). *Control: Sociology's central notion*. Urbana, IL: University of Illinois Press.

Gilbert, D. G., & Connolly, J. J. (Eds.) (1991). *Personality, social skills, and psychopathology: An individual differences approach*. New York: Plenum.

Goldberg, L. R. (1992). The development of markers for the Big-Five factor structure. *Psychological Assessment, 4*, 26–42.

Goldberg, L. R. (1999). The Curious Experiences Survey: A revised version of the Dissociative Experiences Scale: Factor structure, reliability, and relations to demographic and personality variables. *Psychological Assessment, 11*, 134–145.

Goldberg, S., Muis, R., & Kerr, J. (Eds.) (1995). *Attachment theory: Social, developmental, and clinical perspectives*. Hillsdale, NJ: Analytic Press.

Goldfried, M. R. (1982). *Converging themes in psychotherapy: Trends in psychodynamic, humanistic, and behavioral practice*. New York: Springer.

Goldfried, M. R. (1999). Role of theoretical bias in therapeutic interventions: To see or not to see? *Journal of Clinical Child Psychology, 28*, 544–547.

Goleman, D. (1995). *Emotional intelligence*. New York: Bantam Books.

Gollwitzer, P. M. (1999). Implementation effects: Strong effects of simple plans. *American Psychologist, 54*, 493–503.

Gorall, D. M., & Olson, D. H. (1995). Circumplex model of family systems: Integrating ethnic diversity and other social systems. In R. H. Mikesell, D. D. Lusterman, & S. H. McDaniel (Eds.), *Integrating family therapy: Handbook of family psychology and systems theory* (pp. 217–233). Washington, DC: American Psychological Associaton.

Gordon, R. E., & Gordon, K. K. (1981). *Systems of treatment for the mentally ill: Filling the gaps*. New York: Grune & Stratton.

Gordon, T. (1970). *Parent effectiveness training*. New York: Wyden.

Gottman, J. M. (1979). *Marital interaction: Experimental investigations*. New York: Academic Press.

Gottman, J. M. (1999). *The marriage clinic: A scientifically based marital therapy.* New York: W. W. Norton.

Gottman, J. M., Fainsilber, L., & Hooven, C. (1997). *Meta-emotion: How families communicate emotionally.* Mahwah, NJ: Earlbaum.

Gould, R. L. (2001). A feedback-driven computer program for outpatient training. In L. L'Abate (Ed.), *Distance writing and computer-assisted interventions in psychiatry and mental health* (pp. 93–111). Westport, CT: Ablex.

Greenberg, L. S. (1991). Research on the process of change. *Psychotherapy Research, 1,* 3–16.

Greenberg, L. S. (1994). The investigation of change: Its measurement and explanation. In R. L. Russell (Ed.), *Reassessing psychotherapy research* (pp. 114–143). New York: Guilford.

Greenberg, L. S., & Paivio, S. C. (1997). *Working with emotions in psychotherapy.* New York: Guilford.

Greene, R. L., & Clopton, J. R. (1999). Minnesota Multiphasic Personality Inventory (MMPI-2). In M. E. Maruish (Ed.), *The use of psychological testing for treatment planning and outcomes assessment* (pp. 1023–1050). Mahwah, NJ: Earlbaum.

Greene, S. M., & Anderson, E. R. (1999). Observed negativity in large family systems: Incidents and reactions. *Journal of Family Psychology, 13,* 372–392.

Griffiths, M. (1998). Internet addiction: Does it really exist? In J. Gackenbach, (Ed.), *Psychology and the Internet: Intrapersonal, interpersonal, and transpersonal implications* (pp. 61–75). San Diego, CA: Academic Press.

Grohol, J. M. (1998). Future clinical directions: Professional development, pathology, and psychotherapy on line. In J. Gackenbach (Ed.), *Psychology and the Internet: Intrapersonal, interpersonal, and transpersonal implications* (pp. 111–140). San Diego, CA: Academic Press.

Gross, J. J. (1999). Emotion and emotion regulation. In L. A. Pervin & O. P. John (Eds.), *Handbook of personality: Theory and research* (pp. 525–552). New York: Guilford.

Guerney, B. G., Guerney, L., & Cooney, T. (1985). Marital and family problem prevention and enrichment programs. In L. L'Abate (Ed.), *Handbook of family psychology and therapy* (pp. 1179–1277). Pacific Grove, CA: Brooks/Cole.

Gurman, A. S., & Kniskern, D. P., & Pinsoff, W. (1986). Research on the process and outcome of marital and family therapy. In A. S. Gurman & D. P. Kniskern (Eds.), *Family therapy* (pp. 565–624). New York: Brunner/Mazel.

Gurman, A. S., & Kniskern, D. P. (Eds.) (1991). *Family therapy. Volume II.* New York: Brunner/Mazel.

Gurtman, M. B., & Balakrishnan, J. D. (1998). Circular measurement redux: The analysis and interpretation of interpersonal circle profiles. *Clinical Psychology: Science and Practice, 5,* 344–360.

Haaga, D.A.F. (2000). Introduction to the special section on stepped care models in psychotherapy. *Journal of Consulting and Clinical Psychology, 68,* 547–548.

Halleck, S. L. (1988). Which patients are responsible for their illnesses? *American Journal of Psychotherapy, 42,* 338–353.

Halverson, C. F., Jr. & Wampler, K. S. (1997). Family influences on personality development. In R. Hogan, R. J. Johnson, & S. Briggs (Eds.), *Handbook of personality theory* (pp. 241–268). San Diego, CA: Academic Press.

Haney, C., & Zimbardo, P. (1998). The past and future of the U.S. Prison policy. *American Psychologist, 53*, 709–727.

Hansen, J. C. & L'Abate, L. (1982). *Approaches to family therapy*. New York: Macmillan.

Hanson-Kahn, P., & L'Abate, L. (1998). Cross-cultural couple therapy. In F. M. Dattilio (Ed.) *Case studies in couple and family therapy: Systemic and cognitive perspectives* (pp. 278–302). New York: Guilford.

Harper, R. A. (1975). *The new psychotherapies*. Englewood Cliffs, NJ: Prentice-Hall.

Hartlage, S., Arduino, K., & Alloy, L. B. (1998). Depressive personality characteristics: State dependent concomitants of depressive disorder and traits independent of current depression. *Journal of Abnormal Psychology, 107*, 349–354.

Havik, O. E., & VandenBos, G. R. (1997). Limitations of manualized psychotherapy for everyday clinical practice. *Clinical Psychology: Science and Practice, 4*, 264–267.

Hayes, S. C., Follette, V. M., Dawes, R. M., & Grady, K. E. (1995). *Scientific standards of psychological practice: Issues and recommendations*. Reno, NV: Context Press.

Hayes, S. C., Nelson, R. O., & Jarrett, R. B. (1987). The treatment utility of assessment: A functional approach to evaluating assessment quality. *American Psychologist, 42*, 963–974.

Hayes, S. C., Strosahl, K. D., & Wilson, K. G. (1999). *Acceptance and commitment therapy: An experiential approach to behavior change*. New York: Guilford.

Hayes, S. C., Wilson, K. G., Strosahl, K., Gifford, E. V., & Follette, V. M. (1996). Experiential avoidance and behavioral disorders: A functional dimensional approach to diagnosis and treatment. *Journal of Consulting and Clinical Psychology, 64*, 1152–1168.

Heckhausen, J. (1999). *Developmental regulation in adulthood: Age-normative and sociostructural constraints*. New York: Cambridge University Press.

Heckhausen, J., & Dweck, C. S. (Eds) (1998). *Motivation and self-regulation across the life span*. New York: Cambridge University Press.

Heeter, C. (1999). Aspects of presence in telerelating. *CyberPsychology & Behavior, 2*, 325–335.

Heimberg, R. G. (1998). Treatment manuals in clinical practice: Introduction to the series. *Clinical Psychology: Science and practice, 3*, 387–390.

Hendrick, B. (1998). Peace of mind. *Atlanta Journal-Constitution*, May 2nd, C1.

Henley, A. R. (1987). *Phobias: The crippling fears*. New York: Avon Books.

Hermann, C., Blanchard, E. B., & Flor, H. (1997). Biofeedback treatment for pediatric migraine: Prediction of treatment outcome. *Journal of Consulting and Clinical Psychology, 65*, 611–616.

Hersen, M., Kazdin, A. E., & Bellack, A. S. (Eds.) (1991). *The clinical psychology handbook*. Second Edition. New York: Pergamon.

Hersen, M., & Last, C. G. (Eds.) (1990). *Handbook of child and adult psychopathology: A longitudinal perspective*. New York: Pergamon.

Hetherington, E. M. (1998). Relevant issues in developmental science: Introduction to the special issue. *Amercan Psychologist, 53*, 93–94.

Hill, C. E. (1989). *Therapist techniques and client outcomes: Eight cases of brief psychotherapy*. Newbury Park, CA: Sage.

Hill, C. E., & Stephany, A. (1990). Relation of nonverbal behavior to client reactions. *Journal of Counseling Psychology, 37*, 22–26.

Hinde, R. A. (1997). *Relationships: A dialectical perspective*. East Sussex, UK: Psychology Press.

Hogan, R., Johnson, J., & Briggs, S. (Eds.) (1997). *Handbook of personality theory*. San Diego, CA: Academic Press.

Hogue, A., Liddle, H. A., Rowe, C., Turner, R. M., et al. (1998). Treatment adherence and differentiation in individuals versus family therapy for adolescent substance abuse. *Journal of Counseling Psychology, 45*, 104–111.

Hojjat, M. (1997). Philosophy of life as a model of relationship satisfaction. In R. J. Sternberg & M. Hojjat (Eds.), *Satisfaction in close relationships* (pp. 102–126). New York: Guilford.

Holman, T. B. (1992). Prevention programs for families and children. *Family Relations, 41*, 141–191.

Horowitz, M. J. (1997). *Stress response syndromes: PTSD, Grief, and Adjustment Disorders*. Northvale, NJ: Aronson.

Horwitz, A. V. (1990). *The logic of social control*. New York: Plenum.

Howard G. S., Nance, D. W., & Myers, P. (1987). *Adaptive counseling and therapy: A systematic approach to selecting effective treatments*. San Francisco, CA: Jossey-Bass.

Howard, K. I., Krause, M. S., & Orlinsky, D. E. (1986). The attrition dilemma: Toward a new strategy for psychotherapy research. *Journal of Consulting and Clinical Psychology, 54*, 106–110.

Hoyt, M. E. (1999). Comments on L'Abate. *The Family Journal: Counseling and Psychotherapy with Couples and Families, 7*, 224–226.

Huang, M. P. (1999). Introduction: Beyond presence. *Cyberpsychology & Behavior, 2*, 321–324.

Hughes, M. J. (2000). Intervention versus punishment: Efficacy in juvenile desistance from crime. *Offender Programs Report, 4*, 3–4, 10–13.

Hurt, S. W., Reznikoff, M., & Clarkin, J. F. (1991). *Psychological assessment, psychiatric diagnosis, treatment planning*. New York: Brunner/Mazel.

Hurtug, J., Audy, J. R., & Cohen, Y. A. (Eds.) (1998). *The anatomy of loneliness*. New York: International Universities Press.

Hussong, A. M. (2000). Distinguishing mean and structural sex differences in adolescent friendship quality. *Journal of Social and Personal Relationships, 17*, 223–243.

Huston, T. L., & Rempel, J. K. (1989). Interpersonal attitudes, dispositions, and behavior in family and other close relationships. *Journal of Family Psychology, 3*, 177–198.

Iaccino, J. F. (1993). *Left brain-right brain differences: Inquiries, evidence and new approaches*. Hillsdale, NJ: Earlbaum.

Imber, S. D. (1992). Then and now: Forty years of psychotherapy research. *Clinical Psychology Review, 12*, 199–204.

Isen, A. M. (2000). Positive affect and decision making. In M. Lewis & J. M. Haviland-Jones (Eds.), *Handbook of emotions. Second Edition* (pp. 417–435). New York: Guilford.

Jensen, P. S. (1999). Links among theory, research, and practice: Cornerstone of clinical scientific progress. *Journal of Clinical Child Psychology, 28*, 553–557.

Jensen, P. S., Josephson, A. M., & Frey, J., III. (1994). Informed consent as a framework for treatment: Ethical and therapeutic considerations. *American Journal of Psychotherapy, 48*, 378–386.

Jerome, L. W., DeLeon, P. H., James, L. C., Folen, R., Earles, J., & Geney, J. J. (2000). The coming of age of telecommunications in psychological research and practice. *American Psychologist, 55*, 407–420.

John, O. P., & Srivastava, S. (1999). The Big Five Trait taxonomy: History, measurement, and theoretical perspectives, In O. P. John & L. A. Pervin (Eds.), *Handbook of personality: Theory and research* (pp. 102–138). New York: Guilford.

Johnson, J. L. (1994). *Professional manual: Symptom Scale-77*. Department of Psychology, Louisiana Technological University, Ruston, LA.

Johnson, S. M. (1991). *The symbiotic character*. New York: Norton.

Johnson, S. M., & Greenberg, L. S. (1985). Emotionally focused couples therapy: An outcome study. *Journal of Marital and Family Therapy, 11*, 313–317.

Johnson-Laird, P. N., & Oatley, K. (2000). Cognitive and social construction in emotion. In M. Lewis & J. M. Haviland-Jones (Eds.), *Handbook of emotions. Second Edition* (pp. 458–475). New York: Guilford.

Johnston, T. B., Levis, M. M., & L'Abate, L. (1987). Treatment of depression in a couple with systematic homework assignments. *Journal of Family Psychotherapy, 2*, 117–128.

Joiner, T. E., Jr., Steer, R. A., Beck, A. T., Schmidt, N. B., Rudd, M. D., & Catanzaro, S. J. (1999). Physiological hyperarousal: Construct validity of a central aspect of the tripartite model of depression and anxiety. *Journal of Abnormal Psychology, 108*, 290–298.

Joinson, A. (1998). Causes and implications of disinhibited behavior on the internet. In J. Gackenbach (Ed.), *Psychology and the Internet: Intrapersonal, interpersonal, and transpersonal implications* (pp. 43–60). San Diego, CA: Academic Press.

Jones, S. G. (Ed.) (1995). *Cybersociety: Computer-mediated communication and community*. Thousand Oaks, CA: Sage.

Jongsma, A. E., & Peterson, L. M. (1995). *The complete psychotherapy treatment planner*. New York: Wiley.

Jongsma, A. E., Peterson, L. M., & McInnis, W. R. (1996). *The child and adolescent psychotherapy treatment planner*. New York: Wiley.

Jongsma, A. E., & Stout, C. E. (1997). *The continuum of care treatment planner*. New York: Wiley.

Jordan, K. B. (2001). Teaching psychotherapy through workbooks. In L. L'Abate (Ed.), *Distance writing and computer-assisted interventions in psychiatry and mental health* (pp. 171–190). Westport, CT: Ablex.

Jordan, K., & L'Abate, L. (1995). Programmed writing and psychotherapy with symbiotically enmeshed patients. *American Journal of Psychotherapy, 49*, 225–236.

Jordan, K. B., & L'Abate, L. (1999). The tape of the mind workbook: A single case study. *Journal of Family Psychotherapy, 10*, 13–25.

Kadzin, A. E. (1997). Validated treatments: Multiple perspectives and issues: Introduction to the series. *Clinical Psychology: Science and Practice, 4*, 216–217.

Kadzin, A. E. (1998). Manual-based treatment in clinical practice: Introduction to the series. *Clinical Psychology: Science and Practice, 5*, 361–362.

Kadzin, A. E. (1999). Current (lack of) status of theory in child and adolescent psychotherapy research. *Journal of Clinical Child Psychology, 28*, 533–543.

Kadzin, A. E., & Weiss, J. R. (1998). Identifying and developing empirically supported child and adolescent treatments. *Journal of Consulting & Clinical Psychology, 66*, 19–36.

Kagan, S. L., Powell, D. R., Weissbound, B., & Zigler, E. F. (1987). *America's family support programs: Prospectives and prospects.* New Haven, CT: Yale University Press.

Kaplan, R. M. (2000). Two pathways to prevention. *American Psychologist, 55*, 382–396.

Karasu, T. B. (1996). The specificity versus nonspecificity dilemma: Toward identifying therapeutic change agents. *American Journal of Psychiatry, 143*, 687–695.

Karpman, S. B. (1968). Fairy tales and script drama analysis. *Transactional Analysis Bulletin, 7*, 39–43.

Katz, R., Katz, J., & Shaw, B. F. (1999). Beck Depression Inventory and Helplessness Scale. In M. E. Maruish (Ed.), *The use of psychological testing for treatment planning and outcome assessments, Second Edition* (pp. 831–870). Mahwah, NJ: Earlbaum.

Kavanaugh, E. R. (1993). Using HELP-software in substance abuse treatment. In *Computer assisted therapy: A guide* (pp. 34–35). Santa Barbara, CA: CATSco.

Kazantzis, N. (2000). Power to detect homework effects in psychotherapy outcome research. *Journal of Consulting and Clinical Psychology, 68*, 166–170.

Kazantzis, N., Deane, F. P., & Ronan, K. R. (2000). Homework assignments in cognitive and behavioral theory: A meta-analysis. *Clinical Psychology: Science and Practice, 7*, 189–202.

Keeney, B. F., & Sprenkle, D. H. (1982). Ecosystemic epistemology: Critical implications for the aesthetics and pragmatics of family therapy. *Family Process, 21*, 1–10.

Kelley, P. (Ed.) (1991). *The uses of writing in psychotherapy.* New York: Haworth.

Kelly, E. J. (1990). *Differential test of conduct and emotional problems.* East Aurora, NY: Slosson Educational Publications.

Kelly, E. J., & Vitali, G. J. (1992). *Conduct problem/Emotional problem intervention: A holistic perspective.* East Aurora, NY: Slosson Educational Publications.

Kelly G. A. (1955). *The psychology of human constructs.* 2 vols. New York: Norton.

Kelly, T. A. (1990). The role of values in psychotherapy: A critical review of process and outcome effects. *Clinical Psychology Review, 10*, 171–186.

Kendall (1998). Directing misperceptions: Researching the issues facing manual-based treatments: *Clinical Psychology: Science and Practice, 3*, 396–399.

Kennedy, J. A. (1992). *Fundamentals of psychiatric treatment planning.* Washington, DC: American Psychiatric Association.

Kennedy-Moore, E., & Watson, J. C. (1999). *Expressing emotion: Myths, realities, and therapeutic strategies.* New York: Guilford.

Kessler, M., Goldston, S. E., & Joffe, J. M. (Eds.) (1992). *The present and future of prevention: In honor of George W. Albee.* Newbury Park, CA: Sage.

Kiesler, D. J. (1966). Some myths of psychotherapy research and the search for a paradigm. *Psychological Bulletin, 65*, 110–136.

Kiesler, D. J. (1994). Standardization of intervention: The tie that binds psychotherapy research and practice. In P. F. Talley, H. H. Strupp, & S. F. Butler (Eds.), *Psychotherapy research and practice: Bridging the gap* (pp. 143–153). New York: Basic Books.

Kiesler, D. J. (1999). *Beyond the disease model of mental disorders.* Westport, CT: Greenwood Publishing.

Kiesler, D. J. (Ed.) (1996). *Contemporary interpersonal theory and research: Personality, psychopathology, and psychotherapy.* New York: Wiley.

Kiesler, S., & Kraut, R. (1999) Internet use and ties that bind. *American Psychologist, 54*, 783–784.

Kimble, G. A. (1999). Functional behaviorism: A plan for unity in psychology. *American Psychologist, 54*, 981–988.

King, D. W., Leskin, G. A., King, L. A., & Weathers, F. W. (1998). Confirmatory factor analysis of the clinician-administered PTSD scale: Evidence for the dimensionality of posttraumatic stress disorder. *Psychological Assessment, 10*, 90–96.

King, S. A., & Moreggi, D. (1998). Internet therapy and self-help groups—The pros and cons. In J. Gackenbach (Ed.), *Psychology and the Internet: Intrapersonal, interpersonal, and transpersonal implications* (pp. 77–109). San Diego, CA: Academic Press.

Kirsch, I., & Lynn, S. J. (1999). Automaticity in clinical psychology. *American Psychologist, 54*, 504–515.

Klerman, G. L., DiMascio, A., Weissman, M. M., Prusoff, B., & Paykel, E. S. (1974). Treatment of depression by drugs and psychotherapy. *American Journal of Psychiatry, 131*, 186–191.

Kliewer, W., Lepore, S. J., Oskin, D., & Johnson, P. D. (1998). The role of social and cognitive processes in children's adjustment to community violence. *Journal of Consulting and Clinical Psychology, 66*, 199–209.

Kobak, K., Dottl, S., & Serlin, R. (1997). Accuracy of PRIME-MD in detecting mental disorders in primary-care patients. *Journal of the American Medical Association, 278*, 905–910.

Kobak, K. A., & Reynolds, W. M. (1999). Hamilton Depression Inventory. In M. E. Maruish (Ed.), *The use of psychological testing for treatment planning and outcome assessment, Second Edition* (pp. 935–970). Mahwah, NJ: Earlbaum.

Kochalka, J., & L'Abate, L. (1997). Linking evaluation with structured enrichment: The Family Profile Form. *American Journal of Family Therapy, 25*, 361–374.

Kokish, R. (1994). Experiences using a PC in play therapy with children. *Computers in Human Behavior, 11*, 141–150.

Kolden, G. G. (1991). The generic model of psychotherapy: An empirical investigation of patterns of process and outcome relationships. *Psychotherapy Research, 1*, 62–73.

Korzybski, A. (1949). *Science and sanity: An introduction to non-Aristotelian systems and general semantics*. Lakeville, CT: Institute of General Semantics.

Kosson, D. S., Steuerwald, B. L., Forth, A. E., & Kirkhart, K. J. (1997). A new method for assessing the interpersonal behavior of psychopathic individuals: Preliminary validation studies. *Psychological Assessment, 9*, 89–101.

Kraut, R., Patterson, M., Lundmark, V., Kiesler, S., Mukopadhyay, T., & Scherlis, W. (1998). Internet paradox: A social technology that reduces social involvement and psychological well-being? *American Psychologist, 53*, 1017–1031.

Krueger, R. F. (1999). The structure of common mental disorders. *Archives of General Psychiatry, 56*, 921–926.

Kyle, J. L. (1993). Using HELP-software for comprehensive community mental health services. In *Computer assisted therapy: A guide* (pp. 29–31). Santa Barbara, CA: CATSco.

L'Abate, L. (1969a). An input-output approach to psychodiagnosis of children. *World Journal of Psychosynthesis, 1*, 68–73.

L'Abate, L. (1969b). The continuum of rehabilitation and laboratory evaluation: Behavior modification and psychotherapy. In C. M. Franks (Ed.), *Behavior therapy: Appraisal & status* (pp. 476–494). New York: McGraw-Hill.

L'Abate, L. (1971). Receptive-expressive functions in kindergarten children and adolescents. *Psychology in the Schools, 8*, 253–259.

L'Abate, L. (1973). The laboratory method in clinical child psychology: Three applications. *Journal of Clinical Child Psychology, 2*, 8–10.

L'Abate, L. (1976). *Understanding and helping the individual in the family*. New York: Grune & Stratton.

L'Abate, L. (1977). *Enrichment: Structured interventions with couples, families, and groups*. Washington, DC: University Press of America.

L'Abate, L. (1981a). Skill training programs for couples and families. In A. S. Gurman & D. P. Kniskern (Eds.), *Handbook of family therapy* (pp. 631–661). New York: Brunner/Mazel.

L'Abate, L. (1981b). Toward a systematic classification of counseling and therapy theorists, methods, and goals: The E-R-A model. *Personnel and Guidance Journal, 59*, 263–265.

L'Abate, L. (1983a). *Family psychology: Theory, therapy, and training*. Lanham, MD: University Press of America.

L'Abate, L. (1983b). Prevention as a profession: Towards a new conceptual frame of reference. In D. Mace (Ed.), *Toward family wellness: The need for preventive services* (pp. 49–62). Beverly Hills, CA: Sage Publications.

L'Abate, L. (1983c). Styles in intimate relationships: The A-R-C model. *The Personnel and Guidance Journal, 63*, 227–283.

L'Abate, L. (1984). Beyond paradox: Issues of control. *American Journal of Family Therapy, 12*, 12–20.

L'Abate, L. (Ed.) (1985a). *Handbook of family psychology and therapy*. Homewood, IL: Dorsey.

L'Abate, L. (1985b). Structured enrichment (SE) with couples and families. *Family Relations, 34*, 169–175.

L'Abate, L. (1986a). Prevention of marital and family problems. In B. A. Edelstein and L. Michelson (Eds.), *Handbook of prevention* (pp. 177–193). New York: Plenum.

L'Abate, L. (1986b). *Systematic family therapy*. New York: Brunner/Mazel.

L'Abate, L. (1987). *Family psychology II: Theory, therapy, enrichments, and training*. Lanham, MD: University Press of America.

L'Abate, L. (1990). *Building family competence: Primary and secondary prevention strategies*. Thousand Oaks, CA: Sage.

L'Abate, L. (1991). The use of writing in psychotherapy. *American Journal of Psychotherapy, 45*, 87–98.

L'Abate, L. (1992a). Family psychology and family therapy: Comparisons and contrasts. *American Journal of Family Therapy, 20*, 3–12.

L'Abate, L. (1992b). *Programmed writing: A self-administered approach for interventions with individuals, couples, and families*. Pacific Grove, CA: Brooks/Cole.

L'Abate, L. (1994a). *A theory of personality development*. New York: Wiley.

L'Abate, L. (1994b) Book review. De Giacomo's *Finite Systems and Infinite Interactions. American Journal of Family Therapy, 21*, 89–94.

L'Abate, L. (1996). Workbooks for Better Living. <*www.mentalhealthhelp.com*>

L'Abate, L. (1997a) Distance writing and computer assisted training. In S. R. Sauber

(Ed.), *Managed mental health care: Major diagnostic and treatment approaches* (pp. 133–163). Bristol, PA: Brunner/Mazel.

L'Abate, L. (1997b). The paradox of change: Better them than us! In S. R. Sauber (Ed.), *Managed mental health care: Major diagnostic and treatment approaches* (pp. 40–66). Bristol, PA: Brunner/Mazel.

L'Abate, L. (1997c). *The self in the family: A classification of personality, criminality, and psychopathology*. New York: Wiley.

L'Abate, L. (1998a). Discovery of the family: From the inside to the outside. *American Journal of Family Therapy, 26*, 265–280.

L'Abate, L. (Ed.) (1998b). *Family psychopathology: The relational roots of dysfunctional behavior*. New York: Guilford.

L'Abate, L. (1998c). Of clocks and rubber bands: On the use of props in family therapy. In T. S. Nelson & T. S. Trepper (Eds.), *101 more interventions in family therapy* (pp. 13–17). New York: Haworth.

L'Abate, L. (1999a). Being human: Loving and hurting. In A. C. Richards & T. Schumrum (Eds.), *Invitations to dialogue: The legacy of Sidney Jourard* (pp. 81–90). Dubuque, IA: Kent/Kendall.

L'Abate, L. (1999b). Decisions we (mental health professionals) need to make (whether we like them or not): A reply to Cummings and Hoyt. *The Family Journal: Therapy and Counseling for Couples and Families, 7*, 227–230.

L'Abate, L. (1999c). Increasing intimacy in couples through distance writing and face-to-face approaches. In J. Carlson & L. Sperry (Eds.), *The intimate couple* (pp. 328–344). Philadelphia, PA: Taylor & Francis.

L'Abate, L. (1999d). Programmed distance writing in therapy with acting-out adolescents. In C. Schaefer (Ed.), *Innovative psychotherapy techniques in child and adolescent therapy* (pp. 108–157). New York: Wiley.

L'Abate, L. (1999e). Structured enrichment and distance writing for couples. In R. Berger & T. Hannah (Eds.), *Preventive approaches in couples therapy* (pp. 106–124). Philadelphia, PA: Taylor & Francis.

L'Abate, L. (1999f). Taking the bull by the horns: Beyond talk in psychological interventions. *The Family Journal: Therapy and Counseling for Couples and Families, 7*, 206–220.

L'Abate, L. (2000). Psychoeducational strategies. In J. Carlson & L. Sperry (Eds.), *Brief therapy strategies with individuals and couples* (pp. 346–396). Phoenix, AZ: Zeig/Tucker.

L'Abate, L. (2001a). Distance writing (DW) and computer-assisted interventions (CAI) in psychiatry and mental health. In L. L'Abate (Ed.), *Distance writing and computer-assisted interventions in psychiatry and mental health* (pp. 3–31). Westport, CT: Ablex.

L'Abate, L. (2001b). Hugging, holding, huddling, and cuddling: A task prescription for couple and marital therapy. *Journal of Clinical Activities, Assignments, and Handout in Psychotherapy Practice*, 1, 5–18.

L'Abate, L. (Ed.) (in press). *The role of workbooks in mental health: A practical resource for clinicians*. Binghamton, NY: Haworth.

L'Abate, L. (submitted for publication, a). *An annotated bibliography of selected self-help mental health workbooks in print.*

L'Abate, L. (submitted for publication, b). Systematically written homework assignments: The case for homework based treatment. In N. Kazantzis, F. P. Doane, K. R.

Ronan, L. L'Abate, & Associates (Eds.). *Using homework assignments in cognitive-behavioral therapy.*

L'Abate, L. (in preparation). Personality: Socialization in the family and other settings.

L'Abate, L., & Bagarozzi, D. A. (1993). *Sourcebook of marriage and family evaluation.* New York: Brunner/Mazel.

L'Abate, L., Boyce, J., Fraizer, L., & Russ, D. A. (1992). Programmed writing: Research in progress. *Comprehensive Mental Health Care, 2*, 45–62.

L'Abate, L., & Colondier, G. (1985). The emperor has no clothes! Long live the emperor! A critique of family systems thinking and a reductionistic proposal. *American Journal of Family Therapy, 15*, 19–33.

L'Abate, L., De Giacomo, P., McCarty, F., De Giacomo, A., & Verrastro, G. (2000). Testing three models of intimate relationships. *Contemporary Family Therapy: An International Journal, 22*, 103–122.

L'Abate, L., & Dunne, E. E. (1978). The family taboo in psychology textbooks. *Teaching of Psychology, 5*, 115–117.

L'Abate, L., & Frey, J., III (1981). The ERA model: The role of feelings in family therapy reconsidered: Implications for a classification of theories of family therapy. *Journal of Marital and Family Therapy, 7*, 143–150.

L'Abate, L., Frey, J., & Holly, J. (1979) Intimacy is sharing hurt feelings: Comparison of three conflict resolution methods. *Journal of Marriage and Family Therapy, 5*, 35–41.

L'Abate, L., Frey, J., & Wagner, V. (1982). Toward a classification of family therapy theories: Further elaborations and implications of the E-R-A-Aw-C model. *Family Therapy, 9*, 251–262.

L'Abate, L., Ganahl, G., & Hansen, J. C. (1986). *Methods of family therapy.* Englewood Cliffs, NJ: Prentice-Hall.

L'Abate, L., & Harrison, M. G. (1992). Treating codependency. In L. L'Abate, J. E. Farrar, & D. A. Serritella (Eds.). *Handbook of differential treatments for addictions*, (pp. 286–306). Boston, MA: Allyn & Bacon.

L'Abate, L., & Hewitt, D. (1988). Toward a classification of sex and sexual behavior. *Journal of Sex and Marital Therapy, 14*, 29–39.

L'Abate, L., & Hewitt, D. (1989). Power versus presence: When complementarity becomes polarity. In J. F. Crosby (Ed.). *When one wants out and the other doesn't: Doing therapy with polarized couples*, pp. 136–152. New York: Bruner/Mazel.

L'Abate, L., Johnson, J., & Weeks, G. R. Forced holding: A technique for treating parentified children. *Family Therapy, 6*, 124–132.

L'Abate, L., & Jurkovic, G. (1987). Family systems theory as a cult: Boom of bankruptcy? In L. L'Abate, *Family psychology II: Theory, therapy, enrichments, and training* (pp. 19–27). Lanham, MD: University Press of America.

L'Abate, L., & Kern, R. (in press). Workbooks, technology, and emotionality. In S. Lepore & J. Smyth (Eds.), *The writing cure.* Washingon, DC: American Psychological Association.

L'Abate, L., & Kunkel, D. (1988). Problems-in-Relationships Scale with undergraduates. Unpublished research. Department of Psychology. Georgia State University, Atlanta.

L'Abate, L., Lambert, R. G., & Schenk, P. W. (2001). Testing a relational model of psychopathology with the MMPI-2. *American Journal of Family Therapy, 29*, 221–238.

L'Abate, L., & McHenry, S. (1983). *Handbook of marital interventions.* New York: Grune & Stratton.

L'Abate, L., & Milan, M. (Eds.) (1985). *Handbook of social skills training and research.* New York: Wiley.

L'Abate, L., Norman, M. A., & Aurandt, H. P. (1972). Modality preference, temporality, and school performance. Unpublished paper. Department of Psychology, Georgia State University, Atlanta.

L'Abate, L., & Odell, M. (1995). Expanding practices and roles of family clinicians. In M. Harway (Ed.), *Treating the changing family: Handling normative and unusual events* (pp. 321–339). New York: Wiley.

L'Abate, L., & Platzman, K. (1991). The practice of programmed writing (PW) in therapy and prevention with families. *American Journal of Family Therapy, 19*, 99–109.

L'Abate, L., & Rupp, G. (1981). *Enrichment: Skill training for family life.* Washington, DC: University Press of America.

L'Abate, L., & Thaxton, L. M. (1981). The differentiation of resources in mental health delivery systems: Implications for training. *Professional Psychology, 12*, 761–768.

L'Abate, L., Ulrici, P., & Wagner, V. (1983). The E-R-A model: A heuristic framework for classification of skill training programs for couples and families. *Family Relations, 30*, 307–315.

L'Abate, L., & Wagner, V. (1985). Theory-derived, family-oriented test batteries. In L. L'Abate (Ed.), *Handbook of family psychology and therapy* (pp. 1006–1032). Pacific Grove, CA: Brooks/Cole.

L'Abate, L., & Wagner, V. (1988). Testing a theory of developmental competence in the family. *American Journal of Family Psychology, 16*, 23–35.

L'Abate, L., & Weinstein, S. E. (1987). *Structured enrichment programs for couples and families.* New York: Brunner/Mazel.

L'Abate, L., & Young, L. (1987). *Casebook of structured enrichment programs for couples and families.* New York: Brunner/Mazel.

Labouvie-Vief, G. (1990). Wisdom as integrated thought: Historical and developmental perpsective. In R. J. Sternberg (Ed.), *Wisdom: Its nature, origins, and development* (pp. 52–83). Cambridge, UK: Cambridge University Press.

Lahey, B. B., Frick, P. J., Loeber, R., Tannenbaum, B. A., Van Horn, Y., & Christ, M. A. G. (1990). *Oppositional conduct disorder: I. A meta-analysis review.* Unpublished manuscript. University of Georgia, Athens.

Lambert, M. J. (1986). Implications of psychotherapy outcome research for eclectic psychotherapy. In J. C. Norcross (Ed.), *Handbook of eclectic psychotherapy* (pp. 436–662). New York: Brunner/Mazel.

Lambert, M. J. (1989). The individual therapist's contribution to psychotherapy process and outcome. *Clinical Psychology Review, 9*, 469–485.

Lambert, M. J. (1998). Manual-based treatment and clinical practice: Hangman of life or promising development? *Clinical Psychology: Science and Practice, 3*, 391–395.

Laszlo, J. V., Esterman, G., & Zabko, S. (1999). Therapy over the Internet? Theory, research, and finances. *CyberPsychology & Behavior, 2*, 293–307.

Lauterbach, W. (1996). The changing structure of Tanya's conflicts: A case of on-line conflict assessment in psychotherapy. *Psychotherapy Research, 6*, 277–290.

Leary, M. R., Springer, C., Negel, L., Ansell, L., & Evans, K. (1998). The causes, phenomenology, and consequences of hurt feelings. *Journal of Personality and Social Psychology, 74*, 1225–1237.

Lefons, E., Pazienza, M. T., Silvestri, A., Tangorra, F., Corfiati, L., De Giacomo, P., & Pierri, G. (1979). Possibilita' di riconoscimento di stati depressivi secondo il test SISCI-I. *Psychiatrica Messanensia, 1*, 25–30.

Leon, S. C. Kopta, S. M., Howard, K. I., & Lutz, W. (1999). Predicting patients' responses to psychotherapy: Are some more predictable than others? *Journal of Consulting and Clinical Psychology, 67*, 698–704.

Lepore, S. J. (1997). Expressive writing moderates the relation between intrusive thoughts and depressive symptoms. *Journal of Personality and Social Psychology, 73*, 1030–1037.

Lepore, S. J., & Helgeson, V. S. (1998). Social constraints, intrusive thoughts, and mental health after prostate cancer. *Journal of Social and Clinical Psychology, 17*, 89–106.

Lepore, S. J., Ragan, J. D., & Jones, S. (2000). Talking facilitates cognitive-emotional processes of adaptation to an acute stressor. *Journal of Personality and Social Psychology, 78*, 499–508.

Lepore, S. J., Silver, R. C., Wortman, C. B., & Wayment, H. A. (1996). Social constraints, intrusive thoughts, and depressive symptoms among bereaved mothers. *Journal of Personality and Social Psychology, 70*, 271–282.

Levant, R. F. (1986). *Psychoeducational approaches to family therapy and counseling*. New York: Springer.

Levinson, H. N. (1986). *Phobia free*. New York: Evans.

Levy, R. L., & Shelton, J. L. (1990). Tasks in brief therapy. In R. A. Wells & V. J. Giannetti (Eds.), *Handbook of the brief psychotherapies* (pp. 145–163). New York: Wiley.

Lewis, M. (1999). On the development of personality. In L. A. Pervin & O. P. John (Eds.), *Handbook of personality: Theory and research* (pp. 327–346). New York: Guilford.

Liberman, R. P., DeRisi, W., & Mueser, K. T. (1989). *Social skills training for psychiatric patients*. Des Moines, IA.: Allyn & Bacon.

Lindaver, P. (1998). Le persone in relazione: Tre modelli teorici a confronto. *Famiglia, Interdisciplinarita' Ricerca, 3*, 101–114.

Linden, W., & Wen, F. K. (1990). Therapy outcome research, health care policy, and the continuing lack of accumulated knowledge. *Professional Psychology: Research and Practice, 21*, 482–488.

Liotti, G. (1999). Disorganization of attachment as a model for understanding dissociative psychopathology. In J. Solomon & C. George (Ed.), *Attachment disorganization* (pp. 291–317). New York: Guilford.

Livesley, W. J., Jackson, D. N., & Schroeder, M. L. (1989). A study of the factorial structure of personality pathology. *Journal of Personality Disorders, 3*, 292–306.

Lofquist, W. A. (1983). *Discovering the meaning of prevention: A practical approach to positive change*. Tucson, AZ: AYD Publications.

Lombard, D., Haddock, C. K., Talcott, G. W., & Reynes, R. (1998). Cost-effectiveness analyis: A primer for psychologists. *Applied & Preventive Psychology, 7*, 101–108.

Lorr, M., Youniss, R. P., & Stefic, E. C. (1991). An inventory of social skills. *Journal of Personality Assessment, 57*, 506–520.

Loukas, A., Twitchell, G. R., Piejak, L. A., Fitzgerald, H. E., & Zucker, R. A. (1998). The family as a unity of interacting personalities. In L. L'Abate (Ed.), *Family psychopathology: The relational roots of dysfunctional behavior* (pp. 35–59). New York: Guilford.

Luborsky, L. (1993). Recomendations for training therapists based on manuals for psychotherapy research. *Psychotherapy, 30*, 578–580.

Luborsky, L., Crits-Christoph, P., Mintz, J., & Auerbach, A. (1988). *Who will benefit from psychotherapy? Predicting therapeutic outcomes.* New York: Basic Books.

Luborsky, L., Singer, B., & Luborsky, L. (1975). Comparative studies of psychotherapies: Is it true that "everyone has won and all must have prices"? *Archives of General Psychiatry, 32*, 995–1008.

Lynam, D. R. (1997). Pursuing the psychopath: Capturing the fledging psychopath in a nomological net. *Journal of Abnormal Psychology, 106*, 425–438.

Lynn, S. J., & Garske, J. P. (Eds.) (1985). *Contemporary psychotherapies: Models and methods.* Columbus, OH: Charles E. Merrill.

Maddi, S. R. (1989). *Personality theories: A comparative analysis.* Chicago: Dorsey.

Magdol, L., Moffitt, T. E., Caspi, A., Fagan, J., & Silva, P. A. (1997). Gender differences in partner violence in a birth cohort of 21-year-olds: Bridging the gap between clinical and epidemiological approaches. *Journal of Consulting and clinical Psychology, 65*, 68–78.

Magnusson, D. (1999). Holistic interactionism: A perspective for research on personality development. In L. A. Pervin & O. P. John (Eds.), *Handbook of personality: Theory and research*, (pp. 219–247). New York: Guilford.

Maheu, M. (2000). Telehealth: The furthering of psychology as a profession. Available on the World Wide Web: <telehealth.net/articles/further.html.>

Maheu, M., Allen, A., & Whitten, P. (2001). *E-health, telehealth, and telemedicine: A practical guide to startup and success.* San Francisco, CA: Jossey-Bass.

Mahoney, M. J. (1991). *Human change processes: The scientific foundations of psychotherapy.* New York: Basic Books.

Mahrer, A. R. (1999). Embarassing problems for the field of psychotherapy. *Journal of Clinical Psychology, 55*, 1147–1156.

Marks, I., Shaw, S., & Parkin, R. (1998). Computer-aided treatments of mental health problems. *Clinical Psychology: Science and Practice, 5*, 151–170.

Marlowe, H. A., & Weinberg, R. B. (Eds.) (1985). *Competence development: Theory and practice in special populations.* Springfield, IL: Charles C. Thomas.

Marques, C. (1998). Manual-based treatment and clinical practice. *Clinical Psychology: Science and Practice, 3*, 4030.

Maruish, M. E. (Ed.) (1994). *The use of psychological testing for treatment planning and outcome assessment.* Hillsdale, NJ: Earlbaum.

Mascolo, M. F., & Griffin, S. (Eds.) (1998). *What develops in emotional development?* New York: Plenum.

Mash, L. J., & Barkley, R. A. (Eds.) (1996). *Child psychopathology.* New York: Guilford.

Masten, A. S., & Coatsworth, J. D. (1998). The development of competence in favorable and unfavorable environments: Lessons from research on successful children. *American Psychologist, 53*, 205–220.

Mayer, J. D., & Salovey, P. (1995). Emotional intelligence and the construction and regulation of feelings. *Applied & Preventive Psychology, 4*, 197–208.

McAdams, D. P. (1988). *Power, intimacy, and the life story: Personological inquiries into identity*. New York: Guilford.

McAdams, D. P. (1996). Alternative futures for the study of human individuals. *Journal of Personality Research, 30*, 374–388.

McCrae, R. R. (1994). A reformulation of Axis II: Personality and personality-related problems. In P. T. Costa, Jr., & T. A. Widiger (Eds.), *Personality disorders and the five-factor model of personality* (pp. 303–309). Washington, DC: American Psychological Association.

McCubbin, H. I., Thompson, A. I., Kretzschmar, H. O., Smith, F. A., Snow, P. A., McEwen, M. A., Elver, K., & McCubbin, M. A. (1992). Family systems and work environment predictors of employee health risk: A discriminant function analysis. *American Journal of Family Therapy, 20*, 123–144.

McCullough, M. E., Pargament, K. I., & Thorensen, C. E. (Eds.) (2000) *Forgiveness: Theory, research, and practice*. New York: Guilford.

McFall, R. M. (2000). Elaborate reflections on a simple manifesto. *Applied & Preventive Psychology, 9*, 5–21.

McFarlane, W. R. (1991). Family psychoeducational treatment. In A. S. Gurman & D. P Kniskern (Eds.), *Handbook of family therapy. Volume II* (pp. 363–395). New York: Brunner/Mazel.

McGuire, W. J. (1997). Creative hypotheses generating in psychology: Some useful heuristics. *Annual Review of Psychology, 48*, 1–30.

McGurrin, M. C. (1992). *Pathological gambling; Conceptual, diagnostic, and treatment issues*. Sarasota, FL: Professional Exchange.

McLellan, H. (2000). Experience design. *CyberPsychology & Behavior, 3*, 59–69.

McMahan, O., & L'Abate, L. (2001). Marital adjustment and programmed distance writing with seminarian couples. In L. L'Abate (Ed.), *Distance writing and computer-assisted interventions in psychiatry and mental health* (pp. 135–156). Westport, CT: Ablex.

McMahan, O., & L'Abate, L. (in preparation). Individual background, personality adjustment, and marital functioning in seminarian couples.

McMullin, R. E. (1986). *Handbook of cognitive therapy techniques*. New York: Norton.

Mikesell, R. H., Lusterman, D. D., & McDaniel, S. H. (Eds.) (1995). *Integrating family therapy: Handbook of family psychology and systems theory*. Washington, DC: American Psychological Association.

Miller, I. J. (1989). The therapeutic empathic communication (TEC) process. *American Journal of Psychotherapy, 48*, 531–545.

Miller, M. J., Hammond, K. W., & Hile, M. G. (Eds.) (1996). *Mental health computing*. New York: Springer.

Mills, J. A. (1998). *Control: A history of behavioral psychology*. New York: New York University Press.

Mirin, S. M., Gossett, J. T., & Grob, M. C. (Eds.) (1991). *Psychiatric treatment: Advances in outcome research*. Washington, DC: American Psychiatric Press.

Moen, P., Elder, G. H., Jr., & Luscher, K. (Eds.) (1995). *Examining lives in context: Perspectives on the ecology of human development*. Washington, DC: American Psychological Association.

Moncher, F. J., & Prinz, R. J. (1991). Treatment fidelity in outcome studies. *Clinical Psychology Review, 11*, 247–266.

Moras, K. (1993). The use of treatment manuals to train psychotherapists: Observations and recommendations. *Psychotherapy, 30*, 581–586.

Moras, K., Di Nardo, P. A., & Barlow, D. H. (1992) Distinguishing anxiety and depression: Reexamination of the reconstructed Hamilton scales. *Psychological Assessment, 4*, 224–227.

Morey, L. C. (1999). Personality Assessment Inventory. In M. E. Maruish (Ed.), *The use of psychological testing for treatment planning and outcome assessment, Second Edition* (pp. 1083–1122). Mahwah, NJ: Earlbaum.

Morey, L. C., & Henry, W. (1994). Personality Assessment Inventory. In M. E. Maruish, (Ed.), *The use of psychological testing for treatment planning and outcome assessment* (pp. 185–216). Hillsdale, NJ: Earlbaum.

Mrazek, P. J., & Haggerty, R. J. (Eds.) (1994). *Reducing risks for mental disorders: Frontiers for preventive intervention research.* Washington, DC: National Academy Press.

Mueser, K. T., Curran, P. J., & McHugo, G. J. (1997). Factor structure of the Brief Psychiatric Rating Scale in Schizophrenia. *Psychological Assessment, 9*, 196–204.

Murray, B. (1998). The latest techno tool: Essay-grading computers. *Psychological Monitor*, August Issue, p. 43.

Murray, E. J., Lamnin, A. D., & Carver, C. S. (1989). Emotional expression in written essays and psychotherapy. *Journal of Social and Clinical Psychology, 8*, 414–429.

Murray, E. J., & Segal, D. L. (1994). Emotional processing in vocal and written expression of feelings about traumatic experiences. *Journal of Traumatic Stress, 7*, 391–405.

Nathan, P. E. (1997). Validated forms of psychotherapy may lead to better-validated psychotherapies. *Clinical Psychology: Science and Practice, 4*, 251–255.

Nathan, P. E. (1998). Pactice guidelines: Not yet ideal. *American Psychologist, 53*, 290–299.

Nathan, P. E., & Gorman, J. M. (Eds.) (1998). *A guide to treatments that work.* New York: Oxford University Press.

Neimeyer, G. J., & Lyddon, W. J. (1993). Constructivist psychotherapy: Principles into practice. *Journal of Cognitive Psychotherapy, 7*, 183–194.

Newcomer, P. L., Barenbaum, E. M., & Bryant, B. R. (1994). *Depression and Anxiety in Youth Scale.* Austin, TX: Pro-Ed.

Newman, M. G. (2000). Recommendations for a cost-offset model of psychotherapy allocation using generalized anxiety disorder as an example. *Journal of Consulting and Clinical Psychology, 68*, 549–555.

Newman, M. G., Kenardy, J., Herman, S., & Barr-Taylor, C. (1997). Comparison of palmtop-computer-assisted brief cognitive-behavioral treatment to cognitive-behavioral treatment for panic disorder. *Journal of Consulting and Clinical Psychology, 65*, 178–183.

Nicholson, I. R. (1998). Schizophrenia and the family. In L. L'Abate (Ed.), *Handbook of family psychopathology* (pp. 280–210). New York: Guilford.

Nickelson, D. W. (1998). Telehealth and the evolving health care system: Strategic opportunities for professional psychology. *Professional Psychology: Research and Practice, 29*, 527–535.

Norcross, J. C. (Ed.) (1986). *Handbook of eclectic psychotherapy.* New York: Brunner/Mazel.

Norcross, J. C., & Goldfried, M. (Eds.) (1992). *Handbook of psychotherapy integration.* New York: Basic Books.

Nystrand, M. (Ed.). (1977). *Language as a way of knowing: A book of readings.* Toronto: Ontario Institute for Studies in Education.

Nystrand, M. (1986). *The structure of written communication: Studies in reciprocity between writers and readers.* Orlando, FL: Academic Press.

Oaksford, M., & Chater, N. (1998). *Rationality in an uncertain world: Essays on the cognitive science of human reasoning.* Hove, England: Psychology Press Ltd.

O'Donohue, W., & Krasner, L. (Eds.) (1995). *Handbook of psychological skills training: Clinical techniques and applications.* Boston, MA: Allyn & Bacon.

Ogles, B. M., Lambert, M. J., & Masters, K. S. (1996). *Assessing outcome in clinical practice.* Boston, MA: Allyn & Bacon.

Oher, J. M., Conti, D. J., & Jongsma, A. E., Jr. (1998). *The employer assistance treatment planner.* New York: Wiley.

Okun, B. F. (1990). *Seeking connections in psychotherapy.* San Francisco, CA: Jossey-Bass.

Oliver, P. J., & Srivastava, S. (1999). The big five trait taxonomy: History, measurement, and theoretical pedrspectives. In L. A. Pervin & O. P. John (Eds.), *Handbook of personality: Theory and research* (pp. 102–128). New York: Guilford.

Olson, D. H. (1993). Circumplex model of marital and family systems. In F. Walsh (Ed.), *Normal family processes* (pp. 104–137). New York: Guilford.

Omer, H. (1989). Specifics and nonspecifics in psychotherapy. *American Journal of Psychotherapy, 43,* 181–192.

Orbach, I., & Mikulincer, M. (1998). The body investment scale: Construction and validation of a body experience scale. *Psychological Assessment, 10,* 415–425.

Orlinsky, D. E. (1994). Research-based knowledge as the emergent foundation for the clinical practice in psychotherapy. In P. F. Talley, H. H. Strupp, & S. F. Butler (Eds.), *Psychotherapy research and practice: Bridging the gap* (pp. 99–125). New York: Basic Books.

Orlinsky, D. E., & Howard, K. I. (1995). Unity and diversity among psychotherapies: A comparative perspective. In B. Bongar & L. E. Beutler (Eds.) *Comprehensive textbook of psychotherapy: Theory and practice* (pp. 3–23). New York: Oxford University Press.

Ornstein, R. (1997). *The right mind: Making sense of the hemispheres.* New York: Harcourt Brace & Co.

Orvaschel, H. (1999). Does theory have value in clinical child psychology? *Journal of Clinical Child Psychology, 28,* 548–549.

Otto, M. W., Pollack, M. H. & Maki, K. M., (2000). Empirically supported treatment for panic disorder: Costs, benefits, and stepped care. *Journal of Consulting and Clinical Psychology, 68,* 556–563.

Parks, E. D., & Balon, R. (1995). Autobiographical memory of childhood events: Patterns of recall in psychiatric patients with a history of alleged trauma. *Psychiatry—Interpersonal and Biological Processes, 59,* 199–208.

Parks, M. R., & Roberts, L. D. (1998). "Making Moosic": The development of personal relationships on line and a comparison to their off-line counterparts. *Journal of Social and Personal Relationships, 15,* 517–537.

Parloff, G. (1998). Is psychotherapy more than manual labor? *Clinical Psychology: Science and Practice, 3,* 376–381.

Pearson, L. (Ed.). (1965). *The use of written communication in psychotherapy*. Springfield, IL: Charles C. Thomas.

Pelfry, M. (1993). Using HELP-software in a psychiatric hospital. In *Computer Assisted Therapy: A Guide* (pp. 41–44). Santa Barbara, CA: CATSco.

Pennebaker, J. W. (1997). *Opening up: The healing power of expressing emotions*. New York: Guilford.

Pennebaker, J. W. (2001). Explorations into the health benefits of disclosure: Inhibitory, cognitive, and social processes. In L. L'Abate (Ed.), *Distance writing and computer-assisted interventions in psychiatry and mental health* (pp. 33–44). Westport, CT: Ablex.

Pennebaker, J. W., & King, L. K. (1999). Linguistic styles: Language use as an individual difference. *Journal of Personality and Social Psychology, 77*, 1296–1312.

Peplau, L. A., & Perlman, D. (Eds.) (1982). *Loneliness: A sourcebook of current theory, research, and therapy*. New York: Wiley.

Pereira, O. G., & Ferreira, C. P. (1985). Applicazioni del modello di De Giacomo e Silvestri in psicologia. In C. Cipolli & A. Silvetri (Eds.), *Comunicazione e sistemi*. Milano, Italy: Angeli.

Perry, J. C., Banon, E., & Ianni, F. (1999). Effectiveness of psychotherapy for personality disorders. *American Journal of Psychiatry, 156*, 1312–1321.

Perry, J. N., & Butcher, J. N. (1999). Butcher Treatment Planning Inventory (BTPI): An objective guide to treatment planning. In M. E. Maruish (Ed.), *The use of psychological testing for treatment planning and outcome asssessment, Second Edition* (pp. 1157–1172). Mahwah, NJ: Earlbaum.

Perry, S., Frances, A., & Clarkin, J. (1990). *A DSM-III-R casebook of treatment selection*. New York: Brunner/Mazel.

Pervin, L. A. (Ed.) (1990). *Handbook of personality theory and research*. New York: Guilford.

Pervin, L. A. (1996). Personality: A view of the future based on a look at the past. *Journal of Personality Research, 30*, 309–318.

Pervin, L. A., & John, O. P. (Eds.) (1999). *Handbook of personality: Theory and research*. New York: Guilford.

Petronio, S. (2000). Preface: Meaning of balance. In S. Petronio (Ed.), *Balancing the secrets of private discosures* (pp. xiii–xvi). Mahwah, NJ: Earlbaum.

Phillips, E. L. (1990). The delivery system as a prime therapeutic determinant. In J. K. Zeig & W. M. Munion (Eds.), *What is psychotherapy? Contemporary perspectives* (pp. 115–119). San Francisco, CA: Jossey-Bass.

Phillips, E. L., & Wiener, D. N. (1966). *Short-term psychotherapy and structured behavior change*. New York: McGraw-Hill.

Pine, B. J., III, & Gilmore, J. H. (1999). *The experience economy: Work is theater and every business a stage*. Cambridge, MA: Harvard Business School.

Plutchik, R. (1993). Emotions and their vicissitudes: Emotions and psychopathology. In M. Lewis & J. M. Haviland (Eds.), *Handbook of emotions* (pp. 53–66). New York: Guilford.

Plutchik, R., & Conte, H. R. (Eds.) (1997). *Circumplex models of personality and emotions*. Washington, DC: American Psychological Association.

Polanyi, M. (1964). *Science, faith, and society*. Chicago, IL: University of Chicago Press.

Prager, K. J. (1995). *The psychology of intimacy*. New York: Guilford.

Pransky, J. (1991). *Prevention: The critical need.* Springfield, MO: Burrell Foundation & Paradigm Press.

Prentice, D. A. (1987). Psychological correspondence of possessions, attitudes, and values. *Journal of Personality and Social Psychology, 53*, 993–1003.

Primakoff, L., Epstein, N., & Covi, L., (1986). Homework compliance: An uncontrolled variable in cognitive therapy outcomes research. *Behavioral Therapy, 17*, 443–446.

Prochaska, J. O. (1984). *Systems of psychotherapy: A transtheoretical analysis*, Chicago, IL: Dorsey.

Progoff, I. (1975). *At a journal workshop*. New York: Dialogue House Library.

Progoff, I. (1980). *The practice of process mediation: The intensive journal way to spiritual experience*. New York: Dialogue House Library.

Quattrone, G. A. (1985). On the congruity between internal states and action. *Psychological Bulletin, 98*, 3–40.

Rabasca, L. (1998). Study probes how patients are affected by telehealth. *Psychological Monitor*, August, p. 31.

Rapee, R. M. (Ed). (1996). *Current controversies in the anxiety disorders*. New York: Guilford.

Reed, R., McMahan, O., & L'Abate, L. (2001). Workbooks and psychotherapy with incarcerated felons. In L. L'Abate (Ed.), *Distance writing and computer-assisted interventions in psychiatry and mental health* (pp. 157–161). Westport, CT: Ablex.

Reichenbach, H. (1936). *Experience and prediction*. Chicago: University of Chicago Press.

Reid, E. (1998). The self and the internet: Variations on the illusion of one self. In J. Gackenbach (Ed.), *Psychology and the Internet: Intrapersonal, interpersonal, and transpersonal implications* (pp. 29–42). San Diego, CA: Academic Press.

Reiss, D. (1981). *The family's construction of reality*. Cambridge, MA: Harvard University Press.

Reynolds, M., Brewin, C. R., & Saxton, M. (2000). Emotional disclosure in school children. *Journal of Child Psychology and Psychiatry, 41*.

Richards, J. M., Beal, W. E., Seagal, J. D., & Pennebaker, J. W. (2000). The effects of disclosure of traumatic events on illness behavior among psychiatric prison inmates. *Journal of Abnormal Psychology, 109*, 156–160.

Rierdan, J. (1999). Internet-depression link? *American Psychologist, 54*, 781–782.

Riordan, R. J. (1996). Scriptotherapy: Therapeutic writing as a counseling adjunct. *Journal of Counseling and Development, 74*, 263–269.

Roberts, M. C., & Peterson, L. (Eds.) (1984). *Prevention of problems in childhood: Psychological research and applications*. New York: Wiley.

Robins, R. W., Norem, J. K., & Cheek, J. M. (1999). Naturalizing the self. In L. A. Pervin & O. P. John (Eds.), *Handbook of personality: Theory and research* (pp. 443–479). New York: Guilford.

Rogers, C. R. (1957). The necessary and sufficient conditions of therapeutic personality change. *Journal of Consulting Psychology, 21*, 95–103.

Ross, C. A., & Pam, A. (1995). *Pseudoscience in biological psychiatry: Blaming the body*. New York: Wiley.

Roth, A., & Fonagy, P. (1996). *What works for whom? A critical review of psychotherapy research*. New York: Guilford.

Royce, W. S., & Muehlke, C. V. (1991). Therapists' causal attributions of clients' problems and selection of intervention strategies. *Psychological Reports, 68*, 379–386.

Rueter, M. A., Scaramella, L., Wallace, L. E., & Conger, R. D. (1999). First onset of depressive or anxiety disorders predicted by the longitudinal course of internalizing symptoms and parent-adolescent disagreements. *Archives of General Psychiatry, 56*, 726–732.

Russell, L. B. (1986). *Is prevention better than cure?* Washington, DC: The Brookings Institution.

Russell, R. L. (1989). Language and psychotherapy. *Clinical Psychology Review, 9*, 505–519.

Ryan, E. B. (1994). Memory for Goblins: A computer game for assessing and training working memory skill. *Computers in Human Services, 11*, 213–217.

Ryan, R. M., & Deci, E. L. (2000). Self-determination theory and the facilitation of intrinsic motivation, social development, and well-being. *American Psychologist, 55*, 68–78.

Rychlak, J. F. (1975). Dialectical versus demonstrative conceptions of mental illness and its cure. In D. Bannister (Ed.), *Issues and approaches in the psychological therapies* (pp. 27–46). New York: Wiley.

Saarni, C. (1999). *The development of emotional competence.* New York: Guilford.

Safran, J. D., & Muran, J. C. (1998). *The therapeutic alliance in brief psychotherapy.* Washington, DC: American Psychological Association.

Salovey, P., Rothman, A. J., Detweiler, J. B., & Steward, W. T. (2000). Emotional states and physical health. *American Psychologist, 55*, 110–121.

Salovey, P., & Sluyter, D. (1997). *Emotional development and emotional intelligence: Educational implications.* New York: Basic Books.

Salvo, R., Cusinato, M., & Rossetti, N. (1996). Attaccamento e relazione di coppia. *Famiglia Interdisciplinarieta', Ricerca, 1*, 5–16.

Salzen, E. A. (1995). Why there are eight primary emotions? *ASCAP Newsletter, 8*, 8–11.

Sanders, M. R. (1998). The empirical status of psychological interventions with families of children and adolescents. In L. L'Abate (Ed.), *Family psychopathology: The relational roots of dysfunctional behavior* (pp. 427–465). New York: Guilford.

Sanford, K. (1997). Two dimensions of adult attachment: Further validation. *Journal of Social and Personal Relationships, 14*, 133–143.

Sarason, I. G., Sarason, B. R., & Pierce, G. R. (1996). Editorial: Views of the future. *Journal of Personality Research, 30*, 447–453.

Satir, V. (1964). *Conjoint family therapy.* Palo Alto, CA: Science & Behavior Books.

Sauber, S. R. (1983). *The human services delivery system: Mental health, criminal justice, social welfare, education, health services.* New York: Columbia University Press.

Sauding, K. J., & Plomin, R. (1996). Personality and behavioral genetics: Where have we been and where are we going? *Journal of Personality Research, 30*, 335–347.

Scheel, M. J., Forsythe, N., Kristjansson, S., Pranata, H., Packard, T., & Packard, K. (2000). Marital enrichment: Linking research with practice. *The Family Psychologist, 12*, 6–10.

Schroeder, M. I., Wormsworth, J. A., and Livesley, W. J. (1992). Dimensions of personality disorder and their relationships to the Big Five dimensions of personality. *Psychological Assessment, 4*, 47–53.

Schultheis, G. M. (1998). *Brief therapy homework planner*. New York: Wiley.

Schultz, D. (1990). *Theories of personality*. Belmont, CA: Brooks/Cole.

Schwebel, A. I. (1993). Family defense mechanisms: The concept and its utility to family scientists, practitioners, and educators. *The Family Journal: Counseling and Therapy for Couples and Families, 1*, 31–41.

Scott, E. M. (1998). *Within the hearts and minds of prisoners: An in-depth view of prisoners in therapy*. Springfield, IL: Charles C. Thomas.

Segal, D. L., Bogaards, J. A., Becker, L. A., & Chatman, C. (1999). Effects of emotional expression on adjustment of spousal loss among older adults. *Journal of Mental Health and Aging, 5*, 297–310.

Segal, D. L., & Murray, E. J. (2001). Comparison of distance emotional expression with psychotherapy. In L. L'Abate (Ed.), *Distance writing and computer-assisted interventions in psychiatry and mental health* (pp. 61–75). Westport, CT: Ablex.

Seligman, L. (1990). *Selecting effective treatments*. San Francisco, CA: Jossey-Bass.

Seligman, M.E.P. (1998). Why therapy works. *Psychological Monitor*, December Issue, p. 2.

Seligman, M.E.P., & Csikszentmihalyi, M. (2000). Positive psychology: An introduction. *American Psychologist, 55*, 5–14.

Shapiro, D. (2000). *Dynamics of character: Self-regulation in psychopathology*. New York: Basic Books.

Shapiro, D. A. (1996). "Validated" treatments and evidence-based psychological services. *Clinical Psychology: Science and Practice, 4*, 256–259.

Shapiro, D. A., Startup, M., Bird, D., Harper, H., Reynolds, S., & Suokas, A. (1994). The high-water mark of the drug metaphor: A meta-analytic critique of process-outcome research. In R. L. Russell (Ed.), *Reassessing psychotherapy research* pp. 1–35). New York: Guilford.

Shapiro, D. H. & Astin, J. (1998). *Control therapy: An integrated approach to psychotherapy, health, and healing*. New York: Wiley.

Shapiro, J. S. (1999). Loneliness: Paradox or artifact? *American Psychologist, 54*, 782–783.

Shaw, N. F., Elkin, I., Yamaguchi, J., Olmstead, M., Vallis, T. M., Dobson, K. S., Lowery, A., Sotsky, S. M., & Watkins, J. T. (1999). Therapist competence ratings in relation to clinical outcome in cognitive therapy of depression. *Journal of Consulting and Clinical Psychology, 67*, 837–846.

Shelton, J. L., & Levy, R. L. (1981). *Behavioral assignments and treatment compliance: A handbook of clinical strategies*. Champlain, IL: Research Press.

Shoda, Y., & Mischel, W. (1996). Toward a unified, intra-individual dynamic conception of personality. *Journal of Personality Research, 30*, 414–428.

Silverman, T. (1999). The Internet and relational theory. *American Psychologist, 54*, 780–781.

Silverman, W. M. (1996). Cookbooks, manuals, and paint-by-numbers: Psychotherapy in the 90's. *Psychotherapy, 33*, 207–215.

Simon, L. (1998). Do offender treatments work? *Applied & Preventive Psychology, 7*, 137–159.

Simpson, J. A., & Rholes, W. S. (Eds.) (1998). *Attachment theory and close relationships*, New York: Guilford.

Singleton, W. T., Spurgeon, P., & Stammers, R. B. (Eds.) (1979). *The analysis of social skills*. New York: Plenum.

Smyth, J. M. (1998). Written emotional expression: Effect size, outcome types, and moderating variables. *Journal of Consulting and Clinical Psychology, 66*, 174–184.

Smyth, J. M., & L'Abate, L. (2001). A meta-analytic evaluation of workbook effectiveness in medicine and mental health. In L. L'Abate (Ed.), *Distance writing and computer-assisted interventions in psychiatry and mental health* (pp. 77–90). Westport, CT: Ablex.

Snyder, D. K. (1981). *Manual for Marital Satisfaction Inventory*. Los Angeles, CA: Western Psychological Services.

Snyder, D. K., & Aikman, G. G. (1999). Marital Satisfaction Inventory—Revisited. In M. E. Maruish (Ed.), *The use of psychological testing for treatment planning and outcomes assessment, Second Edition* (pp. 1173–1210). Mahwah, NJ: Earlbaum.

Snyder, D. K., & Costin, S. E. (1994). Marital Satisfaction Inventory. In M. E. Maruish (Ed.), *The use of psychological testing for treatment planning and outcome assessment* (pp. 322–351). Hillsdale, NJ: Earlbaum.

Snyder, D. K., Lacher, D., & Wills, R. M. (1988). Computer-based interpretation of the Marital Satisfaction Inventory: Use in treatment planning. *Journal of Marital and Family Therapy, 14*, 397–409.

Sobell, M. B., & Sobell, L. C. (2000). Stepped care as a heuristic approach to the treatment of alcohol problems. *Journal of Consulting and Clinical Psychology, 68*, 573–579.

Sober, E., & Wilson, D. S. (1998). *Unto others: The evolution and psychology of unselfish behavior*. Cambridge, MA: Harvard University Press.

Spanier, G. (1976). Measuring dyadic adjustment: New scales for assessing the quality of marriage and similar dyads. *Journal of Marriage and the Family, 38*, 15–28.

Spanier, G., & Thompson, L. (1982). A confirmatory analysis of the Dyadic Adjustment Scales. *Journal of Marriage and the Family, 2*, 731–738.

Spence, D. P. (1994). The failure to ask the hard questions. In P. F. Talley, H. H. Strupp, S. F. Butler (Eds.), *Psychotherapy research and practice: Bridging the gap* (pp. 19–38). New York: Basic Books.

Spence, S., & Shepherd, G. (1983). *Developments in social skills training*. New York: Academic Press.

Sperry, L., Brill, P. L., Howard, K. I., & Grissom, G. R. (1996). *Treatment outcomes in psychotherapy and psychiatric interventions*. New York: Brunner-Mazel.

Sperry, L., & Carlson, J. (1996). *Psychopathology and psychotherapy: From DSM-IV diagnosis to treatment*. Philadelphia, PA: Taylor & Francis.

Spiegel, J. (1971). *Transactions: The interplay between individual, family, and society*. New York: Science House.

Spiegel, D., & Wissler, T. (1983). Perceptions of family environment among psychiatric patients and their wives. *Family Process, 22*, 537–547.

Spielberger, C., & London, P. (1982). Rage boomerangs. *American Health, 1*, 52–56.

Spielberger, C. D., Reheiser, E. R., & Sydeman, S. J. (1995). Measuring the experience, expression, and control of anger. In H. Kassinove (Ed.), *Anger disorders: Definition, diagnosis, and treatment* (pp. 49–67). Philadelphia, PA: Taylor & Francis.

Spielberger, C. D., Sydeman, S. J., Owen, A. E., & Marsh, B. J. (1999). Measuring anxiety and anger in the State-Trait Anxiety Inventory (STAI) and the State-Trait Anger Expression Inventory (STAXI). In M. E. Maruish (Ed.), *The use of psychological testing for treatment planning and outcome assessment, Second Edition* (pp. 993–1022). Mahwah, NJ: Earlbaum.

Sprafkin, R. P., Gershaw, N. J., & Goldstein, A. P. (1993). *Social skills for mental health: A structured learning approach.* Boston, MA: Allyn & Bacon.

Stamm, B. H. (1998). Clinical applications of telehealth in mental health care. *Professional Psychology: Research and Practice, 29*, 536–542.

Startup, M., Shapiro, D. A. (1993). Therapist treatment fidelity in prescriptive vs. exploratory psychotherapy. *British Journal of Clinical Psychology, 32*, 443–456.

Steketee, G., & Chambless, D. L. (1992). Methodological issues in prediction of treatment outcome. *Clinical Psychology Review, 12*, 387–400.

Sternberg, R. J. (1987). *The triangle of love: Intimacy, passion, commitment.* New York: Basic Books.

Sternberg, R. J. (1996). *Successful intelligence.* New York: Simon & Schuster.

Sternberg, R. J., & Barnes, M. J. (Eds.) (1988). *The psychology of love.* New Haven, CT: Yale University Press.

Sternberg, R. J., & Kaufman, J. C. (1998). Human abilities. *Annual Review of Psychology, 49*, 479–502.

Sternberg, R. J., & Swerling, L. S. (1998). Personal navigation. In M. Ferrari & R. J. Sternberg (Eds.), *Self-awareness: Its nature and development* (pp. 219–245). New York: Guilford.

Stevens, F. E., & L'Abate, L. (1986). Structured enrichment (SE) with a couple. *Psychotherapy and the Family, 2*, 59–67.

Stevens, F. E., & L'Abate, L. (1989). Validity and reliability of a theory-derived measure of intimacy. *American Journal of Family Therapy, 17*, 359–368.

Stiles, W. B., Shapiro, D. A., & Harper, H. (1994). Finding the way from process to outcome: Blind alleys and unmarked trails. In R. L. Russell (Ed.), *Reassessing psychotherapy research* (pp. 36–64). New York: Guilford.

Straus, M. B. (1999). *No-talk therapy for children and adolescents.* New York: Norton.

Stricker, G. (1997). Are science and practice commensurable? *American Psychologist, 52*, 442–448.

Strosahl, K. (1998). The dissemination of manual-based psychotherapies in managed care: Promises, problems, and prospects. *Clinical Psychology: Science and practice, 3*, 382–386.

Strupp, H. H., & Anderson, T. (1997). On the limitations of therapy manuals. *Clinical Psychology: Science and Practice, 4*, 76–82.

Szapocznik, J., Kurtines, W., Foote, F. H., Perez-Vidal, A., & Hervis, O. (1989). Conjoint versus one person family therapy: Some evidence for the effectiveness of conducting family therapy through a person. *Journal of Consulting and Clinical Psychology, 51*, 881–889.

Szapocznik, J., Murray, E., Scopetta, M., Hervis, O, Rio, A., Cohen, R., Rivas-Vasquez, A. Posada, V., & Kurtines, W. (1989). Structural family versus psychodynamic child therapy for problematic Hispanic boys. *Journal of Consulting and Clinical Psychology, 57*, 571–578.

Szell, E. (1994). *Comparison of therapeutic interactions between face-to-face and telemediated communication conditions.* Ph.D. dissertation, University of Miami, Florida.

Talley, P. F., Strupp, H. H., & Butler, S. F. (Eds.) (1994). *Psychotherapy research and practice: Bridging the gap.* New York: Basic Books.

Taylor, S., Kuch, K., Koch, W. J., Crockett, D. J., & Passey, G. (1998). The structure of posttraumatic stress symptoms. *Journal of Abnormal Psychology, 107*, 154–160.

TherapyWorks* Products. (1998). *Empirically-supported treatment programs*. San Antonio, TX: Psychological Corporation.

Theye; W. (1993). Computer enhanced counseling at Ohio Northern University. In *Computer Assisted Therapy: A guide* (pp. 22–28). Santa Barbara, CA: CATSco.

Thompson, L. (1990). Negotiation behavior and outcomes: Empirical evidence and theoretical issues. *Psychological Bulletin, 108*, 515–532.

Tolan, P. H., Quintana, E., & Gorman-Smith, D. (1998). Prevention approaches for families. In L. L'Abate (Ed.), *Family psychopathology: The relational roots of dysfunctional behavior* (pp. 379–400). New York: Guilford.

Trabin, T. (1996). *The computerization of behavioral healthcare: How to enhance clinical practice, management, and communications*. San Francisco, CA: Jossey-Bass.

Ulrici, D., & Wagner, V., & L'Abate, L. (1981). The E-R-A model: A heuristic framework for classification of skill training programs for couples and families. *Family Relations, 30*, 307–315.

U.S. Department of Health and Human Services (1999). *Mental Health: Report of the Surgeon General*. Rockville, MD: Author.

Van Etten, M. L., & Taylor, S. (In press). Comparative efficacy of treatments for post-traumatic stress disorder: A meta-analysis. *Clinical Psychology & Psychotherapy*.

Vetter, H. J. (1970). *Language behavior and psychopathology*. Chicago, IL: Rand McNally.

Vitelli, R. (1993). The computerized adjunct to psychotherapy program at Millbrook Correctional Centre. In *Computer Assisted Therapy: A guide* (pp. 36–38). Santa Barbara, CA: CATSco.

Vosen, B. F. (1991). *The effect of the Therapeutic Learning Program on health care costs and member retention in an HMO*. Unpublished Ph.D. dissertation, University of Southern California.

Waterhouse, J. H. (1993). Using HELP-software in a private mental health practice. In *Computer Assisted Therapy: A guide* (pp. 13–14). Santa Barbara, CA: CATSco.

Watson, D. (2000). *Mood and temperament*. New York: Guilford.

Watters, E., & Ofshe, R. (1999). *Therapy's delusions: The myth of the unconscious and exploitation of today's walking worried*. New York: Scribner.

Weeks, G. R., & L'Abate, L. (1982). *Paradoxical psychotherapy: Theory and practice with individuals, couples, and families*. New York: Brunner/Mazel.

Wegner, D. M., & Wheatley, T. (1999). Apparent mental causation: Sources of the experience of will. *American Psychologist, 54*, 480–492.

Weiner, B., & Graham, S. (1999). Attribution in personality psychology. In L. A. Pervin & O. P. John (Eds.), *Handbook of personality: Theory and research* (pp. 605–628). New York: Guilford.

Weiner, I. B. (Ed.) (1976). *Clinical methods in psychology*. New York: Wiley.

Weintraub, M. D. (1981). *Verbal behavior: Adaptations in psychopathology*. New York: Springer.

Weissman, M. M. (1995). *Mastering depression: A patient's guide to interpersonal psychotherapy*. San Antonio, TX: Psychological Corporation.

Weissman, M. M. (1998). *Patient assessment forms: Workbook for interpersonal psychotherapy program*. San Antonio, TX: Psychological Corporation.

Weissman, M. M., & Markowitz, J. C. (1995). Interpersonal psychotherapy: Current status. *Archives of General Psychiatry, 51*, 599–606.

Wells, R. A., & Giannetti, V. J. (Eds.) (1990). *Handbook of the brief psychotherapies*. New York: Plenum.

Weston, H. E., Boxer, P., & Heatherington, L. (1998). Children's attributions about family arguments: Implications for family therapy. *Family Process, 37*, 35–49.

Wiggins, J. S., & Trobst, K. K. (1999). The fields of interpersonal behavior. In L. A. Pervin & O. P. John (Eds.), *Handbook of personality: Theory and research* (pp. 653–669). New York: Guilford.

Wildman, R. W., II (1992). Gambling. In L. L'Abate, J. E. Farrar, & Serritella (Eds.), *Handbook of differential treatments for addictions* (pp. 211–229). Boston, MA: Allyn & Bacon.

Wildman, R. W., II (1998). *Gambling: An attempt at integration*. Edmonton, AL, Canada: Wynne Resources.

Wildman, R. W., II (1999). *Gambling decisions: A self-help guide to help you control your gambling*. Reno, NV: Author.

Wildman, R. W., II, & L'Abate, L. (1979). The AVOM: A modality derived, age-limited and theory-related test of intellectual functioning. *Psychology in the Schools, 16*, 408–413.

Williams, J.B.W., & Spitzer, R. L. (1984). *Psychotherapy research: Where are we and where should we go?* New York: Guilford.

Williams, R. B., Boles, M., & Johnson, R. E. (1995). Patient use of a computer for prevention in primary care practice. *Patient Education and Counseling, 25*, 283–292.

Wilson, G. T. (1997). Empirically validated treatments: Reality and resistance. *Clinical Psychology: Science and Practice, 4*, 241–244.

Wilson, G. T. (1998). Manual-based treatment and clinical practice. *Clinical Psychology: Science and Practice, 3*, 363–375.

Wilson, G. T., Vitousek, K. M., & Loeb, K. L. (2000). Stepped care treatment for eating disorders. *Journal of Consulting and Clinical Psychology, 68*, 564–572.

Wilson, K. A., de Beurs, E., Palmer, C. A., & Chambless, D. L. (1999). Beck Anxiety Inventory. In M. E. Maruish (Ed.), *The use of psychological testing for treatment planning and outcome assessment, Second Edition* (pp. 971–992). Mahwah, NJ: Earlbaum.

Wilson, S. A., Becker, L. A., & Tinker, R. H. (1997). Fifteen-month follow-up of eye movement desensitization and reprocessing (EMDR) treatment for posttraumatic stress disorder and psychological trauma. *Journal of Consulting and Clinical Psychology, 65*, 1047–1056.

Wincze, J. P., & Barlow, D. H. (1997). *Client workbook: Enhancing sexuality: A problem-solving approach*. San Antonio, TX: Psychological Corporation.

Wine, J. D., & Smye, M. D. (Eds.) (1981). *Social competence*. New York: Guilford.

Winter, D. G., & Barenbaum, N. B. (1999). History of modern personality theory and research. In L. A. Pervin & O. P. John (Eds.), *Handbook of personality: Theory and research* (pp. 3–27). New York: Guilford.

Wittchen, A. U., Hofler, M., & Merikangas, K. (1999). Toward an identification of psychological processes? *American Journal of Psychiatry, 56*, 929–931.

Wolff, H. D. (1993). Using HELP-software in a private psychiatric practice. In *Computer Assisted Therapy: A guide* (pp. 15–12). Santa Barbara, CA: CATSco.

Wolpe, J. (1961). The systematic desensitization of neuroses. *Journal of Neuroses and Mental Diseases, 132*, 189–203.

Zeig, J. F. (Ed.) (1997). *The evolution of psychotherapy: The third conference*. New York: Brunner/Mazel.

Index

About the Author

LUCIANO L'ABATE is a Professor Emeritus of Psychology at Georgia State University. He is the author, editor or co-editor of 31 books, including *Distance Writing and Computer-Assisted Interventions in Psychiatry and Mental Health* (Ablex, 2001).

Lightning Source UK Ltd.
Milton Keynes UK
172631UK00017B/93/P